J. I. Packer

An Evangelical Life

Leland Ryken

CROSSWAY
WHEATON, ILLINOIS

For Crossway editors,
past and present

• • • • • • • • •

J. I. Packer: An Evangelical Life

Published by Crossway
1300 Crescent Street
Wheaton, Illinois 60187

Cover image & design: Josh Dennis

First printing 2015

Printed in the United States of America

All emphases in Scripture quotations have been added by the author.

Trade paperback ISBN: 978-1-4335-9934-7
ePub ISBN: 978-1-4335-4255-8
PDF ISBN: 978-1-4335-4253-4
Mobipocket ISBN: 978-1-4335-4254-1

Library of Congress Cataloging-in-Publication Data
Ryken, Leland.
J. I. Packer : an evangelical life / Leland Ryken.
pages cm.
Includes bibliographical references and index.
ISBN 978-1-4335-4252-7 (hc)
1. Packer, J. I. (James Innell) 2. Church of England—Biography. 3. Evangelists—Biography. I. Title.
BX5199.P22R95 2015
283.092—dc23 [B] 2015001676

Crossway is a publishing ministry of Good News Publishers.

"This book offers a full and balanced portrait of a diligent and faithful theologian. But because J. I. Packer's theology has always been pastoral, practical, catechetical, and eminently readable—instead of recondite, esoteric, or merely academic—it is appropriate that this welcome volume is itself down-to-earth, accessible, and reader friendly. Leland Ryken, as a veteran student of the Puritans, is the ideal author to write about the most influential Puritan of our time."

Mark A. Noll, Francis A. McAnaney Professor of History, University of Notre Dame; author, *Protestantism: A Very Short Introduction*

"This book is a fascinating, insightful, and, to my mind, precisely accurate portrait of the same Jim Packer whom I have known for more than thirty-five years. What a joy to read this book and be challenged by Packer's remarkable life!"

Wayne Grudem, Research Professor of Theology and Biblical Studies, Phoenix Seminary

"Without a doubt, this is now the definitive, most up-to-date biography of J. I. Packer, and it deserves high praise. With the sensitivity, wisdom, and sheer humanity that a fine biographer needs, Leland Ryken allows us to see the life, mind, and heart of this quiet but highly influential man. Traversing the notoriously complex and hazardous terrain of UK and US evangelicalism with impressive sure-footedness, Ryken not only helps us understand the man and his context, but ourselves as evangelicals."

Michael Reeves, Director of Union and Senior Lecturer, Wales Evangelical School of Theology

"A friendly portrait of a great evangelical, the man behind the headlines, full of insight into Packer's genius as a brilliant communicator of the Reformed faith."

Andrew Atherstone, Tutor and Latimer Research Fellow, Wycliffe Hall, University of Oxford

"It is such a pleasure to read Leland Ryken's biography of Dr. Jim Packer. Personally, I have been deeply blessed by Dr. Packer's writing and teaching ministry for over fifty years since, as a student, I picked up *"Fundamentalism" and the Word of God*. I can also testify that his *Knowing God* was most often nominated by my seminary students as a work that profoundly influenced them. To be able to read about the man himself and to understand how God gifted and shaped him has been a moving and edifying experience. This is a good book about a great man."

Peter Jensen, Former Archbishop, Sydney, Australia; Former Principal, Moore Theological College

"J. I. Packer is chief among the cadre of impressive British thinkers who have had a shaping influence on evangelical Christianity in North America over the past half-century. Indeed, his influence girdles the globe, and it shows no sign of abating as this great theologian approaches his tenth decade. This new biography builds on earlier Packer studies, but it offers distinctive insights into the humanity and ministry of a life lived well, with grace abounding and wisdom from above."

Timothy George, Founding Dean, Beeson Divinity School; General Editor, Reformation Commentary on Scripture

"For evangelicals, J. I. Packer stands as one of the foremost theological leaders of this generation. His writings have illuminated the minds of countless Christians with the clarity of the Bible's teaching. He has answered our questions, provoked our thinking, expanded our understanding, and always pointed us to Christ. I'm so glad that Crossway has produced this biography of the man behind the words."

Phillip D. Jensen, Evangelist and Bible Teacher, Two Ways Ministries

Contents

List of Photographs

Introduction

I became acquainted with J. I. Packer as a college sophomore in 1962, when I was browsing in a Christian bookstore in my hometown of Pella, Iowa. For reasons known only to God, I was led to purchase a paperback entitled *"Fundamentalism" and the Word of God*. I am the more amazed that I found the book, because it was a thin paperback that could have easily been lost on the shelf. This became one of the most influential books in my life, with my original underlining indicating what made it such a landmark for me.

In the years that followed, my reading of Packer was sufficiently thorough that as I was completing my book *Worldly Saints: The Puritans as They Really Were*, it occurred to me to ask Packer to write a foreword. Although we had never met in person, I had the audacity to write him and make the request. It is a tribute to Packer's generosity that he agreed to write it, even though my stature as an author was modest. Furthermore, Packer did not write a perfunctory foreword, but a full-fledged essay entitled "Why We Need the Puritans" (which I was happy to see reappear in some of Packer's own subsequent publications).

I met Packer in person as I was waiting for the promised foreword to appear. On that occasion, I served as Packer's driver between a local motel and the campus of Wheaton College, where he delivered an address on the Puritans as part of an academic conference. His first words to me after we had exchanged greetings was the assurance that I "was next on [his] list," meaning that he was ready to write the foreword. Packer was comically overprepared for his address on the Puritans, running out of time (apparently to his genuine surprise) after finishing his introduction. He then summarized his main points in the inimitable impromptu Packer manner.

I next spent time with Packer approximately fifteen years later, when we both served on the translation committee for the English Standard Version. During the next five years, Packer was a constant presence in my life, both in person when the committee met and by his comments in translation proceedings conducted in print.

What Kind of Biography Is This?

My goal in writing this biography was to enable my readers to know J. I. Packer and to get a picture of his varied roles and accomplishments. It is the man that I wanted my readers to encounter. I therefore rejected the model of the documentary history, which so overwhelms readers with factual data about events and people that the subject of the biography disappears from sight. I have not written a history, but a biography.

Because my goal was to present Packer the man, it quickly became evident that a strictly chronological arrangement of the data was insufficient as a format for the biography. A biography does, indeed, involve a life, so in the first part of this book, I unfold the story of Packer's life. But many aspects of Packer the man span whole eras in his life. Trying to fit them into a strict chronological framework would obscure them.

For purposes of illustration, I offer the following examples. J. I. Packer is a latter-day Puritan. It is important to chronicle the beginning of Packer's passion for the Puritans and to locate its origin in his life story. But once Packer had embraced the Puritans, they were a continuous presence in his life, and my consideration of his admiration for them could not be divided into segments that corresponded to changes in his external life. Similarly, a published history of the Tyndale Fellowship for Biblical and Theological Research in England shows that Packer was a continuous participant in the work of that fellowship for three decades. But it would have been completely artificial to attempt to match Packer's involvement with the Tyndale Fellowship to the succession of academic positions he held during those three decades. I would note in passing that biographers who attempt to fit the life themes of their subjects into a chronological flow keep stopping the flow to digress on the themes.

The only plausible organizing framework that would allow my readers to know J. I. Packer the man was a combination of chronological biography and thematic biography, and I have accordingly followed that paradigm, with an interspersed unit that paints a portrait of the man.

Every biography is an interpretation of a person, as well as a collection of information about the person. However, this biography is light on the interpretive and evaluative side. My goal was to present J. I. Packer and leave my readers to engage in as much or as little assessment as they wished. I have made no evaluations of whether Packer did the right or wrong thing in regard to his beliefs and actions. Much has been written in particular about Packer's loyalty to the Church of England when others separated from it and about his involvement in the movement known as Evangelicals and Catholics Together. Much has also been said about Packer's withdrawal from Canada's Anglican Church when others stayed within it. I had no interest in making evaluations of Packer's stand on the issues that drove these events. It strikes me that to attempt to do so would have been out of place in a biography, and a violation of the Puritan principle that a person is bound by his conscience before God.

Signposts for What Is to Follow

Many biographies end with a chapter of "conclusions," in which the author casts a retrospective glance over the material that has preceded and extracts some leading themes from the data. I chose to begin with a series of signposts so my readers can look for evidence of them as they read this biography. The following are themes that emerged as I lived with the material and that I want my readers to look for in my account.

1. *Paradoxes.* Right at the start of my research for this biography, I was handed a very useful piece of theory regarding biographical writing. It is the idea that people are paradoxical and mysterious creatures. Identifying the paradoxes is a useful framework for understanding the subject of a biography, even if the apparent contradictions remain mysterious. J. I. Packer's life embraces a more-than-ordinary number of paradoxes, including the following:

- Packer is theologically and temperamentally a Puritan, and in his college days, he was influenced by the Plymouth Brethren strain in British evangelicalism; yet he remained devoted to the Anglican Church throughout his life, and he has affiliated with movements sympathetic to Roman Catholicism.

- Packer is quintessentially British, yet he has lived nearly half of his adult life in Canada, and (to extend the paradox even further) his sphere of greatest influence is the United States.
- Packer is one of the most famous modern evangelicals, yet he has never held high-visibility positions such as prestigious pulpits or professorships at large universities.
- Packer is by nature a peacemaker and a gentle man, yet he has had a career of controversy in the sense that much of his writing has been polemical and his stand on religious issues has often made him the object of criticism.
- Throughout his life, Packer refused to bolt from the Anglican Church when pressed to do so, yet he ended up withdrawing and in effect being expelled from the Anglican Church of Canada.
- Packer loves specialized scholarship, yet most of his writing has been oriented to the general Christian public and ranks as "mid-level" work.

Paradox is thus one of the underlying themes that I want my readers to note as this book unfolds.

2. *Selfless Service.* Another unifying theme in Packer's life is his overriding sense of calling to serve the church—both the church as an institution and as the worldwide community of Christians. At every turn, Packer has primarily accepted tasks and positions that have been helpful to Christians in their walk with God, with no concern for professional advancement. Packer is utterly devoid of concern about professional advancement. A look at the nature of his publications (both books and articles) is one way to see this. But Packer's speaking career likewise shows his propensity to say yes to virtually every invitation that has come his way. Those who have seen this willingness to agree to speaking and interview invitations marvel that Packer has been such a prolific writer in spite of the inroads on his time that he has allowed.

3. *Quiet Service.* Despite his high visibility among evangelical Christians, much of Packer's investment of time and ability has been behind the scenes. I was alerted to this right at the outset of my writing of this book, and I have seen it at every turn. One cannot even imagine how many meetings of Church of England committees Packer attended during his years as a semi-official evangelical representative on such panels. For several decades, Packer has not only served as an advisor to

Christianity Today, but has also critiqued every issue of the magazine, including its advertising and graphics. In fact, he has continued these critiques to the present day, even after the magazine's finances made it a voluntary activity. Again, Packer is on record as saying that his work on the translation of the English Standard Version of the Bible is his greatest scholarly achievement, but all that the public at large sees of this is the notation that Packer was the general editor of the translation.

4. *Varied Roles*. Another theme that emerges in this biography is the many-sided nature of Packer's life and achievements. The range of roles that he has filled is breathtaking. Along with this trait is his transcendence of labels. The most customary category into which I see Packer placed is that of theologian, but other categories seem equally natural to me based on my acquaintance with him: church historian (Puritan scholar), classicist, writer on topics of Christian living (implying a scope that the label *theologian* does not quite capture), academician, consultant, Bible translator, churchman, and editor.

Packer's career has been a case study of entering the open doors that God and people have placed before him. This is obvious in the academic positions that he has held (particularly in England before he moved to Canada), the books and essays he has published, and the speaking engagements he has discharged. Relatively few of the items that appear in Packer's *vita* were part of a planned program or professional path. Instead, Packer has trusted to providence in accepting invitations that were placed before him, governed by the impulse to minister to God's people. I note therefore the aptness of the title of a *festschrift* that was composed in Packer's honor: *Doing Theology for the People of God*. Packer did not enter theology for the sake of "making a scholarly contribution," as the academy tends to conceive of a scholarly career, but "for the people of God."

5. *Setbacks and Successes*. A final theme that I will flag here at the outset is the degree to which Packer has risen above calamity and disappointment to achieve greatness. One thinks most immediately of his life-changing physical injury at age seven. Packer has not held the high-visibility professional positions that most scholars of his ability enjoy, and there were setbacks in his academic career in England for which he was not responsible. Yet the world became Packer's classroom through

his writing, and the Christian world has been immeasurably enriched by his speaking in modest venues as well as prestigious ones.

Acknowledgments

I wish to express my sincere gratitude to the following people and to acknowledge the published sources to which I am particularly indebted. Lane Dennis, president of Crossway Books, is the "only begetter" of this biography in the sense that he asked me to write it. In turn, neither Lane nor I would have felt free to pursue the venture without the approval and help of Packer himself. In addition to the telephone interviews with Packer that I list as sources for the early chapters, every chapter in this biography bears the imprint of two days of conversation that I had with him at the Crossway offices on June 16–17, 2014. Although I have not noted this source of information in my summaries at the end of the book, I drew heavily on these conversations, which I count among the greatest privileges of my life. I also could not have written this biography without the pioneering and monumental work of Alister McGrath in his masterful book *J. I. Packer: A Biography* (Grand Rapids: Baker, 1997). Here, too, I would not have felt free to write my biography without the blessing of McGrath, whose permission was immediately and warmly extended to me. In the acknowledgments in his book, McGrath notes that just under three hundred people (half of whom he names) gave him access to data. This primary research was invaluable to me. I also owe an immense debt to a source that might seem inconsequential compared to McGrath's book, but that was nonetheless worth its weight in gold: "Bibliography of the Works of J. I. Packer," in *J. I. Packer and the Evangelical Future: The Impact of His Life and Thought*, ed. Timothy George (Grand Rapids: Baker, 2009), 187–230.

Part 1

THE LIFE

A biography is more than the story of a person's life, but it is not less than that. The events that have made up J. I. Packer's life to date are the starting point for understanding him and his work. We might think of them as the plotline on which the person and his activity for the kingdom of God are fleshed out.

Packer's life is promising material for a story. He has done so many different things that his life sometimes reads like an adventure story. As with any adventure story, there have been striking and abrupt shifts in location. The stakes have sometimes been very high. And there have been ups and downs.

But this adventure story is a narrative of divine providence, reminiscent of the story of Joseph in the book of Genesis and perhaps of Hamlet in William Shakespeare's masterpiece. In the most famous speech on the subject of providence in Shakespeare's play, Hamlet expresses the sentiment that "there's a divinity that shapes our ends." That is the ultimate pattern in the story that makes up Part 1 of this biography.

Early Life and College

(1926–1948)

1

Childhood and Teen Years

(1926–1944)

When we consider great and famous people, it is natural to think of them as having always been great and famous. After all, that is how we know them.

The J. I. Packer that we know certainly ranks as a great and famous man. In 2005, *Time* magazine included Packer in a list of "The 25 Most Influential Evangelicals in America," and entering the name J. I. Packer on an Internet search engine yields over seven hundred thousand hits. When we consider data like that, it is natural to believe that Packer has always been great and famous.

But, of course, this is untrue. Great and famous people are not born so, but as ordinary specimens of humanity. James Innell Packer was no exception.

Early Years

Packer was born on July 22, 1926, in the village of Twyning, near the city of Gloucester. His childhood home was in the heart of Gloucester, which is located in a region of England known as the South West, not far from the border of Wales. Packer calls Gloucester a market town. It is also a cathedral city, which means that the church has a more-than-usual institutional visibility on the local scene. Cathedral cities in

England perpetuate the external rituals of the Anglican faith, creating plenty of scope for nominal Christianity.

At the time of Packer's upbringing, Gloucester was also a rail center of some importance in England, and his father, James Percy Packer, oversaw the general office of the Great Western Railway at Gloucester. By Packer's account, his father was unsuited for major responsibility and was comfortable with the fact that his duties mainly involved dealing with such matters as lost luggage claims. The office staff consisted of only two people beyond Percy—a junior clerk and a typist. The Second World War increased the workload enormously, and at the age of fifty-two, Packer's father suffered a temporary mental collapse leading to early retirement.

The Packers were thus a lower-middle-class family, and we can say that J. I. Packer came from humble roots. In fact, a generation or two earlier, his ancestors had farmed in Oxfordshire. Throughout his life, Packer has retained what Britons call "a West Country burr," which one dictionary defines as a way of speaking English in which the "r" sound is more noticeable than in ordinary pronunciation.

People who know Packer can attest that he has never lost the common touch. One friend recounts that Packer commended a local restaurant to her with the statement: "This place has a homespun feel. That's why I like it." I recall that when the translation committee that produced the English Standard Version met in Cambridge, England, the committee members occasionally ate the noon meal in a restaurant, and Packer was faithful in making the waitress feel appreciated. Similarly, when Packer ate the evening meal in my home on the occasion of my first meeting him in Wheaton, he inquired of my wife what the main dish was called and commended her for its deliciousness.

Throughout his childhood years, Packer lived in a modest rented home. On the ground level were what former generations called a "front room" (a living room for receiving guests), a dining room, a kitchen, a pantry, and what in England is called a "scullery" (an all-purpose kitchen and laundry room). There was a piano in the front room. The upstairs consisted of three bedrooms and a bathroom. Gas lighting was replaced by electricity when Packer was six.

Packer was the firstborn child in his family, with his sister, Margaret, being born three years later. His middle name, Innell, sounds nearly aristocratic, and the initials J. I., by which Packer became known, are immediately impressive (perhaps especially to American ears). Innell is a Packer family name, and its choice as a middle name is an endearing piece of family history. An unmarried second cousin of Packer's father bore the surname of Innell, but she was the last in a family line. Packer's father acquiesced in her request to give his newborn a middle name that would perpetuate her family name.

Packer describes his early years as uneventful. The family's house had fenced-in front and back lawns, where Packer engaged in normal boy's play. His father's employment by the Great Western Railway made steam trains a fascination to him, and one of his favorite toys was a train set. He also played with a construction kit, drew pictures, and read.

From his early years, Packer was a shy boy who did not mingle easily with his peers. When asked in his eighties what he most remembers about his childhood, he replied, "Solitariness." While Packer was a self-described introvert, his sister was the opposite. Margaret had many friends, but Packer had "very few" (his own testimony). However, Packer claims that he has "always been able to be happy on my own."

People who have written biographically about Packer all describe him as a loner, solitary, and isolated in his childhood. Packer himself has shared that when he first felt the call to ministry during his second year in college, he hesitated because he saw himself as "an odd person, somewhat solitary and, as I thought and felt, very poor at human relationships." However, he has also recorded that God "overpowered me, telling me I must trust him and go ahead."

People who have known Packer in his adult years find it hard to picture him as anything but sociable and gregarious. When the translation committee of the English Standard Version met in Cambridge, it faced a daily choice between eating a catered lunch at Tyndale House or walking to a restaurant on the Cam River. An excursion to the restaurant extended the time to a whopping two hours, but Packer was a consistent advocate of the more sociable amble and sit-down lunch.

When I noted to Packer that people who know him today find him a gregarious person, he offered two explanations for the apparent contradiction. One is that introverts "don't enjoy being introverts" and find ways to compensate and even behave like extroverts in social situations. Second, when Packer became a Christian, the words *love* and *fellowship* became, he said, "heavyweight words" for him, and he consciously cultivated "the habit of fellowship."

The Packer family enjoyed an annual summer holiday, and their preferred vacation was vintage British—renting a bed-and-breakfast house on the seacoast. Except for one Welsh holiday, the family regularly went to Cornwall. Packer says the family enjoyed the Cornwall coast and saw no need to vary the routine. The family traveled with "privilege tickets" that were free to employees of the train company.

When Packer's academic ability became increasingly obvious as the years unfolded, his father was proud of his son's accomplishments, but he did not have the background to understand them. His mother, however, grasped what was happening and continuously showed interest in what Packer was learning at school.

Packer's maternal grandmother had been widowed in her forties and had retrained herself as a "district nurse" who visited patients. Her drive and initiative lived on in Packer's mother, whom Packer calls "a remarkable person, clearheaded and strong-willed." She attended a teacher training college and then had a successful teaching career at two or three schools before marrying Packer's father. Unfortunately, she suffered from anemia during Packer's growing-up years, an era when little help for the disease was available. She therefore led what Packer calls "a quiet life," resting on the dining room couch between two and four o'clock every afternoon.

Packer considers his mother to be the dominant parental influence in his life. She attained what Packer believes to have been saving faith at college, but it was of an Anglo-Catholic, "high-church" nature, expressed by what the Puritans called "formalism" (performing the standard rituals of the church).

A Momentous Accident at School

In September 1933, Packer began to attend the local "junior school." It was a difficult adjustment for the seven-year-old, who was subjected to bullying from other students. On the fateful day of September 19, a schoolmate chased Packer out of the school grounds and onto a busy street (London Road). Packer was hit by a bread van and thrown to the ground. The accident resulted in injuries that have affected Packer every subsequent day of his life.

Packer was taken to the Gloucester Royal Infirmary and rushed into surgery. The primary injury was trauma to the head. The external damage was a dent in the skull, which is a feature of Packer's physical appearance to the present day. The formal diagnosis was what Alister McGrath (quoting the surgeon's memorandum) calls "a depressed compound fracture of the frontal bone on the right-hand side of his forehead." Naturally, there was fear of damage to the brain, but it proved to be much less severe than might have been expected.

Packer spent three weeks in the hospital and then six months at home for recuperation, returning to school near the end of the academic year. For three years after the accident, he spoke slowly and with a drawl, and he never regained any memory of what had happened immediately before and after the accident. Two years afterward, the boy who had chased Packer from the playground (named Arthur Oliver Cromwell!) identified himself, which Packer received as new information.

The injury had huge repercussions for Packer, but as bad as the accident was, it was a story of providence and grace as well, beginning with the sparing of Packer's life. But the marvel goes further. The surgical procedure that was immediately performed required the extraction of fragments of bone from inside the skull to relieve pressure on the brain. The resident surgeon in the Gloucester hospital had just returned after an extended time in Vienna, where he had specialized in this very type of surgery.

Of course, the accident was traumatic for Packer's parents, who took every possible precaution to prevent further injury to their son's head. They curbed his physical activities in the years that followed and discouraged bicycle riding. Even more confining was a black aluminum plate, held in place by an elastic band, that Packer wore on his head from the time of the accident until the age of fifteen, when, he says, he "went on strike" and refused to wear it any longer. Packer refers to his appearance while wearing the plate as that of "a speckled bird."

A Reader Is Born

Packer's solitary nature intensified in the days following the accident. He felt marginalized; though he found a niche as a good learner who would help others (even those who bullied him) with their homework, he never fully participated in schoolyard games. Reading had always been more natural to Packer than sports. He recalls that he was a prodigious reader already at the age of four and always remained such, characterizing himself as "something of a bookworm." In the wake of his accident, this appetite for reading only accelerated.

A year or so after the accident, Packer's grandmother took him for a weeklong vacation to the coastal resort town of Torquay to help him recover from a bout of bronchitis (to which he was prone). The weather was rainy and unsuitable for walking on the beach. The boardinghouse where the pair stayed provided books for just such occasions. Deprived of his construction set and toy train, Packer began to read the books that were in his room.

He began with a collection of short stories by Agatha Christie entitled *The Hound of Death*. His grandmother then lent him some of her own Christie books. In his adult years, Packer became such a zealous reader of older spiritual classics that it is natural for us to think of those books as his primary reading material. But when *Christianity Today* conducted a poll of its contributors on the ten best religious books of the twentieth century, a nomination by J. I. Packer stood out. He chose the *Lord of the Rings* trilogy by J. R. R. Tolkien, with a supporting comment: "A classic for children from 9 to 90. Bears constant re-reading."

A Writer Is Born

While reading might be an expected result of an enforced convalescence, the path by which Packer became a schoolboy writer is less expected. That avenue was an ordinary typewriter.

Packer's fascination with typewriters began when he accompanied his father to the railway office on Saturday afternoon "catch-up" trips. There were two typewriters in the office, and Packer was allowed access to one of them. At the age of eight, he taught himself to type using four fingers. The subject matter of his typing was highly unusual—copying poems such as Henry Wadsworth Longfellow's "Hiawatha" and Robert Southey's "The Inchcape Rock," although it was not the poetry but the act of typing that he found rewarding.

Packer's passion for typing did not escape the notice of his parents, partly because it solved a problem in the making. A bicycle was the toy of choice among boys in Packer's milieu, where receiving a bike around the age of eleven was a virtual rite of passage. But Packer's parents were fearful of any physical activity that might further injure their son's head.

On the morning of his eleventh birthday, Packer hastened to the living room, where the family made a practice of placing birthday presents. He had given hints that he wanted a bicycle and expected to receive one. What he found was a used typewriter that seemed to him to weigh half a ton. Yet, old as it was, it had been well serviced.

For his eleventh birthday in 1937, J. I. Packer was given a used Oliver typewriter, similar to the one pictured here.

If the birthday boy was disappointed, he did not let it show. He at once put paper into the typewriter and began to type. According to McGrath, the typewriter became "the most treasured possession of his boyhood." Its legacy was long lasting: to this day, Packer types his books and correspondence on a typewriter instead of a computer.

The acquisition of a typewriter gave impetus to Packer's early writing. He began to compose stories about school and space travel, two genres that youngsters of the time read in weekly publications. Packer contributed his stories to "magazines" produced by friends at school. It can be hard to pinpoint when an eventual author first contracts the "infection" of writing and publishing, but my theory is that the seeds are planted early. I have no intention of being overly dramatic when I ask what Packer's life and career would have been like if he had received a bicycle instead of a typewriter for his eleventh birthday.

Some sixty-five years later, Packer was able to see the hand of providence in his parents' decision not to give him a bicycle (he did receive a bicycle on his thirteenth birthday, when he was physically able to handle it). In this, Packer "came to discern that what he had experienced was outstandingly good parenting, though it had not felt like that at first." Packer added that he "cannot forget that the head injury became a happy providence eleven years later," excluding him from conscripted military service at the age of eighteen and enabling him to go to Oxford

University, where he became a Christian, which Packer thinks "would hardly have happened to him in the army."

In September 1937, not long after that memorable eleventh birthday, Packer made the transition from the local "junior school" to the Crypt School in Gloucester. The school was prestigious, having been founded in 1539, the approximate time when King Henry VIII broke with the Church of Rome and established the Church of England. Ironically, in view of Packer's nominal Christianity at the time, but prophetically in view of what he became, the Crypt School counted among its former students the English preacher and evangelist George Whitefield.

At the Crypt School, Packer chose to specialize in "classics." This involved the study of the language, literature, and history of ancient Greece and Rome. A double significance might be seen in this decision. First, when Packer went on to Oxford University, he again chose the track known as classics. Second, Packer was the only student in his class at the Crypt School to choose classics. It was an early indication of his willingness to travel less-trodden roads, a tendency that has led many to judge him to be "in a class by himself."

The Religious Climate at Home and Church

Packer came from a churchgoing family, but the Christian commitment was nominal rather than genuine. The Packer family regularly attended a local Anglican church (St. Catharine's), but Packer recounts that his parents did not require him to attend Sunday school, no one "talked about the things of God" at home, and there was no prayer at mealtimes. In my conversations with Packer, he said that it was considered "in bad taste to talk religion" in his home. He recalls a three-year span in his teen years when he "wondered what is real in Christianity." His home environment did not provide adequate answers.

In nominally Christian families in the Church of England, there is a strong impetus to perform longstanding church rituals, and this was true in the Packer family. One of the benchmarks in the Anglican Church is confirmation, a rite of initiation in which children who were baptized as infants claim oneness with Christ as their own experience based on faith in the gospel. When Packer was fourteen, his mother expressed the desire that he be confirmed. In her background lay the influence of the Anglo-Catholic (high church) revival of the nineteenth century. Packer agreed to be confirmed, even though he did not possess saving faith in Christ and, as he says, "indeed did not know what it was."

It was not an ordinary confirmation, however; Packer missed the application deadline, which meant he did not attend the regular confirmation classes offered by the vicar of the church. However, the church had a new curate, a young man named Mark Green, who offered to teach Packer in a one-on-one tutorial. The instruction followed a high-church path, so the focus was moral rather than spiritual. Talk also centered on preparation to receive Holy Communion, but nothing was said about personal conversion. Green recalls Packer as a "shy and reserved" teenager who was nonetheless "very receptive and attentive" to the instruction.

Religious Encounters at School

Although Packer did not receive what we today call a Christian education, the religious influence at school was important in his life. Significantly, it was in school that Packer first encountered the writing of C. S. Lewis.

A teacher at the Crypt School was in charge of Packer's class during one time slot per week devoted to "general studies." He needed a book that would stimulate discussion among his students. He chose the recently published *The Screwtape Letters*, thereby introducing Packer to Lewis. Lewis, who was just beginning to attract the attention of the British public, had originally published the thirty-one chapters of this book as a series of articles in a religious newspaper. The format of the book—imagined letters from one devil to another—could hardly have been more captivating to a schoolboy.

We can see in this encounter with a book authored by Lewis yet another example of divine providence. Was the teacher a Christian? Packer's remembrance is that "it does not seem so."

There was another religious influence at school of a more indirect nature. Packer began to play chess with the son of the local Unitarian minister. As they played, Packer's classmate attempted to convert him to Unitarianism. The arguments struck the fifteen-year-old Packer as illogical. In Packer's words, "Unitarianism affirms the ethic of Jesus as the most wonderful thing since ice cream and negates the divinity of Jesus as superstition." Packer could not help wondering why, if his Unitarian friend believed part of the New Testament, he did not believe more of it. Why deny something so central as the deity of Jesus?

This way of formulating an issue became a lifelong paradigm for Packer. For example, in a 1981 essay entitled "Is Christianity Credible?" Packer asks, with regard to such modern influencers as Friedrich Schleiermacher, Albrecht Ritschl, Adolf von Harnack, and Ernst Troeltsch: "Why, if this man believes so much, does he not believe more? but if he believes so little, why does he not believe less?"

Packer's Anglican churchgoing had given him a rudimentary understanding of the Christian faith, though without any inner conviction regarding it. The sparring with his Unitarian friend prompted Packer to start thinking seriously about what constituted religious truth. In his own words, "My mind had been grabbed by the question, What is *true* Christianity?"

Reading the Bible was a starting point for answering that question. Lacking a Bible of his own, Packer used his grandmother's copy of the King James Version. He read it avidly. At the same time, Packer encountered another newly published book by Lewis entitled *Mere Christianity*. Later readers of this landmark book (as influential in my own life as Packer's *"Fundamentalism" and the Word of God*) know that it began as a series of fifteen-minute wartime radio talks on the BBC (British Broadcasting Corp.), which subsequently were published as three short books before being combined in a single volume in 1952. Packer witnessed the birth of the book as described, reading the trilogy as the individual books were published.

What was the nature of Lewis's influence on Packer? He has answered that question in a series of articles and interviews. One of these articles, written in 1988 on the occasion of the twenty-fifth anniversary of Lewis's death (and after Packer had been reading Lewis for forty-five years), shows that the religious impact of Packer's early reading of Lewis was more subliminal than direct. Packer writes that he "enjoyed *Screwtape Letters* and *Mere Christianity* more for their manner than their matter, for Lewis's writing style made him seem both a fellow schoolboy and a wise old uncle simultaneously." After Packer's conversion, Lewis seemed "more grandfatherly," a change that Packer ascribes more to himself than to Lewis. A decade later, Packer attributed somewhat more significance to his encounter with the two Lewis books, saying that they "brought me, not indeed to faith in the full sense, but to mainstream Christian beliefs about God, man, and Jesus Christ, so that now I was halfway there." According to Packer's analysis, the long-term effect of his encounter with Lewis was that he came to see the reasonableness of the Christian faith, the moral demands of discipleship, and the reality of heaven as a home.

Planning for College

Given Packer's lower-middle-class background, it was not a foregone conclusion what he would do when he reached college age. His headmaster at the Crypt School, David Gwynn Williams, had received his college education at Corpus Christi College, part of Oxford University, and was convinced that Packer had the ability to be accepted at Oxford. Of course, a series of factors, including finances, needed to fall into place for this to happen. (Being poor, Packer's parents had always made it clear that advanced education would depend on his getting scholarships.)

In March 1943, Packer's last year in what North Americans call high school, the *Oxford University Gazette* published details of scholarships for classics students applying to Corpus Christi College. Oxford University scholarships fell into two categories—those for students who belonged to certain named groups (such as sons of Anglican clergy) and those that placed no restrictions on applicants ("open" scholarships). Corpus Christi College advertised two open scholarships for the upcoming academic year. Both were for 100 pounds, small by today's standards but substantial at the time. The awarding of the two scholarships would be based on a competitive examination to be administered in Oxford in September 1943.

Packer sat for the examination over a two-day span. It was his first genuine trip to Oxford (though he had once bicycled from Gloucester to Oxford and back in a single day on one of his numerous long and solitary cycling ventures, a total distance of about a hundred miles). It is in keeping with Packer's temperament that he returned to Gloucester thinking that his performance on the exams was undistinguished. Nonetheless, he received the Hugh Oldham Scholarship, which would enable him to attend Oxford University.

Waiting for College

Even though Packer had been accepted into college, he was only seventeen, which was considered too young to begin his Oxford education. This left him with free time, though technically he was still enrolled in his "sixth form" at school. With characteristic industry, Packer made it a year of intellectual advance. The academic distinctions that Packer received at this era of his life were a tribute to his intellectual ability, but they were also signposts that he was destined to achieve great things.

To begin, the Crypt School named him head prefect. This title is part of the school system in England, where schools sometimes name a "head girl" and "head boy." It is partly an honorific position that signals the esteem with which the school regards the recipient, though the post brings tasks as well.

Also at this time, Packer began his lifelong process of self-education. He spent the year largely in self-directed reading, and trips to the public library were a regular feature of his life. Packer's reading program showed not only the seriousness of his intellectual quest, but also his continuing interest in religious matters. He read Sigmund Freud and Carl Jung, as well as Russian novels by Fyodor Dostoyevsky (*The Idiot*; *Crime and Punishment*; *The Brothers Karamazov*; and *The Devils*, a title more often translated as *The Possessed*). These novels with Christian premises seemed more truthful to Packer than Freud's attempt to explain Christianity away. Packer told me that he became "a Dostoyevsky addict," much impressed by how the Russian novelist "takes the skin off his characters and allows us to see what they are like."

A schoolboy friendship with Eric Taylor was also an important part of Packer's final year at the Crypt School. While Packer spent his third year in "sixth form," Taylor made the transition to the University of Bristol. During that year, Taylor became a Christian, and he wrote letters to Packer about his new-found faith. Packer did not fully understand the letters, especially one that contained an exposition of the final verses of Romans 3, on justification by faith. Packer also was puzzled by references to "saving faith." During the following summer vacation, Taylor and Packer had a series of conversations about the Christian faith. The discussions left Packer feeling that something was lacking in his life, but he was mystified as to what it was. Although Taylor did not lead Packer to faith, he did the next best thing by encouraging Packer to make contact with the Oxford student group called the Christian Union.

One of the most revealing statements that Packer has made is that he went to Oxford University actually believing himself to be a Christian. The basis of that belief was that in school debates with atheists, he had found himself defending Christianity as a belief system. However, in his first year at Oxford, Packer would realize his true spiritual state and experience conversion to Christianity, after which, he has said, he was "very conscious of wasted years and was trying to catch up."

Summary

Any Christian reading the foregoing account of J. I. Packer's pre-college life can see it as a story scripted by God's providence. It is nothing less than a "hound of heaven" story. Packer's life-changing accident diverted him from dreams of being a cricket player to being a more devoted reader and a writer. He did not grow up in a believing family, but he had continuous contact with the basic doctrines of the Christian faith at home and church. He was a seeker with spiritual promptings. And he had a Christian friend who wanted him to pass from spiritual death to life. All the ingredients were in place that would lead Packer to take the step into personal faith.

2

The College Years

(1944–1948)

When J. I. Packer arrived at Oxford, he was doubly prepared to make the most of the experience. Academically, he had long been a serious student and possessed the intellectual spark. Spiritually, a foundation had been laid for the conversion that happened almost immediately after his arrival.

Oxford University as Packer Found It

Packer made the trip to Oxford in early October 1944, in the midst of the Second World War. He traveled by train, using a free ticket available to him as a family member of a Great Western Railway employee. With his suitcase in hand, he walked the mile from the train station to Corpus Christi College in central Oxford.

To catch the flavor of Packer's college experience, we need to assemble a picture of what Oxford was like during the war. The university bore the signs of being in crisis. The war was in its late stages, but not yet over. The Oxford student body was still almost entirely male, and most of the surviving able-bodied men were in the army. Blackouts made the city dark at night, creating a sense of a place under siege. Most colleges were carrying on at a greatly reduced level, with sections of some completely shut down.

Packer was eighteen years old, and during the war, most entering

The main entrance and Pelican Sundial (built in 1581) of Corpus Christi College at Oxford University, where J. I. Packer studied from 1944 to 1948. (Photo © Godot13. License: http://creativecommons.org/licenses/by-sa/3.0/legalcode)

students of that age enrolled in six-month courses before going into military service. Packer was one of a few eighteen-year-olds who were enrolled as full-time students, expecting to be in college for three or four years. Corpus Christi College had dwindled to an enrollment of twenty-four undergraduate students, divided equally between full-time students and short-term students from the armed forces. Not only students were away at war: so were young professors. Two of Packer's professors had been brought out of retirement to teach the classics courses.

Life in the colleges was austere. Heat in the rooms was inadequate and the food poor. The heat in dorm rooms was provided by coal fireplaces, but coal was in short supply because of the war effort. The fact that the library was well heated was a mixed blessing: it encouraged study by those who were serious students, but it also attracted those in search of warmth rather than books and desks. The library was always packed, and students often had to sit on the floor.

Packer was a student in the classics track, meaning that the content of his studies was classical literature, history, and philosophy. It was a rigorous path, taking four years in contrast to the three years required for other tracks. The classics curriculum included language study, as well as reading of the great texts. One of Packer's duties within his college was to recite from memory a long Latin prayer before formal dinners in the dining hall.

The classics curriculum at Oxford University was (and remains) systematic and fixed. The program is divided into two categories, with the second building on the first. The first category occupies five terms and the second seven terms, adding up to four academic years. With three terms per academic year, the system is equivalent to what in the United States is called a quarter system, as distinct from a semester system. The first segment is mainly the study of ancient Greek and Latin. The method of education consists primarily of weekly one-on-one "tutorials" with a master or tutor, supplemented by voluntary attendance of lectures sponsored by the university at large. In a tutorial, a student reads aloud an essay he has written, which the tutor then critiques. The second part of the program consists of reading primary texts in a wide range of subjects stemming from the Greek and Roman cultures, including ancient history and ancient and modern philosophy.

Although Packer gave priority to the Christian side of life and the activities of the Christian Union, he was not impatient with the time he spent on Greek and Latin language study and the reading of masterworks in those languages. Packer had come to enjoy the Greek and Latin languages, finding that they "have their strengths and fascination," with the result that mastering and using them provided "a rather good feeling." He entered Oxford with a well-developed grasp of both Greek and Latin, giving him a head start on his college studies. By his own testimony, he "had the ability to become a classical scholar," and several professors attempted to influence him in that direction. But the bent of his being following his conversion was in the direction of Christian scholarship and ministry.

The classical author whom Packer "most admired" was the Greek dramatist Aeschylus, whom Packer regarded as a master of language, similar to William Shakespeare in English literature. In Packer's words,

"Aeschylus handled language in a forcible way, and I always admire writers who handle language in a forcible way." Packer also enjoyed reading Homer, though not with the same passion with which he read Aeschylus. Among Latin authors, the historian Livy was Packer's favorite on the strength of the vividness of his writing.

Only one professor touched Packer deeply. He was a displaced Jew named Eduard Fraenkel, affiliated with Packer's own college (Corpus Christi). Fraenkel was a legendary classical scholar of his era whose name lives on today. Packer attended only one Fraenkel course, on the Latin poet Horace, but he was awed by Fraenkel's extemporaneous lecturing as he roamed up and down the aisles of the classroom.

The classics curriculum bore fruit in Packer's later life and career, and we can say with confidence that his Oxford education served him well. In his role as general editor of the English Standard Version of the Bible, Packer sometimes dazzled other committee members with his knowledge of Greek and the nuances of classical rhetoric. Additionally, he benefited from the Oxford model of individualized education and frequent presentation of essays, a model that is designed to produce a certain quality of mind, including precision of thought and expression, and careful organization of material. Packer's writings display a quality possessed by another Oxford classics student, C. S. Lewis, namely, the ability to follow a line of thought to its logical conclusion, breaking the main topic into its constituent parts and making complex ideas clear to the general reading public.

In conversation with me, Packer described the Oxford method as "throwing a student into the deep end and seeing how he does." For a classics student such as Packer, this was, he said, "the best education I could have had." However, it is not the model Packer followed in his own teaching, since he realized that most students need help in learning the basic ways of philosophical thought.

I entitled this section "Oxford University as Packer Found It"; I want to end it by reversing that to consider J. I. Packer as Oxford University found him. Packer's self-portrait as an entering college student reveals "a man of like passions such as we are" (see James 5:17), not the commanding figure that he became. Here are formulas that Packer later used when he cast a retrospective look at himself as an Oxford student:

- ". . . an immature and churned-up young man, painfully aware of himself, battling his daily way, as adolescents do, through manifold urges and surges of discontent and frustration."
- "I was an oddity. I was bad at relationships, an outsider, shy, and an intellectual."
- ". . . an eighteen year-old oddball, . . . emotionally locked up."
- ". . . a shy, introverted, and awkward young man."

This picture is so different from the J. I. Packer that we know that we need to accept the self-portrait as carrying the authority of the person who observed himself firsthand.

Packer's Conversion

As noted in the preceding chapter, Packer's school friend Eric Taylor had urged him to seek out the Christian Union (an Inter-Varsity organization) when he arrived at Oxford. It so happened that Packer did not need to do this.

Christian student groups at Oxford and Cambridge Universities were highly active in the middle of the twentieth century. The Christian Union at Oxford followed a practice of arranging social events in the respective colleges for new students at the beginning of each academic year. These were informational meetings designed to attract students to participate in the gatherings of the Christian Union of the university as a whole. Nearly everything at Oxford University is traditional, and the opening recruitment meetings of the term happened specifically on the Thursday evening before the start of the academic year. Ralph Hulme, the Corpus Christi representative for the Oxford Inter-Collegiate Christian Union, contacted Packer and invited him to the introductory Thursday meeting.

I will note in passing that as I did the research for this biography, I was pushed to the limit by the dozens of acronyms that make up the history of evangelical organizations in England during the twentieth century. On my trips to Oxford through the years, I had heard references to OICCU (too oddly pronounced to reproduce it here, though "oi-kew" comes close) and to a sister organization, CICCU ("kick-you"), at Cambridge University. In the United States, we would prosaically refer to either of these groups as "the local InterVarsity chapter"!

Packer accepted Hulme's invitation, having already determined that he would attend. The first meeting was eminently forgettable, as evidenced by the fact that the only thing Packer remembers about the event is that it failed to spark his interest!

Despite the low wartime enrollments at the University, OICCU President David Mullins (a medical student) was determined to maintain the evangelistic thrust of the Christian Union. The weekly agenda was ambitious. On the university level, there was a Bible exposition every Saturday evening and an evangelistic sermon every Sunday evening (known as "Sunday evening sermon"). Individual colleges then sponsored weekly Bible studies and prayer meetings. Packer learned about these options at the informational meeting. The first week, he decided to attend the Saturday evening Bible exposition, but not the Sunday evening evangelistic service. He did, however, attend the evangelistic service the next Sunday, October 22, 1944, a service that would change his life eternally.

The service occurred at St. Aldate's, an Anglican church in the center of the city. It was one of the larger Oxford churches and was noted for its student ministry. St. Aldate's is just a "stone's throw" from Pembroke College, where bygone Crypt School alumnus George Whitefield attended college and was converted. "Dim-out" conditions were in effect, so care was taken not to allow any light to emanate from the church building. Spiritual light, however, shone within the church.

The service began at 8:15. The preacher was an elderly Anglican parson, the Rev. Earl Langston, from the resort town of Weymouth. The first half of the forty-minute sermon consisted of biblical exposition that left Packer bored. But the second half was a personal narrative of how Langston had been converted at a boys' camp. The key component of that conversion had been a challenge posed to the youthful Langston by a camp leader, who had asked whether he was a Christian. Langston had been jolted by this question to conclude that he was not actually saved. That, in turn, led to his coming to personal faith in Christ as Savior.

This autobiographical narrative was riveting to Packer, who had entered Oxford believing himself to be a Christian. He suddenly saw his own story in Langston's narrative and realized that he was not a believer. It was a traumatic realization that was accompanied by an imagined picture, which Alister McGrath describes as follows: "He found a picture arising from within his mind. The picture was that of

The interior of St. Aldate's Anglican Church in Oxford, England, around 1940. J. I. Packer was converted at an evening service at the church on October 22, 1944. (Photo courtesy of St. Aldate's Anglican Church)

someone looking from outside through a window into a room where some people were having a party. Inside the room, people were enjoying themselves by playing games. The person outside could understand the games that they were playing. He knew the rules of the games. But he was outside; they were inside. He needed to come in."

Packer was particularly convicted by the latter awareness: "I need to come in." So by the Spirit's prompting, he came in. The sermon ended as most evangelistic services in the Oxford milieu (and more universally) did—with the preacher emphasizing the need for his hearers to commit themselves to Christ and the singing of the hymn "Just As I Am." Packer states simply, "I had given my life to Christ." He also recounts, "When I went out of the church I knew I was a Christian." More than half a century later, Packer could attest, with regard to his conversion, that "I remember the experience as if it were yesterday."

After sharing his conversion story, Langston added that he had afterward written to his parents to tell them what had happened. So when Packer went back to his room at Corpus Christi, he followed that example and wrote his parents about the step he had taken. In a return letter, Packer's mother expressed that she was glad he had found what he had found.

The preceding chapter pieced together various threads of Packer's life, and those threads all converged on the night of October 22, 1944. The foundation of belief had been laid. Packer had even defended the Christian faith on an intellectual level. What he needed was a catalyst. As is nearly always the case, the preaching of the gospel brought conviction. In keeping with the paradigm expressed in the Bible itself and Christian doctrine based on the Bible, the process of conversion began with an awareness of his lost state. Packer's friend Eric Taylor had been unable to fully show Packer that he lacked saving faith, but he had asserted the need for Packer to attain it. Nor should we miss the crucial role played by what we familiarly call a personal testimony (in this case, the preacher's).

Believing the Bible

A colleague once observed to me that before he became a Christian, the Bible seemed to him to be full of contradictions, but after his conversion, these seeming contradictions fell away. Something similar happened in Packer's life. As we reconstruct his first few weeks at Oxford, it is obvious that changes were happening to him with dizzying speed.

Packer began the life of genuine faith with his inherited view of the Bible. It was the attitude of theological liberalism, which Packer had imbibed from his nominally Christian, "high-church" background and from his random religious reading. Packer's description of his view of the Bible, as recorded by McGrath, is that it was "a mixed bag of religious all-sorts, of which one could not accept more than the general outlines." As a collection of religious sentiments, however, the Bible of course commended itself as a book of devotional reading. Accordingly, during the first few weeks after his conversion, Packer continued to read the Bible in an attitude of what he labels "partial skepticism," though some of it lit up for him in a new way.

Packer began to attend the Saturday evening Bible expositions sponsored by the Christian Union. Doing so required him to give up the opportunity to play clarinet in a jazz band that he had joined. The turnaround in Packer's attitude toward the Bible occurred six weeks after his conversion. It happened at the Saturday evening meeting, when "an eccentric old man from Cambridge" gave an exposition of a chapter from the book of Revelation (Packer believes that it may have been Revelation 12—in my view, very promising material). At the beginning of the meeting, Packer retained his longstanding liberal skepticism about the Bible; at the end, he believed that the Bible is God's Word about the world and God himself, and that it expresses the truth about every reader of the Bible. Packer later said, "I can still remember the feeling of surprise—and gladness—as I left the meeting because I knew that *I knew* that the Bible is the Word of God."

Completing the Academic Program

Two stories unfolded during Packer's years at Oxford. One was the spiritual journey—the life of faith. The other was the academic life of the mind. It would be wrong to set these two stories up as rivals. They both carried God's approval, and both were important to Packer's future life and ministry.

Packer's academic success was of the very highest order. In his second year at Oxford, he took his first public examination. He achieved what is known as a "first" or "the first class" in Oxford and Cambridge circles. This means "first-class honors" and is equivalent to the U.S. *summa cum laude*. Bruce Harris, who arrived at Oxford as a student two years after Packer matriculated, recalled that Packer's academic achievements and intellectual brilliance were already legendary among students. In his lifestyle, Packer was what I call "a serious student." He split his life between studies and Christian service, and did not take time to socialize in the Common Room. His head injury prevented him from participating in sports, but he would not have had time for it anyway.

Packer's final examinations came at the end of his time at Oxford, in the spring of 1948. He was expected to receive what at Oxford is called a "double first"—first-class honors in two subjects on the same set of examinations. Packer did not quite make it, being awarded second-class honors in both ancient history and philosophy.

Even to this early point, as we have seen, Packer's life was a case study in seeming setbacks that God used for good. We can see this in such a small detail as his housing during his time at Oxford. Four-year students at Corpus Christi were ordinarily allowed to live on campus for three years, but they needed to find off-campus housing for the additional year. Although Packer looked forward to being in his familiar room for his third year (1946–47), the influx of returning soldiers into the student body led college officials to allot Packer's room to a new student. Packer managed to find a room in a house on Lincoln Road, off the busy Abingdon Road leading south from the city center. Thus, for his last two years in college, Packer enjoyed the scholarly advantage of having a living room ("front room") and an upstairs bedroom for his own use. The daily walk to college and the Bodleian Library took thirty minutes, and I can easily picture Packer making the walk. When the ESV translation committee met in Cambridge, Packer regularly chose a fast thirty-minute walk between the Arundel House Hotel and Tyndale House (site of the committee work) over an available van ride. To this day, I can see the seventy-year-old Packer in the first wave of walkers, setting a lively pace and conversing the entire way.

Church Affiliations during the College Years

It is common for Christian college students to find their weekly religious affiliations something of a problem. The options include spiritual nurture from a student group and some type of Sunday experience at a local church. Usually, multiple groups and churches compete for the allegiance of students. Packer's post-conversion religious experience in Oxford followed this familiar pattern.

As Packer sized up the church situation in which he found himself, he began with disillusionment regarding the Anglican Church, in which he had been raised. That church had let him down. He had grown up in the church, yet nothing had been clearly said about the need for conversion and personal union with Christ. Packer had left his Gloucester Anglican parish as a latter-day Nicodemus—a stranger to what was best in his own tradition, not even knowing the basics of the new birth. Yet, despite his disillusionment with the Anglican Church, he did not entirely abandon his connections with it after his conversion. In fact, he stated in a 2014 conversation that he "never thought of leaving the Anglican Church on a permanent basis."

Given the uneasy state of his alliance with the Anglican Church, also known as the Established Church, we can discern two threads in Packer's church affiliations at Oxford, both of them signposts for paths that he has taken throughout his life. If we are looking for broad labels, we might call them Anglicanism and what historically has been called the nonconformist tradition in England, including an evangelical parachurch strand, encompassing organizations such as the Christian Union.

As is still true today, there were two evangelical Anglican churches in the vicinity of the college in center city Oxford. It has always seemed a little unfortunate to me that they are so close to one another (one block apart). The two churches are St. Ebbe's and St. Aldate's. In Packer's day, as today, the two churches represented distinctly different styles within evangelicalism.

In the mid-1940s, St. Ebbe's was characterized by what Americans call fundamentalism—a rigidly conservative orientation (in Packer's phrase) suspicious of culture and disapproving of "worldly" practices. Packer found the preaching style cool and detached. According to McGrath, Packer regarded St. Ebbe's as "a cold and unwelcoming place." Packer recalls that attendance at St. Ebbe's during his first two years in college was so low that the church was "very empty" at worship services. St. Aldate's was more attractive to Packer. The preaching was ardent. During Packer's first year at Oxford, he sometimes attended St. Aldate's with his Corpus Christi Christian Union representative, Ralph Hulme.

During the first two years following his conversion, Packer gravitated toward the local Plymouth Brethren assembly, located off Cowley Road on the outskirts of the college part of Oxford. The content of the preaching was biblical and substantial, in contrast to the preaching at St. Aldate's. Several leaders in the Christian Union were Plymouth Brethren people. Two of these became very important in Packer's life—James Houston (one of the founders of Regent College in British Columbia and its first president) and Donald Wiseman (who became a noted archaeologist and also played an important role in the history of Tyndale House in Cambridge).

However, starting in his third college year, Packer attended St. Ebbe's, where an interim minister and then a long-term minister had rejuvenated the church. The long-term minister, Maurice Wood, was a commanding figure who attracted students to St. Ebbe's (Wood later became principal of Oak Hill Theological College in London and then bishop of Norwich).

Packer's attendance at Anglican churches during his college years had an effect that proved prophetic of Packer's later life: it made him suspect in the eyes of non-Anglican evangelicals. The Oxford Christian Union at that time was, in Packer's estimate, "an extremely conservative evangelical organization." When Packer was nominated as a candidate for the Executive Committee of the Christian Union, the suggestion was dismissed because Packer then attended St. Aldate's, which was considered theologically "unsound" by the senior members of the committee (a stigma that was less true of St. Ebbe's).

The Oxford Inter-Collegiate Christian Union

The church loyalties sketched above were supplemented by Packer's involvement in the Christian Union, which today we would call a parachurch organization. Having been converted through the work of the student-led group, Packer stayed active in its work throughout his years at Oxford. He became involved in *daily* prayer meetings sponsored by the Christian Union. According to McGrath, Packer in later years has had "no hesitation in affirming that he gained all his spiritual nurture from the OICCU at this stage," a verdict that Packer confirmed to me.

An organization this important in Packer's life deserves further attention. What kind of group was it? It was an evangelical melting pot. Prominent in the leadership were Plymouth Brethren students who were committed to an understanding of the Christian life known as the Keswick view of holiness (see below). But this does not mean that evangelical Anglicans were absent from the group. In fact, Packer was among those Anglicans.

What was the spiritual tenor of the group? Lady Elizabeth Catherwood (daughter of D. Martyn Lloyd-Jones and a student at Oxford when Packer was there) remembers it as being "pietistic and not strong doctrinally—cheerful but not very profound." Lady Catherwood believes that the Christian Union that she knew could fairly be characterized as "anti-intellectual."

Perhaps this explains why a group of four or five intellectually inclined students spontaneously generated an informal supplemental group of their own. They met at a local restaurant on Wednesday nights after the missionary prayer meeting of OICCU. The group was comprised of Elizabeth Lloyd-Jones and another woman, along with Packer, O. Raymond Johnston, and sometimes an additional male student. This group discussed issues of the Christian life. Lady Catherwood remembers the group as "a great mix" in which everyone brought something to the table. She brought a superior biblical knowledge, whereas Packer brought a philosophical temperament that asked what the biblical data meant. Lady Catherwood recalls Packer being "by nature a philosopher," someone who "had a very sharp mind in getting to the basis of an issue," and someone of whom it could be said that "everything he said was interesting." The meetings of the group were intellectually invigorating, "but also very touching."

In addition to the Plymouth Brethren influence in the OICCU, there was a group known as the "Bash campers." This movement had been formed by the Rev. Eric Nash, who organized summer camps known as the "Varsity and Public School" camp. Admittance to the camps was limited to boys who attended what in the United States would be called private schools or "college prep schools," which in England were known as public schools. The students at these schools were boys from privileged and wealthy families. Packer says these upper-class boys knew that they belonged to an aristocracy of talent from which future leaders would come.

The "Bash campers" were an evangelical branch of the broader social phenomenon of British upper-class values and lifestyles. Nash called them "the best boys from the best schools." They, too, were a group within the Oxford Christian Union. David Mullins, the student president of the OICCU from 1943 to 1946, was a Bash camper. Likewise, Wiseman, who overlapped with Packer at Oxford, claims that during their time there, the Christian Union was "under something of a 'Bash' influence." Lady Catherwood and Packer both affirm that they were aware of not belonging to this group of insiders and that they were viewed as "not measuring up" to the Bash standards. Lady Catherwood concludes that the Bashers were "a divisive element" in the Christian Union—a group that "did a great deal of good and a great deal of harm."

Puritanism and the Keswick School

The affiliations noted above give us the external story of Packer's religious development during his time at Oxford. But much was going on in Packer's spiritual life beyond those affiliations. The story of this internal life anticipates important themes in Packer's later life. Two encounters in particular were especially formative—Puritanism (as encountered in books) and a pietistic association known as the Keswick movement.

The history of Packer's interaction with the Puritans is the subject of a later chapter in this biography. All that we need to note here is that the Puritan influence began early—at the end of Packer's first term in college in December 1944. Being a devotee of the idea that all education is ultimately self-education, Packer resolved not to cease studying simply because the academic term was over. So when he went home for Christmas vacation, he resolved to learn more about George Whitefield, who had attended the same school in Packer's native Gloucester where Packer himself had been a student. Packer went to the public library and checked out a two-volume biography of Whitefield. He later called his reading of this biography a milestone in his spiritual development.

Two permanent influences flowed from this landmark experience. One was the Puritan theology of Whitefield. The second was Whitefield's transdenominational orientation. Whitefield *was* an Anglican, but we rarely think of him as such. Rather, we think of him as transdenominational. In America, we might think of him as a mainstream evangelical—the way we think of Billy Graham. Whitefield became a role model for Packer in highlighting the ecumenical advance of the gospel.

Packer's encounter with the Puritans had a lifelong influence on him, evident in both his thinking and his career as a speaker and writer. By contrast, the second significant encounter that he experienced in the year following his conversion produced a rejection rather than an embrace. This encounter was with the movement known in England as the Keswick view of the Christian life, which goes more particularly by the label "victorious living" (also known as the "higher-life" experience). To understand what all this means, we need to conduct a brief historical inquiry.

Keswick is a town in the Lake District of northern England. It became important to British evangelicalism (with spillover influence in America) starting in 1875. The most visible institutional "scaffolding" for the movement was an annual summer convention held in a tent in Keswick. For people who remember or still attend an annual "summer camp," we might think of the Keswick convention as a high-octane version of that evangelical institution. The Keswick conference has attracted "big name" evangelical speakers throughout its history, right to the present day. The conference has been important to missionaries and laypeople, but it also attracted the allegiance of British university students in the middle of the twentieth century, and this is how the movement entered the life of the newly converted J. I. Packer.

The keynote of the Keswick teaching was the promise of a deeper spiritual life (or "victorious Christian living") for people who followed its principles. This, in turn, was part of a long Christian tradition known as the quest for personal holiness. The promise held out was a version of triumphalism, or conquest over sin in one's life, along with the prospect of a closer walk with Christ. The path to such triumph was full surrender to Christ, with the implication that people who did not experience freedom from sin were deficient in this surrender. The favored motto by which to express this surrender was "Let go and let God." The other model of the quest for holiness—a resolved obedience to follow God in the spiritual warfare between good and evil—was dismissed by the Keswick school of theology as a form of legalism. In the Keswick view, instead of being a long obedience in the same direction, the Christian life took the form of continuous consecrations and reconsecrations, and the genre of the "consecration sermon" became a standard part of the picture.

The victorious-living view of the Keswick movement was prominent among students at Oxford in Packer's time there. It did not have the approval of the local Anglican churches (including St. Ebbe's and St. Aldate's), but it was the dominant strand in the student-led Christian Union. Packer could not possibly avoid the impact of the Keswick view. It precipitated the first emotional and theological crisis of his newly found faith, and throughout his life, he has criticized the Keswick view of holiness with unusual vehemence.

The nature of the crisis can be described as follows. Packer knew himself to be a genuine Christian, wholly committed to follow Christ. He wanted the peace that the Keswick people dangled in front of him. So he reconsecrated himself as the paradigm encouraged him to do.

However, in his words: "It didn't work and that was a deeply frustrating and depressing thing. . . . In fact, it was driving me crazy." Packer claims that he felt like the "poor drug addict" whom he once saw trying to walk through a brick wall, as well as like someone who kept "missing the bus." He experienced all of this as "an immature and churned-up young man." He later subjected the experience to a mature understanding and offered this critique of the Keswick view of sanctification: "It offers a greater measure of deliverance from sin than Scripture anywhere promises or the apostles themselves ever attained." According to McGrath, Packer came to believe that "the Keswick teaching encouraged believers to expect too much and too little"—too much in terms of freedom from sin in this life and too little in terms of the need to advance in the daily spiritual battle against evil.

The destructive effects of the Keswick philosophy remained a permanent theme in Packer's life and writing. He first took aim at Keswick theology in an oft-cited article published in 1955 (see the notes at the end of this book). In 1979, Packer compared himself to a child who has been burned and thereafter dreads the fire, in the same sentence describing his "hatred of the cruel and tormenting unrealities of overheated holiness teaching" as something "that remains in his heart to this day." In 1984, Packer claimed that if one takes the Keswick paradigm seriously, "it will tend not to help you but to destroy you." As recently as an interview in 2004, Packer restated the account of his tumultuous encounter with the Keswick view in college and his critique of that view as not teaching the truth about the need for repentance, thereby producing "a quite misleading account of the Christian's inner life."

Obviously Packer's negative encounter with Keswick triumphalism was a traumatic experience that permanently affected him. The corrective came in the form of Packer's encounter with the Puritans, especially (at this early stage) John Owen. This encounter also set a direction for the rest of Packer's life, as we will see in the later chapter devoted to the history of Packer's assimilation and advocacy of the Puritans.

Summary

College is a life-transforming experience for most young people, but it was preeminently so for J. I. Packer. We might think of his Oxford experience as a series of forks in the road. At the first fork, Packer turned from nominal Christianity to genuine faith. Then, almost immediately, he turned from skepticism about the Bible to belief that it is God's authoritative Word. Packer gained a firm foundation in the evangelical church scene and (more important) the Christian Union, but while standing on that foundation, he needed to decide between the Keswick theology of victorious living and the Puritan theology of repentance. Finally, no one drifts into academic success; Packer's seriousness about the intellectual life as a classics student was a deliberate choice.

Theological Education and Ministry

(1948–1954)

3

The Post-College Year

(1948–1949)

It is a common pattern in the academy for students to become so absorbed in their academic routine that they are diverted from planning for the next stage of their lives. It is therefore not uncommon for new college graduates to spend a year getting their bearings and planning their next moves. Some, however, are fortunate enough to have good interim employment fall into their laps. By God's providence, J. I. Packer was one of those fortunate people.

Packer Lands a Teaching Position

Midway through his years at Oxford University, Packer reached a well-thought-out decision to seek ordination in the Church of England. (The steps leading to that decision and the story of its implementation are chronicled in a later chapter.) Packer also reached a decision as to where he would attend seminary (known in England as "theological college"). Wycliffe Hall in Oxford was the college of choice.

Initially, Packer assumed that he would begin his study at Wycliffe Hall immediately after graduating from college, but then he developed second thoughts. Again following a common paradigm, in his final two terms as an undergraduate, Packer became restless with being confined in the college environment, which seemed to him to have taken on an air of isolation from "real life" and the larger culture. In Packer's word, he had come to feel that the intellectually rarified air of Oxford was "stuffy." Packer also remembers that in the circles in which he moved, it

J. I. Packer spent a year teaching Greek and Latin at Oak Hill Theological College in London. (Photo courtesy of Carl Dorey)

was generally assumed that gaining personal experience outside of formal education was a valuable thing for a future cleric to do. Of course, it is one thing to decide to take the familiar "year off" and another to find a meaningful and financially viable way of doing it.

As is often the case, what we today call networking was God's means of providing for Packer's employment in his first post-college year. The Oxford Christian Union had its own library of seminal Christian books, received as a bequest from an elderly Anglican clergyman who had built up a collection that was especially rich in religious classics from the sixteenth and seventeenth centuries. The senior librarian of the collection was the Rev. John Reynolds, curate of St. Clement's, an evangelical Anglican church on the outskirts of Oxford. During Packer's second year in college, Reynolds latched on to him as a book lover who could be trusted to serve as junior librarian to the collection.

What began as a shared interest in Christian books led to an unforeseen turning point in Packer's professional life. As final examinations were approaching, Packer and Reynolds crossed paths at a daily prayer meeting sponsored by the Christian Union. Reynolds had just received a letter from the principal of Oak Hill Theological College in north London, announcing his need to find someone to teach Greek and Latin for one year. Oak Hill had been founded in 1932 for the benefit of "training persons who are desirous of obtaining ordination in the Church of England and are without adequate means."

The possibility of a one-year teaching position seemed too good to be true to someone who possessed only an undergraduate degree. Nevertheless, Packer immediately wrote to the principal. An interview followed, and at the end, Packer was offered the position. The problem of the interim year was providentially and unexpectedly solved.

The Teaching Life

The position that Packer had landed was ideal for the young college graduate. The offered salary was room and board, plus two hundred pounds. The room and board, moreover, continued during vacation periods (which are extensive in the British educational system). This enabled Packer to stay in London instead of needing to return to Gloucester when classes were not in session.

Oak Hill was a small college, and the atmosphere was very different from the elite air of Oxford University. At the time, the Oak Hill faculty consisted of three permanent professors, supplemented by part-time lecturers such as Packer. As Packer's academic life unfolded, he became so thoroughly the theologian and biblical scholar that we need to let it sink in that during his year at Oak Hill, Packer taught in what American colleges might call the foreign languages department, not the Bible or theology department.

For scholars who become academicians, the first teaching assignment is formative for the future, and this was surely the case in Packer's life. The first important consequence of his one-year tenure at Oak Hill was his discovery that he possessed the teaching instinct. Geoffrey Chaucer captured the essence of that instinct in his magical one-liner about the Oxford "clerk" (student) on the pilgrimage to Canterbury: "gladly would he learn, and gladly teach." Packer's account of what happened during his year at Oak Hill is that "I discovered that nobody needed to teach me how to teach."

Students' responses to the new faculty member confirmed that Packer was a "natural" in the classroom. Alister McGrath polled some of these students and discovered that they found Packer to be "meticulous" and "careful." One remembered Packer as someone who "got the best out of his students" without ceasing to be caring and considerate.

To this day, Packer speaks in a slow and thoughtful style, producing the impression that everything is well thought out. Packer's students regarded this style as an asset for classroom instruction.

New teachers also gradually find their most natural areas of expertise. Packer was hired to teach Greek and Latin, and he was qualified by his Oxford degree to teach ancient history and philosophy as well. But institutions of higher education have a way of eliciting broader interests from teachers and students. During his year at Oak Hill, Packer began to teach students the Greek text of Ephesians, something that his advanced study of Greek at Oxford had equipped him to do, and this in turn allowed him to indulge his theological orientation.

Packer began his year at Oak Hill planning to seek ordination in the Church of England. He did not abandon that intention, but when he ended the year, teaching at a theological college had emerged in his mind as a natural direction for him to take. In typical fashion, Packer raised the bar high in regard to a possible career of theological teaching. He decided that it would require a doctorate in addition to what in the United States is called a seminary degree. This ran counter to the situation in England, where seminary teachers were not required to have doctorates. But in Packer's view, the cause of evangelicalism in Britain would require theological research as a prerequisite to becoming academically respectable and influential.

Forming Professional Relationships

A final sphere in which Packer's year at Oak Hill proved formative was the friendships and professional contacts that emerged, starting with the small faculty at the college. When asked what he remembers most vividly about his year at Oak Hill, Packer replied, "The friendships." Among these friends was Alan Cole, a fellow short-term tutor who confirmed Packer's abilities as a teacher and theologian. Packer also formed a lifelong friendship with Alan Stibbs, himself a leader of British evangelicalism in the mid-twentieth century (Packer later called him "for many years the best theological mind serving British evangelicals"). During Packer's year at Oak Hill, Stibbs and Packer took walks together and conversed about future directions that Packer's life might take.

Additionally, during the year in London, Packer renewed contact with O. Raymond Johnston, who had been a member of the small group of Oxford students who met for food and fellowship after Wednesday evening missionary prayer meetings. During Packer's year at Oak Hill, Johnston was a student at the University of London, so he and Packer reconnected. One of the bonds that Packer and Johnston shared was a passion for the Puritans. In fact, Johnston had just published an article on John Owen.

This Puritan interest, in turn, led to another important contact that Packer made during his time at Oak Hill, namely, D. Martyn Lloyd-Jones. Lloyd-Jones was a towering British evangelical, having succeeded the famous G. Campbell Morgan as preacher at the Westminster Chapel. By the end of the 1940s, his sermons and teaching had made Westminster Chapel a center for Reformed theology in England. Packer already knew Lloyd-Jones, having heard him speak to students at Oxford. Furthermore, Elizabeth Lloyd-Jones, daughter of the minister, had been a member of the same small Oxford student group that included Packer and Johnston. During his year at Oak Hill, Packer quickly adopted the practice of attending the Sunday evening worship service at Westminster Chapel (having attended a morning service at a local church). Packer provides an interesting slant on his attendance at Westminster Chapel despite being a committed Anglican, saying it was "enriching because it was different."

This informal connection with Lloyd-Jones took a more specific form when Packer and Johnston summoned the nerve to approach the "elder statesman" with a plan for an academic conference on Puritan life and thought. Of course, such a conference would require a platform from which to launch it. Part of that platform was to be the support of the Tyndale Fellowship for Biblical and Theological Research, associated with the Tyndale House enterprise in Cambridge. In addition to administering the house in Cambridge as a center for biblical research, this organization sponsored lectureships and study groups. The Tyndale Fellowship agreed to support Packer and Johnston's conference idea, but more help was needed to give the conference visibility, and a place for the meeting also had to be secured.

So the pair asked Lloyd-Jones for his help. "The Doctor" was enthusiastic about the possibility and offered Westminster Chapel as the location for the conference. Thus was formed the Puritan Studies Group of the Tyndale Fellowship, more familiarly known as "the Puritan Conference." The first conference was held in the church parlor of Westminster Chapel in December 1950, the year following Packer's teaching stint at Oak Hill.

McGrath provides the following analysis of the nature and scope that the Puritan Conference eventually attained:

> A rising generation of theological students and younger ministers were being offered a powerful and persuasive vision of the Christian life, in which theology, biblical exposition, spirituality and preaching were shown to be mutually indispensable and interrelated. It was a vision of the Christian life which possessed both intellectual rigour and pastoral relevance. . . . The Conferences offered those who attended them theological stimulation, pastoral reflection and Christian fellowship.

Given that the Puritan Conference eventually wielded great influence in sparking a revival in British evangelicalism, it is entirely possible that the idea for it was Packer's greatest accomplishment during his interim year. It would have been an honor for an established scholar to have been in on the ground level of such an auspicious project. For a recent college graduate to be a cofounder of the movement seems nearly unthinkable.

The truth is that Packer had already caught the attention of evangelical leaders in Britain. An entry in the history of Tyndale House and Fellowship speaks volumes: "In July 1949 a significant decision was taken to follow Geoffrey Bromiley's suggestion that different leaders could organize specialist reading parties. . . . It was suggested that James Packer might organize a study group on the Puritans." In July 1949, Packer was only twenty-two years old, yet already he was seen as the right person to organize an "interest group" of the Tyndale Fellowship.

Summary

McGrath is right to caution against treating Packer's year at Oak Hill Theological College as a mere interlude. Perhaps no other year in Packer's life surpassed this one in codifying future directions in his life. Packer discovered that he had the gift of teaching. He matured as a person while filling the public role of college teacher. He began to feel a calling to be a scholar as well as a minister. He forged important professional relationships. And he succeeded in finding support for a Puritan conference, and immediately found a niche in the intellectual world of British evangelicalism. He then returned to Oxford to resume his studies with a sense of purpose and a self-confidence he did not possess just a year earlier, when he graduated with his undergraduate degree. The lines had fallen in pleasant places for the twenty-two-year-old Packer.

4

Graduate Student in Oxford

(1949–1952)

Following his year of teaching at Oak Hill Theological College, Packer was ready to begin "theological college" (called "seminary" in the United States). The year of teaching had gradually convinced him of his need for more than a seminary education, but he did not abandon his commitment to earn such a qualification leading to ordination in the Church of England. Accordingly, Packer entered Wycliffe Hall in September 1949.

Wycliffe Hall as Packer Found It

Wycliffe Hall is something of an enigma to Americans, inasmuch as it does not fit the usual paradigm of a North American seminary and is not one of the regular Oxford University "colleges." The list of Oxford University institutions today consists of two groups—thirty-eight "colleges" and six "Permanent Private Halls," which are of religious foundation. Wycliffe Hall falls into the latter category. This in no way means that Wycliffe Hall is anything other than a full-fledged Oxford institution, and I note in passing that such prestigious Oxford institutions as Regent's Park College and Campion Hall are also among the six "halls."

Wycliffe Hall was founded in 1877 to provide theological education for people headed for ordination in the Church of England. It was

Wycliffe Hall in Oxford, England, the theological college where J. I. Packer completed his graduate studies. (Photo © Jpbowen. License: http://creativecommons.org/licenses/by-sa/3.0/legalcode)

named after John Wycliffe, an early reformer and master of Balliol College in the fourteenth century. Through the years, Wycliffe Hall has been regarded as an evangelical institution, but the expression of this has varied from one era to another. The Wycliffe Hall website highlights the "distinctive status" of the college as an official, degree-granting part of Oxford University that at the same time is governed by an independent council whose members must sign the Hall's Trust Deed, thereby safeguarding the college's evangelical commitment.

Alister McGrath was principal of Wycliffe Hall for more than a decade (beginning in 1995) and is obviously an authority on the history of the institution. In his biography of Packer, McGrath gives the following portrait of the college during the era of Packer's enrollment there: Although Wycliffe Hall was strongly evangelical in its first forty years, after the First World War, it became a liberal institution; in fact, during the period of 1935–1970, "Wycliffe Hall was widely regarded as a liberal Protestant college, with little genuine evangelical commitment." Packer confirms this verdict and remembers being "somewhat depressed" when he realized the extent of liberalism at the college.

One index to the prevailing liberalism is that during Packer's time at

Wycliffe Hall, the contingent of Christian Union students was a minority within the student body. The more liberal Student Christian Movement (SCM) was the dominant student group on campus. And yet, even though the institution was a "middle-of-the-road Church of England" college (McGrath's description), it was characterized by a thoroughgoing "low church" bias, as signaled (for example) by the fact that the officiating minister at Communion services stood on the north side of the communion table instead of facing east. The theological spectrum of the Oxford milieu was sufficiently broad that a student needed to be grounded in his convictions in order to maintain an evangelical viewpoint.

The mixed theological picture of the student body was matched by the faculty members at Wycliffe Hall. The principal, Julian Thornton-Duesbery, was viewed as more liberal than other staff members because of his involvement with a European movement called Moral Rearmament, which reached its greatest influence in the 1940s. It championed the belief that society needed to rearm itself morally rather than militarily. It thus produced a moral rather than spiritual view of the Christian life. According to Packer, other faculty and staff members at Wycliffe Hall were also more liberal than evangelical. We should note in passing that C. S. Lewis was at the height of his Oxford career during this era, though there is no record of him speaking to evangelical student groups at Oxford. Packer observes that Lewis was, after all, an Anglo-Catholic rather than an evangelical.

My concern for the moment is to find connections between Wycliffe Hall and the J. I. Packer that we have come to know. When Packer began his graduate study in the fall of 1949, he was one of fifty-four students enrolled at Wycliffe Hall. This small enrollment produced a closely knit circle of kindred spirits. The daily routine was tightly organized: morning prayer at seven thirty; quiet time at eight; breakfast at eight thirty; lectures beginning at nine and ending at one; lunch at one; free time after that (including time for sports); afternoon tea at four; evening prayer at six thirty; dinner at seven; and then time devoted to study. Saturday was a regular teaching day, and Sunday was set aside for church attendance and ministry in local churches. This routine exactly fits the picture of Packer that I have gained based on personal acquaintance with him.

Something else that fits Packer is the austerity of life in post-war Oxford (including Wycliffe Hall). Many college buildings were unheated. Food rationing was still in effect. The smell of boiled cabbage became a fixture in the reading room close to the kitchen of Wycliffe Hall. An American student who kept his California parents apprised of the food scene at Wycliffe Hall reported that the meals were "mostly potatoes, bread, cereals and soup." Packer says the same, adding jam and peanut butter to the inventory of staples. "Care packages" from home were even more welcome then than they are today. Packer relishes life and the festivity of meals, but he is not an extravagant man. He took the austerity of post-war Wycliffe Hall in stride.

Packer the Student, 1949–50

Packer threw himself back into the academic life with zest. He was an editor of the college newspaper (*The Lollard*) and served a stint as captain of the Wycliffe Hall table tennis team. His roommate during that initial year, Ralph Thomas, described Packer as "a friend to us all." Thomas later remembered Packer's towering intellectual abilities and unusual knowledge of the Bible, Christian theology, and the Thirty-Nine Articles of the Church of England.

A particularly endearing picture of Packer comes from an encounter with a fellow student at the very first meal of the term in the dining hall at Wycliffe Hall. Packer himself recounted the event in his 1981 book *God's Words* (see note on sources at end of this book). It was a "vintage Packer" experience:

> We were all strangers to each other, and conversation was exploratory, hearty and random. I told the man opposite me, a grinning little Welshman, that I was a Puritan addict. He asked why. I told him the Puritans had done me good; they went deep, and were magnificent on mortification. "Mortification!" he said. "Let's have a talk after the meal."

So the two talked about mortification—for two hours! They went to the adjacent University Parks and walked on the banks of the River Cherwell, discussing John Owen on mortification of sin. It turned out that the student, John Gwyn-Thomas, had struggled with the same brand of "higher life" perfectionism that Packer had repudiated a few years earlier. Gwyn-Thomas had eventually left the "overheated community" of perfectionists and was in every way a kindred spirit to Packer. College friendships are often formative experiences, perhaps those at Oxford preeminently so, and I note that forty years later, Packer wrote an introduction to a commentary on Philippians authored by the person who sat across the table from him at their first meal at Wycliffe Hall.

In a characteristic move, Packer had used the vacation times during his year of teaching at Oak Hill to work ahead on the required readings for his Old Testament course of study during his first year at Wycliffe Hall. This advance reading coincided with a policy at Oxford that allowed graduate students to complete their theology degrees in one year if they could meet all requirements. The official title of the degree program falls strangely on American ears: Oxford University Final Honour School of Theology. The knowledge base with which Packer entered his year of "seminary" education included competence in Greek, familiarity with the Greek New Testament, and a good grasp of church history and philosophy. Much of that competence flowed from the noble practice of self-education.

Packer's formal education at Wycliffe Hall took the following contours. The vice principal at Wycliffe, Jim Hickinbotham, was Packer's tutor in patristics (history of early Christian thought). His New Testament tutor was Douglas Jones, who allowed Packer to follow his own plan of study and made himself available as a resource person as needed. Packer also took a course in the philosophy of religion from the chaplain of Balliol College. In addition, he attended lectures by the famous Oxford scholar Austin Farrer (a friend of C. S. Lewis, to whom Lewis dedicated his book *Reflections on the Psalms*). Farrer was a stunning model for Packer—"a class A genius" who had mastered philosophy of religion, New Testament scholarship, and systematic theology. Where one attends college and graduate school *does* make a difference, and the Oxford milieu where Packer was educated filled his life with images of greatness, including people of towering intellect, and with beautiful surroundings as well.

At Oxford University, earning a degree does not depend on completion of course work; it depends instead on passing examinations. Packer took his examinations in June 1950. A fellow student named Geoffrey

Shaw (who later became principal at Wycliffe Hall) recalled walking with Packer in the gardens of Wycliffe Hall in the minutes before the exams were scheduled to start. When Shaw returned to his room for some last-minute cramming, Packer continued to meander through the gardens, eating the apple that constituted his lunch. Packer's self-confidence was validated when he attained a "first" (first-class honors) on the examinations.

Transition to Doctoral Study

Packer's innate brilliance and exemplary work ethic not only produced honors on his examinations; they also helped to solve the problem of how to finance his doctoral education, which began immediately after his initial year at Wycliffe Hall. Packer had been the beneficiary of financial support from the Church of England during his first year at Wycliffe, but that support did not extend to doctoral studies. However, because of Packer's performance on his exams, he was invited to teach biblical theology and philosophy of religion at St. Michael's House, a few minutes' walk up Banbury Road. St. Michael's House was a school for women preparing for ministry. It had an enrollment of some thirty students. It so happened that the course in biblical theology that Packer composed for this teaching assignment was the same course that he would later teach in his career in Bristol.

Packer's diligence paid off when he received two scholarships that helped to make the completion of his doctoral degree possible. One of these came on the strength of his superior showing on the examinations that climaxed his first year at Wycliffe Hall. It was known as the Liddon Theological Studentship, intended to finance theological research at Oxford, and named after an esteemed nineteenth-century British theologian and churchman named Henry P. Liddon. The two-year scholarship was supplemented by a grant from the Local Education Authority of Packer's hometown of Gloucester.

Graduate education at Oxford University is different from the model followed at American universities. In the United States, a graduate student starts by taking ordinary courses and then gradually moves toward identifying an area of specialization for the dissertation. At Oxford, one begins with the specialization already established. The important hurdle then becomes finding the right supervisor for the dissertation. Another difference that should be noted is that whereas a doctoral degree in the United States is called a PhD ("doctor of philosophy"), the designation at Oxford is DPhil.

Packer began his quest for the doctorate in the enviable position of having already identified a subject that had seized the sovereignty of his mind. That subject was the English Puritan Richard Baxter (1615–1691). But Baxter was a double-edged sword: the corpus of his writings is voluminous (at the end of his life, Baxter offered the verdict on his writings that "fewer well studied and polished had been better"), which meant that material was plentiful, but it also would be easy for Packer to lose his way in the sheer quantity of it all. However, Packer already had a specific area of inquiry in mind: the doctrine of salvation.

Packer also had a preferred dissertation director in mind, but he was not a faculty member of Oxford University. This posed a potential problem. The scholar whom Packer regarded as the best candidate was Geoffrey F. Nuttall, an established Puritan scholar who had graduated from Oxford University in the 1930s, after which he became a Congregational minister (following in the footsteps of his grandfather and father). Of Welsh origin, Nuttall in 1945 became the second nonconformist theologian to receive a doctor of divinity degree from Oxford University. Nuttall's landmark book *The Holy Spirit in Puritan Faith and Experience* (Basic Blackwell, 1946) had put him on the map in the broader world of church history scholarship. By the time Packer wished to study under him, Nuttall had begun a long tenure as a lecturer in church history at New College in London.

Packer's persistence in securing the approval of Nuttall as his dissertation director tells us something important about him. In Packer's mind, Nuttall was the most qualified person to direct his study, and Packer is disinclined to settle for second best. Still, getting approval for someone not on the faculty at Oxford University was a hurdle.

I speak personally when I say that a Christian scholar's career is typically a chain of providential links in which one thing leads to the next, and we can see this in the process by which Packer was enabled to write his dissertation under Nuttall. Packer began his quest to jump this hurdle by paying a visit to an esteemed and long-established Regius professor at Oxford named Claude Jenkins. Initially, Jenkins offered the opinion that Nuttall's non-faculty status would make him ineligible to direct a dissertation. But it so happened that Jenkins had served on the committee that had assessed Nuttall's doctoral dissertation, leading to his receiving the doctor of divinity degree, and had formed a high opinion of Nuttall. So he advocated for Nuttall to oversee Packer's dissertation, despite his initial uncertainty about the arrangement.

Soon after his meeting with Jenkins, Packer received a formal letter from the committee on graduate studies of the Oxford University Faculty of Theology informing him that his topic had been approved—and so had his request to study under Nuttall, whose degree from Oxford gave him sufficient connection with the Faculty of Theology to allow the arrangement. Packer was instructed to make contact with Nuttall to arrange the logistics.

Nuttall recalled to McGrath that the arrangements for supervision were "very unusual." It was agreed that Packer and Nuttall would meet regularly each term, either in Nuttall's home or at Williams's Library in central London, famous for its Puritan (also called nonconformist) holdings.

Writing the Dissertation

The eventual title of Packer's dissertation was "The Redemption and Restoration of Man in the Thought of Richard Baxter." It ran to 499 pages. For several reasons, it was not published as a book until half a century later (in 2003).

Packer began his research in September 1950. Once the university clock started ticking in regard to the timetable for writing the dissertation, Packer had seven terms (two years) to complete the project. According to Packer, in the early stages, the research was unfulfilling. The protocol for any dissertation is to begin with the mandatory "review of scholarship." The secondary literature on Baxter was unsatisfying to Packer, who became increasingly impatient with how scholars had failed to hit the target. Nuttall proved his worth as a director by encouraging Packer to stay the course. By the time Packer left Oxford to assume parish duties in December 1952 (see next chapter), he had completed his exhaustive research.

The completion of the dissertation occurred while Packer was a minister in a church in Birmingham. Following the familiar protocol for all doctoral dissertations, Packer submitted his successive chapters to his supervisor, who critiqued them, leading to eventual revision. Packer beat the deadline for submitting three copies of his final dissertation by a mere three days. This happened in the week of Packer's marriage to Kit Mullett. My son Philip Ryken, who wrote an Oxford dissertation on the Puritan Thomas Boston, has told me that it became virtually a hallowed ritual among evangelical scholars studying in Oxford to ask that Packer's dissertation be "fetched from the stacks" for them to hold in their hands. Philip also informs me that the list of people who have thus checked out the dissertation reads likc a who's who of well-known scholars.

Handing in a dissertation is a rite of passage for academicians, but there is a sense in which the oral examination (U.S.: "oral defense") is even more determinative of a scholar's future. In European universities, the oral defense is called a *viva* (Latin *viva voce*, meaning "with living voice" [i.e., oral]). Packer's defense occurred at Regent's Park College (of Baptist origin) on Wednesday, December 1, 1954, at 2 in the afternoon. It lasted only one hour.

An Oxford oral exam is conducted by two examiners, neither of whom is the director of the dissertation. Packer's examiners were the principals of Mansfield College, John Marsh, and Regent's Park College, R. L. Child. As is often the case in oral defenses, the examiners were not experts in the subject of the dissertation. As a result, Packer's examiners were left to judge the dissertation on how well it was written, on Packer's ability to defend his arguments, and on Packer's knowledge of theology more generally. Packer recalls that one of the examiners came alive when the subject moved to Anselm of Canterbury (eleventh century) and how Baxter could have been descended from Anselm. There was never any question that Packer would pass, and he was quickly informed that he had earned his doctorate. This is the longed-for consummation of every graduate student, and Packer experienced it as such. His dissertation director, Nuttall, praised the dissertation as "one of the best theses I have ever supervised or examined."

What the Dissertation Tells Us about Packer

The climax of Packer's graduate education was the dissertation that he wrote, so it is appropriate to take a brief excursion into what we can know about J. I. Packer in his mid-twenties based on his dissertation.

The most immediate thing that we notice is the ambitiousness of the project. The reprinted works of Baxter are a library of twenty-three volumes, and this is only about two-fifths of his total output! Baxter is what we familiarly call "a bigger-than-life figure," but so is Packer. It would have been possible for him to choose a lesser Puritan or to base the dissertation on selected texts, but Packer essentially took on the entire Baxter corpus.

We can note secondly the choice of a very specific theological dimension of Baxter as the topic of study—the doctrine of salvation. Baxter is an encyclopedic figure who wrote on much besides theological topics. In my own book on the Puritans, Baxter is one of my most frequently quoted Puritan authors, but almost none of those references are to theological themes. They deal instead with what I call practical Christian living—topics such as work, money, and education. In Packer's choice of subject, we can see that he is at heart a theologian. McGrath's conclusion is that in the dissertation, Packer set for himself the task of providing "a full, sympathetic exposition of Richard Baxter's doctrine of man, created and fallen; of his redemption by Jesus Christ; and of the restoration in him of the image of God through the obedience of faith by the power of the Holy Spirit."

Additionally, we should not overlook the obvious: Packer is an expert on Puritanism. It has been a life passion, dating from his second year in college. It was nearly inconceivable that Packer would not choose a Puritan subject for his doctoral dissertation. In the dissertation itself, before Packer explicates Baxter's theology of man and redemption, he reconstructs the Puritan context within which Baxter wrote. As always, Packer writes about Baxter and the Puritans in a polemical vein, defending them against detractors.

Finally, I note the specialized or technical nature of the dissertation. Packer has not built his publishing career on this type of writing, showing that his impulse to make theology and other subjects plain to ordinary educated Christians has been a conscious choice, even though other options were open to him in the direction of specialized academic scholarship. Here is a specimen of the prevailing style of the dissertation (taken from the conclusion): "In his Arminian analysis of the work of Christ, Baxter went beyond the earlier Calvinistic advocates of universal redemption, the followers of Cameron and Amyraldus in France and of

Usher and Davenant in England." Again, "'hypothetical universalism' . . . sought to combine a Calvinist view of the nature of the atonement with an Arminian view of its scope." Packer has the intellectual inclination to thrive in such theological discourse, but his sense of vocation to the ordinary Christian has led him away from it (even though his own thinking is undergirded by specialized knowledge).

Summary

There is a tendency in some circles to be fully aware of the formative influence of education at the grade school, high school, and college levels, while viewing graduate education as an activity pursued by those whose formation is virtually complete. In such a view, the years in graduate school are largely devoted to proving scholarly competence en route to an advanced degree. This is a misconception, as most people with PhDs will attest. The three years that Packer spent at Wycliffe Hall were years of formation, both intellectually and personally. He was permitted the luxury of largely self-directed study and research. He sharpened his ability to conduct theological argument, and he built a firm foundation on which to stand as a Puritan scholar the rest of his life. Packer left Oxford not only with a credential, but also with a habit of mind that served him well from then on.

5

Ministry

(1952–1954)

Even though J. I. Packer is known as an academician rather than a minister, he felt an early call to the ministry. There are ways in which Packer never abandoned a pastoral calling, even though his venues of service have been the college and the published word rather than the church. I am reminded of a parallel provided by John Milton. As a Cambridge University student, Milton was theoretically headed for the ministry, but he was denied a church position because of his Puritan convictions. Miltonists have long theorized about when Milton changed his vocation from being a minister to being a writer. I was intrigued by the thesis of a book that claimed that Milton never abandoned his early sense of calling to the ministry; he simply shifted the venue from the pulpit to the published word.

The Decision to Enter the Ministry

Packer was decisively converted as a young adult. A year after his conversion, he began to feel a call to the ministry. Acquaintances had suggested the ministry as a possible direction for his life. In fact, a year before his entrance to Oxford and his conversion there, the mother of his friend Eric Taylor had predicted that he would become a minister! Since Packer was not even a genuine Christian, he was hardly in a position to take the suggestion seriously. Still, the seed was planted in his mind.

After Packer's conversion, the possibility of becoming a minister gradually seized the sovereignty of his mind. During his third year in college, Packer devoted a Sunday afternoon to wrestling with the issue. He even compiled lists of reasons for and against entering the ministry. By the end of this momentous afternoon, Packer had reached an inner conviction that he should eventually seek ordination.

There were obstacles in such a path. One was Packer's sense of limitations regarding his qualifications for being a minister. By the end of his year of teaching at Oak Hill, he had proved himself as a teacher, but the things that made for success in the classroom were not by themselves the ones that would make for success in the pulpit or the teaching of young people. Packer viewed himself as shy and handicapped in relating to others, especially children.

Another issue was the need to determine his denominational loyalty. Packer had felt betrayed by the Church of England for not giving him the whole truth of the gospel. Furthermore, neither of the two evangelical Anglican churches in Oxford (St. Ebbe's and St. Aldate's) had impressed Packer very favorably (though this was more an assessment of the two rectors than the churches per se). Packer felt at home in the Brethren church on the outskirts of Oxford. Nonetheless, he chose to cast his lot with the Church of England, the church of his roots.

The Process of Pursuing Ordination

The Church of England has an elaborate protocol for anything having to do with the institutional church. This was certainly true of the process on which Packer embarked during his third year as an undergraduate at Oxford. The process leading to ordination was supervised by the Central Advisory Council on Training for the Ministry (CACTM, and I again record how my head swam with acronyms when I explored the ecclesiastical and evangelical history of England in the middle of the twentieth century). The secretary of the council turned out to be the same curate who had taken Packer under wing in the instruction leading to his confirmation in Gloucester. Also, one of those who recommended Packer was the former vicar of his church in Gloucester; in keeping with the nominal Christianity that had prevailed in Packer's home church, this minister commended Packer as "a faithful churchgoer," not as a vibrant Christian (for example).

After Packer approached his former curate about beginning the process of ordination, the process unfolded smoothly. The first step was attendance at a selection conference early in 1947. The conference was a formidable one, lasting three days. The time was spent with other candidates and five selectors. The candidates were interviewed individually by each of the five selectors, who then conferred and reached decisions about them. Packer was questioned about his motivation for seeking ordination, about his self-assessment of his qualifications for ministry, and about his educational foundation for ministry. He left the conference with such a strong sense of calling to the ministry that he resolved that if his request were denied, he would immediately reapply. However, within a week, Packer was informed that he had been accepted for training for the ordained ministry.

It is impossible to overstate the difficulties that faced a conscientious evangelical entering the ministry in the Church of England in the middle of the twentieth century. The dominant ideology of the Anglican Church at that time was classic liberalism. The supernaturalism of the Bible and the Christian faith was discredited, and the Bible itself was regarded as a human book, not a divine revelation.

Concurrent with this story of the liberalism of the Anglican Church, we can trace the state of evangelicals as a group within the broader Anglican Church in the second half of the twentieth century. (More is said about that story later in this biography.) When Packer decided to seek ordination, evangelicalism in Britain had reached a low ebb. Its numbers within the Anglican Church were statistically insignificant. Furthermore, it was dominated by a pietistic strain that was impatient with serious theological inquiry, including the Christian past. An isolationist mentality held sway in the movement. Not surprisingly, evangelicals were treated dismissively by academic theologians. They had no prominence within the Church of England, where they were regarded as "fundamentalists" and made to feel like outcasts. For these reasons, ordination in the Anglican Church was an unlikely course for Packer to choose, but he entered the path without evident hesitation.

The Search for a Ministerial Position

As Packer neared completion of his work at Wycliffe Hall in 1952, he became increasingly concerned about finding a place to serve. He had a very high regard for two churches in London. One was Westminster Chapel, a nonconformist (non-Anglican) church where D. Martyn Lloyd-Jones was minister. Technically, Westminster Chapel was a Congregationalist church and, as such, was not an option for the Anglican J. I. Packer. The Anglican church in London that Packer found most appealing was All Souls, located in central London at Langham Place, where John Stott was rector (parish minister). The prospect of serving there was sufficiently attractive to Packer that he wrote to Stott inquiring about the possibility of becoming a curate (American "assistant minister") at the church. In the words of Alister McGrath, Stott's reply was "courteous and affirming—but not affirmative." When I asked Packer if it was a great disappointment to be turned down for a position at All Souls, he said that it was not, because he is not a person who characteristically has only one option.

With the door closed at All Souls, Packer looked for guidance to the principal of Wycliffe Hall, Julian Thornton-Duesbery. The latter had just learned that a vicar (another term for a parish minister, somewhat equivalent to an American "senior minister") in Cheltenham was looking for a curate. Cheltenham is close to Gloucester, where Packer's parents still lived, and therefore appealed to him, so he made a trek to Cheltenham to explore the possibility. However, the vicar was liberal in orientation, and Packer returned to Oxford with the realization that the Cheltenham opening was not an option for him. His situation was becoming increasingly urgent as he neared the end of his education.

As is often the case, networking became the avenue by which Packer landed a clerical position. During his year of teaching at Oak Hill Theological College, Packer had become a close friend of Alan Stibbs, a colleague on the faculty. Stibbs had heard of an opening at Harborne, a suburb of Birmingham. The minister was an evangelical named William Leathem and Harborne was a conservative evangelical parish. It was an ideal position for Packer. He accepted the position of curate for a salary of 315 pounds per year.

To "seal the deal," Packer needed to undergo a formal interview with the bishop of Birmingham. The bishop, Ernest W. Barnes, was a theological and social liberal. His goal was to extirpate medieval "superstition" from the church. Barnes was seventy-eight years old—someone whom Packer remembers as a "doddering old man." The main topic covered during the interview was the importance of evolution for the church! I find it highly humorous that, in McGrath's words, "Packer remembers the interview being amiable, even though he was conscious that they both had very different understandings of what they were talking about." In confirmation of the liberal orientation of the church hierarchy, Barnes asked Packer to write an essay on "The Use of Reason in Theology" (not "the use of the Bible," we should note). The essay was read by an examining chaplain, who expressed "profound distaste" for Packer's theology, which he called "intellectual bulldozing."

It is obvious that Packer was in a common position for evangelicals in denominations dominated by liberalism. He had landed a position at an evangelical oasis in a liberal desert. Packer was fortunate to have found a conservative evangelical parish pastored by an evangelical preacher.

The process of searching for and finding a job climaxed with a formal ordination service. Ordinarily, the Church of England schedules its ordination services to correspond to the academic calendar. The two common times are the end of the academic year (late June or early July), when an entering minister's education would be complete, and the end of summer vacation. Because Packer had followed a somewhat irregular pattern in his seminary education, his ordination was an "Advent ordination," occurring on December 21, 1952. The service was not held at Harborne, where the parish church had been destroyed by bombing during the war, but in the parish church of Handforth. The presiding minister was Bishop James Henry Linton, taking the place of the ailing Bishop Barnes. Everything was conducted according to Church of England protocol. Packer's official title was that of ordained deacon. A year later, on December 20, 1953, Packer would be ordained as a priest at a service conducted in Birmingham Cathedral.

Parish Life

The parish church at Harborne was officially called St. John's. The environment there was distinctly Protestant—more Puritan than Anglican. Before coming to Harborne, Leathem, the vicar, had served a church in Preston (northern England) that was known for the length and Protestant substance of its sermons. The presiding ministers at Harborne preached in the black gowns used in free (nonconformist) churches instead of the clerical vestments typical of the Anglican Church. The original church building had been destroyed during the bombing of the Second World War, with the result that during Packer's tenure, the church met at the local Memorial Hall.

Life was busy for the new curate, who was one of several students living at the vicarage with the Leathem family. Leathem was a lively intellectual companion for Packer. The two typically spent an hour together every morning, praying and reading the Bible, determining the business of the day, and conducting theological conversations. Packer found these times highly rewarding.

Packer also did his share of preaching, filling the pulpit every other week. He had become a devotee of Lloyd-Jones's style of painstaking exposition of Bible passages. Packer's first sermon was an exposition of Matthew 5:3 ("Blessed are the poor in spirit"). An intended twenty-five-minute sermon actually took thirty-five minutes to deliver (reminding me of the Puritan address at Wheaton College that was my first exposure to Packer as a speaker). After six months, Leathem offered Packer a critique of his preaching. He told Packer that some people found his sermons hard to follow. Leathem also said: "Look, you are too serious when you preach for anyone to take you seriously. God gave you humor. Use it." Packer accepted the challenge, claiming many years later that "I've been planting jokes in my sermons ever since, and I rather think it is a good idea."

Teaching was an important part of Packer's duties at Harborne, and this task felt more natural to him than preaching. Packer initiated a weekly doctrine class for young people. The goal was to introduce attendees to the basics of Christian doctrine. Some who found the content of Packer's sermons difficult to follow remember the clarity with which he expounded ideas in the theology class. Later in life, Packer offered the verdict that "the best of all I did" during his two years in parish ministry was the weekly doctrine class. He remembered fondly that "all the youngish people wanted to learn about their faith, and I introduced them to their heritage. They loved it. I gave them something they discovered they wanted."

Packer's job was not that of youth minister, but his duties evolved in that direction. The Birmingham branch of Boys' Brigade was based at St. John's, and it had become a custom for the curate of the church to serve as chaplain at the annual summer camp of this group. Packer stepped to the plate and accompanied the boys to a seaside resort in Somerset. He gave the evening addresses, designed to bring each day to a close. In a manner that paralleled his own story, Packer explained the way of salvation to one boy who knew the content of the gospel (having attended a Baptist church for many years) but had never been told about the need to make a commitment to Christ.

The truth is that Packer was better at relating to people than he believed. He did fine with young people. Mrs. Leathem, who organized the women's meetings at St. John's, recalled how popular Packer's teaching was with the older members of the group. Forty years later, parishioners at St. John's continued to maintain contact with Packer, who, with good reason, remembered his brief career as a parish minister as an affirming and growing time in his life.

Although Packer was a parish minister for only two years, the subjects of preaching and the ministerial calling are ones on which he has spoken and written throughout his career. I devote a separate chapter to these topics later, but I note for now that Packer's theory of preaching and ministry was rooted in his early experience as a parish minister.

Packer's Scholarly Life at Harborne

Packer actually wore "two hats" during his years at Harborne. He was the local curate, but he was also a scholar. The fact that he found time for both is a tribute to his work ethic. He had left Oxford in December 1952 with the research for his dissertation virtually complete, but did the writing while serving full time in the church. Packer composed the dissertation largely in his room at the vicarage. It is hard for the computer generation to imagine someone's typing a five-hundred-page dissertation or storing information on notecards, but I can attest that this is how it was done. There were not even Xerox copiers to aid the process.

Given that he was a full-time curate, it is hardly surprising that Packer came close to the wire in regard to meeting the deadline for submission of his dissertation. He handed it in a mere three days before the due date. Leathem was compassionate in regard to Packer's situation. During the final month of composition, he relieved Packer of all non-Sunday duties. Packer spent his time reaching closure on the dissertation, supervising its typing, and then proofreading the final copy.

Amazingly, writing the dissertation was not the only scholarly activity in which Packer engaged during his time at Harborne. Two additional things were unfolding in his life as a scholar. One was his publishing career. Packer did what enterprising graduate students always do—he started submitting articles based on aspects of his dissertation to journals. In Packer's case, this subject was Richard Baxter and the Puritans. The first published article is a rite of passage for a scholar, and for Packer it was "The Puritan Treatment of Justification by Faith," an article published in *Evangelical Quarterly* in July 1952. Half a year later, *The Christian Graduate* published "Sanctification—Puritan Teaching." Then, six months later, a more prestigious journal—*Theology*—published "Great Pastors: Richard Baxter."

But that was only one of two "extracurricular" scholarly enterprises that Packer was pursuing. As noted earlier, during Packer's year of teaching in London, he and a fellow student had successfully enlisted the cooperation of Lloyd-Jones to initiate a Puritan conference. The first conference was held in December 1950, when Packer was enrolled at Wycliffe Hall. The series then continued for two decades. For our purposes, I note that during Packer's years at Harborne, he not only helped to organize the annual conference, but also delivered two addresses in 1952, three in 1953, and two in 1954.

Summary

Every early phase of J. I. Packer's life was formative for his future. While a parish minister in suburban Birmingham, Packer developed skill in the pulpit that has served him well throughout his life. He discovered that his true gift lay in teaching, but not divorced from the context of the church locally and globally. In a situation in which it would have been easy to let his dissertation slide, Packer showed both perseverance and brilliance of mind in completing the 499-page work. He also published three articles and spoke seven times at the Puritan Conference.

6

Courtship and Marriage

(1952–1954)

There is a proverb about a "storybook romance." I personally think that the courtship of J. I. Packer and Kit Mullett gives substance to the proverb. Like the biblical story of Ruth and Boaz, the story that I am about to recount was governed by remarkable providences (to use a Puritan formula) and marked by captivating moments. I have heard Packer retell the story multiple times in a way that shows that he himself knows the story to be a "classic" (at least in entertainment value).

The Seminary Student and the Nurse

We have already had occasion to note Packer's self-assessment that he was an awkward person from childhood. His verdict on himself as an undergraduate student was that he was "an immature and churned-up young man, painfully aware of himself." When he first contemplated the possibility of becoming a minister, he hesitated because he felt himself to be "an odd person, somewhat solitary . . . very poor at human relationships." Additionally, Packer felt that he should not marry if he could not support a wife financially, and he was in no position to do so during his years of college and graduate education.

Despite the obstacles, Packer possessed the normal romantic longings of a young man. According to Alister McGrath, "As a young Christian, [Packer] gave considerable thought and prayer to the question of whom he should marry." We can thus picture Packer as a seminarian in quest for a wife, a not uncommon phenomenon. An early foray happened in 1945. At a Christian summer camp near Bath, Packer met a young woman from Bradford with whom he subsequently corresponded. The romance was short-lived. As the young woman later confided to her eventual husband, she "couldn't understand a word" of Packer's letters!

Someone who *could* understand the intellectually inclined Packer was Kit Mullett. She was Welsh, from the town of Llandebie in the county of Dyfed. In 1946, she had been converted at an Inter-Varsity evangelistic crusade in the nearby Welsh town of Ammanford. By the time she and Packer met, she was a nurse in training at St. Bartholomew's Hospital in London, within sight of St. Paul's Cathedral and across the street from where the blind John Milton lived in hiding while working on *Paradise Lost* after the fall of the Puritan cause.

The Most Productive Double Booking in History

The occasion that brought Packer and Kit together was a weekend conference, which Packer long afterward described as an event "that neither of us by rights should have been at." Kit's half of the equation is as follows: she was scheduled to work at St. Bartholomew's on the weekend of the conference (held at Pentecost 1952). But when Kit reported for duty on the momentous day, her "ward sister" (head nurse on the floor) observed that Kit had an inflamed eye that might be infectious. The head nurse told Kit, "You must go off the ward and not come back until that eye inflammation is gone."

The weekend conference had been arranged to bring together the two Christian Unions at St. Bartholomew's Hospital. One was for nurses and the other for doctors. Approximately thirty people from the hospital staff attended the conference, which was held in rural Surrey at a Methodist campground. With Kit's work for the weekend cancelled, attending the conference was suddenly a possible and attractive option for her. In Packer's account, "With a few hours' notice she packed her bag and came to the conference."

Packer's half of the equation centers around a development that was as unanticipated as Kit's sore eye. Packer was a student at Wycliffe Hall. One of his friends at the college, John Harwood, was the scheduled speaker for the Christian Unions conference. As the event approached, he discovered that he had scheduled himself to speak at two events on the same weekend. Packer's account is that Harwood "gave me the hospital conference." Packer was apparently a resourceful speaker, as evidenced by McGrath's account of what followed: "At this stage, Packer was still a student at Wycliffe Hall, with a reasonable amount of spare time at his disposal. He packed his clothes and a set of four talks on Paul's letter to the Philippians, and headed off to Surrey." Packer's laconic comment on the event at which he and Kit should not have been is that "there we were, and we just met."

A Compassionate Nurse

The conference started on Friday evening. Packer delivered the opening address, after which he found himself standing alone. The attendees, meanwhile, knew each other and were enjoying conversation in small groups. Kit noticed what was happening and "felt sorry for the speaker" (McGrath's summary of the situation). She went to his table and engaged in small talk. What kind of small talk? Kit told the speaker that she was a great admirer of the preaching of D. Martyn Lloyd-Jones and a regular attendee of services at Westminster Chapel. Both of those facts were also true for Packer. It is hard to imagine a greater compliment than Kit's observation to Packer that he spoke "remarkably like my minister, Dr. Martyn Lloyd-Jones." In fact, Kit said that she had never heard an Anglican speak like this!

In later years, Kit gave Wendy Zoba the inside story of why she went to speak to Packer. Kit thought that it was a "terrible rudeness" to leave a visiting speaker standing by himself while others conversed. She explained further: "I was affronted by the fact that everybody else around me was ignoring the speaker. We Welsh people generally try to make strangers at ease."

Kit's sociability extended to the next day. On Saturday afternoon, the conference attendees went for a walk on the trails of the North Downs. With a bond having been established on Friday evening, Kit and Packer gravitated to each other on the afternoon walk. Little things mean a lot, and half a century later Packer was still enthralled by something that happened as they walked. He recalled in an interview, "I remember walking with her on a Saturday afternoon and seeing her kick off her shoes and walk barefoot, which, in a mild way, was intriguing to me."

One of the conventions of a love story, whether in real life or fiction, is that at first the couple seems unlikely to fall in love and get married. In later life, Kit confided regarding Packer: "When he took an interest, I was surprised. I still am." Packer, in turn, wrote in 2008 regarding Kit that "she was not in the least like the wife I had imagined myself finding someday."

After the Conference

On the Sunday afternoon of the conference, Packer recalls, it was "time for us all to go home, and that seemed to be the end of it." But it was not the end of it. Packer returned to Wycliffe Hall and found that he could not sleep! He recalls: "I couldn't get her out of my mind. I realized something pretty drastic had happened." In the circles in which I move, young men speak somewhat facetiously and metaphorically about being in quest for a Proverbs 31 wife. For Packer, this was quite literal. He got up at 2 in the morning and read the encomium in praise of the virtuous wife found in Proverbs 31. Packer's recollection is that "I could see her in every verse." When asked by an interviewer if it was "love at first sight," he replied: "I guess the realization of it didn't come until forty-eight hours after it had happened. Call it the depth-charge effect."

Packer reached the conclusion that he needed to "devise a respectable and responsible reason for getting in touch with her and maintaining our acquaintance." Recalls Packer, "I knew right away that this woman was it, and something must be done." Packer was accustomed to go on walking "holidays" (vacations) with an acquaintance, so he wrote to the Welsh Kit Mullett, asking for advice about a trip to Wales. Half a century later, Packer could laugh at the ruse. Kit took it in stride and replied to the letter. Packer adds that "we kept writing." Of course, correspondence by itself would not suffice, and the relationship did not stop there.

Courtship and Engagement

A happy love story requires initial secrecy about the relationship, along with a secret rendezvous or two, and the Packer-Mullett courtship ran true to form. At the beginning of the fall term that would bring Packer's time at Wycliffe Hall to an end, he arranged a Saturday meeting with

Kit in London. Packer was still concerned to keep the friendship a secret at this stage, so he planned to meet Kit at the Paddington train station (the station for trains running between London and Oxford). Secrecy was not as easy as he had imagined, however. At the Oxford train station, Packer was joined by the wife of a teacher at Wycliffe Hall! She was en route to London for a singing lesson. Of course, the two sat together on the train, and Packer spent the entire journey wondering how to keep matters secret at Paddington Station. With resourcefulness, however, he managed to meet Kit undetected. The couple spent a happy day together at Kensington Gardens in London.

As the autumn unfolded, Kit paid two daylong visits to Oxford, and Packer then went to London for a further one-day visit. The first visit in Oxford contained a memorable moment. Kit arrived during a heavy snowfall. She was wearing old shoes, and by the time the couple had walked from the train station to Wycliffe Hall (a very long walk indeed), Kit's feet were soaking. The resourceful Packer prepared a bowl of hot water, and Kit sat warming her feet in Packer's room. An Oxford friend who was active in the Puritan Conference stopped by, saw a woman in Packer's room soaking her feet, and withdrew in embarrassment.

Packer felt a certain urgency to become engaged to Kit. By December 1952, he was ready to move to Birmingham to begin his ministerial duties. He needed a time and place to propose to Kit. The third annual Puritan Conference at Westminster Chapel, scheduled for the end of December, seemed a suitably dramatic venue for the proposal. Packer was on the program for two addresses, but they were not primarily what was on his mind. He was given the use of a friend's apartment as a place to propose. On the evening of the engagement, after the event had occurred, Packer met Elizabeth Lloyd-Jones, daughter of Martyn and a close Oxford friend, at a tube stop; Elizabeth nearly fell onto the track in her excitement about the news.

The engagement was transacted on a Tuesday evening. The next day, Kit came to the Puritan Conference at Westminster Chapel, where she attended church, to hear her fiancé speak. When Lloyd-Jones saw two females in the audience, he offered the opinion to Packer that the women who were attending the conference were there "only for the men." When Packer said that he was engaged to marry one of the women, Lloyd-Jones replied that it was as he had said.

The Wedding in Harborne

Packer had just begun his ministry in suburban Birmingham. He was living in the home of the senior minister. Mrs. Leathem, wife of the minister, did not even know that Packer had a girlfriend. Once, when the phone rang for Packer at the Leathem residence while he was at a meeting, Mrs. Leathem answered and asked if she could take a message for him. Kit's reply was, "Tell him it's Kit." When Packer made an appearance and was asked who Kit was, he replied, "She's my fiancée." A formal introduction to the mystery woman occurred in the spring of 1953.

Things fell into place quickly. When Kit completed the requirements to become a fully qualified nurse, she had the good fortune to land a nurse's position at a hospital two miles from Harborne. She remained employed at the hospital until her marriage on July 17, 1954.

The wedding of J. I. Packer and Kit Mullett occurred at the local Memorial Hall, the temporary location of St. John's Church. William Leathem officiated. The ceremony was a Puritan-style wedding, lasting two hours! As was the custom of Puritans, there was a full-length sermon (preached by Alan Stibbs). The serving of Communion also added to the time required for the service. No one complained.

The Marriage

What do we know about the couple whose lives had been brought together so providentially and dramatically? My wife, a retired counselor, insists that in romance and marriage, people are searching for that which will complete what is lacking in them. I tell my students that most people marry their temperamental opposites, so there is every reason to believe that they will in due course do the same. I laughed and laughed when I heard Jill Briscoe, speaking in a chapel service at Wheaton College, tell the students that most people discover in their first year of marriage that they have married someone with whom they are incompatible. Packer adds that "achieving a happy compatibility of incompatibles is part of the maturing effect that marriage is meant to have." Of course, a successful marriage also requires a strong common bond, starting with the spiritual.

According to Zoba, it is important in Kit's thinking that "she's Welsh; he's English." On their Saturday afternoon walk at the conference in Surrey, Packer liked the "individuality" represented by Kit's taking her shoes off, but his own shoes remained on his feet. On walks together, Kit has always meandered, wanting to see the birds and the flowers. She carries binoculars. Packer is businesslike, ready for the trek to move on or be over. My friend Wendell Hawley tells me that when he visited a botanical garden with the Packers in Vancouver, Kit was alive with information about the plants, while Packer merely looked on approvingly.

According to Zoba: "Kit possessed all those qualities that [Packer], in his bookish way, seemed to lack. She was practical, relational, lively, and independent." Kit feels comfortable in challenging Packer's ideas and debating them. Packer claims to be an "analyst" instead of a debater.

To round out the portrait of their marriage and family, I share the following gleanings from Packer's books.

- "For Kit." The dedication in Packer's best-known book, *Knowing God* (Downers Grove, IL: InterVarsity, 1973).
- "For Ruth, Naomi and Martin [the Packers' adopted children], with their father's prayers that they will make their own all that I have written about here." The dedication in Packer's book *God's Words: Studies of Key Bible Themes* (Downers Grove, IL: InterVarsity, 1981).
- "The phrase 'hanging on' makes me think of the time many years ago when my wife Kit and I were taking a little-used path to see a waterfall. . . . Kit did not have any problem with it because she has always been very agile; she is like a mountain goat on unstable terrain. I am different. I was always clumsy." *Praying* (Downers Grove, IL: InterVarsity, 2006), 207.
- "I am enormously grateful to my daughter Naomi, who labored at some inconvenience to herself to put the book on computer, and to my wife Kit, who was willing to be neglected for a time so that it might be born." Preface to *Rediscovering Holiness* (Ann Arbor, MI: Servant, 1992).

Professional Life in England

(1955–1979)

7

Tyndale Hall, Bristol

(1955–1961)

J. I. Packer felt called to ordination in the Church of England, but not exclusively to parish ministry. After two years as a local minister, he moved into the academic life that would be the primary arena of his ministry for the rest of his life. Compared to the stable professional life that Packer enjoyed after moving to Canada in 1979, his quarter century as an academician and Anglican spokesman in England is a story of intermittent instability. As I tell that story, my American readers need to keep in mind that evangelicals in England from the mid-twentieth century on have lacked the critical mass that characterizes evangelicalism in the United States. The institutions for which Packer worked were small and often found themselves in stressful situations.

Relocating

Packer was beloved by his parishioners in Harborne, but his two years as a minister there left him with a growing conviction that his gifts lay in the direction of teaching theology in an academic setting. Additionally, both Packer and Kit had their family roots in the west of England and in adjacent Wales. A move in that direction would suit them well.

As Packer's second year of service in Birmingham neared its end, a teaching position opened at Tyndale Hall, a theological college (seminary) in Bristol. There was much to make the position appealing to

Packer. The college was located in the "west country," on the Bristol Channel, across which lay Wales. What today we would call the job description lay in Packer's area of expertise, that of "lecturer in theology."

Bristol has been on the "evangelical map" for more than two centuries, right to the present day (with Trinity College located there). It became a hotbed of evangelicalism and Methodism in the middle of the eighteenth century, and it played a key role in the Evangelical Revival, being the city where John Wesley reached a decision to emulate George Whitefield's practice of preaching in the fields.

Tyndale Hall before Packer Arrived

In order to understand this phase of Packer's life, we need to reconstruct the nature of the college to which he was called. It was founded by an evangelical group that had broken away from an organization known as the Church Missionary Society. That society had been founded in 1799 as a network of Anglican and Protestant evangelistic organizations working together to foster worldwide missionary activity, especially in Africa and the East. The "Clapham Sect" had provided the initial impetus, and William Wilberforce had been asked to be the first president (he declined, but accepted the position of vice president). As theological liberalism became entrenched in the Anglican Church in the twentieth century, the inevitable division between conservative and liberal factions arose. The conservative wing left the organization in 1922 and formed the Bible Churchman's Missionary Society. The purpose of the breakaway group was to be "the rallying ground for true scriptural evangelicalism at home and in the mission field."

The group perceived that this mission would require theological education. So, just three years after its formation, in 1925, the organization acquired property in a suburb of Bristol, where it founded the Bible Churchmen's Missionary and Training College. The setting was fabulous—across from parkland evocatively called the Downs and extending for a mile from the college. The park even offered views of the Avon Gorge and the Bristol Channel. Two years later, the college achieved recognition by the Church of England as a theological college designed to prepare men for ministry in the Anglican Church. The vision kept expanding, as a college named Dalton House was formed to educate women for missionary service.

Unfortunately, division struck the new institution within just a few years. In 1931, the principal of the college came into conflict with the executive committee over matters of discipline. The disagreement escalated to the point where the principal (or president) and staff resigned and formed their own college a short distance away. The new college was named Clifton Theological College. The original college made a moderately quick recovery, and within three years was again a viable college with a new faculty and student body. Nonetheless, the resulting situation was extremely awkward: three evangelical colleges in the same part of the city, with a history of hostility and suspicion toward one another.

J. I. Packer, around the time of his first teaching position, at Tyndale Hall in Bristol, England. (Photo courtesy of Regent College)

As a barometer of the unsettledness, J. Stafford Wright (who had been educated at the original college) joined the faculty of Clifton Theological College under the new principal, W. Dodgson Sykes (who headed the college from 1932 to 1951). But Wright soon left the faculty as a result of a dispute, only to return in 1951 to succeed Sykes as principal.

In 1952, the college changed its name to the more manageable Tyndale Hall, named after the English reformer William Tyndale (who had been born and raised in nearby Gloucestershire). The new name signaled a commitment to biblical scholarship and to the Reformation tradition. The Reformation flavor of the college was enhanced by the naming of individual residence halls after the reformers Thomas Cranmer, Hugh Latimer, and Nicholas Ridley.

Despite the college's shaky early history, by the time Packer joined the staff full-time in January 1955, Tyndale Hall was on the rise as an evangelical college in England. A key figure in that rise was a biblical scholar named Geoffrey W. Bromiley. Bromiley had earned his MA at

Cambridge University and his doctorate at the University of Edinburgh. All of this is par for the course in colleges and seminaries today, but at the beginning of the 1950s in England, most tutors (professors) were what Alister McGrath terms "enthusiastic amateurs"—teachers who would serve three- to five-year teaching stints before moving on to parish ministry. Bromiley was thus something of an anomaly among evangelical educators in England at the time in having earned a doctorate. He had been a student at Tyndale Hall and had returned to the college from 1946 to 1955, teaching and serving as vice principal. Though Bromiley soon decided to move on (eventually teaching at Fuller Seminary in California for three decades), there is a sense in which he had paved the way for Packer to succeed him as a professional biblical scholar.

As already noted, amateurism was the dominant mode in evangelical education in England at the time. According to McGrath, the idea of conducting what in the United States is called a national search was unheard of. Networking was the means by which jobs were filled. Packer had already been the beneficiary of this method at Oak Hill Theological College, and now it happened again.

William Leathem, Packer's senior minister, was a key player in the chain of events by which Packer landed his first permanent teaching position. Leathem had been active in the Bible Churchmen's Missionary Society. He had also commuted from Birmingham to Bristol regularly to lecture at Tyndale Hall on the Book of Common Prayer and Anglican worship. Thus, Leathem was naturally one of the first to know about the opening for a theology professor. He alerted Packer to the opportunity.

Tyndale Hall needed the new professor (tutor) to start in September 1954. However, the protocol of the time required curates in the Church of England to remain in a position for a minimum of two years. Packer would not reach that point until the end of December 1954.

The first step down the path by which Packer left parish ministry for the academy was a trip that Packer and Kit made to Bristol to explore the nature of the position and the degree of their interest in making a move. Because of Leathem's sympathy toward Tyndale Hall, the requirement for Packer to remain at Harborne was handled in a flexible manner. Leathem freed Packer to spend two days each week serving as "visiting lecturer" at Tyndale Hall while retaining his curacy in Birmingham. The schedule was rigorous, with Packer taking an early train to Bristol, teaching for the day, staying overnight, and returning to Birmingham the next day.

Tyndale Hall as Packer Found It

Packer became "resident lecturer" in January 1955. McGrath has ascertained that the official records of the Anglican Diocese of Birmingham list January 8, 1955, as Packer's last day of employment at St. John's Church in Harborne. Moving day was memorable for its wintry conditions. The Packers did not own a car, so they rode from Birmingham to Bristol in the moving van. They rode through sleet and snow.

Packer and Kit lived on campus in student housing. Their apartment was on the first floor of Ridley House. By today's university standards, the living arrangement seems appealing. The couple's apartment was over the college's chapel and lecture rooms. Dormitory rooms for six or seven students were above them. The apartment included a large room that Packer used as a study. The physical arrangements were a good launching pad for his academic career.

The living situation made interaction with students inevitable, and Packer quickly became "an institution" among them. The faculty members did not eat lunch with the students, but Packer circumvented that segregation by eating breakfast with them. The students evolved a protocol whereby he was allowed to finish his first cup of coffee uninterrupted. Then a student would pose what McGrath calls the "profound theological question of the day." Packer is a person of distinctive traits, and one of them emerged from the scenario I have just described: he would put his coffee cup down, put his hands to his head, wait for ten seconds, and then give an impromptu dissertation having three to five points!

The teaching assignment was well suited to Packer's interests and areas of expertise. On the church history side, Packer taught early church history and the history of the Reformation. On the theological side, he taught biblical theology. He was also a sometime teacher of doctrine for the General Ordination Examination, which applicants for the ministry in the Anglican Church were required to take.

Tyndale Hall was a normal-sized theological college for the time. Its enrollment was fifty-five to sixty students, most of whom were preparing to become Anglican clergymen. The demographics of the student body showed a disproportionate number from the northern part of England (especially Lancashire) because that region was a stronghold of the Bible Churchmen's Missionary Society, which had founded the college. The academic calendar was the same as Packer had known at Oxford, consisting of three ten-week sessions. The daily schedule would have reminded Packer of his Wycliffe Hall days: morning prayer in the chapel from seven thirty to eight; quiet time from eight to eight thirty; breakfast at eight thirty; classes from nine to one; and studying and class preparation after that.

McGrath, an expert on evangelical education in England, paints a very positive picture of the faculty at Tyndale Hall when Packer taught there, calling the staff "unusually talented." Wright, the principal of the college, was popular with the students. More prominent in the history of evangelicalism in Britain was John Wenham, who was an expert in New Testament Greek; in fact, his textbook on that subject had been published by Cambridge University Press and was the standard text of the time.

The Beginning of Packer's Academic Career

For most professors, the first year or two is a time of testing in which they need to prove their excellence and in which "the die is cast," setting the trajectory for their future careers. This was certainly true for J. I. Packer.

One strand in the scenario was Packer's popularity as a teacher and the ease with which he moved among students. According to McGrath, "Most Tyndale students of the late 1950s were quite convinced that they had the strongest teaching staff of any theological college in the country, and regarded Packer as the best among them." As would become true at Regent College later in his career, Packer was the reason why many students chose Tyndale Hall over other options. Of course, there is always the possibility of envy among colleagues when a professor elicits the popularity that Packer attracted from the student body. Nothing was expressed publicly, but McGrath notes that the students believed that at least one other staff member was somewhat envious.

I remarked earlier in this book that the first time I heard Packer deliver a public lecture, he was caught completely off guard by the quickness with which his allotted time on the program came to an end. According to McGrath, this Packer trait surfaced as early as his teaching at Tyndale Hall: "Packer never seemed to quite manage to fit all his lecture material into the time available." McGrath attributes this tendency partly to Packer's desire to answer students' questions in such a way as to reveal the process by which answers evolved rather than giving them only the product of his thinking.

As Packer's teaching was hitting its stride, his publishing and speaking were in the early stages of what we now see as his career path. Packer became a regular speaker on the Inter-Varsity circuit, traveling around the country to speak for Christian Union groups. He early evolved a pattern in which his publishing grew out of his speaking and teaching. A later chapter will trace Packer's career as a writer; here we need only note that his first book, *"Fundamentalism" and the Word of God*, came into being when Packer was asked to "write up a talk at pamphlet length."

While "tending the shop" at his college in Bristol, Packer remained active in two evangelical scholarly networks—the Puritan Conference and the Tyndale Fellowship. Packer delivered an address at each Puritan Conference held during his years at Tyndale Hall. The topics were Puritan evangelism, the witness of the Holy Spirit, Sunday observance, the Puritans as interpreters of Scripture, the Puritan view of preaching the gospel, and Jonathan Edwards and the theology of revival. In addition, Packer composed a frequently referenced introduction to the published addresses for the 1958 conference. The introduction was a "position paper" in which Packer articulated how the Puritan Conference viewed the Puritans as models that contemporary Christians might profitably emulate. Through the years since 1958, this document has been the touchstone for how modern-day Puritans view their prototypes.

Technically, the Puritan Conference was under the auspices of the Cambridge-based Tyndale Fellowship for Biblical and Theological Research. Packer was a "ranking member" of this group as well. In May 1961, as Packer was nearing the end of his time at Tyndale Hall, an important strategy session was held in London, attended by leaders of the Tyndale Fellowship. The suggestion had been put on the table that the Puritan Conference cease to be part of the Tyndale Fellowship. The broader subject of the one-day planning session was whether or not the

Fellowship would concentrate on specifically biblical scholarship, to the exclusion of broader theological and church history scholarship. Packer argued strongly for the inclusion of broader theological and historical interests, but his viewpoint was defeated.

Academicians at the start of their publishing careers often agree to write articles for dictionary projects. In this way, too, Packer followed a familiar path. He served as one of four consulting editors and the author of eighteen articles for *The New Bible Dictionary* (a book that I purchased at the outset of my teaching career and that served me as an "old standby" for four decades). This standard evangelical reference book was conceived and produced under the auspices of the Tyndale Fellowship. J. D. Douglas was the general editor. It is a tribute to the public stature of the youthful Packer that he was asked to serve on the editorial team with well-known scholars such as F. F. Bruce and D. J. Wiseman.

The eventual contours of Packer's publishing career were established during his formative years at Tyndale Hall. His first two major books were produced during this era—*"Fundamentalism" and the Word of God* (1958) and *Evangelism and the Sovereignty of God* (1961). Additionally, Packer began publishing articles in a wide range of "popular" religious magazines (as distinct from specialized scholarly journals), a trend that has continued throughout his career. Thus, we find Packer articles on a range of religious subjects in such magazines as *Evangelical Quarterly, Christianity Today, Faith and Thought, Bible League Quarterly,* and *Churchman*. He has built his publishing career out of entering the doors that God has opened, accepting opportunities to publish articles on the criterion of usefulness to the church.

Controversy

One of these articles occasioned the first major chapter in Packer's career as a controversialist. On the surface, a book review in a religious periodical called *Evangelical Quarterly* would seem to be an unlikely instrument for stirring up a hornet's nest, but the controversy was so intense that it might have led to Packer's dismissal from Tyndale Hall.

The book that Packer reviewed was authored by Wheaton College professor Steven Barabas (with whom I eventually overlapped on the faculty at Wheaton College). It was entitled *So Great Salvation: The*

History and Message of the Keswick Convention (1952). Packer had struggled with and repudiated the Keswick view of Christian triumphalism during his college years at Oxford, but it was the rallying point for a major segment (perhaps *the* major segment) of British evangelicalism at the time. I note in passing that Keswick is a town in northern England, and that the largest segment of the student body and constituency of Tyndale Hall was from northern England.

Packer wrote a thirteen-page review of the book on the Keswick movement. It was a scathing attack on the Keswick theology, which Packer declared to be "false to Scripture and dishonouring to God." And that was only part of the attack! Packer himself has called the review a "fiery onslaught" against the Keswick viewpoint. He based his attack on sophisticated theological arguments, claiming, for example, that Keswick theology was essentially Pelagian, adding this "is the natural heresy of zealous Christians who are not interested in theology." This kind of theological vocabulary carried weight with the more theologically oriented segment of British evangelicalism. On the other side, Packer's theologically laden arguments confirmed the more pietistic strain in British evangelicalism in its suspicion of advanced theological scholarship.

The review produced a firestorm of protest from adherents of the Keswick movement (though Packer quickly became a hero with an emerging generation of English evangelicals). The reaction was particularly negative at Tyndale Hall. The largest segment of the student body and constituency of Tyndale Hall was from northern England, where the town of Keswick is located. That constituency included many Keswick loyalists. For instance, the chairman of the Tyndale Hall Council was a prominent Keswick leader. The financial support of these people was needed to sustain the college. It became a common sentiment in some quarters that Tyndale Hall would be better off without J. I. Packer on the faculty. McGrath concludes that "it was a serious crisis for Packer, and it was far from clear what would happen." However, Leathem successfully intervened on Packer's behalf.

The spirit of the book review by the thirty-year-old Packer contrasts with his later style of dealing with intellectual opponents. Someone who lived through the event has called Packer's attack "shockingly presumptuous." Packer revisited the subject three decades later in his book *Keep in Step with the Spirit*. In that book, he discusses the Keswick view for nearly twenty pages. It is a detailed critique of the viewpoint, closely reasoned and with continuous analysis of passages from the New Testament epistles. But the critique is preceded by two pages on "Keswick's strengths," prefaced by the lead-in, "Some words of appreciation ought to be spoken before we go any further."

Apologist for the Bible

The first published book is a rite of passage for scholars, and the event is doubly significant if the book becomes a major success. Packer was fortunate in having his first book, *"Fundamentalism" and the Word of God* (1958), become a landmark in twentieth-century evangelicalism.

McGrath has described the context of the book in greater detail than fits my purpose here. The brief story is as follows. The occasion for Packer's book was the debate that was swirling in England between liberals and conservatives. High-visibility Anglicans were combative in attacking evangelicals—complaining that Billy Graham was allowed to speak at Cambridge University, for example, and dismissing the evangelical view of Scripture with the put-down label of "fundamentalist." From the beginning of his career, Packer's speaking and writing were "occasional"—occasioned by the hot topics of the day, on which he was asked to speak or write. In his own words, as an author, he has been "obliging, writing what I was asked to write." Packer's first book grew out of an address to a graduate group in London, which resulted in an invitation to turn the address into a pamphlet that became a book instead.

The core of *"Fundamentalism" and the Word of God* is its defense of the authority of the Bible. In this book, Packer lays out the three traditional views of religious authority and provides proof, from Scripture itself and the testimony of Jesus, that the Bible is the final authority for belief and practice.

The book fell on receptive minds. McGrath presents evidence that it gave a generation of British evangelicals new confidence in their view of the Bible and Christian doctrine based on it (that is exactly the effect that the book had on me as a "farm boy" college student in central Iowa). Professor Valentine Cunningham of Oxford University attested that "it felt good to have Packer on one's side." A former editor of

Evangelical Times recalled that the effect of the book was to lift the "drooping heads" of the upcoming generation of evangelicals.

The book established Packer as an expert on the authority of the Bible (later, of course, he came to be viewed as a "go-to" evangelical on numerous topics). One small evidence of this is that in 1958, the two-year-old *Christianity Today* carried two articles by Packer on views of revelation and one on fundamentalism in England.

Packer's speaking and writing have always formed a symbiotic relationship, and this was already evident as he was getting started in his profession at Tyndale Hall. A particularly important example occurred as a result of the public visibility that *"Fundamentalism" and the Word of God* achieved among British students. Late in the fall term of 1958, the Student Christian Movement (not the Christian Union) at Oxford University arranged a debate on the subject of the authority of the Bible. Packer, of course, was the person of choice to defend the evangelical view. His opponent was Christopher Evans, the dean of Corpus Christi College. The event was scheduled for the church hall of the Wesley Memorial Church in center city Oxford. The eight o'clock event attracted a crowd of eight hundred, which necessitated moving the debate to the sanctuary of the church. By the time the transition had been effected, it was nine o'clock!

Evans made a tactical mistake in deciding that he would not present prepared remarks, but would respond to Packer's presentation. Packer spoke for seventy-five minutes! Evans puttered away at such minutiae as the relationship between Matthew and Mark in the Synoptic Problem. The moderator of the debate called a halt to it at eleven o'clock because attendees needed to catch their buses home.

Evangelical students in the audience felt that they had been given a place to stand. Packer and his Bristol contingent drove home exhilarated that the evangelical view of the Bible had been defended at Oxford University. As they talked, something even more important than the evening's debate began to take shape, namely, the possibility of establishing an evangelical research institution at Oxford.

Reaching Closure at Tyndale Hall

Packer remained at his first permanent academic position for six years. He weathered the crisis of his attack on the Keswick movement, but scars from the battle were part of his history at Tyndale Hall. Certainly Packer was a major component in the ongoing success of the college. Tyndale Hall proved to be an entirely adequate base of operation for his career as a writer and speaker, though without the heavy teaching load, he naturally could have done more publishing. The claim is sometimes made that the class system of England worked against Packer, in contrast to someone like John Stott, but there is no evidence that Packer was hampered by his roots while at Tyndale Hall. He forged his reputation the way a beginning scholar always does—through hard work, innate ability, and eagerness to please.

Still, a certain ethos was entrenched at Tyndale Hall that militated against long-term commitment. Packer and his colleague John Wenham believed in the idea of the career theology teacher, but the prevailing custom at British seminaries of the time was for clergymen to take time out from parish ministry to teach for a few years, then return to the pulpit. Furthermore, Tyndale Hall was a relatively small college, and Bristol is in no way at the crossroads of England. Given these factors, it is not surprising that Packer was at Tyndale Hall for the relatively short time of six years.

Summary

In retrospect, we can see the foundation being laid for Packer's high visibility as an evangelical spokesman during his time at Tyndale Hall. On the strength of his speaking and publishing, Packer was already becoming well known in England, the United States, and Australia. Of course, a professor has to "make it" in the classroom as a prerequisite to becoming a publicly acclaimed speaker and author. McGrath's research revealed that among many Tyndale Hall students, Packer *was* the college, and also that he was regarded as the most knowledgeable of the Tyndale teachers. To achieve that degree of excellence in teaching and breadth of knowledge in scholarship requires that one pay one's dues in terms of research and class preparation. That represents the behind-the-scenes Packer, without which the public figure would not exist.

The early years in a professor's academic life carry their own stresses, and we can picture how this operated in Packer's life. We need to remember that a college with an enrollment of sixty students is never secure financially. Additionally, Packer took on an unexpected burden of conflict by publishing his attack on the Keswick movement right at the outset of his teaching career at Tyndale Hall; it was not the kind of thing that the Keswick contingent at the college would forget. Finally, there was the sheer busyness involved in simultaneously being a scholar/researcher, a speaker, and a published writer. Life at Tyndale Hall was exhilarating, but taxing.

8

Latimer House, Oxford

(1961–1970)

J. I. Packer's six years at Tyndale Hall are a kaleidoscope of developments in his life and that of the college. But by comparison with the next phase of Packer's life, they are a picture of serenity and stability. Packer's decade with Latimer House in Oxford represented a broadening of the sphere in which he exercised his gifts, and the accompanying lifestyle was very different from that of a college professor.

I need to begin by defining an English academic "house." To call a college a "hall" is an oddity to Americans, but to speak of a "house" leads to total bewilderment. The label "study center" is a good starting point for understanding the institution. It can also be thought of as a "think tank," a place where upper-echelon minds give their best thinking to a shared agenda of interests. Tyndale House in Cambridge is an example: it is a building that houses a library, study tables and cubicles, a common room, a large lecture room, offices for employees, meeting rooms, and dormitory rooms and apartments. It also offers a supporting program of activities, including lectureships, chapel services, afternoon tea, and informal conversations. The people who use Tyndale House are not students but established scholars from around the world. Of course, there is a built-in difficulty with the institution, namely, the fact that there are no students who pay tuition and thereby help to keep the institution afloat financially.

Latimer House in Oxford during Packer's time of employment there did not exactly match the description of Tyndale House that I have just given, but Tyndale House is a close enough approximation to provide an early glimpse of what this phase of Packer's life was like.

The Personal Context for Packer's Tenure at Latimer House

It is impossible to overstate the formative effect of Packer's time at Tyndale Hall in Bristol. It gave him the professorial satisfaction of being a successful teacher. Success in the classroom is the necessary foundation for a good scholarly career. In addition, Packer was fast becoming a well-known author among evangelicals on three continents and an established lecturer among Christian groups in England.

J. I. Packer during his tenure as warden of Latimer House. (Photo courtesy of Fuller Theological Seminary)

These spheres of influence were beginning to establish the identity of British evangelicalism at the beginning of a new decade. Evangelicals had long been a beleaguered and maligned group on the British religious scene, but when people such as Packer began to defend evangelicalism in the public arena, it instilled new hope in them. And it was not only a matter of confidence: theological positions were being defined by individuals and groups. Puritanism had emerged in many people's minds as a preferred alternative to the Keswick school of theology. Excitement about Christian doctrine stood a chance of replacing pietistic separatism.

For Packer, the prospect of enlarging his voice on the national scene naturally held an appeal. An academic house (as defined above) would not only provide time for research, writing, and speaking; it would also be a center to which evangelicals would look for leadership—a "default" source of information and theological guidance.

The Evangelical Context

Packer went to Latimer House at a time when British evangelicals were at a defining moment in their history. Of course, the label "evangelical" covered a broad swath, even encompassing a liberal group whose members called themselves "liberal evangelicals" in an effort not to completely abandon the gospel. For our purposes, the two strands that comprised the evangelical scene were the same ones that had dominated the religious landscape in England since the Restoration—the nonconformist or free church wing and the Anglican wing. Packer decisively affiliated with the Anglican Church, but his influence extended to the nonconformist segment of British evangelicalism, partly on the strength of his books and speaking.

To understand why the institutional Anglican Church attracted Packer's best efforts, we need to distance ourselves from the now-familiar picture of dwindling evangelical influence in the liberal Anglican Church in England and North America (accompanied by a huge gap between evangelical churches and the pronouncements of official boards and denominational leaders). In the 1960s, evangelicals within the Church of England were making amazing strides. Hopes ran high that evangelicals would become an influential minority capable of capturing the allegiance of local parishes. Here are a few statistics:

- At a conference held early in 1966 for young evangelical Anglican clergymen, an informal poll of those present showed a hundred evangelicals who had been appointed to parishes where, up to that point, the ministers had been non-evangelicals.
- In the late 1960s, a fifth of Anglican clergymen were considered to be evangelical in some sense.
- In 1972, a third of Anglican ordinands (people intending to enter the ministry) were enrolled in evangelical colleges.

Expanding evangelical influence in the Anglican Church was the churchmanship task to which Packer gave himself during the 1960s. It was a very different calling from his teaching at Tyndale Hall and a testimony to his versatility.

The Formation of Latimer House

Latimer House was the visible and institutional manifestation of the spirit that I have described. It was the brainchild of three Tyndale Hall professors—Packer, John Wenham, and Richard Coates—who had traveled to Oxford and back in the fall of 1958 to attend the debate between Packer and Christopher Evans on the authority of the Bible. Wenham had been active in the formation of Tyndale House in Cambridge. He was keen on the possibility of establishing a similar research center in Oxford, and Packer came to share his enthusiasm for the idea. So the two began to brainstorm.

Within a few weeks, Wenham had codified a vision for the Oxford Evangelical Research Centre. The goal was to make the evangelical viewpoint visible and persuasive in the Church of England and beyond. Part of that goal was to counter the views of theological liberalism, thereby giving evangelicals a place to stand in the wars of truth. Whereas Tyndale House in Cambridge was (1) non-denominational and (2) oriented specifically toward biblical scholarship, Wenham proposed (1) an Anglican institution where (2) scholars would discuss doctrine, worship, and issues involving the institutional church (and not just the Bible). It was a bold vision.

When Wenham handed over his statement of vision to Packer, the latter added a rationale for why an Anglican study center should be established and situated in Oxford. Packer called the idea of a research or study center "a strategic requirement of the very highest priority." The influence of liberalism would go unchecked if evangelical scholars were not given the time and resources to formulate rebuttals. One of Packer's most interesting points was that throughout church history, "the best theological work has been done under pressure of controversy and urgent need." Accordingly, "doing theology" (as we call it today) at the proposed center would have a practical aim—to address "actual present-day needs of Anglican evangelicalism." Oxford, Packer said, was the best location for the center (even though the vision was formulated by scholars in Bristol) because of its library resources and because Oxford was at the intellectual crossroads of the world.

The vision began to take shape with amazing rapidity. The trio from Bristol met with evangelical leaders in Oxford on the evening of December 29, 1958, just a month or two after the Packer-Evans debate, forming a committee to guide the formation of the study center. The committee met in the rectory of St. Ebbe's Church. Within two months of that meeting, the committee met again, taking the further step of naming Coates to direct the center when funds made its establishment possible. Another committee member, Philip Edgecumbe Hughes, was designated to be the second employee when funds allowed it. A mimeographed letter was mailed to prominent evangelicals, informing them of the new study center, and donations began to trickle in. Someone donated a large collection of books for the center's eventual library. A parent organization called the Oxford Evangelical Research Trust was formed, and in a very significant development, John R. W. Stott agreed to serve as chairman of the trust.

Thereafter, things happened very quickly. A meeting of the committee was held in London on January 12, 1960. Coates was confirmed as the first warden, a position that in the United States would go by the title of director. Hughes was named librarian. Both the warden and librarian were given three-year appointments. Equally important was the purchase of a large house on Banbury Road, close to Wycliffe Hall.

Packer had every reason to feel gratified by this outcome of his debate with Evans. The eventual influence of Latimer House, especially through its publications, far exceeded the three modest goals of the house at its inception: (1) to provide opportunities for staff members to study and write, (2) to enable Anglican scholars to work together on projects, and (3) to strengthen the evangelical witness in Oxford. By April 1960, Latimer House, replete with library, funding, warden, and librarian, was functional.

Before I tell the story of how Packer became librarian and then warden at Latimer House, I need to note the sequence of events that opened the door for his appointment. The house on Banbury Road was sufficiently large to accommodate the Coates family on the ground level and the Hughes family on the upper level. But by June, the relationship between Coates and Hughes had unraveled, ostensibly over the living arrangements.

First, Coates withdrew his acceptance of the position of warden. Then Hughes threatened to resign as librarian. An attempted solution to the tension came in the form of a suggestion that Hughes move with his family to another house in Oxford, but Hughes rejected the idea and resigned. To leapfrog for the moment over the steps by which Packer became librarian at Latimer House, we need to note that the day after Packer settled into the upper floor of the house with his family as the new librarian, Coates informed Packer that he was resigning as warden! When I asked Packer how he felt about that announcement, he replied, "Rather glum."

From Bristol to Oxford

Packer had already established a track record of starting a new position before leaving one. He was still a doctoral student when he assumed his parish position at Birmingham. He was a commuting professor at Bristol while serving as a minister. It can hardly be a surprise to learn that starting on April 1, 1960, Packer was released by Tyndale Hall to work two days each week at Latimer House in Oxford as a contributor to the work of the center.

We have noted that Hughes had resigned his position as librarian almost immediately after Latimer House had opened. The situation was viewed as desperate. On July 2, 1960, the committee made a decision to offer the position of librarian to Packer, who in turn noted the obvious—that he had another year left on his contract to teach at Tyndale Hall. The committee was undeterred and undertook negotiations with Tyndale Hall. As a result, Packer divided his time for the 1960–61 academic year between Tyndale Hall and Latimer House, moving to Oxford to assume full-time employment at the center in April 1961.

It has already been noted that the day after Packer's arrival, the warden of Latimer House, Coates, dropped the bombshell on Packer that he intended to resign. But because Coates had not given a date by which he would move on, the committee did not dare to name a successor. In September 1961, Coates announced his departure date (the next January), and the search for a warden was officially on. The initial list of eight candidates that the committee considered did not include the name of J. I. Packer. However, on June 13, 1962, Packer was selected to be the next warden of Latimer House. Packer's choice for librarian, Roger T. Beckwith, was confirmed several months later.

In the remainder of this chapter, I will tell the story of what Packer did during his decade as warden at Latimer House in Oxford. I need to say, by way of anticipation, that later chapters in this biography will be devoted to Packer the writer and Packer the Anglican, so I will touch lightly on those aspects of his life during the Latimer House era. Additionally, I have resolutely refused to get sidetracked into retelling the minutely trodden history of the evangelical split in England during the 1960s and of various evangelical committees within the Church of England during the 1960s and 1970s. My purpose in this chapter is to tell the life story of J. I. Packer as it relates to his directorship of Latimer House from 1962 to 1970.

Overseeing Latimer House

When Packer assumed the wardenship in 1962, Latimer House was a work in progress. The exact role of the house was still being determined. One thing that was in place was a conviction that Latimer House did not fit the paradigm of Tyndale House in Cambridge, which was a study center where established evangelical scholars from around the world could pursue specialized biblical scholarship. The business of Latimer House was practical theology as it was useful to evangelicals in the Church of England.

Latimer House is regularly referred to as a think tank, but this is somewhat misleading. The thinking that was generated by Latimer House was not new research and scholarship, but the harnessing of established truth in the interests of the Church of England and evangelical Christians generally. Packer claims that the house's intrachurch endeavors occurred at a less rigorous intellectual level than those undertaken by the academic theological guild. He also describes himself as being "an ideas man in those days."

The first task that Packer needed to accomplish as warden was to mobilize the daily work at the center. In a 2014 conversation, Packer told me that initially he found the assignment "very amorphous." No daily record of events exists, but we know that much of what Packer did in his role as warden was of a behind-the-scenes nature. He did less publishing of articles and books than might have been expected after he had left a teaching position to oversee a study center. The reason is that Packer was busy nurturing the work of others and directing projects that impacted the Church of England. The main roles he discharged as warden of Latimer House were those of public spokesman on church and religious issues; convener of Anglican study groups designed to produce pamphlets and group study guides on various issues; speaker; church committeeman; and author. It is also part of any director's job description to undertake assignments and cultivate contacts that will assure the ongoing financial viability of the institution.

Public Spokesman on Critical Issues

Latimer House was conceived as representing a trusted evangelical response to the cultural crosswinds that were blowing in the tumultuous 1960s. An early opportunity to exercise such leadership came to Packer near the beginning of his tenure as warden. In March 1963, an Anglican bishop named John A. T. Robinson published a 150-page book entitled *Honest to God*. The book was a brief exposition of theological liberalism that proposed to replace the traditional view of God (especially his transcendence) with a more existentialist view. What now seems like a slight book made an immediate sensation. It sold 350,000 copies in a mere seven months. This was partly due to the fact that an Anglican bishop had composed such an attack on traditional Christian belief, and partly because the book captured the rebellious and iconoclastic spirit of the 1960s.

Of the many evangelical critiques of Robinson's bombshell, the one by Packer is the best known. The response came in the form of a twenty-page booklet, and in this we see the preferred format of publications produced by Latimer House. The booklet, entitled *Keep Yourselves from Idols*, was an expanded version of an article originally published in *The Church of England Newspaper* (and again we should note how many of Packer's publications throughout his life have appeared in religious magazines). Today the title *Keep Yourselves from Idols* is baffling, but its purpose was to draw upon the apostle John's warning in 1 John 5:21: "Little children, keep yourselves from idols." The idol in this case was the false God that Robinson had created. While purporting to give the public a new view of Christianity, Robinson's proposal actually formulated a new religion.

Packer's short book was produced on short notice. The genre—theological journalism—was a new venture for Packer, though it became a leading aspect of his professional life (as seen especially in his eventual work for *Christianity Today*). The booklet sold 20,000 copies within a few months.

The religious periodical in which the first version had appeared, *The Church of England Newspaper*, became a regular outlet for Packer during his years at Latimer House. The journalistic mode, however, posed challenges in the sense that responding quickly to crises and opportunities was a diversion from conducting business according to a planned schedule. The hope had been that Latimer House could undertake activities according to its own agenda and timetable. The intrusion of "the *Honest to God* debate" (as posterity has labeled it) even led Packer to say in a report to his committee that the event had shown that Latimer House was "vulnerable to unforeseen developments."

A second issue that siphoned off vast amounts of Packer's time and mental energy grew out of the ecumenical spirit that ran high in the late 1950s and early 1960s. Mainline denominations in the West came to be dominated by this spirit, especially under the influence of the World Council of Churches. In England, this movement crystallized in the early 1960s around a proposed merger between the Methodist Church and the Church of England. In the abstract, such a merger now seems preposterous, but the ecumenical euphoria over the possibility of institutional unity was uncontrollable. Of course, doctrinal differences were ignored under the World Council of Churches' banner that "doctrine divides; ministry unites." (Later in Packer's life, that motto carried more weight for him than it did in 1963.)

Discussions about the proposed merger produced a document entitled *Conversations between the Church of England and the Methodist Church*. However, evangelicals within the Anglican Church were opposed to any union with a denomination that had become as theologically liberal as the Methodist Church. In his role as warden of Latimer House, as well as his acknowledged theological leadership of evangelicals in England, Packer became the point person for evangelical resistance to the merger. On short notice, he edited two books responding to the proposal—*The Church of England and the Methodist Church* (1963) and *All in Each Place: Towards Reunion in England* (1965).

These two books were published by a local press called Marcham Manor Press. Inter-Varsity Press could hardly be expected to publish Packer's books dealing with denominational issues. Yet Latimer House needed an outlet. In the next decade (the 1970s), Latimer House published a series of monographs under its own imprint, but in the 1960s,

Latimer House books and monographs were regularly published by Marcham Manor, a private publishing house established by an Anglican layman and entrepreneur named Gervase Duffield. Duffield ran his publishing house out of his home near Abingdon, south of Oxford.

I note in passing that in this same era, Duffield printed an extremely important series of scholarly books called the Courtenay Library of Reformation Classics. The Editorial Advisory Board consisted of some of the best-known Puritan scholars and church historians of the day. Packer was one of them. He also wrote the introduction to the volume on Thomas Cranmer. The introduction is a triumph of scholarship. It is thirty-six pages long, including a bibliographic essay on secondary sources and another on Cranmer's primary sources. It is also a goldmine of specialized information about and analysis of Cranmer and his work. Surely this project was a welcome oasis of scholarly research and writing in the sea of church issues that occupied Packer in his day-to-day duties as warden.

Speaker and Editor on Anglican Issues

As a spinoff from his role as the evangelical voice on issues that grabbed public attention, Packer found himself increasingly on the speaking circuit (and away from the typewriter, we should observe). To cite just one example, in the autumn of 1968, Packer spoke at twenty-one events devoted to the subject of the proposed Methodist-Anglican merger. And that was not all: he also spoke at two private consultations and a conference organized by a group of young Anglican clerics known as the Eclectics. It was a wearying enterprise, but it was driven by a sense of duty that is a hallmark of Packer.

Directors of institutions, as well as presidents of colleges and seminaries, need to keep up their speaking engagements as a way of placing their institutions in the public eye, partly to advance the stature of the institutions and partly to garner financial support for them. In regard to the first of these, all those who have written on British evangelicalism in the middle of the twentieth century stress that the efforts of leaders such as J. I. Packer and John Stott were changing the public perception of evangelicals. This was such a momentous enterprise that it produced its own energy and rewards. Still, speaking engagements came to occupy more and more of Packer's time. Alister McGrath paints this picture: "Packer was constantly in demand to speak at all kinds of conferences on theological issues, to address Diocesan Evangelical Unions on matters of theology and church politics, and to preach at friendly churches." The Packer that I have known finds it hard to decline an invitation to speak, and that was even truer when he was warden of Latimer House.

Appointments to official church committees came in the wake of Packer's role as public spokesman on church issues. Those assignments, too, absorbed a great deal of time. Examples included the Archbishop's Doctrine Commission, the Faith and Order Advisory Group (which formulated suggestions on Anglican ecumenical issues), and various dialogue groups between the Church of England and other churches (mainly the Presbyterian and Methodist).

The Puritan Conference during the 1960s

During his decade at Latimer House, Packer naturally maintained his involvement in the annual Puritan Conference held at Westminster Chapel in London. These conferences had been an important part of Packer's religious and intellectual life from their very beginning. From 1961 to 1969, Packer prepared and delivered annual addresses on topics that were dear to his heart—the Puritan idea of communion with God, the Puritan conscience, the Puritan approach to worship, John Calvin as servant to the Word, Martin Luther, John Owen on communication from God, the Puritans on spiritual gifts, "Arminianisms," and the Puritan doctrine of justification. But 1969 was the last year when Packer spoke at the Puritan Conference, and therein lies an important development in his life.

The great split in British evangelicalism in 1966 has produced an enormous quantity of analysis, and it is not the purpose of this biography to get sidetracked from the story of J. I. Packer to this history of evangelicalism in England. What we need to know about the broader story is the following. The two key players in the division were D. Martyn Lloyd-Jones and John Stott (which is not to deny that Packer also played a very important role). The context was the growth of liberalism in mainline denominations in both England and America. Denominational boards and the official policies that flowed from them were usually controlled by the liberal factions within the denominations. The

Westminster Chapel in London, where Dr. D. Martyn Lloyd-Jones was minister from 1939 to 1968, was the site of the Puritan Conference from 1950 to 1969. (Photo © Foreveryounger. License: http://creativecommons.org/licenses/by-sa/3.0/legalcode)

same was true for local churches, though on a kind of sliding scale (by which I mean that local churches were dominated by a liberal philosophy to varying degrees). The question then became whether individuals and churches should remain within liberal denominations or withdraw from them.

Lloyd-Jones, minister of the Congregational or independent Westminster Chapel in London, was a leading exponent of the separatist model. He brought things to a head at a 1966 conference called the Second National Assembly of Evangelicals, held in the famous and imposing Methodist Central Hall, across the street from Westminster Abbey. Lloyd-Jones gave the opening address at the conference. It changed the face of evangelicalism in England. Lloyd-Jones issued a call for evangelicals to leave the Church of England and form an association of evangelical churches. People who attended the meeting remember the atmosphere as being "electric."

Stott was chair of the session at which Lloyd-Jones spoke. He was alarmed by what Lloyd-Jones had said and feared its impact on many evangelical Anglicans in the audience. So he used his position as chair of the session to express his disagreement with Lloyd-Jones, encouraging evangelicals to remain within the Church of England. Stott hoped to avert a crisis of secession, and in a sense he did. But the evening could equally be viewed as exposing an existing crisis in British evangelicalism.

Packer was completely opposed to the secessionist position of Lloyd-Jones, as I will explore in a later chapter on Packer's lifelong Anglicanism. His unwillingness to follow Lloyd-Jones dampened the relationship between the two, but it did not bring it to an immediate end. The Puritan Conference continued to meet through 1969, with Packer presenting a paper every year. However, no conference was held in 1970, and when the series resumed a year later, it bore the title of the Westminster Conference.

The trigger for the name change was not Packer's unwillingness to agree with Lloyd-Jones on the separation issue, but rather an ecumenical book entitled *Growing into Union*, of which Packer was one of four authors. This book laid out common ground between two factions within the Church of England who opposed the Anglican-Methodist merger. Those two groups were the evangelicals and the Anglo-Catholics. Packer was criticized by many evangelicals for the positions he advocated in this book, but perhaps preeminently by Lloyd-Jones. An unexpected casualty of the disagreement was the two-decades-old Puritan Conference.

In a letter dated July 7, 1970, Lloyd-Jones informed Packer that pursuant to a conversation he had had with two other free-church members of the planning committee, a decision had been reached not to hold a conference in 1970. The reason was that the doctrinal position outlined in *Growing into Union* was considered to be neither evangelical nor Puritan, with the result that cooperation with Packer would "cause great confusion in the minds of all Free Church evangelical people." It is interesting to note that a sidelight in the letter is Lloyd-Jones's lament that Packer had "become involved in ecclesiastical affairs" instead of producing "a major work in the Warfield tradition"; for Lloyd-Jones, this was "nothing less than a great tragedy and a real loss to the Church." Lloyd-Jones ended by saying that "after all these years I am saddened at the thought that we shall not meet regularly year by year at the Conference and at other odd times; but I sincerely hope that we shall be able to maintain some personal contact."

Packer replied in a letter two days later. He reiterated that Lloyd-Jones's arguments regarding separation had "never convinced" him. He also stated, "My respect for you and my gratitude for what God has given me through you in the past remains undimmed." A few months later, Lloyd-Jones and Packer held a face-to-face conversation on the matter, but agreement proved impossible. A decade after this parting of ways, when Packer lived in Canada, Packer wrote to Lloyd-Jones, proposing that he pay a visit to his one-time collaborator on Puritan projects during a forthcoming trip to England. Lloyd-Jones agreed, but he died before Packer could visit him.

Five years after Lloyd-Jones's death, Packer contributed a major and now well-known essay entitled "A Kind of Puritan" to a volume of commemorative essays on "the Doctor." The only reference to the breach between them is Packer's muted comment that the pressure Lloyd-Jones exerted on evangelicals to leave the Church of England "led to individual estrangements, from which the present writer was not exempt."

I write as a student of the Puritans when I say that the termination of the annual Puritan Conference was a great tragedy for Puritan studies. During the two decades of its existence, the Puritan Conference provided the impetus for Packer to compose an annual essay on the Puritans. A look at his bibliography shows that virtually all of his Puritan essays (including those later reprinted in his 1990 book *A Quest for Godliness*) were composed before 1970.

I note finally that Packer's exclusion from the new Westminster Conference was matched by other closed doors in his professional life. Packer had been a regular contributor to a periodical called *Evangelical Magazine*. In fact, the content of his later book *Knowing God* was originally published in this magazine as a series of articles. By the late 1960s, *Evangelical Magazine* refused to print articles by Packer, and he was removed from the editorial board. But the alienation between Packer and the free-church segment of British evangelicalism came to extend far beyond the immediate response to the ecumenical views expressed in *Growing into Union* and his continuing loyalty to the Anglican Church. Westminster Seminary professor Carl Trueman paints the following picture of what he encountered in his days in nonconformist circles in England: "The suspicion and the bile that was directed toward Packer in post-1966 nonconformist circles in so many informal ways, over cups of tea after church, in conversations, in sermonic asides, and so on, is by its very nature not documentable but was nonetheless real, tangible, and in my experience as a young Christian, pervasive in churches led by men who looked to Lloyd-Jones as their mentor."

The Keele Congress of 1967

As already hinted, Latimer House was a beehive of activity that reached in many directions. We can think of it as a clearinghouse of Anglican projects and publications. However, it was not the only center of Anglican evangelical energy. For instance, a group of evangelical clergymen in the northern part of England had begun to hold regional conferences known as the Northern Evangelical Conference. McGrath writes regarding those conferences that "the effect on evangelical morale was significant."

By 1964, a committee chaired by Stott brought together representatives of the Northern Evangelical Conference and evangelical leaders from other parts of England. The goal was to mobilize evangelical laypeople and ministers in Anglican parishes that were open to evangelical influence. Plans evolved to hold a National Evangelical Anglican Congress at the University of Keele in early April 1967. Historians who write about the event speak of it in shorthand fashion as "Keele." The most important thing about this conference for purposes of Packer's life story is that, in his words, "Keele was the child of Latimer House."

The Keele Congress would be attended by a thousand people—519 clergy and 481 laypeople. The logistics involved in running a conference of that size were of course monumental, but so was the groundwork that preceded the conference.

Latimer House had already begun publishing pamphlets on topics that were relevant to evangelical revival in the Church of England. Once the agenda for Keele became codified, a book edited by Packer was composed and published in 1967, on the eve of the conference. It was entitled *Guidelines: Anglican Evangelicals Face the Future*. The essays that comprised the book were planned by the authors at meetings held at Latimer House. Publishing and distributing the book to introduce the conference was a last-minute decision; the original intention had been that the book would be released following the conference.

But *Guidelines* was not the only preconference publishing program undertaken by Latimer House. Equally impressive was a series of eighteen "study kits" that were jointly published by Latimer House and the Church Pastoral Aid Society. These study kits were Bible studies that more than seven hundred Anglican churches incorporated into their winter teaching programs. Another preconference event was a meeting in 1966 of two hundred younger evangelical ministers in the Church of England. The theme of that conference was "Facing the Future." The group affirmed the importance of Latimer House, suggesting an increase in its funding and unofficially charging it with identifying the important issues facing the Anglican Church and convening study groups on those issues. Within two years, fourteen study groups with 142 members were up and running at Latimer House. All of this activity raised the visibility of Latimer House and, indirectly, of its warden.

The Keele Congress was an imposing event. Nine speakers, all of them "leading evangelical luminaries" (McGrath), delivered the plenary addresses. Packer spoke on "The Good Confession: Our Crisis and God's Christ." It was a major address, running to twenty-five pages in its printed form. He began with a biblically based definition of confession and followed with reasons why confession was needed in a day of secularism and cultural syncretism. An additional context into which Packer placed his remarks was two weaknesses within the Church of England—naturalism and pietism. The last third of the address took up the content of genuine confessional renewal; here Packer developed the themes of the gospel, theism, a Trinitarian element, and an evangelistic thrust. Of course, the overall context for all of the addresses at Keele was the need for evangelicals within the Church of England to assert their convictions—to "make the good confession."

According to Timothy Dudley-Smith, Packer came to Keele with limited expectations, but found his hopes rising as the congress tackled its task. Stott later recalled that as the two of them walked from one room to another between meetings, Packer remarked that it was evident that the conference was an epoch-making event.

Keele was one of Packer's most important achievements to that point. The congress was a high point of modern evangelicalism in England. Perhaps at no other point had the evangelical influence in the Church of England risen so high since the days of the original Puritans (who were, we need to remember, the English branch of the Protestant Reformation). It appeared that evangelicals might become a major influence in the Anglican Church. When Packer was interviewed a month after the conference, he stressed two positive effects. One was that the congress had achieved its goal of bringing Anglican evangelicals together spiritually and ideologically. A second result was that the conference had projected an image of evangelical vitality to the outside world, including the liberal majority in the Church of England. As warden of Latimer House, Packer was naturally seen as a leading figure (along with Stott) of the evangelical revival in the national church.

Packer, Stott, and Evangelical Anglican Leadership

Indeed, Stott and Packer were the two most prominent evangelical leaders in the Church of England during the 1960s and 1970s. Since much has been said and speculated about the relationship between these two leaders and the nature of their respective influence, I need to take an excursion into the subject. The following description is my codification of what emerged in an extended discussion with Packer. The overall assessment is mine, not his. The umbrella under which I explore the subject is Packer's sense that he and Stott to some extent represented alternative leadership options among evangelicals in the Church of England.

This difference should not obscure the fact that the two had much in common. According to Packer, both he and Stott thought of leadership as a burden of responsibility generated by circumstances, not as a personal goal. Additionally, in most matters, the two were warm-hearted, cooperating colleagues. In fact, Stott was the first chairman of the Latimer House Council.

At the same time, there were distinct differences in the roles that Packer and Stott filled. Stott was raised in an upper-class family. His father was a Harley Street physician. Stott himself was educated at boarding schools starting at age eight, and eventually he attended the famed Rugby School. He received his college and theological education at Cambridge University. But these are only part of Stott's upper-class connections. As a youth, he attended the "Bash camps," started and then superintended by Rev. Eric Nash. Attendance at these camps was by invitation only. Nash invited boys from what he considered the top thirty public (American "private" or "prep") schools in England. If upper-class parents asked Nash to see that their sons did not associate with boys from the working classes, he acquiesced. To complete this picture of privilege, Stott served for a quarter of a century as rector at All Souls Anglican Church, located in central London at Langham Place, adjacent to the BBC (which sometimes broadcast sermons from All Souls).

What kind of theology did such privilege produce? It resulted in an outlook that reflected a certain social grooming. This does not mean that people like Stott and Nash denied human sinfulness. It means that Stott's aristocratic upbringing, reinforced by the Bash camps, led to a relatively optimistic way of describing human nature. His upper-class lifestyle isolated him from much of the seamier side of life. (John King, in his book *The Evangelicals*, notes that the paradigm that Stott and then many other "Bashers" followed enabled them to reach the ministry without leaving the world of privilege: elite public school education, summers at the Bash camp, college and theological education at Cambridge University, and ordination in the Anglican Church.) Additionally, the Puritans, who have been such an important influence in Packer's life, were less likely to hold interest for someone with an upper-class orientation. After all, the Puritans were scornful of aristocratic privilege and deeply conscious of human sinfulness.

By contrast, Packer belongs to what Americans call the working class. Packer declines to use this designation because in his milieu, "working class" denoted "working with one's hands." He himself uses the terms "blue collar" and "lower middle class" for his background. He has described his family as "a quiet, unobtrusive lot, rural in our style." Packer was bullied on the school field. His opportunity to receive an Oxford education depended on his ability to land scholarships, inasmuch as his parents were unable to afford such an education for him. Additionally, Packer is of Puritan temperament. John Owen's book on the mortification of sin led him out of his first spiritual crisis.

On the theological front, Packer viewed himself as supplementing what Stott represented. For Packer, Stott's approach to evangelical renewal in the Church of England was "too bland for the reality of our pastoral world." In particular, it lacked a sufficient view of human sinfulness. There was an additional dimension as well: Packer's approach to the Christian faith, both theologically and at the parish level, was more intellectual than Stott's, despite the latter's reason-oriented sermon style. Stott and his followers stressed pietistic community based on experience, while Packer stressed the importance of thinking in the parish.

The foregoing is the foundation of divergent leadership styles and spheres of influence. Stott took the initiative in filling leadership roles in groups that became his followers. The "Bash camp" clerics, for example, looked upon Stott as their leader. Packer's perception was that this group viewed him as "eccentric and an outsider." Additionally, in 1955, Stott revived an eighteenth-century clerical group called the Eclectic Society. This organization was comprised of under-forty Anglican clerics. It started with twenty-two of Stott's friends, and within a decade, it had a thousand members divided into seventeen regional branches. The group held regular conferences at which Stott spoke. According to Alister Chapman, Stott "decided who joined (at least in the early days), ensuring that they were theologically conservative and loyal. Limiting members to clergy under forty kept out senior evangelicals, whose presence would have diluted his leadership." A fraternity developed, with Stott at the center. Fellowship was a high priority. In Packer's view, the Eclectics were a pietistic group that emphasized conversion and prayer, but not doctrine and sin. All that I have sketched confirms Packer's assessment that Stott's genius was his gift for organization.

What, then, was the nature of Packer's influence (surely equal to Stott's during Packer's Latimer House years)? In my conversation with Packer, he told me that he has "not cultivated being a leader" and has "never wanted to be a leader." He also insists that he has always avoided recruiting followers. By his own estimate, he has "admirers but not followers." Packer was never in the circle of Eclectics. It is a fair inference that he became a leader on the strength of his writing and speaking

More important than the "how" of Packer's Anglican leadership is the nature of that leadership. For starters, evangelical Anglicans who looked to Packer as their leader were not the same as those who viewed Stott as their leader. Packer has always regarded the Puritans as a brand of Anglicans, but in recent years, few Anglicans have claimed the Puritans as kin to themselves. This means that people who shared Packer's Puritan beliefs and orientation were united by an intellectual kinship rather than by institutional ties. Packer believes that he has influenced ministers theologically. He is also of the opinion that he has appealed to the more intellectually inclined clerics and laypeople.

As noted above, Stott's followers stressed piety, conversion, and fellowship, based on experience, while Packer's followers emphasized doctrine, especially sin and its implications. In Packer's words, "With my Puritan roots, I was offering something else" than what the Stott circle represented. Says Packer, "Pietists want experience and feelings first; I want convictions." He did not have a network of conferences as Stott did, nor a pulpit located in the middle of London across the street from the BBC studios. Packer's influence depended directly on his words, both written and spoken.

Packer rejects the suggestion that he and Stott were rivals. They simply represented alternative leadership styles and filled different niches. The contrast was a difference of temperament and philosophy of ministry. We can formulate the difference of philosophy in terms of a trickle-down strategy and a grassroots strategy. Dating all the way back to his "Bash camp" days, Stott was committed to the principle of influencing the leaders at the top in the belief that the layperson would reap the benefit. In Wendy Zoba's words, "Stott orchestrated central conferences for leaders to gather for fellowship and refreshment, with the hope that the inspiration would trickle down into their churches."

Packer's alternative is well embodied in his efforts at Latimer House, where he oversaw committees and publishing projects designed to impact local churches. Packer was committed to thinking through the doctrinal and ecclesiastical issues relevant to the Church of England and then equipping clergy and laity with the results of that thinking. In Packer's last years in England, his vision became a minority viewpoint among Anglican clerics, and Stott's organizational leadership ensured the acceptance of his agenda. Packer has declared informally that in the 1970s he "hadn't got any kind of leadership role" in Anglican circles, leaving him to "wonder what good I am, really, to the Christian world." Stott was protective of his leadership among Anglican evangelicals, but that became something of an irrelevance when he turned to the Third World as his primary sphere of ministry, which he did at approximately the same time that Packer moved to Canada.

Packer's Publishing during the 1960s

In the abstract, being released from teaching duties might have been expected to result in an increase in essays and books from Packer. Because of the duties associated with heading up Latimer House, this expectation proved incorrect. Still, the list of Packer's publications during this era is an important part of his intellectual life and career. We can divide Packer's output published during the 1960s into definite categories.

One category is pamphlets and monographs that discussed Anglican issues. Most of these grew out of Packer's duties as warden of a house devoted to reclaiming the Church of England for evangelicalism. Specimen titles include *The Thirty-Nine Articles* (a forty-six-page compendium of six articles originally published in *The Church of England Newspaper*); *Keep Yourselves from Idols* (a twenty-page response to Bishop Robinson's *Honest to God*); *The Gospel in the Prayer Book* (an eight-page booklet originally published in a parish magazine); and *The Thirty-Nine Articles Today*. While these were certainly topics of interest to Packer, they also represented a fulfillment of duties related to the position of warden.

A second category is essays published in either church magazines or in anthologies of essays (some of them edited by Packer). Examples of books edited by Packer are *Eucharistic Sacrifice: Addresses Given at the Oxford Conference of Evangelical Churchmen, September 1961*; *All in Each Place: Towards Reunion in England: Ten Anglican Essays with Some Free Church Comments*; and *Guidelines: Anglican Evangelicals Face the Future*. Essays appearing in books edited by others bear such titles as "The Origin and History of Fundamentalism," "The Nature of the Church," and "Calvin the Theologian."

Additional categories that eventually made up a major part of Packer's complete bibliography of publications made an appearance during the 1960s. One category was articles written at a popular (as opposed to scholarly) level and published in religious periodicals such as *Church-*

man, *Christianity Today*, *Eternity*, and *The Presbyterian Guardian*. The latter three show the growing influence of Packer in the United States. Packer also published book reviews in abundance. Eventually he became a prolific writer of prefaces and introductions to books authored by others, but this category does not yet appear during the 1960s.

Packer's major work during his tenure as warden at Latimer House was *God Has Spoken: Revelation and the Bible*. It was published by Hodder & Stoughton in 1965 and underwent revisions in 1979, 1993, 1998, and 2005. In 1965, the book was published in the United States by Westminster Press under the title *God Speaks to Man: Revelation and the Bible*. I personally own the 1979 version, which was published by InterVarsity Press, showing what an amazing series of permutations this book has undergone. The book is a triumph of comprehensiveness combined with readability. In just 150 pages, Packer covers all the important aspects of the subject. There are many echoes of *"Fundamentalism" and the Word of God*, and I note in passing that one of the strokes of genius in Packer's publishing career has been his ability to perpetuate the content of his previously published books in new ways.

Packer's Legacy at Latimer House

The primary thing that Packer achieved during his decade at Latimer House was to shore up and advance the presence of evangelicalism in the Church of England during the turbulent 1960s. Evangelicals made amazing gains in the Anglican Church, perhaps because traditional values were crumbling on many fronts. Packer later summed up his achievement at Latimer House by saying that the enterprise corrected a public perception of evangelicals as being isolated from the Anglican Church and lacking in intellectual sophistication. For Packer, the Keele Congress, perhaps the crowning accomplishment of his time at Latimer House, had laid a foundation for "a constructive reforming agenda" within the Anglican Church.

Packer's assessment of the first decade of Latimer House is corroborated by the statements of others. McGrath believes that "by late 1968, Latimer House had established itself as the leading evangelical think-tank and resource centre for evangelicals within the Church of England." And John Wenham, who had helped to found Latimer House and who succeeded Packer as warden, paints this picture of what Latimer

House achieved during its first decade of existence: "The tiny staff had done a remarkable work reinforcing the growing band of Evangelicals in many directions. They had set up fifteen study groups which had been working on publications in the fields of Liturgy, Patronage, Missionary Theology, Church and Ministry, Tradition, Law and Morality, Ecclesiastical Polity, Preaching, Church and Community, Pastoral Reorganisation, Church and Sacraments, Ecumenism, Sex and Marriage, Race Relations, Roman Catholicism and Eastern Orthodoxy."

A word needs to be said about the subsequent history of Latimer House. Packer remained involved with certain aspects of the house during the decade following his time there. His 1978 monograph *The Evangelical Anglican Identity Problem: An Analysis* was published in the series called Latimer Studies. Nineteen titles are listed adjacent to the title page, headed by the information that J. I. Packer was the consulting editor for the series. Anyone who has edited an essay or monograph authored by someone else knows that it usually takes as much time to oversee the material as it would take to write the essay oneself; I say that only to correct a common misperception that serving as an editor is merely honorific and does not represent a significant outlay of time and expertise.

Packer was succeeded in the position of warden by three distinguished men—Packer's sometime colleague Wenham (1969–73); Packer's choice for librarian when he himself became warden, Roger Beckwith (1973–1994); and a scholar on the Puritan Richard Hooker named Nigel Atkinson (1995–1998). As the decade of the 1990s moved to its conclusion, financial difficulties at Latimer House resulted in the disbanding of the house. The books and journals were relocated to Oak Hill Theological College in London and remain under the control of the Latimer Trust.

Lecturer in America

During his decade at Latimer House, most of Packer's speaking was local and related to Anglican issues. However, it is important to note that his growing visibility around the world resulted in trips to the United States. Overseas speaking invitations required an official policy decision before Packer could accept them. When he received an invitation to travel to California in May 1965 to deliver the annual Payton Lectures at Fuller Seminary, the Latimer House Council raised objections, feeling that such engagements were not in line with the primary mission of Latimer House. Packer believed that his speaking in the United States would raise the public stature of Latimer House and would be enriching to him personally. Packer did deliver the Fuller Seminary lectures, his first foreign speaking assignment of many.

During subsequent speaking trips to the United States, Packer was impressed by Westminster Theological Seminary in Philadelphia. He even served a short stint as a visiting professor at Westminster in 1966. He also developed connections at Trinity Evangelical Divinity School in Deerfield, Illinois, and Gordon-Conwell Theological Seminary in Wenham, Massachusetts, both of which became interested in Packer's joining their faculties.

Reaching Closure at Latimer House

Packer's tenure at Latimer House was a unique era in his life. Although he remained active in ecclesiastical concerns, no other phase of his career was devoted so singlemindedly to the institutional Anglican Church. During this decade, Packer poured his best efforts into the Church of England and had the satisfaction of seeing that church become somewhat more sympathetic to evangelicalism than it had been when he went to Latimer House in 1960. Packer's work at Latimer House exercised some of his gifts, but left other aspects of his life unfulfilled. According to McGrath, Packer "felt that he was going dry, and hence that Latimer House was going dry as well." He needed the stimulation that he had once received from the classroom experience at Oak Hill Theological College and Tyndale Hall. These feelings drove his decision to step down as warden.

Nevertheless, Packer left Latimer House with a sense of closure. The house was firmly established as a clearinghouse for evangelical concerns in the Anglican Church. Its programs were in place. A competent administrator could coordinate the work of the house for the foreseeable future. This left Packer pondering his options for the next phase of his life.

9

Return to the Academic Life

(1970–1972)

J. I. Packer made a decision to leave Latimer House before he had secured a new job. He had achieved what he had set out to accomplish. When he left Latimer House, the council commended him for the "significant contribution" he had made "to the contemporary growth of evangelicalism within the Church of England." Packer could have maintained the status quo in his life by keeping an efficient machine running smoothly, but to do that would have been the very antithesis of his personality. Nonetheless, he could not have envisioned the difficult path that lay ahead of him when he decided to leave.

Weighing the Alternatives

Today we think of Packer so thoroughly as an academician, author, and speaker that we tend to assume that returning to parish ministry would not have been a live option for him as he took stock at the end of his years at Latimer House. It is not quite that simple, however. During his tenure at Latimer House, Packer had been involved in the ministry of one of four evangelical Anglican churches in Oxford—St. Andrew's, up the street from Latimer House and Wycliffe Hall. As an ordained minister, Packer has always felt the pull of ministerial involvement in the local church. So he considered a return to parish ministry at this stage.

But Packer also possesses the instincts of the scholar; he does specialized scholarship very well indeed. Just as he was contemplating his next professional move, the prestigious Lady Margaret Chair of Divinity at Oxford University became vacant. Friends encouraged Packer to apply. In a highly significant statement about how he perceives his calling, Packer offered this opinion: "I really am called . . . to make ministers and establish consciences, rather than to advance learning as an Oxbridge professor should." When I asked Packer if it was anxiety-producing to resign from Latimer House before he had landed a position elsewhere, he replied that it was not, because his strong sense of calling "preempted any sense of anxiety." He said that his "real business was theological education with special attention to tomorrow's clergy," with the result that returning to teaching was "getting back to [his] own proper work."

If theological education was Packer's calling, one path open to him was to teach in a North American seminary. Packer's friend and colleague John Wenham became so worried about this possibility that he wrote in a 1968 letter about "Jim Packer's probable departure to America." Wenham regarded that possibility as "perhaps the greatest disaster that has ever overtaken the Evangelical cause in the Church of England." Wenham also offered the highly significant assessment that "Jim is head and shoulders above all other Evangelicals in his influence in the Church of England."

Packer did not leave for North America. He was committed to unfinished work in England. Nonetheless, finding the right theological college at which to serve proved elusive. Because of the stature Packer had achieved at Latimer House, accepting a junior position at a theological college would have been inappropriate. The position for which he was most qualified was that of principal (or president) of a theological college. Such a position would carry the possibility of maximum influence on the future direction of evangelicalism in the Church of England through the formation of young clergymen and would provide Packer with a public platform from which he could speak (as Latimer House had done).

A Closed Door

In June 1968, Packer informed the Latimer House Council that he intended to apply for the position of principal of the London College of

Divinity, an evangelical theological college or seminary. The college had been located in London, but was in the process of relocating to Nottingham. The college's board of governors advertised the vacant position, an unusual procedure in England at the time. Initially, both Packer and the board of governors were positive about his candidacy, but the interview process took a turn that disappointed Packer.

In brief, the short list of candidates (one of whom was Packer) was augmented by one when a professor at Nottingham University (with the support of the bishop of London) imposed an additional candidate on the board of governors. Then, in still more irregularity, the governors did not reach a decision directly on the basis of the interviews that they had conducted. Michael Green, who was already on the faculty of the London College of Divinity, received the appointment. However, Green attached conditions to his acceptance of the position. One of those conditions was the appointment of Packer as "director of studies," a new position. Packer accepted the offer and informed the Council of Latimer House about it in December 1968.

Michael Green and J. I. Packer would seem to have been a "dream team," being two of the most prominent evangelicals in the Anglican Church. But things began to unfold in a manner reminiscent of the early days of Latimer House. Packer found the job description of "director of studies" to be vaguely conceived. A subsequent statement by the governors would seem to have left a lot unstated: "The London College of Divinity and the Rev. Dr. J. I. Packer jointly announce that Dr. Packer has decided to withdraw his acceptance of the post of Director of Studies at the College following its move to Nottingham in the Summer of 1970. The College accepts this with very great regret."

Packer's conviction that he needed to change jobs was stronger than the fears that were produced by the possibility of being without a job for the immediate future. Packer shared his conviction with the Latimer House Council at its July 1969 meeting. At that time, he announced that he would leave Latimer House sometime during 1970.

The Naming of Packer as Principal of Tyndale Hall, Bristol

In a move that no one could have foreseen, Packer was appointed principal of the very college at which he had begun his permanent teaching career—Tyndale Hall in Bristol. However, Tyndale Hall had undergone a tumultuous history during the decade when Packer served as warden of Latimer House. The brief version of that history is as follows.

We saw in an earlier chapter that Tyndale Hall was founded in 1925, that it largely dissolved in 1931 when the principal and faculty left to found the nearby Clifton Theological College, and that it had successfully reconstituted itself within three years of that traumatic event. Tyndale Hall and Clifton Theological College coexisted within a mile of each other for nearly four decades, but the close proximity caused some discomfort.

While Packer was dealing with ecumenical mania over church mergers during his tenure as warden of Latimer House, a parallel clamor for the merger of Anglican colleges was unfolding. In fact, in 1968, the Church of England published a document entitled *Theological Colleges for Tomorrow*. Among its proposals was one for a minimum enrollment of eighty for theological colleges (with 120 regarded as optimal). According to the report, these figures could be reached through the merging of colleges. Naturally, Tyndale Hall and Clifton Theological College were candidates to merge. Unfortunately, the attempt failed, at least partly due to lingering mistrust over "the events of 1965," as they are called in Bristol circles.

The first crisis occurred at Clifton Theological College, where, at eleven o'clock at night (note well) on February 11, 1965, three of five faculty members were summoned before the college council (equivalent to an American board of trustees) and told that they were dismissed. They were not told why. Shortly thereafter, two other staff members resigned in a sympathy move. The people who had been fired were the ones who had attracted students to Clifton. As word spread, criticism began to mount in evangelical circles. Packer was among the critics. So was respected Tyndale Hall professor Colin Brown, a friend of Packer.

As Alister McGrath reconstructs the series of events, turmoil at Clifton spread to nearby Tyndale Hall, whose faculty members were on close terms with their counterparts at Clifton Theological College. Additionally, for reasons that are unclear, tension developed between the faculty and council of Tyndale Hall.

Within this climate of unrest, the proposal for a merger between Tyndale Hall and Clifton Theological College ran its course. A meeting to consider a merger was imposed on the two faculties. This meeting, a tense one, took place in June 1968. Pursuant to that meeting, the faculty of Tyndale Hall requested that the merger efforts be abandoned. The council of Clifton Theological College kept its faculty informed about continuing plans for a merger, but during summer vacation, the Tyndale Hall Council said nothing to its faculty. When classes resumed in the fall of 1968, the Tyndale faculty was told that the merger was "on" and that two well-known evangelical Anglicans, Michael A. Baughen and John B. Taylor, were scheduled to be interviewed for the position of principal. The Tyndale Hall faculty expressed its "dismay and grave concern" over this bombshell.

One chaotic event led to another. Brown was singled out for exclusion from the faculty of the merged colleges. Additionally, it was announced that the doctrinal statement that had given Tyndale Hall its theological distinctiveness would be dropped. And then there was the very important question about who the new principal would be. Of course, Packer's name was bandied about, but the "word on the street" was that he would go to the London College of Divinity or be rejected as a candidate because he had been critical of the 1965 firings at Clifton Theological College and supportive of Brown.

The Tyndale Hall Council pressed forward with the merger, leaving the faculty to find out what was happening through the pages of *The Church of England Newspaper*. Baughen was named principal of the new college. Brown was given his walking papers. Wenham resigned in protest. The *Church Times* used the word *fiasco* to describe the turmoil in Bristol. The Tyndale Hall faculty drew up a memorandum critical of both the merger and the path by which it had been engineered. Applications for new students virtually dried up. The Church of England, meanwhile, proceeded to announce that the new college would be called Trinity College.

Opponents of the merger had a trump card, however. Tyndale Hall was answerable to two governing bodies. These were the Tyndale Hall Council and the organization that had founded the college—the Bible Churchmen's Missionary Society. The proposal to drop the doctrinal statement carried weight with the latter body. After multiple committee meetings, the BCMS passed a resolution stating that it could not "give the support asked for the proposed merger unless all present staff appointments be re-examined, with great weight given to the primacy of theology." That proved to be the death blow to the proposed merger. The councils of Tyndale Hall and Clifton Theological College admitted defeat.

The foregoing records only *some* of the chaos that took place at Tyndale Hall in the months before Packer was named principal. Baughen had been in line for the position of principal in the envisioned new college, but that did not materialize when the merger fell through. The then-current principal of Tyndale Hall resigned two weeks after the announcement that the merger had been called off in protest against the "breach of faith towards the Rev. Michael Baughen and Clifton Theological College." The council immediately advertised for a new principal. Packer refused to apply for the position, but expressed a willingness to consider it if offered. Things moved quickly, and by the beginning of August 1969, Packer had been approved by both the council of Tyndale Hall and the ruling committee of the Bible Churchmen's Missionary Society as the principal of Tyndale Hall.

Tyndale Hall as Packer Found It

It is hard to know what descriptors to use for Tyndale Hall as it re-opened its doors in the fall of 1969, but the name of a street in York, England, comes to my mind—The Shambles. The enrollment had fallen to twenty-eight students. Deficits were projected for the 1969–70 academic year, as well as the following one. Emotional scars from the preceding several years ran deep in both faculty and students.

There was also a glitch in the timing of Packer's assuming his new duties. He was named principal in the summer of 1969, but January 1, 1970, was the date on which he was scheduled to begin his new position. This lag was required because an early autumn lecture tour was in place for Australia and New Zealand, from which Packer would return in late September. However, as was typical for Packer, he got started in his new job before the official start date.

We can say without hesitation that the faculty of five that Packer inherited was of the very highest quality. Even to an outsider like me, the list reads like a who's who of British evangelical scholarship from that era, with such names as Alec Motyer, Colin Brown, and Anthony Thiselton. All that was needed for the viability of the college was a few years to allow Packer's planned educational reforms to have their effect and an expansion of the student body to forty-five or fifty.

Packer as Educational Reformer

A whole new side of Packer emerged when he became a college administrator. He immediately became an educational reformer. Packer had had enough contact with North American educational institutions to conclude that the British system was deficient. He saw in the American system a more democratic arrangement, in which the faculty and not just the president (British "principal") played a key role. Already in 1968, Packer had written an article in which he had criticized the hierarchical British system of theological education. In this article, Packer argued for a greater degree of faculty governance, with the principal serving as chairman of a board or as a "leader of a team of ministry specialists."

Tyndale Hall was in such disarray when Packer became principal that there is a sense in which it provided a good opportunity for him to test his new ideas about how to structure a college. A main problem that needed to be addressed was the recent history of the Tyndale Hall Council (the governing body) working in isolation from the faculty. So even before Packer officially assumed his duties, he began a process of educational reform at the college. He named a working committee from within the college to oversee a revision of governance of Tyndale Hall. This committee met twice in the fall of 1969. After the second meeting, Packer sent a letter to the college's constituency outlining proposed changes to the college's mode of operation. A summary of the changes follows:

- An entirely new governing body would be formed, called the Tyndale Hall Association. This governing body would elect a fourth of the college's council (board of directors).
- All faculty members would serve on the college's council *ex officio*. This step was intended to ensure that those who were charged with implementing the college's policies would have a voice in determining those policies. This provision was also a direct response to the breakdown of communication that had occurred in 1968 in regard to the proposed merger.
- The college's curriculum and ministerial training program would be reviewed to ensure its relevance to the known needs of the church. Packer reaffirmed the college's primary emphasis on theology.

A new wind was blowing at Tyndale Hall, and Packer was the mastermind behind it. This is a side of Packer that most people do not know and is a tribute to his versatility in doing well whatever he sets himself to.

When Packer officially assumed his duties in January 1970, optimism ran high. The ruling committee of the Bible Churchmen's Missionary Society met and approved the proposed structural changes. Although the college faced immediate financial difficulties, there were hopes that student enrollment would begin to rise. As McGrath notes: "All that was needed was time to allow things to settle, and Tyndale's new vision to become more widely known and appreciated. But, as events would prove, time was something Tyndale would not be allowed to have."

The Ax Falls

What Packer and his college had not factored into the equation was the machinations of the Anglican Church. We have already noted that at the end of the 1960s, the Anglican committee in charge of theological education had begun to advocate the merger of colleges. A committee called the Joint Planning Group issued a report laying out two models for Anglican theological colleges. One was to allow student numbers to determine the continuation of colleges; the other was control by the church—"a policy of consultative planning, which would carry the full authority of the church." What the second proposal really meant was that a church board would determine which colleges would be allowed to continue.

McGrath reconstructs the moves and countermoves that occurred as 1970 ran its course in fuller detail than serves my purpose. Despite a frenzy of meetings and proposals, the fate of twenty-one Anglican theological colleges was actually going to be determined by forces beyond the colleges and their constituencies. More specifically, the final decisions would be made by the Anglican House of Bishops. For purposes of this biography, all that needs to be said is that Tyndale Hall did not "make the cut." The "bottom line" document reads as follows:

> In the opinion of the House of Bishops, the continuation of training of ordinands at Bristol is only possible if Tyndale Hall, Clifton and Dalton St Michael's [the women's college] agree to amalgamate on

> the Clifton site. . . . The House, therefore, asks that the Governing Bodies of the colleges concerned should immediately explore this possibility and submit their decisions to the House of Bishops not later than 1 May 1971.

A further stipulation was that all staff members at the three colleges resign their positions. This is a standard procedure, but it raised the possibility that not all faculty members would be hired at the new college.

The Move toward a Merger

The first joint meeting of representatives of the three colleges was held at Bristol Cathedral on March 3, 1971. The bishop of Bristol, Oliver Tomkins, served as chair of the meeting. The name of the new college was determined to be Trinity College. Working committees were formed. Give and take ensued. Tomkins came to a personal conclusion that a genuine gap existed between Tyndale Hall (Calvinist, working class) and Clifton Theological College (Arminian, privileged [public school summer camps]). The leadership of the new college was conceived as a triumvirate of officials from the respective colleges, to be known as a dean of studies, a dean of students, and a dean of women. Packer was tabbed for dean of studies, though as matters fell out, this suggestion did not materialize.

Misunderstanding ran high and the negotiations were stormy. Packer's efforts were sometimes considered helpful and sometimes obstructive. Eventually it became clear that the Clifton Theological College Council did not want Packer to be part of the administrative team of the new college. After the dust had settled, Motyer, who had taught at both Tyndale Hall and Clifton Theological College (where he was vice principal at the time of the notorious "events of 1965"), was named principal of Trinity College, and a position of associate principal (not dean of studies) was created for Packer. The latter was understood to be a senior position. In this role, Packer was charged with developing theological education and maintaining links with seminaries in England and abroad. The position was envisioned as allowing him to play a major role in shaping the future of the college while also giving him time to write. We should note in passing that Joyce Baldwin, a well-known name in evangelical circles in England and the United States, was named dean of women (being the senior representative from Dalton House), and Gervais Angel, a junior member of the Clifton faculty, became dean of studies.

There is an additional, little-known story that Wallace Benn, a retired Anglican bishop, has shared with me. At a meeting of the student body at Clifton Theological College, students expressed overwhelming support for the proposed merger of the colleges. A student of liberal persuasion stood up and announced that Packer would never agree to teach at a college of which he was not principal. Benn, who was a Clifton student at the time, and two other students marched over to Tyndale Hall and were given an audience with Packer, who denied the allegation. Benn regards Packer as being characteristically humble in agreeing to serve at Trinity College under the principalship of his friend Motyer.

Trinity College and Packer's Place in It

Trinity College officially began on January 1, 1972. The formal letter announcing its formation to the constituencies of the three predecessor colleges hints at the sense of weariness that came to surround its founding: "It has not been an easy road to travel and some have paid no small price in the ebb and flow of negotiations in these recent years." The letter also confided that "the 'whole story' . . . is too lengthy and complex to record here."

Yet on balance, the new college opened on a note of muted optimism. The official letter claimed that "the final realization of Trinity College may properly be described as a story of death and resurrection." The formal announcement of the merger encouraged interested parties to "join us in worshipping, praising, and loving" God. There was, in fact, much relief and much gratitude to God. In the end, no faculty members lost their jobs in the merger.

Matters that had been a cause for anxiety fell into place. The campus of the former Tyndale Hall became student apartments. The new college began with approximately eighty students. That rose by one for the next year, and by the 1980–81 academic year (the last of Motyer's principalship), the number had risen to 132.

The official letter sent to the constituencies in 1972 spoke of "the wonder-working, gentle and sovereign hand of God" in the events leading up to the formation of the new college. That is an accurate account of how things ended up for Packer as well. There is no doubt that he had been on an emotional roller coaster for two years. There were certainly times when it appeared that his vision for reforming college education had been lost. But it turned out that many of Packer's reforms were carried over to Trinity College. Additionally, Packer's teaching responsibility at the new college was relatively light, and he was relieved of the emotional wear and tear of the administrative life. The academician finally had leisure to pursue the scholarly life for which he was gifted and temperamentally suited.

Summary

Externally considered, the two years following Packer's departure from Latimer House were years of testing and disappointment. They began with a rejected application for the position of principal of the London College of Divinity (renamed St. John's College), followed by an abortive appointment as dean of studies at this same college. Then an enormous outlay of time and emotional energy in an attempted rescue of Tyndale Hall proved to be largely a wasted effort. Tyndale Hall was in some sense protected, but only at the cost of great personal anxiety and defeated efforts at many points in the journey. But at the end of the arduous path, Packer regarded the sequence of events as an exodus from Egypt—a very long journey with a promised land at the end of it. He emerged from the two years as principal of Tyndale Hall like a wounded soldier who had returned home and was ready to resume a normal life.

10

Trinity College, Bristol

(1972–1979)

The most important fact about J. I. Packer's new teaching arrangement was that it represented the end of a season of turmoil. Packer had devoted a major part of his life to theological education in Bristol. For a brief time, that investment had been threatened. As the newly formed Trinity College gained stability, theological education in Bristol was no longer precarious; it had been secured, much to the relief of Packer and others.

Helping to Make Trinity College a Success

It is always invigorating to be on a winning team, and to play a major role in the success of a team is even more rewarding. This accurately describes Packer's situation as a faculty member at the new theological college. At undergraduate colleges around England, Packer and Trinity College Principal Alec Motyer became a draw to Christian Union members anticipating a ministerial career. One person who lived through the era writes: "Up till [the early 1970s] it had been almost automatic [for evangelical seminarians] to go to either Wycliffe Hall, Oxford, or Ridley Hall, Cambridge. Now the great attraction was in [Trinity College]. . . . Here the students sat at the feet of Jim Packer and Alec Motyer, and Bristol became the launching pad to send bright young men into the ministry of the Church of England."

What were the ingredients of the education that these students received? A look at Packer's writings shows how intellectually rigorous his teaching is, whether in the classroom or a book. The knowledge base is broad, especially in regard to the Bible, but also to historical texts. Additionally, though, Packer's orientation from the time of his book *"Fundamentalism" and the Word of God* had been in the direction of responding to topics of current importance in the surrounding culture. So a practical element was built into the teaching that occurred at Trinity College, reinforced by Packer's lifelong commitment to the ministry of the local church.

The practical bent of Packer's teaching was reinforced by the nature of Trinity College as a seminary designed to prepare students for vocational service in the Anglican Church. The Thirty-Nine Articles of the Church of England were a constant point of reference for Packer, and therefore for his students. I note in passing that in 1961, Packer had published a forty-six-page monograph entitled *The Thirty-Nine Articles* (Falcon Books), and that later (in 1984) he published *The Thirty-Nine Articles: Their Place and Use Today* with Latimer House. The points of reference in Packer's courses were not the latest "hot-topic books," but works of the traditional English theologians, lending a distinctly Anglican flavor to the courses.

Retired Anglican Bishop Wallace Benn remembers an event from the 1971–72 academic year that is a barometer of Packer's willingness to engage in debate in the public arena. All of the religious institutions in Bristol (including Trinity College, a Baptist college, a liberal Methodist college, and the very liberal University of Bristol) sponsored a public forum on the authority of the Bible. Packer was the speaker. Benn recalls the attendance as being more than four hundred. In the question-and-answer session following the address, a senior lecturer from the University of Bristol took an aggressive stance and said, in effect, that Packer surely could not ignore what Friedrich Schleiermacher had written on the Bible. The challenger remained standing with a copy of a Schleiermacher book in his hand! Packer rubbed the dent in his head and then began his reply by asking, "Are we in agreement as to what Schleiermacher said?" Packer proceeded to give his questioner a brief tutorial on Schleiermacher, replete with references to specific pages in Schleiermacher, after which he developed the thesis that "Schleiermacher was wrong, for the following eight reasons." The hostile challenger withered and slunk in his seat. Packer's students, says Benn, "felt like carrying him home on [their] shoulders."

Packer's Personal Routine at Trinity College

As noted earlier, the position of associate principal had been designed to give Packer time to speak and write. In regard to the former, Packer secured an arrangement by which he would teach during the autumn and spring terms, and travel to North America during the winter term. Some of these trips lasted ten weeks. They greatly enlarged Packer's visibility in the United States, with appearances now supplementing his books and articles as a means of personal influence.

Packer's writing and publishing also picked up speed during his years at Trinity College. The blockbuster was Packer's book *Knowing God* (1973), which became one of the best-known books by an evangelical author in the twentieth century. But there were additional books that became a standard part of the Packer canon, including *I Want to Be a Christian* (better known today under the reissued title *Growing in Christ*) and *Knowing Man* (one of four books carried in the first book catalog of Crossway Books). Approximately three dozen articles and essays appeared under Packer's name during this era. The category of "forewords, introductions, and prefaces" made a major appearance in Packer's bibliography for the first time.

Packer has never been able to pursue his professional life without doing some form of active ministry in the church that he attends. In Bristol, that church was St. Edyth Sea Mills, an Anglican parish. Alister McGrath describes the vicar of the time, George Cassidy, as "a genial Irishman."

Packer's Teaching Duties at Trinity College

For an academician, the foundation of a successful publishing career is a successful teaching career. If one does not "make it" in the classroom, he or she will not even stay employed. Packer has always "made it" big in the classroom, and the key to his success is that he is (to use a favorite Puritan adjective) "a painful teacher." *Painful* here means "painstaking." Benn remembers Packer's courses as being distinctive for their superior content and breadth of learning. He also characterizes Packer as "big-minded" in his Reformed theology and a "courteous listener" to students who expressed their viewpoints in the classroom.

Among the many ways in which I find Packer a kindred spirit, one is that he is a devotee of class handouts. Both Packer and I began our careers before the days of Xerox copiers. This means that we typed our pages of notes on stencils that were then duplicated. To add a touch of class, Packer ran his sheets off on pink paper! McGrath claims that "countless early sermons delivered by Trinity Graduates" found their origin in Packer's "pink sheets."

Packer's teaching load consisted of what in the United States would be called four courses (British "courses of lectures"). In turn, each of these was made up of twenty lectures (in prosaic American usage, "class meetings"). Packer's classroom style was to speak slowly and deliberately, endearing him to students who were conscientious in taking notes. In his chapter on Packer at Trinity College, McGrath asserts that Packer's material regularly exceeded the time slot, and that he either "ran over" or omitted material in his lectures. (I am reminded again of the first public lecture that I heard by Packer.)

One of Packer's courses was entitled "An Introduction to Theology," a subject tailor-made to Packer's interests and expertise. This course was considered foundational for his three other courses. Packer began the course by discussing the tasks and tools of theology. It is instructive that Packer saw three functions for theology—(1) to deepen our understanding of the Bible, God, people, the church, and the world, (2) to control the thinking and living of Christians, and (3) to enable Christians to communicate their faith in mission and evangelism. Packer conceived of theology as an activity, and to drive the point home, he spoke of "theologizing"—a verb more than a noun. Theology consists of discovering and explicating what already exists, especially the nature of God as revealed in the Bible.

With the nature and importance of theology thus established, Packer turned to a history of Christian doctrine. Packer believes that the history of theology unfolded as a series of doctrinal debates, so he made these debates an organizing principle of his introductory course. Although we think of Packer as preeminently a Puritan scholar, he actually gave a great deal of attention to the patristic period as well. Of course, the Bible was the central text.

Packer's three other courses were "God, Christ, and Creation," "Sin and Salvation," and "Church, Sacraments, Last Things." Packer's teaching has always fed his writing; it is easy to see that the courses I have described formed the content of his books, including the major book of this era (and of Packer's writing life)—*Knowing God.*

The foregoing gives a picture of the baseline of Packer's week-to-week life during this time. What rises from this baseline to rank as landmark events in Packer's career at Trinity College? Five things: delivering the Tyndale Lecture of 1973; serving on a liberal Doctrine Commission of the Anglican Church; becoming a regular speaker on the lecture circuit in North America; participating in the Nottingham Congress of 1977; and playing a leading role in the debate on biblical inerrancy (with a 1978 conference being particularly important).

The 1973 Tyndale Lecture on the Atonement

The Tyndale Fellowship for Biblical and Theological Research and Tyndale House in Cambridge have exercised a very important influence on evangelical biblical scholarship in England from the mid-1940s to the present day. The published history of Tyndale Fellowship shows that Packer was a regular member and committeeman in that organization from 1949 until his departure for Canada in 1979. This means that Tyndale Fellowship was Packer's most continuous professional affiliation during his years in England, continuing a decade longer than the Puritan Conference, which went defunct after 1969.

Tyndale Fellowship early evolved a program of study groups (interest groups) that met in July of every year. There were also plenary lectures in the various interest areas. In 1973, Packer was invited to deliver the annual address in the area of biblical theology at Tyndale House in Cambridge on July 17. To be asked to give the annual lecture was an honor. Packer turned it into a memorable occasion both in his own life and in the history of evangelicalism in England in the 1970s. He chose as his subject the nature of Christ's atonement, and more specifically, the theme of penal substitution. The title of the address became famous: "What Did the Cross Achieve? The Logic of Penal Substitution."

It was entirely in keeping with Packer's temperament and practice that he chose a topic that was a subject of debate between liberals and conservatives. The context of the debate was as follows. The idea that

Tyndale House in Cambridge, England, where J. I. Packer delivered a major address on the atonement of Christ in 1973. (Photo © Magnus Manske. License: http://creativecommons.org/licenses/by-sa/3.0/legalcode)

Christ's atonement was a substitute for sinners had been the dominant view through the centuries until the advent of nineteenth-century liberalism. In 1962, a Cambridge professor named Geoffrey W. H. Lampe had published an essay that argued that the idea of substitutionary atonement was outdated and offensive. Predictably, this view appealed to many evangelicals. Packer's goal was a familiar one—to steer evangelicals toward the traditional view as opposed to the modernist view.

The address was a vintage Packer performance. He spoke with urgency because he saw a threat to the truth. He viewed himself as holding the line against modernist subversion of a traditionally held doctrine. The essay form of the address is a long one in which Packer (as always) pursues his ideas to their logical conclusion in a carefully organized manner. He weaves together references to the Bible, classic theological texts from the past, and contemporary liberal theology. The subject, said Packer, "takes us to the very heart of the Christian gospel," and nothing elicits Packer's intensity more than that. In his lead-in, Packer said, "I welcome the opportunity of commending my conviction by analysis and argument." The agenda that Packer set for himself was typically ambitious:

> First, to clear up some questions of method, so that there will be no doubt as to what I am doing; second, to explore what it means to call Christ's death substitutionary; third, to see what further meaning is added when Christ's substitutionary suffering is called penal; fourth, to note in closing that the analysis offered is not out of harmony with learned exegetical opinion.

Packer had been given a major responsibility and honor, and he stepped to the plate fully prepared.

McGrath has lavishly praised the address, and this is entirely appropriate. He calls it "a remarkable piece of constructive theology, showing a deep awareness of the development of Christian theology, along with a shrewd and critical awareness of the theological trends of the 1960s." McGrath adds that "many regard it as one of Packer's finest essays." People expressed a hope that it might be expanded into a book.

What insight does the address afford into Packer as a professor at the newly founded Trinity College? It shows first that Packer took his theological vocation seriously. Repeatedly as I read Packer's writing and see how packed the material is, I say to myself that he has gone "above and beyond" what was strictly required. A lesser scholar would not have done as much research and thinking as Packer did for his address on the atonement. His academic post gave him the time and resources to perform the assignment thoroughly.

However, there is also a practical impulse at work, namely, a desire to defend old versions of the truth against inroads of liberal theology. At this point, we can see that Packer was employed at a theological college, not a university. A university professor might have made the case for substitutionary atonement, but not with the same sense of urgency that the future of the evangelical church was at stake that drove Packer as a theological educator.

Finally, Packer based his theology courses at Trinity College partly on a conviction that the best theology has been formulated within the context of debate. The stance that Packer adopted in his Tyndale Lecture was that of holding up his half of a debate.

The Church of England Report Called *Christian Believing*

A second foray into public debate produced less positive results. Starting during his years at Latimer House, Packer had been a member of the Church of England's Doctrine Commission. The commission had little authority and served mainly as a platform for floating the currently fashionable doctrinal ideas of the liberal "establishment" in the Church of England. The Keele Congress of 1967 had been a moment of euphoria for evangelical Anglicans, but the evangelical influence did not extend to high-visibility theologians and the official church boards, including the Doctrine Commission.

Several liberal assaults on evangelical belief clustered in the middle of Packer's tenure at Trinity College. The year 1977 saw the publication of books by two influential liberals—*Fundamentalism*, by James Barr, and *The Myth of God Incarnate*, a collection of essays edited by John Hick. A 1976 report assembled by the Anglican Doctrine Commission had been cut from the same cloth. The commission was chaired by an Oxford Regius professor of divinity named Maurice Wiles, who had published his own attack on traditional Christian belief in a 1974 book entitled *The Remaking of Christian Doctrine*. Most of the commission members gave no credence to traditional views of the authority of the Bible and the person and work of Christ.

The two evangelicals on the commission were Packer and Michael Green (by then rector of St. Aldate's Church in Oxford). They hoped that they might exercise a restraining influence on more extreme views, but they were completely outvoted. The meetings of the commission in the mid-1970s eventuated in a book entitled *Christian Believing*, ironically published by S.P.C.K.—the Society for Promoting Christian Knowledge. The "joint report" expressed total skepticism toward historic Christian beliefs. In fact, the Christian life was described as "an adventure, a voyage of discovery, a journey, sustained by faith and hope, towards a final and complete communion with the Love at the heart of all things." The supernaturalism of the Bible was summarily dismissed. Eight commission members added individual statements in an appendix to the main report, but Packer and Green were not among them (by their choice).

The report would ordinarily have been viewed by evangelicals as confirmation of what they already knew—that the upper echelon of the Church of England was completely dominated by theological liberals. But there was more to the story. Evangelical Anglicans knew the commission included two evangelicals, but there was no evidence of their influence in the final report. According to McGrath, "Packer was singled out for particular criticism by some evangelicals, who felt that he had failed to ensure that evangelical distinctives were clearly defended and enunciated." For instance, John Wenham published an article that was critical of Packer for inadequately upholding the evangelical position.

Packer defended his work on the commission. He believed that it was important that the evangelical voice be represented. In a 1978 Latimer House book entitled *The Evangelical Anglican Identity Problem: An Analysis*, Packer offered the following postmortem on his participation on the commission: the *Christian Believing* report "has the character of a graceful guide to a confused noise"; it gives "information about what different folk do and do not believe and why," but it was not intended by a divided commission to express what Anglicans must believe; all reviews by evangelicals, however, "treated it as if it ought to be normative, and were therefore more or less hostile, as was natural."

In the controversy surrounding *Christian Believing*, we can again see a pattern that has been part of Packer's temperament and practice throughout his life. He does not believe in avoiding the public eye. The impulse to enter the public square on controversial issues has regularly included his participation in movements and service on committees that have been unpopular among mainstream evangelicals. As part of this pattern, Packer has not shrunk from deliberately doing things that have damaged his standing in the evangelical world. Of course, he has done more to strengthen his standing among evangelicals than he has done to subvert it. I note in passing that the concept of being true to one's conscience has been a particular hallmark of the Puritan temperament.

Lecturing in North America

The background chorus against which the era at Trinity College unfolded was Packer's growing familiarity and stature in North America. We should recall that Packer had arranged his annual schedule in such a way as to free up the winter term for lecture trips abroad, chiefly North America. McGrath believes that Packer "was by now regarded in North America as the best-known and most highly respected British evangelical theological writer."

Packer's career as a lecturer in North America does not consist of individual landmarks, but the cumulative weight of a series of visits.

McGrath lists the following seminaries as places where Packer spoke or taught: Westminster Theological Seminary; Fuller Theological Seminary; Trinity Evangelical Divinity School; Regent College; and Gordon-Conwell Theological Seminary.

In addition to these visits to academic institutions, Packer spoke in church settings. In 1975, he made his entry into the highly visible annual conference called the Philadelphia Conference on Reformed Theology. It is no surprise that on that occasion, Packer spoke on the subject "On Knowing God," a reference to his best-selling book *Knowing God*, first published two years earlier. Packer later became a regular speaker at the Philadelphia Conference.

The external culmination of Packer's growing stature in North America was Gordon-Conwell Seminary's conferring of an honorary doctor of divinity degree upon him. This landmark event occurred on May 27, 1978, a year after the disappointing Nottingham Congress.

Nottingham 1977

A fourth event that rose above the surface of Packer's life during his years at Trinity College was the National Evangelical Anglican Congress that met at Nottingham University in 1977. This was a sequel to the Keele Congress of 1967. Packer did not play the central role that he had filled at the previous congress, and its effect in his life was negative. The guiding spirit for the second event was John Stott, who convened a committee in 1975 to discuss the possibility of a ten-year anniversary meeting. Packer was, of course, invited to the committee meeting, but he was not enthusiastic about the conference, believing that the "hype" generated by large conferences tended to divert evangelical energy at the parish level.

At a second committee meeting, fissures began to appear. Packer proposed that a follow-up conference should focus on a specific theme of importance to the church. He argued that there had been a resurgence of evangelical scholarship, so a study conference devoted to a specific subject was now the correct model. Stott, however, wanted another general conference that followed the model of Keele. He won the debate. Packer then offered the opinion that if a broad range of topics was to be covered, the conference should not produce a report, since the coverage would be necessarily thin and the report would seem simplistic. Packer also lost this vote, as three broad topics (with study guides) were approved—*The Lord Christ*, *The Changing World*, and *The People of God*.

It is beyond my purpose for this biography to give a detailed account of the Nottingham Congress. What matters is how it affected Packer. At a personal level, the conference "left Packer feeling isolated and low" (McGrath's summary). I will note three effects of the conference that explain why he came away feeling defeated.

First, a discernible gap opened between Packer's generation of evangelicals and a younger generation. One dimension of this gap was that there emerged from the conference a new preoccupation with hermeneutics (principles of interpreting the Bible). Packer's writings show at every turn that he is aware of interpretive issues, but conference speaker Anthony Thiselton had opened the door for focusing on hermeneutics itself. In particular, Thiselton warned against using the Bible to answer modern questions to which the text does not specifically speak. In Packer's view, the congress sent attendees away with questions about the Bible rather than answers, especially in regard to biblical authority. Benn believes that Thiselton's emphasis on hermeneutics became an excuse to deny the infallibility of the Bible.

Second, and again in the area of hermeneutics, one of the study guides for the conference proposed a new approach to applying the Bible. The author of the guide disparaged how evangelicals had "traditionally . . . done their theology." That method was labeled "deductive" and was said to consist of deriving doctrines from the Bible and then "applying those principles to the question under discussion or seeking to discover their practical implications." The approach adopted by the conference "runs in the opposite direction," being an inductive approach in which a contemporary issue is "analysed in depth to see what is at stake in it and how Christian truth can be related to it." In principle, there is nothing wrong with either approach; the sting was in the combative disparagement of what "traditionally" had been done and the alternative that "runs in the opposite direction." By the very nature of the case, Packer's generation was stigmatized as doing theology according to "the older method."

A third feature of the Nottingham Congress was the disparagement of the Reformation heritage that Packer had championed. This, too, might have had a generational edge to it. A speaker named David Watson said in his address that "the Reformation was one of the greatest tragedies that ever happened to the church." We can readily imagine how this fell on the ears of Puritan enthusiast J. I. Packer.

To Packer, the Nottingham Congress was "a dud." Whereas the Keele Congress had projected an image of evangelicals as energetic and united in purpose, Nottingham, according to Packer's former Tyndale Hall colleague John Tiller, projected an image of evangelicals as ignorant "on many issues" and "obviously divided, uncertain or uninformed." Benn labels the congress "a total disaster," opening the door to a more liberal evangelical leadership during the 1980s.

The Debate over Inerrancy

Nottingham was not the last major conference in Packer's life during his years at Trinity College, however. We should not exaggerate the role of the Nottingham Congress in his life, for there were many compensating events going on (including those noted above). If the Nottingham Congress was a defeating experience, a conference held in the United States the next year was an invigorating one.

The meeting of the International Council on Biblical Inerrancy that Packer attended in Chicago in 1978, the year after the Nottingham Congress, was part of a debate that preoccupied evangelicals in America for two decades. The origin of the debate was the advent of modern theological liberalism, and Packer himself had contributed to the debate in his famous 1958 book *"Fundamentalism" and the Word of God*. The terms of discussion in the 1970s were set by a 1976 best seller entitled *The Battle for the Bible*, authored by Harold Lindsell. Lindsell gave a vigorous defense of the inerrancy of the Bible. The word *inerrant* means "without error." For Packer and others, it makes no sense to speak of the Bible as infallible while at the same time objecting to the word *inerrant*. Nonetheless, the concept of inerrancy was seen by most British evangelicals as an aberration of Americans, with associations of fundamentalist obscurantism.

For this reason, Packer created a stir in England by carrying the torch for inerrancy. His defense of the term and concept of inerrancy never left his agenda following the publication of his 1958 book. In June 1966, when Packer was still at Latimer House, he was one of a handful of British scholars invited to a conference on inerrancy that met at Wenham, Massachusetts. And he attended the meeting of the International Council on Biblical Inerrancy in Chicago in 1978. (In his own history of this organization, Packer laconically notes that the word *International* in the name of the group was due solely to him, since he was the only non-American in the group).

Packer was very active in the work of the council. He attended all of its major conferences—three "summit" meetings and two "congress" meetings over the span of a decade. He drafted the position papers (called "Expositions") for the 1978 and 1982 meetings. The 1978 summit produced a very famous and influential document called the Chicago Statement on Biblical Inerrancy. When Packer wrote about the work of the council in 1990, he made it clear that he regarded it is a triumph. He wrote, "By God's grace, the inerrancy line was held and its strategic significance was made plain. . . . I continue to thank God as I remember ICBI."

I noted earlier that the theme of the substitutionary atonement of Christ excited Packer's intensity because it is central to Christian belief. Packer believes in "first things"—things of first importance. It is obvious that the inerrancy of the Bible is in this category for him. The "Exposition" that Packer wrote for the 1978 meeting of the council was printed in later editions of *God Has Spoken*. He asserted that the concepts of infallibility and inerrancy "explicitly safeguard crucial positive truths." He lamented "the casual, inadvertent, and seemingly thoughtless way in which a belief of such far-reaching importance has been given up by so many in our day." A very great danger is that "if for the time being basic evangelical doctrines are still held, persons denying the full truth of Scripture may claim an evangelical identity while methodologically they have moved away from the evangelical principle of knowledge."

McGrath correctly notes that "Packer has always been a peacemaker in terms of the controversies into which he has been drawn," and this can be seen in his pronouncements on the inerrancy of the Bible. The title of a follow-up book published in 1980 hints at this—*Beyond the Battle for the Bible*. That title could be misinterpreted as meaning that the battle for the Bible is unimportant and misguided, but this is not what Packer meant. His point was that just as a nation at war can become fixated on winning the war and not give thought to what needs to be done after the war, the same thing could happen to people fighting the battle over the

Bible's inerrancy. So the focus of Packer's book was "the task of restoring the Bible to its rightful place in the lives of present-day Christians and churches—a task which extends beyond the battle for the Bible." This should not be construed as meaning that Packer did not throw himself into the battle for the Bible. In the 1990 summary of his position, he wrote that "inerrancy goes far to settle the shape of one's biblical scholarship and the content of one's eventual beliefs. North American evangelicals as a body have seen this, and they have confessed accordingly."

I believe that it is possible to see three additional characterizing traits of J. I. Packer in his involvement in the inerrancy debate. One is the way in which he has thrown himself into causes in which he passionately believes. He believed in the importance of the inerrancy of the Bible, so he became a crusader in its defense. Second, Packer has an ability to remain a lifelong defender of a position without becoming permanently fixated at a given point. He defended the Bible and still does, but he moved on. He did not keep fighting the same battle and become stagnant in the process. Finally, I took particular note when Packer used the metaphor of "holding the line" for inerrancy. Much of Packer's public life has consisted of holding the line for traditional viewpoints against modern and liberal ones.

Summary

The 1970s were a kaleidoscopic period for Packer. The decade began with Packer's move from a settled life at Latimer House in beautiful and exciting Oxford to the stress of reconstituting a college on the brink of closure. Just as that crisis seemed to have been weathered, the college, Tyndale Hall, was merged with two other colleges, a move that was accompanied by acrimony as well as by the enthusiasm that accompanies cooperation in a shared venture.

Once the dust settled, Packer led a normal academic life for seven years. His teaching was rewarding to him and his students. Annual excursions to America energized him and made his life interesting. The scope of Packer's influence beyond his campus shifted from the Church of England to the broader evangelical world. His life became international after having been very national during the Latimer House years. On balance, life during Packer's later forties and early fifties was good, despite stresses and disappointments.

Professional Life in North America

(1979 to the Present)

11

From England to Canada

(1978–1979)

So much has been written and theorized about J. I. Packer's move to Canada that I enter the subject with trepidation. Some see the move as a sinister event in which Packer was pushed out of the British evangelical subculture. Among these are some who do not hesitate to "name names." On the other end of the spectrum are those who see the move as Packer's having the good fortune to land a dream job.

A preliminary point is that while certain developments in Britain provide a helpful context for understanding Packer's life (in some measure, quite apart from the question of the move), people today have a way of assuming that if we describe the context within which something happens, we have explained *why* that thing happened. I propose that a context is not the same as a cause.

How Packer Viewed the Move

Before I look at the British context in which Packer found himself in 1979, we should listen to what Packer himself says about the move. In 2008, he wrote a revealing autobiographical column in *Christianity Today* in which he organized his life into a series of five surprises—"happy surprises, from the hand of a very gracious God." Packer calls these surprises "the high spots of my life" and "the turning points of my life."

The first important fact that Packer establishes regarding his move to Canada is that "nothing was further from my mind at that time than leaving England, despite some awkwardnesses there." So there we have it: Packer was not desperate to leave his native country. Second, Packer "had already turned down some invitations to relocate." In other words, Packer did not go to Regent College in Vancouver because he could not move elsewhere. Why, then, did he go to Regent College when, in the eyes of many, more attractive options existed? Because he was "'head-hunted' . . . by [his] oldest Oxford friend, James Houston, to join the faculty of Regent College, Vancouver." Also, the move to Regent College was the beginning of something very positive, not an escape from a sinking ship. In Packer's words, he moved "into a situation in which I have spent, beyond all question, the best 28 years of my life so far."

I have no desire to excise the British context from the picture, and I will take the matter up shortly. Packer's reference to "some awkwardnesses" deserves an exploration. Nonetheless, Packer is obviously the person who knows the inside story of his move. In a 1996 essay, he reiterated that despite the difficulties he faced in England, he "expected to soldier on where I was till retirement."

The Process by Which Packer Chose Regent College

By 1979, Regent College was an established graduate school with an excellent reputation. The moving spirit behind the founding and early direction of Regent College (at its origin in 1968, an essentially Plymouth Brethren institution) was Houston, whom Packer had known during his undergraduate years at Oxford University. The first two faculty members hired at Regent College had been Old Testament specialist Carl E. Armerding and New Testament scholar Ward Gasque. They had been joined in 1974 by theologian Clark H. Pinnock. When Pinnock departed for McMaster Divinity School, a major hole existed at the flourishing college.

In 1976, Houston took stock of his situation and telephoned Packer, who received the call at 11:10 a.m. as he sat in his office at Trinity College in Bristol. Packer had a routine for turning down job offers, so he asked Houston to put his offer into words and mail it. The letter arrived a week later.

Packer's familiarity with Regent College and sympathy with its mission are important factors for us to understand. Packer had already visited the college. Significantly, Regent had an important goal that Packer had hoped would also happen at Trinity College, namely, the theological education of laypeople as well as prospective clergy. Additionally, the governance model at Regent was exactly what Packer had championed—a democratic arrangement in which faculty members and administrators functioned as peers. Also, the proposed position was a teaching post only, without administrative duties. It would allow more time for writing than Packer's current position did, and doors continuously were opening to him for publishing.

The prospect of living in Canada added to the attraction. The Packers viewed Canada as a cultural compromise between England and the United States. This was more attractive to them than the United States would have been. It is revealing of Packer's attitude toward Canada that in the early 1970s, he had encouraged John Stott to consider relocating to Toronto to establish a church modeled on All Souls at Langham Place.

Additionally, the interdenominational nature of Regent suited Packer's theological temperament. It is true that up to this point he had been thoroughly enmeshed in the Church of England, but that had not proved as satisfactory as envisioned, and Packer had also been a part of the free church scene (even though his presence there had decreased following the split with D. Martyn Lloyd-Jones). The Anglican connection would be easy to maintain in Vancouver, but so would a ministry to non-Anglican evangelicals in the United States.

Packer's family situation was favorable as well. His mother had died in 1965, and his father had passed seven years later. Everything considered, the Regent offer had much to commend it.

All of the foregoing considerations prompted Packer to give Houston a verbal "yes," but with the proviso that he could not come in 1977. Why not? At this point, the story takes on the nature of an adventure tale. Packer did not wish to leave immediately before the Nottingham Congress of 1977, lest he seem to be walking out on the Church of England. He also did not wish to leave immediately after Nottingham, lest it seem that he was leaving in a huff. The more time he had to mend fences with free church evangelicals after his split with Lloyd-Jones, the less likely he would appear to be abandoning them.

As the process slowly moved forward, an element of secrecy entered to make the story even more like a mystery. While on a lecture trip to North America, Packer went to Regent College for a one-day secret visit! Later, he discovered that well-known evangelical Klaus Bockmuehl, who was teaching in Switzerland, was also being interviewed for a faculty position (Bockmuehl ended up joining the Regent faculty two years before Packer did). Packer decided to play a waiting game.

The adventure story entered a new phase during the summer of 1978, when Packer taught a two-week summer course at Regent. We should pause to give credit to the innovative summer course module that became a hallmark of Regent College (and under which I taught in the summer of 1979). The summer in Vancouver allowed Kit to test the waters in regard to the culture and weather of Vancouver. The visit unfolded so positively that Packer agreed to accept a position and return in the fall of 1979.

One additional confirming sign was that in 1978, a noted evangelical Anglican cleric named Harry S. D. Robinson became rector at a local Anglican Church (St. John's Shaughnessy). Robinson offered Packer an honorary assistantship in his parish. This removed an obstacle to Packer's coming to Vancouver, namely, uncertainty about where he might serve in a local church.

There is also a more general American context than I have sketched above, and I am indebted to Alister McGrath's analysis of it. Quite apart from Packer's declining influence in England (see below), he was riding a high tide in the United States. In fact, McGrath does not hesitate to say that "Packer was being lionized in North America" on the strength of his books and lecture trips. In this regard, we need to state the obvious: the number of evangelicals in the United States dwarfs the number of evangelicals in England. So, too, do the number of seminaries and their students: by comparison, the numbers in England are statistically insignificant. In terms of a sphere of influence and advantages of academic situation, what theology professor would not want to be in North America if other factors were conducive as well?

When Packer returned to Bristol, he informed his principal, Alec Motyer, of his plan to move to Canada. Because Packer had kept his possible move a secret, the announcement came like a bombshell. People close to Packer were devastated at the thought that England would lose one of its evangelical leaders. They also tended to assume that England was a Christian center and Vancouver a backwater, a view that Packer never accepted. Of course, neither Packer nor his supporters could quite envision what a large base of operations Regent College would afford him.

The foregoing account of why Packer decided to move to Regent College strikes me as a completely satisfactory account of what happened. Far from bolting from England, Packer prolonged the decision process and delayed the actual departure by two years. I know that some people view the matter differently. Even if I am right, however, the British context and Packer's place in it at the end of the 1970s are important factors for understanding Packer's life. There is no doubt that there were (as Packer himself called them) "certain awkwardnesses" in his situation. He was, in significant ways, a prophet without honor in his own country.

Diminished Evangelical Prospects within the Church of England

The turn of events at the Nottingham Congress (noted in the preceding chapter) was not a concern for Packer alone. It is not part of my task to trace in detail the fallout from Nottingham, so I will simply summarize the fully documented account given in Alister Chapman's biography of Stott, *Godly Ambition: John Stott and the Evangelical Movement*. Whereas Packer's disillusionment with Nottingham was immediate, only a few additional years passed before others began to feel negatively about new directions that followed the conference. The unity that had prevailed at Keele unraveled on many fronts in the years following Nottingham. Chapman's summary statement is that "Stott's attempt to unite Anglican evangelicals around a theologically conservative program to change the church was a failure."

The relevance of this failure to Packer's biography is that the Church of England ceased to be the fruitful field for labor for him that it had been in the 1960s. Packer had never backed off from combat in the wars of truth, but the prospects for accomplishing something permanent in the Church of England had greatly declined.

It is customary to contrast Packer and Stott at this point, and to regard Stott as having pushed Packer out. But Stott followed a parallel path to Packer's. According to Chapman, when the president of the Eclectics told Stott in 1975 that he wished the latter would spend more time with evangelicals in England, Stott replied that he now regarded his chief ministry to be in the Third World. In other words, Stott also came to see England as a comparatively inhospitable place in which to exert his efforts. Stott relinquished his chairmanship of the sponsoring organization of Keele and Nottingham (the Church of England Evangelical Council) in 1984, having offered to step down as early as 1971. He was replaced as chair by Jill Dann, a member of the Church of England's General Synod.

Chapman makes this revealing statement about the similarity of situations for Stott and Packer: "As with Jim Packer, Stott gave himself to Anglican politics but in the end tired of them. Neither had an obvious, appealing role to fill in England. Both were in demand elsewhere. The result was that two of England's most gifted evangelicals spent most of the end of their careers serving the church beyond England's shores."

The Puritans Fall from Favor

One of the most unexpected pieces of information that emerged for me while writing this biography was the degree to which the renewed interest in the Puritans in the mid-twentieth century in England revived the spiritual lives of individuals and churches where that interest took root. The annual Puritan Conference was not simply a professional meeting where a coterie of specialists indulged an intellectual passion. Instead, the writings and ideas of the Puritans held the key to the spiritual renewal and vitality of whole churches, starting with their ministers. The Puritans had played exactly that role in Packer's life (as I will discuss in a later chapter).

It is painful to think of the effect on Packer and his guild of Puritan enthusiasts when the Puritans suddenly became passé to many evangelicals in England. This shift, fully evident at Nottingham, was in part generational. Questions of hermeneutics grabbed the allegiance of younger evangelicals. The Puritans seemed outdated and irrelevant. David F. Wells paints this picture of what had happened:

> By 1977 the revival in Puritan spirituality . . . had more or less run its course. Perhaps the task of translating Puritan concepts into modern terms in the end proved too daunting, but the thirst for

> Puritan spirituality had also abated. What had once seemed so invigorating, now looked stilted and disagreeable, and the Calvinism that had lent such substance to the evangelical confession seemed to vanish overnight.

At this point, a new dimension emerges in regard to Packer's falling out with Lloyd-Jones. The revival that sprang from a rediscovery of the Puritan classics had been located much more in the nonconformist segment of British evangelicalism than in the Anglican wing. Although Packer still had friends in the free church world, his contact with that group was greatly diminished after the mid-1960s.

Lack of an Institutional Role within the Church of England

In addition to this shift of interest away from the subjects that interested Packer most, his institutional role within the Church of England had largely dried up. Latimer House had been designed to strengthen and be of service to evangelicals in the Church of England. The position of warden had given Packer an immediate entrée onto committees. The publishing of Latimer House had been an important instrument for evangelicals in the Anglican Church, and this, too, had kept Packer in the public eye. But when Packer had left Latimer House, his place in the Church of England had immediately shrunk.

One committee where Packer felt this diminishment was the Church of England Evangelical Council, on which Stott was prominent. Although Packer had become principal of an Anglican college (Tyndale Hall), the need to revive it from extinction had occupied nearly all of his time. When Trinity College was formed and Packer had more time to invest in committee work, he found that the Evangelical Council was almost wholly in the hands of Stott and his sympathizers.

Furthermore, Packer's particular vision for steering the Anglican Church in an evangelical direction failed to gain support. He wanted to nurture local parishes by enhancing the role of the laity in them. The dominant model in the Church of England has always been one that places control in the hands of the clergy, but Packer saw the value of a more democratic structure at the local church level (an ecclesiastical version of the model of seminary governance that he had instituted at Tyndale Hall). Packer spoke of "leadership groups" in local parishes, but the idea did not gain support.

That Packer's vision had merit was implicitly acknowledged by Stott's verdict on Keele. "The promise of Keele was not fulfilled," wrote Stott, because "the follow-on was disappointing." By "follow-on" (what Americans call follow-up), Stott meant attention to Christian nurture at the parish level. Nonetheless, Stott opted for the model of large conferences for church leaders, hoping that their influence would work its way down to local parishes. Because Packer's vision was not shared, he ended up feeling, by his own description, like "a pelican in the wilderness." It was not so much a matter of having been pushed out as it was of being a solitary voice.

Even those who supported the Stott vision knew that Packer's departure was a blow to them. Additionally, they ended up disappointed with what their game plan eventually produced. Stott's biographer, Chapman, provides this assessment:

> Packer had many reasons [for moving to Canada], but one was a sense of unease about the direction that Stott and others were taking Anglican evangelicals. Stott marked his departure in 1979 with an article entitled "Enormous Contribution to the Cause of Christ," and Stott knew that losing him was an enormous blow. Packer was a highly respected, heavyweight, traditional anchor that pulled against more liberal ideas. He had been the brains behind much Anglican evangelical policy. . . . His move was one more sign that the evangelical party in the Church of England was in trouble.

I will allow Packer himself to have the final word on his situation in England during the 1970s (especially at the end of the decade). In 1996, he published the following autobiographical retrospective in an essay on the uses of the Bible in a Christian's life:

> For fifteen years I worked to fulfill a vision of evangelical quickening in England through theological education, spiritual formation, ministerial enrichment, profound preaching, wise evangelism, functional Christian unity, and every-member ministry in local congregations. . . . After fifteen years of actively promoting it came several years during which, through what people with other visions did in perfectly good faith to block, more or less directly, the things I was after, I lost all the vantage-points I had had for implementing the purposes that the vision dictated.

Packer adds that he felt "marginalized, isolated, and required to work for . . . flawed agendas." He lived "with frustration in [his] heart, wondering what God . . . could possibly be up to." Carl Trueman correctly concludes that Packer's "move to Canada must surely be seen as much as indicating the theological and ecclesiastical poverty of Britain as any positive commentary on North America" (and we need to note that Trueman offers an equation—*as much as*—that does not deny that the move was an affirmation of possibilities in North America).

Summary

It would be wrong to exaggerate the disappointments that Packer experienced in regard to the institutional Anglican Church during his final decade in England. The teaching and traveling that he did with Trinity College as a platform were fruitful in the Christian world and rewarding to Packer. Even if clouds had not been gathering on the horizon in the late 1970s, the move to Regent College would have been an attractive option. Everything considered, it was providential that Packer found a receptive home in Canada, but it was equally providential that his situation in England became confining to his spirit, thereby inclining him to make the move to North America.

12

Regent College

(1979 to the Present)

The details surrounding the Packers' actual move to Vancouver fall into the category of "worst-case scenario." The manifest for their possessions arrived four months late! The goods were accordingly impounded by Canadian customs agents. When the container was eventually opened, the damage to the contents came to $1,000. All of that, however, stands as a foil to J. I. Packer's teaching duties at Regent College, which won him from the beginning.

Regent College as Packer Found It

The Regent College that Packer joined as a professor had undergone a series of permutations during its brief history. The college had been founded by members of the Plymouth Brethren. Although the Brethren deny that they are a denomination, their organization has many denominational characteristics. The movement began in Dublin, Ireland, in the late 1820s. In the first half of the twentieth century, the Plymouth Brethren were a leading evangelical force in England. Several famous evangelical leaders were Brethren during their days at Oxford University, where they were members of the Christian Union. Examples include Donald Wiseman and James Houston. Packer attended the Oxford Brethren church during his early student days, finding it more welcoming than the local Anglican churches.

J. I. Packer has taught at Regent College in Vancouver, British Columbia, since 1979. (Photo courtesy of Alexander Grudem)

Vancouver, British Columbia, was a center of Brethren activity in the mid-twentieth century. In the early 1960s, the idea of establishing a graduate school for theological education in Vancouver took root, and a School of Theology Committee was formed in 1965. The impetus was partly to ensure an educated leadership in Brethren assemblies. Because the Brethren do not have a formal position of clergyman, the envisioned institution was not to be a typical seminary preparing future ministers. The motto that was used to describe the college was "a Brethren-oriented seminary for laypeople." Students were expected to be people with occupations in the working world.

As plans for the college progressed, Houston's name rose to the forefront as a possible leader. Houston, an Oxford-educated (MA; DPhil) specialist in geography, was a teacher at Hertford College, Oxford, from 1964 to 1970. However, his first love was theological education, even though he taught geography. He was a friend of C. S. Lewis. As Houston had developed a vision for theological education of the laity, he had come to a realization that Oxford was not a hospitable environment for such a college. At the same time that Houston reached that conclusion, he read an article in a Christian magazine that alerted him to the movement in Vancouver to establish a Brethren theological college.

By the time Houston found his way to Vancouver in 1967 to meet with the School of Theology Committee, he had proposed that the college have three characteristics: it would be adjacent to a university with which it would be affiliated; it would be a graduate school of theology; and it would be broadly evangelical rather than Brethren. The third item ran counter to the original vision for the college, but it won the vote. By 1968, the school had received its charter and its name of Regent College. Houston officially became principal in 1970.

The first formal teaching at Regent consisted of summer schools in 1968 and 1969. Fifty students attended the first summer school, and one hundred the second. The college officially opened in 1970 in rented space (the basement of a United Church of Canada theological college on the campus of the University of British Columbia). The incoming class of ten students became a mere four when the others were killed in a car crash on the first day of classes. But the college survived and then flourished.

In 1972, Regent College forged an affiliation with the Vancouver School of Theology (which had links to the University of British Columbia). A stipulation of the affiliation was that Regent College would not become a competitor to the Vancouver School of Theology by establishing a master of divinity degree, a stipulation that became a point of contention later.

Regent quickly outgrew its rented space. By 1973, the enrollment was sixty-three full-time students. The college bought two vacant fraternity houses on the edge of the University of British Columbia campus. Houston was a visionary, and he eventually negotiated a full-fledged affiliation between Regent College and the University of British Columbia.

Two further developments add to our picture of Regent College as Packer found it. The first is that Houston's winning the vote for Regent

College to be broadly evangelical rather than specifically Brethren came to determine the identity of the college. According to Alister McGrath, starting in the mid-1970s, North American Brethren lost interest in Regent College. At the same time, Regent became venerated in mainstream North American evangelicalism. Perhaps we can say that, despite the Brethren origins of Regent College, Packer went to teach at an evangelical graduate school, not a Brethren college.

Second, the rapid growth in numbers at Regent College in the late 1970s led Carl Armerding (who had succeeded Houston as principal in 1978 after Houston was named chancellor) to establish a master of divinity program. The Vancouver School of Theology saw this as a threat to its interests. The outcome was that the affiliation between the two colleges was terminated. Regent College responded by forming an alliance with a Baptist theological college called Carey Hall.

To recap, Regent College had moved from a committee's vision to a prominent theological college in a mere fifteen years. The energy of the place must have impressed Packer. The enrollment at Regent the year Packer began his teaching career there (1979) was approximately 140.

Teaching at Regent College

Because Packer has been so prolific as an author and speaker during his years at Regent, I had assumed that he taught a reduced load. I have discovered that this was not the case. This leads to the obvious question of how Packer was able to teach a full load and also publish and lecture as much as he has. Loren Wilkinson, Packer's colleague for nearly his entire time at Regent College, describes Packer as "one of those people who are able to get a lot done—mainly by getting up very early (4–5 a.m.)."

Packer was hired as a professor of historical and systematic theology, with the latter subject being his primary teaching area. His teaching load consisted of five courses per academic year. The core courses eventually numbered four, each of which came to bear the main title of "Systematic Theology" (I, II, II, IV). The subtitles of the courses were as follows: (1) "Knowledge of God"; (2) "Doctrine of God, Creation, and Man"; (3) "Christology and Soteriology"; and (4) "Ecclesiology and Eschatology." These courses were similar to those that Packer had taught at Trinity College in Bristol, and on the whole, they followed the familiar contours of courses and books on systematic theology of many years and even centuries past.

As the years unfolded, Packer's course offerings greatly expanded beyond the basic theology routine. Jeffrey Greenman, Packer's student at Regent and now president of the college, gives the following description of Packer's teaching load. In addition to the full-fledged and "very large classes" in theology, there was "a one-semester, very compressed, lightning-speed overview of theology." Packer also taught seminars on major theological figures, traditions, and topics. Examples from Greenman's experience were the Puritans and the atonement. The profile on Packer that appears on the Regent College website lists "Anglican History and Theology" and "Colossians/Ephesians/Philemon" as courses within Packer's teaching repertoire.

Packer did not offer tutorials, but he supervised a steady load of master's theses. He also led a faculty-student advisee group for many years. Greenman describes it as "a social-pastoral care group" in which attractions included bird watching and listening to Packer's collection of jazz records. Greenman also recalls transporting Packer to and from the airport, "as he was often speaking at churches or conferences all over North America."

The flavor of a Packer course is captured by the mimeographed "course packet" for Packer's introductory course on systematic theology. The packet runs to some sixty-five single-spaced pages, carefully outlined. It begins with an overview called "The world of systematic theology," in which Packer outlines "ten recognized theological disciplines" within theology. This is followed by modules on "The topics of systematic theology," "The interests of systematic theology," and "The activity of systematic theology." A two-page bibliography of published sources ensures that students will not run out of things to do! (Of course, there are further "suggested readings" at the beginning of many individual units in the outline.) After these preliminaries, the outline marches through the major topics of systematic theology in the customary order. The references are to traditional creeds and theologians (e.g., the Westminster Confession and Martin Luther), the Bible, contemporary theologians (for example, Packer covers "some influential views of revelation" with excursions into William Temple, Karl Barth, Emil Brunner, and Rudolf Bultmann), and Packer's own views.

An interview with Christopher Hall, now chancellor at Eastern University, yielded a picture of Packer as the overseer of independent projects. Hall recalls a procedure whereby he would read a book, such as Augustine's *Confessions*, and then write an essay on it, which he remembers as "a fun, fruitful, and intimidating exercise." After completing the essay, Hall "would arrive at Jim's office, essay in hand, give the door a knock, hand the essay to him, and sit outside his office door while he read it." Hall states, "I can remember my heart pounding." After fifteen minutes, Packer would come to the door and call Hall into his office. "Within the first minute," Hall remembers, "I would know the verdict." Generally, Packer's assessments were positive, but Hall remembers a session that began with the words, "Chris, I have come to expect better work than this from you," and ended with the statement, "Chris, I want you to know that I'm not averse to prolonging your stay in Vancouver."

Hall characterizes Packer the teacher as someone "with a low tolerance for shoddy thinking and shoddy work." He is adept at gauging strengths and weaknesses, Hall says, and at "pushing [a student] to perform well and occasionally dropping in a word of praise." According to Hall, Packer "demanded much, but the demands were supported by wise insight and a willingness to help in areas where [a student] was weak." Above all, Hall records his gratitude for Packer's willingness to spend time with him.

In 1989, a decade after he joined the Regent faculty, Packer became the first holder of an endowed chair at the college. In December of that year, he was installed as the first Sangwoo Youtong Chee Professor of Theology at Regent College. This chair was evidence of the growing importance of the Chinese Christian community in Vancouver and at Regent. In 1996, Packer's official title changed again, as he became Board of Governors' Professor of Theology. In yet another development, on the occasion of Packer's seventieth birthday, Regent announced the founding of the J. I. Packer Chair of Theology at the college.

Packer taught full time at Regent College until his formal retirement in 1996 at the age of seventy. He has continued to teach part time to the present day, with time off for recuperation from hip surgery, for sabbaticals, and for professional travel.

Packer's work at Regent College extended beyond his teaching. He and Kit embraced the role of pastoral care to students. A "community group" of students met in their home every week. Kit also participated in the college wives' group.

While it is impossible to gauge Packer's role in the growth of Regent College, it stands to reason that his presence was a major ingredient in the college's success. There has been no more famous teacher at Regent College through the years than Packer. When he joined the faculty, the study body numbered 140. By 1985, the enrollment had grown to 450. The Regent College home page records the current enrollment as eight hundred full- and part-time students.

If the students were stimulating to Packer, so were his colleagues. Packer would not have thrived as he did at Regent without knowing that he was on a winning academic team. Regent College has always managed to attract professors whose high profiles exceed what we might expect for a relatively small graduate school that is on the geographic periphery of North America. When I taught a course on the Bible as literature as a relative unknown in the summer of 1979, the other visiting professor was none other than John Stott. As the years unfolded, the full-time and part-time teachers at Regent came to read like a who's who of leading evangelical scholars. The current home page of Regent College lists nineteen full-time professors and twenty-nine visiting and part-time teachers.

Other Aspects of the Regent Years: Speaker, Author, Controversialist

Packer's career as a visiting lecturer and conference speaker had long been robust, but it exploded when he moved to Regent College. The following is a partial list of Packer's lectureships in the 1980s and 1990s, not including myriad speaking engagements at churches:

- "The Bible in America" conference at Wheaton College (1979)
- Canadian Theological Seminary in Regina, Saskatoon (1981)
- The Ryan Lectures at Asbury Theological Seminary (1982)
- The Staley Lectures at the Lutheran Bible Institute in Seattle (1982)
- Conservative Baptist Seminary in Denver (1982)
- The Bible Institute of Hawaii (1983)
- The Day-Higginbotham Lectures at Southwestern Seminary (1985)
- The Leon Morris Lecture, delivered to the Evangelical Alliance in Melbourne, Australia (1990)

- The Reformation Heritage Lectures at Beeson Divinity School (1994)

In addition to lectureships, Packer filled temporary teaching assignments at a similarly impressive list of seminaries: Reformed Theological Seminary in Jackson, Mississippi; New College in Berkeley, California; Westminster Seminary California in Escondido, California; Westminster Theological Seminary in Philadelphia; Gordon-Conwell Theological Seminary in Wenham, Massachusetts; and Trinity Evangelical Divinity School in Deerfield, Illinois. Regarding the expanded range of Packer's influence in these assignments as compared with his prior experiences in England, Mark Noll notes that the British posts were Anglican; the North American posts have been Reformed and evangelical.

Packer's publications also exploded as his years at Regent College unfolded. Anything like a complete survey is out of the question for my purposes, so I arbitrarily chose 1995 as a specimen year. Packer published four books in that year—*Knowing and Doing the Will of God*; *Knowing Christianity*; *Life in the Spirit*; and *A Passion for Faithfulness: Wisdom from the Book of Nehemiah*. Additionally, Packer co-edited *Nelson's Illustrated Encyclopedia of Bible Facts*, a revision of *The Bible Almanac* published fifteen years earlier.

Seven essays in books edited by others covered the subjects of "Anglicanism Today," "Jesus Christ, the Only Saviour," "Crosscurrents among Evangelicals" (published in *Evangelicals and Catholics Together*), "The Love of God: Universal and Particular," "Comprehensiveness in the Church of England," "The Preacher as Theologian," and "The Reformational Revivalism of George Whitefield." One can readily see lifelong passions in this many-sided list—the state of the Church of England, preaching, and historical theology—as well as a catholic or ecumenical orientation, and a complementary Reformed orientation.

Also in 1995, Packer wrote an essay on higher criticism for the *New Geneva Study Bible* and a biographical piece on Robert Aitken for *The Blackwell Dictionary of Evangelical Biography: 1730–1860*. In addition, he perpetuated his mini-career of helping other authors by writing a foreword to a book (Don Dunkerley's *Healing Evangelism: Strengthen Your Witnessing with Effective Prayer for the Sick*). Everything considered, 1995 was a representative Packer year in the area of publishing.

From the time that Packer countered the Keswick view of the

Christian life by circulating a twenty-page summary of John Owen's views among his college friends, he has not hesitated to enter public controversy on issues that matter deeply to him. This practice continued very strongly during his years in Vancouver (some of these controversies will receive fuller attention in a later chapter). A short list of issues on which Packer took controversial stands after he left England includes the following:

- The role of women in the church: Packer took a traditional view that women should not serve the same role as men in the church.
- The charismatic movement: when this movement exploded in the 1970s (making a strong appearance even in Anglican churches), Packer undertook extensive research into the subject of the Holy Spirit and attempted to moderate between charismatics and their critics (culminating in his 1984 book *Keep in Step with the Spirit*).
- The myth of contemporaneity (debunking of the past, on the assumption that everything new is best): Packer continued to base his critique of contemporary cultural and theological aberrations on leaders and documents from the past (e.g., Luther, John Calvin, the Thirty-Nine Articles, and the Westminster Confession).
- The elevation of subjectivity in current views of spirituality: Packer was unwavering in making the case that spirituality must be rooted in theological understanding and the Bible.
- Universalism: when the idea that no one will be condemned to hell suddenly gained popularity among a number of Packer's former colleagues and friends, he argued for the traditional and biblical teaching about hell and the immortality of every person's soul.
- Cooperation with Roman Catholics: Packer took an aggressive role in an organization called Evangelicals and Catholics Together.
- Combatting liberalism in the Anglican Church of Canada: when the Synod of the Canadian Anglican Church sanctioned same-sex unions, Packer was one of a group of clerics who repudiated the decision, and Packer, along with the others, was officially (though ineffectually) suspended as a result. This means that Packer's license to serve in the diocese was withdrawn. The bishop of New Westminster (Vancouver) evidently thought that he was reducing Packer to layman status, but this proved untrue, since almost immediately another bishop relicensed Packer.

The English Standard Version of the Bible (ESV)

In the next chapter, I will present evidence that during Packer's years in Vancouver, he spent so much time working for *Christianity Today* that it became a part-time job. The same is true of his work on the English Standard Version of the Bible, starting in 1998 and continuing to the present day. The ESV is a complete revision of the Revised Standard Version of 1952. Crossway Books secured permission from the National Council of Churches in 1998 to produce the revision that became the ESV.

While the work of translation became a short-term preoccupation for the dozen members of the committee who worked on the project, it was much more than that for Packer. He was named general editor for the translation. This made his involvement more all-absorbing than was true for the other translators (not counting Crossway President Lane Dennis).

Packer's work as general editor brought out his best talents. His mastery of Greek enabled him to comment with particular insight on the language, rhetoric, and thought patterns found in the New Testament. At the meetings of the translation committee, he would make the final comment just before a vote was taken. His powers of persuasion blossomed on those occasions. After the preliminary text had been determined, Packer pored over it with more-than-ordinary intensity. Packer and Dennis forged the masterful preface to the ESV. After the new translation was published, interviews with Packer were considered to be particularly important.

The most striking comment about Packer's involvement with the ESV comes from Packer himself. At a banquet Crossway hosted at the International Christian Retail Show in 2006, Packer said, "Now that I look back on what we did in producing [the ESV], I find myself suspecting very strongly that this was the most important thing that I have ever done for the Kingdom." Considering the impact that Packer's multitudinous books have made, as well as his teaching and public speaking, this is a momentous claim.

Packer's work did not end with the ESV translation. When the *ESV Study Bible* was put together several years later, Packer served as theological editor. He describes his involvement in that project this way: "What that has meant is that I have read the text of every article that has been submitted. There are 1.1 million words in the Study Bible. I don't know who else has read them all, but I know that I have." Packer went on to describe the function of the *ESV Study Bible* in terms of a traditional catechism—teaching "people the truths that Christians live by and [teaching] them how to live by those truths."

Summary

I refer to the post-1979 era as "the Regent College years" because Regent was the home base from which the rest of Packer's professional life flowed. During those years, only half of his professional life was occupied with his college responsibilities. Nonetheless, teaching has always been an important part of Packer's sense of calling, so we need to credit the stable teaching life at Regent College as a central aspect of his life since 1979. Equally, though, we need to stress the breadth of Packer's life that he was able to build on the foundation of his academic employment at Regent College—a life of speaking, publishing, and debate in the public arena.

13

Christianity Today

(1958 to the Present)

When *Christianity Today* magazine published its first issue in October 1956, the opening editorial answered the question "Why *Christianity Today*?" The answer reads like a mission statement for much of J. I. Packer's life: "*Christianity Today* has its origin in a deep-felt desire to express historical Christianity to the present generation. Neglected, slighted, misrepresented—evangelical Christianity needs a clear voice, to speak with conviction and love, and to state its true position and its relevance to the world crisis. A generation has grown up unaware of the basic truths of the Christian faith taught in the Scriptures and expressed in the creeds of the historic evangelical churches."

Packer's first contributions to *Christianity Today* came in the form of three articles published by the magazine in 1958, and two more the following year. Obviously Packer had made a favorable impression on the editors of the magazine. Still, no one could have imagined the major role that *Christianity Today* would one day play in Packer's life. I am sure that many of my readers will be surprised by this chapter devoted to Packer's relationship with *Christianity Today*. Nonetheless, it is relevant, because working for the magazine became the equivalent of a part-time job after Packer moved to Vancouver. Much of this work falls into the category of consulting and advising, and in this we can see the behind-the-scenes nature of much of Packer's contribution to the kingdom.

A Brief History of Packer's Advisory Work for *Christianity Today*

Packer first appeared on the masthead of *Christianity Today* in the September 16, 1983, issue. He was named as a group of "contributing editors" (a group to which John Stott already belonged). The role and duties of the contributing editors were minor. Mainly these "editors" lent luster and credibility to the magazine. Contributing editors were encouraged to submit occasional articles, but they were not required to do so. Despite his five early articles, Packer published only occasionally with *Christianity Today* until the mid-1980s.

The April 19, 1985, masthead signaled a new status for Packer, though it would have taken a detective to pick up the change that had occurred. With this issue, Packer was listed as one of five "senior editors." The others were well-known evangelicals—V. Gilbert Beers, George Brushaber, Kenneth S. Kantzer, and Dennis F. Kinlaw. This change "represented a step up," according to longtime *Christianity Today* editor David Neff. Hence, the new position carried a stipend. Packer stepped to the plate in regard to writing for the magazine, publishing five articles in 1986.

Although the magazine's original intention had been that the five senior editors would serve staggered three-year terms, according to Neff, "it quickly became clear that Ken Kantzer and J. I. Packer had something very special to contribute." They accordingly became permanent members of the advisory board of senior editors, while the others served terms. The function of the senior editors was considered "very important" by the staff of *Christianity Today*. Although Packer never bore the official title of "theological advisor," this is the term that the editors informally used for Packer's role following 1985. Serving as theological guardian was a key contribution, because there was discontent among some evangelical leaders regarding the theological direction of *Christianity Today*.

The unsettledness came to a head in 1990–91. Harold Myra, longtime publisher and president of the magazine, called a conclave to deal with the crisis. The meeting occurred in January 1991 for the purpose of conducting "a close examination . . . of the magazine, in order to evaluate its effectiveness." Staff members at *Christianity Today* remember Packer as being a "key voice" and "very helpful" at the conclave. One of the important decisions reached at the meeting—a decision that was endorsed by the theologians (including Kantzer and Packer)—was that *Christianity Today* could not be a hybrid between a "thought journal" and a newsmagazine in the mold of *Time* and *Newsweek*. The magazine was consciously pointed in the latter direction (having already been on that trajectory).

In my 2014 conversations with Packer, it emerged that the picture is not quite as tidy as the summary in the preceding paragraph indicates. Packer's acquiescence in defining *Christianity Today* as a newsmagazine grew out of his awareness of the pragmatic need for the magazine to become financially solvent. It was not his ultimate vision for the magazine. In his own words, his goal was for *Christianity Today* "to grow out of being a newsmagazine and into a thought journal." Packer believes that over the years the magazine has shown no movement in this direction.

Aftermath of the Conclave

The senior editors held a regular meeting in March 1991, two months after the conclave. They overwhelmingly rejected the calls for *Christianity Today* to be a journal with essays that would appeal to scholars. Packer affirmed the consensus view of the magazine (popular rather than scholarly). At this same editorial meeting, Packer also made an appeal that the tone of the magazine should be "statesmanlike" and not combative. It was also agreed that while *Christianity Today* had begun as a countercultural voice, evangelicals had since become the establishment, so something was needed to "restore the energy" (a formula used by Brushaber).

The vision thus evolved of *Christianity Today* as a magazine attuned to current events and having an urbane rather than strident voice. But one more piece of the puzzle needed to fall into place. The crisis had emerged in the first place because of discontent with the theological stance of the magazine. So the need for someone to exercise a vigilant theological eye on the content of *Christianity Today* was a concern.

Out of this concern was born the concept of a scholar-in-residence program. Packer offered his opinion that such a scholar would bring theological resources to the journalists on the staff, while at the same time engaging in reading and thinking to inform the journalists "about what's coming over the horizon theologically." Doubts quickly surfaced about whether such a program would attract good candidates. Kantzer, who had been editor in chief of *Christianity Today* from 1977 to 1982, offered the opinion that "we've had a great weakness in that we haven't had strong theologians" at the magazine.

Packer's Expanded Role

Christianity Today did not institute a scholar-in-residence program. However, in 1991, Packer was offered a full-time position at *Christianity Today*. He gave the offer careful consideration, but ended up declining it. In the wake of that decline, Myra was intent that *Christianity Today* at least garner as much of Packer's time and involvement as possible. Packer's role was accordingly enlarged.

This expanded role entailed several duties. One was a critique of the content and form of each issue (including graphics and layout). Packer has sent the magazine's staff a critique of every issue from that time to the present day. In January 2002, when the economic downturn started to take its toll on printed media, Neff wrote to Packer to inform him that the magazine needed to reduce his stipend and therefore his workload by twenty-five percent. Packer continued to critique every issue, and eventually did so without payment.

Myra offers the verdict that Packer "provided many insightful cautions, suggestions, and praise. . . . He was very good at critiquing the packaging—the art, photos, headlines and overall ways the layouts drew in and informed readers." He adds that Packer has "good sense as to what news should be covered." Likewise, Neff found that Packer "has good journalistic sense and is a great collaborator."

A second task that Packer's theological leadership involved was a routine of quarterly trips to the magazine's offices in Carol Stream, Illinois (adjacent to Wheaton). These were major, multiday events, as Packer met with numerous people and groups. Myra claims that Packer became "the theological lodestar for *Christianity Today*." The board of senior editors, who met regularly, "constituted the broader lodestar for the content of *Christianity Today*, and Jim was a key person in that group." At these meetings, the senior editors discussed the issues that the magazine should address, the ways in which the articles should be approached, and potential authors for the articles. On his visits, Packer met individually with a number of staff people, including Myra and

Neff. Myra recalls that in his meetings with Packer, the two would conduct "wide-ranging discussions of what was happening in the church and academia as well as personal concerns and interests."

There was also an instructional aspect to Packer's quarterly visits, confirming my claim that *Christianity Today* functioned as an extension of Packer's position at Regent College. Packer usually conducted tutorials with staff members as a group. These tutorials were on subjects of special interest to Packer or topics on which he had been asked to speak. These were not dialogues but lectures in which Packer "would preach his own topic" (Myra).

I saw Packer's instructional contribution in action when *Christian History and Biography* published a special issue on the Puritans. Packer and I were invited to be on the committee that produced the issue. A planning meeting was held in the offices of *Christianity Today*. After the usual business had been conducted, Packer was invited to deliver a lecture on the Puritans. I had never been to a committee meeting like this! Packer spoke from very brief notes. I was totally entranced. The lecture was filled with Packer's wisdom on the Puritans, as he gave an audience of three or four his "take" on the Puritan movement. I was thrilled to have heard the only J. I. Packer classroom-style lecture of my life.

More happened on the quarterly visits than meetings at the *Christianity Today* offices. Packer used these occasions to do additional things in the Wheaton area. He scheduled regular meetings with people such as Wendall Hawley at Tyndale House Publishers and Lane Dennis at Crossway. He preached in local churches and became a "regular" in the pulpits of St. Mark's Episcopal Church in Glen Ellyn and All Souls Anglican Church in Wheaton. He spoke to groups of college students assembled by Jerry Root, then the college pastor at College Church in Wheaton.

Auxiliary Activities

Packer's work for *Christianity Today* spawned several related projects. At the same time that *Christianity Today* formed the senior editorial board, it began the Christianity Today Institute. This consisted of "think tank" conferences that eventuated in supplements printed from time to time in issues of the magazine. The first such supplement appeared in the April 19, 1985, issue, the same issue that listed the senior editors for the first time. An accompanying letter from the editor explained the purpose of the institute: "to speak to critical issues with more depth and breadth" than ordinary articles in *Christianity Today* allowed, and to present "the collective insights [of] . . . the best and most articulate Christian thinkers and practitioners . . . in a readable manner." The first supplement was on the subject of "The Christian as Citizen," and the essays had grown out of a two-day conference. Packer's essay was entitled "How to Recognize a Christian Citizen." Packer went on to participate in multiple Christianity Today Institutes, but did not assume a leadership role in them.

A second project was equally ambitious. Packer was named general editor of an annual book of current scholarly articles reprinted from a vast array of scholarly journals. The nature of the venture was suggested by the main title of the successive books—*The Best in Theology*. Prominent evangelical scholars who were experts in various religious categories oversaw their areas. Packer wrote major introductions to each volume. The market could not sustain such an intellectually elevated venture, and the series ended after four books had been published under the imprint of Christianity Today, Inc.

Packer's Articles in *Christianity Today*

Packer's large role at *Christianity Today* gave him an opportunity to write articles for the largest regular circulation of his life. His articles were relatively brief ones and were not in the same genre as the essays that he had written throughout his scholarly life. Neff looks at these articles from a journalist's perspective and puts them into the category of journalistic writing. Considered in that light, the genre of "column" often seems accurate (the more so because most of his articles were one- or two-page pieces that appeared in the early pages of an issue). I look at the articles as a literary scholar and regard them as informal essays.

Writing columns or informal essays for *Christianity Today* liberated Packer to take risks and be creative. He wrote on an immense range of subjects. The writing was often occasional in nature, sparked by something in the life of the times or in Packer's personal life. A lighter, whimsical side of Packer emerged spontaneously. The following is a sampling of the topics on which Packer wrote for *Christianity Today*:

- Jazz music: an article that grew out of Packer's lifelong love of jazz.
- "The Unspectacular Packers": an autobiographical piece about Packer's family lineage.
- "An Accidental Author": another autobiographical piece about Packer's writing career and philosophy of writing.
- "What Lewis Was and Wasn't": a journalistic "occasional piece" on C. S. Lewis on the twenty-fifth anniversary of his death.
- "What the Puritans Taught Me": an autobiographical article in which Packer analyzed the influence of the Puritans in his life.
- "Let's Stop Making Women Presbyters": a famous and controversial article in which Packer argued against feminist views of women in the church.
- "God's Plumber and Sewage Man": an article with a teasing title that virtually compels one to read the piece (it is about the role of theologians!).
- "The Whale and the Elephant": reflections on D. Martyn Lloyd-Jones and F. F. Bruce as temperamental opposites, and on the need not to let diversity impede unity.
- "Why I Left": the narrative of Packer's early sympathy with the World Council of Churches and his eventual repudiation of it.
- "Reflected Glory: What Does Genesis Mean by Man Being Made in the Image of God?": a theological analysis of an important Christian doctrine.
- "Surprised by Graphics": a piece on communication theory that asserts the need to communicate with and to both sides of the brain, and the need for images to match the thoughts in an article.

This is obviously a very intriguing list, and that is exactly the point: an unexpected benefit of Packer's work with *Christianity Today* is that it unleashed a creative side of him that otherwise might have remained untapped or at least hidden from public view.

A Reciprocal Relationship

It is easy to see what *Christianity Today* wanted from Packer: theological guidance and gatekeeping. It got much more than that. The role of theological editor (his unofficial title around the office) was a behind-the-scenes assignment. Packer's years at Latimer House had prepared him for the tasks of writing journalism on wide-ranging "occasional" topics and writing essays of social and theological critique. But in his quarterly visits, Packer became a friend, tutor, and coach to the staff of *Christianity Today*. Additionally, because Packer was more or less assured of having his submissions published, he was free to be daring and creative (not least of all with his titles).

Until I wrote this biography, it was a great mystery to me why Packer has invested himself so heavily in a magazine rather than a journal, and in a magazine that has regularly struck me as more liberal than Packer is. Now that I have the whole picture in view, it makes sense. If *Christianity Today* was a great beneficiary of the relationship, so was Packer.

First, *Christianity Today* gave Packer a platform in North America. He had been a "household name" in British evangelicalism during his years in his native country. He was much less so in North America. His articles in *Christianity Today* made him a familiar friend to more than a hundred thousand readers. Academic publishing never would have provided that kind of exposure to the Christian public.

Second, the role that Packer filled with *Christianity Today* duplicated and extended what he had done in England, especially at Latimer House. Packer's biography shows how single-mindedly he has channeled his efforts into ensuring the theological integrity of the church. In England, that church was largely the Church of England. With *Christianity Today*, the audience was mainstream evangelicalism. The role of theological guide was exactly the same, but *Christianity Today* was broader in influence and carried a better chance of achieving evangelical goals than the Church of England had done. Packer is an idealist, and according to Myra, Packer saw a chance for evangelicalism to be its best through his efforts at *Christianity Today*.

There were personal needs that *Christianity Today* filled as well. Packer is "a great collaborator" (Neff), and the work at *Christianity Today* provided abundant scope for collaboration. We can rest assured that Packer would not have poured himself into *Christianity Today* if he had not found the fellowship with people there gratifying and invigorating. Myra claims that at *Christianity Today*, "whatever Jim advocated was given careful attention," and that was a welcome contrast to the situation during Packer's last years in England. Finally, Myra observed to me that "Jim always had so much to do," and the articles and visits related to *Christianity Today* offered the welcome prospect of small chunks that could be finished in a timely manner.

I will allow Packer to render a last word on his long relationship with *Christianity Today*. In a conversation with me, he called *Christianity Today* "the icing on the Regent cake," meaning that his foundational calling has been at Regent College, but the *Christianity Today* connection has been a source of continuous fulfillment.

Part 2

THE MAN

A complete biography of a person has three main strands, though no biographer is obligated to cover all three. One strand is the events that make up a person's life. These events are the skeleton on which any biography rests. A biographer can become so enamored of the facts of his subject's life that he ends up writing a documentary, not only of the person but also of the era in which his subject lived (sometimes mainly of the era). The person often disappears in the mass of data that the biographer has collected.

The second ingredient is the person about whom the biography has been written. I have regarded this as my primary purpose in writing a biography of J. I. Packer. I trust that my telling of his life story in Part 1 has already performed part of that task, but in this section of the book, the focus is on the person instead of the events that have constituted his life.

The third ingredient of a biography is an account of the lifelong preoccupations and passions of a person. That will comprise Part 3 of this biography, where the approach can accurately be labeled topical biography.

14

A Portrait of the Man

My goal in writing this biography has been to bring my readers close to the person about whom I write. I want them to feel that they know J. I. Packer. The events of his life and the record of his accomplishments are part of who he is, but not the whole. Hence, this chapter is devoted to Packer's temperament and mindset. There is no chronological sequence to the chapter. It is a mosaic in which the order of the units is somewhat arbitrary. What I intend to emerge is a portrait of the man as we can know him in his public roles.

A Generous Man

No trait of J. I. Packer is more evident than his generous spirit toward others. There are many manifestations of this generosity.

We can start at a professional level, with Packer's endorsements and forewords to books authored by other people. When I was a relative unknown, I had the boldness to write to Packer to request that he write a foreword to my book on the Puritans. Packer wrote a substantial foreword, totally beyond my desert, even though he had never met me. Recently, as I was using my coauthored book *Ryken's Bible Handbook*, my eye fell on the back cover and I received a jolt when I saw that Packer had written an endorsement of the book. For someone as busy as Packer, it was an extremely generous act on his part to find the time to endorse the book.

My story has been retold hundreds of times. Author Mike Mason studied at Regent College for one year as a new Christian in the early 1980s. He took one course from Packer. Shortly after Mason's year at Regent, he completed his first book-length manuscript. Although the book became famous (*The Mystery of Marriage*), Mason was at the time an unknown in publishing circles. He now recalls that he was "bowled over" when Packer agreed to write a foreword to the book and was "deeply grateful for his kind words."

The circle of well-known authors whose annual list of publications includes items in the category of "forewords, introductions, and prefaces" is exceedingly small, but it has been a category of Packer's publications nearly from the start of his career. To these works must be added the book endorsements with which Packer's name is nearly synonymous. They number in the hundreds. Wayne Grudem looks back at his writing career and recalls that Packer "gave gracious and generous endorsements to a number of my books even when I was a young and rather unknown professor."

Packer is equally generous with his time in real-life situations. One of the most endearing anecdotes is the story of teenager Ben Zoba. Packer first came on the Zoba family radar screen when he befriended Wendy Zoba during one of his visits to *Christianity Today*. Packer helped Wendy salvage a failed article; in fact, she attests that "it is not an exaggeration to say that J. I. Packer rescued my writing career." Eventually, Packer became a "regular" at the dinner table in the Zoba home. On one occasion, Wendy's seventeen-year-old son Ben asked his mother if she thought Packer would meet with his junior high small group to talk about "what it means to be a Christian in this world." Packer agreed. The group of boys filled the room. Wendy taped the session, and then more material was added to produce a book entitled *J. I. Packer Answers Your Questions*.

A further side of Packer's generosity is his refusal to hold grievances against people in situations where a lesser person would do so. The first time I saw this in action was when I watched the videotape of the sermon Packer preached at the memorial service for John Stott. In the sermon, Packer praised Stott as "the most modest of men," "one of the friendliest men I have ever met," and "a fifteen-talent man." "Don't stop thanking God for John," Packer told the assembled congregation.

This is even more generous than meets the eye. As noted in Part 1 of this book, when Packer was searching for his first ministry position and asked Stott about the possibility of becoming a curate at All Souls Church, Stott declined to extend an invitation. In the years just before Packer left England for Canada, he was overshadowed as an evangelical influencer in the Church of England by Stott, whose agenda won the day over Packer's. There was no hint of grievance in Packer's tribute at Stott's memorial service.

Even more striking is Packer's forgiving spirit toward D. Martyn Lloyd-Jones. When Packer refused Lloyd-Jones's 1966 call for evangelicals to leave the Church of England and engaged in certain other activities that displayed Packer's Anglican loyalties, Lloyd-Jones shunned Packer. He called an end to the twenty-year Puritan Conference in 1970 and wrote a letter in which he chastised Packer for becoming involved "in ecclesiastical affairs," making it clear "that we shall not meet regularly year by year at the Conference and at other odd times."

With that as a context, one of my very favorite pieces of writing by Packer is his biographical essay on Lloyd-Jones in the 1985 book *Chosen Vessels: Portraits of Ten Outstanding Christian Men*, edited by Charles Turner. I value the essay as much for what it does not say as for what it says. Packer begins by reconstructing the circumstances of the split with Lloyd-Jones over "denominationalism," but without a hint of rancor or self-defense. In fact, Packer ends this opening unit of the essay by saying: "Was either of us right? History will judge, and to history I remit the matter." After that, Packer is completely commendatory in his remembrances of Lloyd-Jones. He ends by saying that Lloyd-Jones "embodied and expressed" the glory of God "more richly than any man I have every known." Packer has repeated that tribute numerous times in a variety of venues, including a 2010 address at Clare College, Cambridge, in which Packer called Lloyd-Jones "the greatest Christian leader of our time."

A parallel example involves R. C. Sproul. Packer had a falling out with Sproul when Packer became active in the movement called Evangelicals and Catholics Together (ECT). The entries in Packer's *Concise Theology* began as intended sidebars in a study Bible edited by Sproul. When Packer became prominent in ECT, Sproul claimed that what Packer had written was not good enough to appear in the study Bible. In light of this snub, the following statement by Packer in the preface to his *Concise Theology* says a lot: "I gratefully acknowledge the hidden hand of my much-admired friend R. C. Sproul, from whom came the germ idea for several of these outlines."

A final aspect of Packer's generosity that I will mention is that for this famous man, no audience is too small or venue too modest to elicit his best as a speaker. Professor Jerry Root of Wheaton College first heard Packer speak at a small, sparsely filled Orthodox Presbyterian church in southern California (Root recalls that Packer spoke for two and half hours, and "it seemed like twenty minutes"). Several years later, when Packer became a regular speaker at the annual Philadelphia Conference on Reformed Theology in Wheaton and also made regular trips to Wheaton as part of his *Christianity Today* duties, it became routine for Packer to speak to Root's college group from College Church in Wheaton. The meetings were usually held in Root's home.

In a similar vein, Vern Poythress of Westminster Theological Seminary recalls an impromptu speaking engagement that Packer accepted when the translation committee of the English Standard Version was meeting in Cambridge, England. When people at a local evangelical Anglican church learned that Packer was in town, they requested that he meet with young people in a parishioner's house after the Sunday evening service. Packer consented. Poythress and his wife smuggled themselves into the group. The living room was so crowded that some young people sat on the floor under the dining room table!

A Man Resigned to What Life Brings

People who know the general outline of Packer's life do not hesitate to speak of the adversity and disappointment that have been ingredients in that life, starting with a life-changing head injury at the age of seven. When I asked Packer if he believes that he has experienced a lot of adversity, his reply was, "To be honest, no." He went on to say that temperamentally he is someone who "takes things in stride," including the head injury. The accident itself was "an aspect of life."

This outlook was sufficiently intriguing to me that I explored it with Packer when we met in the Crossway offices. As the day's conversation unfolded, I cited various events that I thought must have been major disappointments, such as earning a second rather than first on his Oxford exams, not receiving certain academic appointments, and being relegated to a minor role in evangelical Anglican circles during the 1970s. Packer repeatedly assured me that he "took it in stride" and "didn't lose any sleep over it." I was reminded of a famous formula that John Milton introduced into *Paradise Lost.* When the angel Raphael is dispatched by God to give the fallen Adam a vision of future history (in effect, a survival kit for life in a fallen world), he prefaces the vision with the statement that Adam must be prepared to be "equally inured / By moderation either state to bear, / Prosperous or adverse." Packer is accustomed to accept what God sends into his life, prosperous or adverse.

A Knowledgeable and Scholarly Man

Although Packer the author often curtails the quantity of data that he puts into an essay or book, in effect writing under vows of renunciation, his natural bent is toward copiousness of data (though not in a display of specialized scholarship, as I will note below). In the preface to *God's Words*, Packer notes that "some of my material is, I know, packed tight," and then he jokes, "Packer by name, packer by nature." Packer does, indeed, "pack it in" in most of his writing.

Having just now quoted from *God's Words*, I randomly opened the book to pages 110–111, from which I was able to tabulate eleven Bible references. On these same two pages, there are allusions to the curse of Adam, the curse of Cain, and the curse of Babel, which are adduced as a shorthand overview of the preoccupations in modern novels (the loss of integrity, of identity, and of communication). There is a quotation from Puritan Richard Baxter, as well as an analysis of the differences between the old covenant and the new covenant. I think everyone will agree that the knowledge base is very wide for J. I. Packer. This is sometimes concealed from view because Packer usually writes midlevel work for the ordinary reader instead of specialized scholarship.

If we take a quick look at a piece of specialized scholarship, though, we can see exactly how much Packer actually knows about the subjects on which he writes. I am fond of Packer's introduction to Thomas Cranmer's theology in the Courtenay Library of Reformation Classics series. The introduction is a twenty-five-page essay (plus notes and appendix) that covers a wide range of material very succinctly. It begins with a narrative of Cranmer's final refusal to recant his Protestant views and his death at the stake in Oxford. The event had never come alive for me as vividly as in Packer's brief account. Then Packer unfolds the shape of Cranmer's theological career: the theological topics on which he wrote, along with what he claimed about each; his approach to theology; and (as we expect from Packer) a putting-it-all-together summary of the three concerns that unified Cranmer's theological career. The essay is accompanied by sixty-six endnotes, but there is much unsourced material as well. Packer's summary of Cranmer's theological method strikes me as equally true of Packer: "Cranmer's theological genius was not for system-building, nor yet for polemics . . . , but for crystallising a stock of tested material into confessional definitions (the Articles), forms for worship (the Prayer Book) and plain practical expositions." Anyone reading Packer's introduction will have consumed a major document that can be reread over and over without seeming repetitious.

One of the spheres in which Packer's knowledge base is at its most impressive is Greek language and literature. This was very evident in the deliberations of the translation committee for the English Standard Version (of which Packer served as general editor). Poythress recalls an occasion when the committee was discussing an obscure Greek word. Poythress's account is that "lexicons were spread out, and people were reading carefully. Packer had no lexicon in front of him. But he started talking about the particular nuances of this word." Poythress concludes that Packer has such a wealth of knowledge that on this occasion, "he spoke with greater knowledge than what was summarized in the standard lexicons."

Grudem recalls a similar occasion when the translation committee was considering a point on which Grudem had conducted extensive research. He "was astonished that off the top of his head Packer simply blurted out the correct understanding of the expression." Of course, this is a tribute to the amount of time Packer spends in study and to his power of memory—one cannot remember a piece of knowledge without first uncovering it and allowing it to register in one's mind. When Grudem asked Packer how old he was when he started to learn Greek, the reply was twelve.

Packer's expertise in Greek (and Latin) is matched by his feel for English style. Poythress recalls that in 1982, at a meeting of the International Council on Biblical Inerrancy, Poythress was asked to fill in for Sproul at a committee meeting when the latter became ill. As the committee worked its way through a draft of a document, the discussion sometimes got bogged down. Recalls Poythress: "When nothing worked, everyone in the room turned and looked at Packer. Packer would come up with just the right wording. This happened again and again. By the end, I was in awe of Packer. . . . What I did not know [before then] was that Packer was a master of the English language, in concert with his theological acumen."

I will add that this scholarship is something that Packer manages with great humility (Grudem offers the view that Packer "has an immense amount of learning that is nevertheless carried lightly"). On one occasion, when the ESV translation committee was considering an extremely important verse from the New Testament, Packer made a more impassioned plea for a certain rendition than I have ever seen him make, before or since. The vote went against him. Every eye was fixed on him. I was momentarily paralyzed with anxiety about what would happen next. Although I had voted against Packer, I felt guilty for having done so. Packer sat motionless for five seconds as the shock registered. Then the pulse of life returned and everyone moved on. It was a great revelation to me not only in regard to Packer, but also in regard to how I should aspire to live.

A Person of Wide Literary Reading

Because I am a literary scholar, I derive particular enjoyment from Packer's references to imaginative literature. Here, too, his knowledge base is very broad. Some of the references are subtle and require literary sophistication to detect. For example, in the preface to *Knowing God*, Packer recalls the circumstances of the book's origin, namely, the request of the editor of *Evangelical Magazine* that Packer write a series of articles on the subject of God. In the course of paying tribute to the editor, Packer calls her "the person that Shakespeare would have described as the 'onlie begetter.'" What does that mean, and why is the word *only* spelled in an archaic manner? Packer is alluding to one of the most famous statements in English literature. William Shakespeare's sonnet cycle is a landmark in English literature, and in the dedication of the collection to his patron in gratitude for financial assistance, Shakespeare wrote, "To the onlie begetter of these insuing [ensuing] sonnets." Packer could have paid tribute to his editor without alluding to Shakespeare, but he is a literary man who values his literary education.

For a second illustration of Packer's literary allusions, I arbitrarily dipped into the opening pages of *God's Words*. In explaining the methodology of his book (a word study), Packer cleverly quotes from Shakespeare's play *Hamlet*. In that play, Polonius asks Hamlet, "What do you read, my lord?" Hamlet's reply is, "Words, words, words." Packer knows exactly what is going on in *Hamlet*. He correctly identifies Polonius as "that classic compound of senile sententiousness and servile stupidity." He also correctly explains that Hamlet's answer to the question of Polonius "was meant as an insulting non-answer, a put-down and brush-off for a prize specimen of the *genus*, tedious old fools." As a literary person, I relish not only this excursion into one of my favorite plays, but also the literary commentary that Packer has tucked in.

On the very next page of *God's Words*, Packer references Lewis Carroll's classic *Alice in Wonderland*: "Lewis Carroll makes Humpty Dumpty sneer at Alice for her protest at finding that by 'glory' he meant 'a nice knock-down argument.' 'When I use a word,' said he scornfully, 'it means just what I choose it to mean—neither more nor less.'" Five pages later, Packer adduces a word that J. R. R. Tolkien coined in his famous essay "On Fairy Stories"—*eucatastrophe* ("good catastrophe").

What's the point? Packer is a very learned and well-read man, and part of his expansive knowledge consists of acquaintance with the literary classics. He values beauty of words and the exercise of imagination. He would not need to use an allusion in the following statement ("To the Reader" in *Knowing Christianity*), but he does so because he loves literature, believes that it expresses truth more powerfully than everyday discourse, and wants to add a level of pleasure for readers who share his literary knowledge and interest: "Christians are not exempt from what Shakespeare called 'the slings and arrows of outrageous fortune'" (from a soliloquy in *Hamlet*). I will add that Packer has never used a computer with its word-search capability, relying instead on his actual acquaintance with the literary works to which he refers.

We might think that literary allusions would be an impediment to the ordinary person, who is Packer's staple reader. My response is as follows. First, Packer writes out of who he is. He is a well-read man and sees no reason to pretend otherwise. But I think that something else is at work. T. S. Eliot formulated a theory that Shakespeare's plays appeal to readers and theatergoers on several levels—plot, characterization, and style (and potentially more). Eliot's view is that readers and viewers respond at whatever levels their literary education enables them to do *and are not troubled by levels that they cannot grasp*. Something like this seems to happen in Packer's writings, and my guess is that even readers who miss some of the allusions are pleased to see the bar raised high.

One would not expect the following barrage of allusions to appear in an introduction to the Puritans (Packer's *A Quest for Godliness*), and specifically not in regard to the point that "the Puritans made me aware that all theology is also spirituality." But whether we expect it or not, here it is:

> C. S. Lewis's first and, for my money, most dazzling Christian book was his Bunyanesque allegory, *The Pilgrim's Regress* (1933). There he traced the lure of what he called Sweet Desire, and Joy. . . . As Lewis knew, different stimuli trigger this desire in different people; for himself, he talks of . . . the title *The Well at the World's End*, the opening lines of *Kubla Khan*. . . . None of those items produces the full effect for me, though I understand how they could do so for Lewis and others; but I can speak of . . . bits of Bach, Beethoven, Brahms, Bruckner, and Wagner . . . ; plus . . . some touches of rhetoric in . . . Lewis himself, and Williams, and (you saw it coming) seraphic Baxter, dreamer Bunyan, and elephantine Owen.

When Wheaton College professor Jerry Root recalls an earlier era when he spent a lot of time in the car with Packer while serving as his unofficial taxi driver, one thing he remembers is discovering how broadly Packer is educated in the liberal arts.

I will add just a few more literary allusions, because they show an important side of Packer:

- "On March 23, 1631, knowing he was on his deathbed (his life ended eight days later), John Donne, dean of St. Paul's, London, wrote 'Hymn to God, My God, in My Sickness.'"
- "Soldiers who have been through war sometimes end up inwardly numb. . . . They have become, in T. S. Eliot's phrase, 'hollow men.' . . . The description that fits them comes again from T. S. Eliot: 'living—and partly living.'"

- "What of Mrs. Manoah? . . . Life for her was one prolonged put-down, and like Ibsen's Nora in *A Doll's House*, she must have felt it."

It is hard to know what Packer remembers from his formal education and what comes to his consciousness from ongoing literary reading, but in either case, his literary sophistication is well attested.

The Most Important Books in Packer's Life

In the next chapter, I will take an excursion into Packer's recreational reading. For the moment, I want to look at his serious reading. Packer is regularly asked about the major books in his life, and the lists that he generates on those occasions fall into two categories—books that influenced him most and books that he reads every year.

In a recent interview, Packer was asked, "Which books have made the greatest impact on you?" He prefaced his reply with a characteristic bit of understatement: "Well, that's a difficult question because I *have* read a lot of books." The ensuing list is as follows, in the order that Packer followed in the interview: (1) John Calvin, *Institutes of the Christian Religion*; (2) Bishop J. C. Ryle, *Holiness*; (3) John Bunyan, *The Pilgrim's Progress*; (4) Richard Baxter, multiple books, but chiefly *The Reformed Pastor*; and (5) John Owen, *Indwelling Sin* and *The Mortification of Sin*, "but it's a shame not to mention *Justification*; *The Holy Spirit*; and *The Death of Death in the Death of Christ*."

Different occasions have produced slightly different results. When Kent Hughes was writing his book *Disciplines of a Godly Man* (published in 1991), he asked selected Christian leaders to name: (1) the five most influential books in their lives; (2) the one among them that was their favorite; (3) their favorite novel; (4) their favorite biography. Packer's answers were as follows: (1) the five most influential books: Calvin, *Institutes*; Bunyan, *The Pilgrim's Progress*; volumes 3, 6, and 7 in the Goold edition of *John Owen: Works*; Baxter, *The Reformed Pastor*; and Martin Luther, *The Bondage of the Will*; (2) favorite among those: *The Pilgrim's Progress*; (3) favorite novel: Fyodor Dostoyevsky, *The Brothers Karamazov*; and (4) favorite biography: Arnold Dallimore, *George Whitefield*. The choice of Dostoyevsky helps to explain why Packer wrote a brief preface to a book entitled *The Gospel in Dostoyevsky*, where he calls Dostoyevsky "a supersensitive giant of the imagination" who embodies "a uniquely poignant vision of the plight of man and the power of God."

In the 1980s, Root, the college pastor of College Church in Wheaton, regularly asked Packer to share meals with students in his home when Packer came to Wheaton for other responsibilities. The question that Root asked Packer in those days was not what books had influenced him most, but what books he reread every year. The standard answer to that question produced the following list: Calvin, *Institutes*; Baxter, *The Reformed Pastor*; Bunyan, *The Pilgrim's Progress*; Charles Williams, *Descent of the Dove*; and John Owen, *The Glory of Christ*. This list predates the "books of influence" noted above. Root claims that Packer "loves Charles Williams."

After one of Packer's meetings with the students, a young man named Kenny wrote to Packer with some questions. The reply letter answers the question of which Puritan books meant most to Packer by citing Owen's *Indwelling Sin* and *Mortification of Sin*, as well as *The Pilgrim's Progress*. In answer to the question, "What other books?" Packer replied, "Calvin, INST.; A. Kuyper, ENCYCLOPAEDIA (PRINCIPLES) OF SACRED THEOLOGY; Norman Grubb, C. T. STUDD (in my teens). No two lists would ever coincide; it depends where you are when the books cross your path."

In a 2008 interview, Packer was asked which books had influenced him most, but with no prescribed limit to the number of authors he might list. That occasion produced this slightly expanded list: in addition to the "big five" (Calvin, Luther, Bunyan, Owen, and Baxter), Packer cited Abraham Kuyper, C. S. Lewis, "Lewis's buddy Charles Williams," and Ryle. Packer identified Williams as his favorite Inkling (chiefly his fictional writings), though Lewis had given him most.

A Lover of Classical Music

It is no surprise that a person of classical training would love classical music. Packer admits to that love in some of his writings. We read in *Praying* that he "loves classical music and knows a fair amount about it and can talk music with professionals," even though he cannot be called a musician. In one of his books, he tells of sitting next to a couple at a performance of Wagner's *Tannhauser* at the Metropolitan Opera in New York City, talking with the wife about opera during the intermission, and then seeing the possessive husband whisk his wife to another part of the auditorium.

Classical music speaks to Packer's longing for the transcendent. In a 2004 interview, after Packer had explained how jazz music awakened this sense within him, he added: "There are some great classical musicians whose work also led me into this joy. I was slower to get into that but Beethoven reached out and grabbed me when I was in my late teens, and I have gone from there to Mozart, Bach, Schubert, Brahms, Wagner, and Bruckner, all of whom have given me wonderful moments and memories."

A Latter-Day Puritan

At numerous points during my work on the life of J. I. Packer, I was struck by the ways in which his temperament and life story have adhered to the experiences and ideas of the Puritans of the sixteenth and seventeenth centuries. In saying that, I am not thinking of Packer's career as a Puritan scholar (the subject of a later chapter in this biography), but of the uncanny ways in which Packer's own life and viewpoints are identical to what we find in the history and writings of the Puritans.

I think, for example, of Packer's conversion. It was an instantaneous event that happened at a preaching service. Packer was not expecting to be reborn on the night he entered into the kingdom of heaven. He was a nominal Christian (a great aversion of the Puritans) and did not know how to move beyond that state. The first half of the forty-minute sermon totally bored him. But when the retired minister reconstructed his own conversion at a boys' camp, God forever changed the course of Packer's life. He remembers the event today "as if it were yesterday," and he left the church knowing he was a Christian.

The moment I read that account, I was reminded of the conversion story of Cambridge student Thomas Goodwin. A group of fellow students urged Goodwin to attend a funeral service, brought to the students' attention by the tolling of a funeral bell. Goodwin allowed himself to be persuaded to attend the service to hear the sermon, which was about "deferring repentance, and of the danger of doing so." Goodwin's own account is as follows: "So God was pleased on the sudden . . . to alter the whole course of his former dispensation towards me, and said . . . to my soul, Yea, live. . . . This speaking of God to my soul, although it was but a gentle sound, yet it made a noise over my whole heart, and filled and possessed all the faculties of my whole soul." It was a vintage Puritan conversion, as was Packer's.

Another angle to Packer's conversion is that it illustrates the Puritan conviction of the momentousness of life and the belief that God uses the commonplace to accomplish his transformation of people. Puritan Richard Greenham wrote, "Because we know not who is the man, what is the time, where is the place, which is the sermon that God hath appointed to work on us, let us in all obedience attend on the ministry of every man, watch at all times, be diligent in every place, and run to every sermon which we can conveniently, because though the Lord touch us not by this man, in this place, at this time, through such a sermon, yet he may touch us by another."

Packer's retrospective comments on his conversion and on coming to believe soon afterward that the Bible is God's true Word capture exactly this point that God uses seemingly commonplace events to achieve his spiritual design in people's lives. Regarding the singing of "Just As I Am" at the service where he was converted, Packer comments, "There's no more ordinary way of being converted than to receive the Lord while singing 'Just As I Am.'" Similarly, the visiting preacher who unpacked a chapter of Revelation at the service where Packer came to the conviction that the Bible is God's Word was not a high-powered speaker, but an "eccentric old man" from out of town.

The Puritans fostered a democratic spirit, with a "leveling" tendency that ignored upper-class status. William Perkins wrote, "No man is to stand upon his gentility, or glory in his parentage for nobility and great blood, but only rejoice in this, that he is drawn out of the kingdom of darkness." William Dell wrote that "all Christians . . . are made priests alike unto God." I immediately recalled those quotations when I read the following statement that Packer made in a semihumorous article in *Christianity Today*, occasioned by his receiving an invitation to purchase a genealogical book on *The Amazing Book of the Packers of Canada*: "I reflected that while exploring one's lineage need not be sin, to draw one's sense of worth and dignity from his or her place in a human family rather than in God's family of saved sinners could never be right."

At multiple points in this biography, I have had occasion to document that Packer is a champion of the ordinary person. His writing and theologizing have had the layperson in view. Editor Ramona Tucker, who knew Packer when she worked at *Christianity Today*, recounts how insistent Packer was that she be given a place at the table during brainstorming sessions, "a surprise to the very male-oriented culture of *Christianity Today*." As I conducted my research for this biography, Britons kept telling me how important the class issue is in understanding Packer (partly in contrast to upper-class people such as John Stott). My point of the moment is that the Puritans would have loved Packer for his everyday touch and would have embraced him as one of them. Packer has often moved in high circles and been in the public eye, but he is the last person to put on airs.

A final Puritan strand in Packer's makeup that I will note is his bent toward what is practical. Owen claimed that "our happiness consisteth not in *knowing* the things of the gospel, but in the *doing* of them." If I saw that as a freestanding quotation, I might ascribe it to Packer. "The soul of religion is the practical part," wrote Bunyan. This is everywhere the thrust of Packer. He has championed the importance of application in sermons. Professional theologians wonder why Packer has not conducted theology the way they do. The answer is that he regards himself as a catechist—someone who packages theology for the ordinary person. Packer writes in "To the Reader" at the beginning of *Knowing Christianity*, "It is not a technical work but . . . a plain and practical one." I love the title of a book "at various hands" (composed by a team of contributors) that encapsulates the life work of J. I. Packer: *Doing Theology for the People of God*.

Spokesman for the Ordinary Person

I have just discussed the way in which Packer identifies with the ordinary person in a manner reminiscent of the Puritans, and I want to push that in a direction that does not bear a Puritan imprint. When scholars write for fellow scholars, they flaunt their learning. They load their articles and books with footnotes. They cite authorities. They take excursions into the history of ideas. This is not bad. In fact, it is part of the scholarly life. Packer can write that kind of specialized scholarship with the best. But if authors aim to write books that the typical educated person (but non-specialist) will read, they need to write under vows of renunciation. Of course, even then the scholarship needs to be in the background, and the reader needs to know that the author has done his or her homework.

C. S. Lewis had a knack for doing this, and I will note in passing that many people (including me) find themselves reminded of certain qualities of Lewis when they read Packer's writings. Here is the kind of formula that I have in mind, from Lewis:

- "The old Christian teachers said that if man had never fallen, sexual pleasure, instead of being less than it is now, would actually have been greater."
- "A famous Christian long ago told us that when he was young he prayed constantly for chastity; but years later he realized that while his lips had been saying, 'Oh Lord, make me chaste,' his heart had been secretly adding, 'But please don't make it just yet.'"

Who were the medieval Christian writers who said that about unfallen sex, and who was the famous Christian with an addiction to sex? It does not serve Lewis's purpose to say.

I call this the concealment of erudition, and I often find it in Packer's writings. Here are examples:

- "Since the seventeenth century, Reformed theologians have tended to distinguish between regeneration and new birth."
- "When the old Reformed theologians dealt with the attributes of God, they used to classify them in two groups: *incommunicable* and *communicable*."
- "Unlike their predecessors, modern Protestant theologians regularly insist that revelation and Scripture are distinct things."
- "Many Protestants today, both liberals of the older type and spokesmen for the current Barthian and 'biblical theology' movements, reject the Evangelical view of Scripture."

The first thing to note about these summary statements is that each of them could produce a learned article or book chapter. There is a time and place for such essays and chapters. But there is also a time and place to withhold the documentation of a generalization and concentrate on the truth contained in the statement. When I asked Packer if he had consciously chosen to write midlevel scholarship for the general Christian public, he said yes.

Concealing erudition is a means of instructing the general reader without distraction. But paradoxically, the author gets credit for the scholarship without putting it on the table. The mention of "the Reformers" or "modern Protestant theologians" carries weight because readers get the picture that the author *could* provide the documentation if it were important to do so. I would describe this as scholarly writing for the general educated public. It is based on acquaintance with primary sources, but the sources are left in the background because the purpose of the discussion of the moment does not require them, and because they would probably scare off the general public.

I will add that Packer's concern for the ordinary reader surfaced strongly during the deliberations of the translation committee of the English Standard Version. The utterance for which Packer became best known was "Joe the bus driver." Packer championed the cause of Joe the bus driver when the committee considered lexical alternatives for the English language rendering of a Hebrew or Greek word. He wanted the rendition that would be most clear to Joe. Another Packerism was "a good Anglo-Saxon word," meaning a simple (probably monosyllabic) word rather than a Latin-derived polysyllabic word. (I personally felt that this stance sometimes tugged away from the commitment to a dignified rather than colloquial Bible, and also from Packer's background in classics.)

Packer's everyday touch is not limited to his scholarly work and writing. It is how he conducts his life. It is natural to attribute this to Packer's lower-middle-class roots, but the situation is not quite that simple. Packer's father felt gratified to have a calling that involved what he regarded as mental work, as opposed to the "working class," which made its livelihood with its hands (like his son, he was manually clumsy, which would have been a factor). Packer describes his parents as aspiring to rise socially and has used the label "social climbers" for them. He also recalls an occasion when his parents implied that one of his friends was socially below the Packer family, whereas to Packer "he was simply a friend."

A Traditionalist

One does not need to read very far in the Packer canon to sense that his orientation is to the past as the locus of wisdom and truth. It is not a question of his not keeping abreast of contemporary developments; Packer knows all about such things. It is rather that Packer believes that modern culture and theology took a wrong turn two centuries ago, and that within evangelicalism there has been a great erosion of faith and truth in just the past few decades. Packer is not devoted to the past simply because it is the past, but because it is where the truth can still be found.

This orientation toward the past begins, for any evangelical Christian, with the Bible. The Bible represents God's Word once for all delivered. It is the Christian's great primary text. For Packer, the die was cast in this direction right from the start in his Christian life and his scholarly career. *"Fundamentalism" and the Word of God* makes the case for viewing the Bible alone as the authoritative source of Christian belief. The themes that Packer articulates in that book have never been absent from his writing, especially the model that Jesus and the biblical authors give us for regarding the Bible as God's infallible Word. In his 2013 book *Taking God Seriously*, Packer calls the Bible "the revelatory book that God has given us for the forming of our faith."

Looking backward to the postbiblical past is just as characteristic of Packer's basic stance as is looking back to the Bible. This applies especially to the Reformation era, but is not limited to it. Below are specimen statements that reflect Packer's characteristic stance:

- "A robust return to the older wisdom about faith's true object is urgently needed if the Anglican Church in particular is ever to impact the surrounding culture again. The same must be said of other churches with Reformation roots."
- "I shall quote most fully from the Thirty-Nine Articles, Homilies and Book of Common Prayer. . . . But the Lutheran and Reformed foundation-documents all point the same way."
- "This book sets out in short compass what seem to me to be the permanent essentials of Christianity. . . . [My approach] is Reformational and evangelical, and as such, so I maintain, historic and classic mainstream."
- "The great Puritans, though dead, still speak to us through their writings, and say things to us that we badly need to hear at this present time."

How can theological truth be found? According to Packer, by looking backward and applying what we find there to our present situation. At every turn, we can see that Packer's intuitive inclination is to give a vote of confidence to our forebears rather than to our contemporaries.

Packer himself confirms this constitutional bias to look to the past in the preface to *Knowing God*, where he quotes Jeremiah 6:16 (NIV): "Stand at the crossroads and look; ask for the ancient paths, ask where the good way is, and walk in it. . . ." Then he adds: "Such is the invitation which this book issues. It is not a critique of new paths, except indirectly, but rather a straightforward recall to old ones, on the ground that 'the good way' is still what it used to be."

In ascribing a traditional and conservative orientation to Packer, I need to guard against creating a misconception. Packer has never embraced the Roman Catholic and Anglo-Catholic viewpoint that elevates church tradition to the same level of authority as the Bible. When Packer lays out the three answers that Christians have historically given to the question of authority, he disallows reason and church tradition as authorities equal to Scripture. In a 1992 essay entitled "The Comfort of Conservatism" (in *Power Religion*, ed. Michael Horton [Moody Press, 1992]), Packer addressed the question of the place of tradition in Christian belief. In that essay, he defines tradition as "the handing-on process and then secondarily as the sum of what is handed on." The benefits conferred by embracing the value of the Christian tradition are four—roots, realism ("a vantage point for assessing the present"), resources, and reminders.

Packer's Sense of Vocation

The idea of calling or vocation is important to Packer. It could hardly be otherwise for a latter-day Puritan, inasmuch as no subject occupied the Puritans more than the idea of vocation. Having written extensively on Puritan attitudes toward work myself, I will take the prerogative of summarizing what they said so voluminously about vocation: (1) God calls people to their tasks in the world; (2) the goals toward which work must be directed are the glory of God and service to humanity; (3) all honest work is a calling as pleasing to God as the work of a minister preaching in the pulpit; and (4) all work offered to God is a form of worship.

In 2007, Packer was interviewed on the subject of vocation at Laity Lodge in Texas. If the following statements by Packer were presented anonymously as part of a list of Puritan quotations on work, it would be impossible to differentiate the two sources:

- "The heart of vocation is . . . the sense that God has called one to do what one is doing."
- "All honest work is worth doing for the glory of God, and we may find ourselves called to do any honest work that we're fitted for."
- "God made us for honest work. And we glorify him by doing honest work."
- "Worship is honoring God in every appropriate way. When one's labor is labor that one feels called to, then one is fulfilling one's vocation as one pursues it."
- "All work . . . is oriented to the welfare of other people—directly or indirectly. The answer to the question [of how Christians can view their daily work as ministry] is to be conscious of your work as service to people."

As the interview unfolded, it wound its way to the subject of Packer's writing as an important part of his vocation.

Packer has lived out his convictions about calling. The vocabulary of calling comes up naturally when he speaks of his life. During his undergraduate days in Oxford, Packer reached a deliberate and prayerful decision to seek ordination in the Church of England. He has never wavered from that calling. But the sense of calling extends to other spheres of his life as well. When I asked him whether he ever regretted leaving the parish ministry, he replied, "No, because I have had such a strong sense of calling in regard to my academic life." When Packer faced the need to chart his course at the end of his Latimer House decade, he said that "I really am called . . . to make ministers and establish consciences."

One of the great gifts that this Puritan-style sense of vocation confers is that it allows one to focus on one's calling and ward off distractions from it. The doctrine of vocation produces a great sense of purpose and self-confidence in what one is doing. Such a sense of vocation tends to generate a strong work ethic, and I note that the Puritans found it natural to speak of vocation and work at the same time. One need only to look at his quantity of publications and lecture trips to see that Packer has possessed an unusual aptitude for work.

Summary

The public life of J. I. Packer is largely known to his readers and audiences, so we can say that the traits covered in this chapter are not surprising. Packer is generous, scholarly, knowledgeable, cultured, classically oriented, a traditionalist, and a latter-day Puritan with a strong sense of vocation.

15

The Little-Known Packer

The foregoing chapter devoted to J. I. Packer the man covered territory that, while personal to Packer, is nonetheless generally known, or at least not unexpected to someone who knows the public figure. But everyone has a dimension of personality and life that is hidden from public view and known mainly by family members and close acquaintances. In this chapter, I have collected data that belongs to this lesser-known side of J. I. Packer.

Early to Bed and Early to Rise

Packer is known by his acquaintances as a morning person. A typical day begins at four or five in the morning with a cup of tea. Packer's Regent College colleague Loren Wilkinson theorizes that early rising, combined with an exemplary work ethic, is what has enabled Packer to be the prolific author that he has been.

The counterpart of rising early is that Packer fades in the evening, something that he knows and to which he accommodates himself. When author Mike Mason was Packer's student at Regent, he was once invited to Packer's home for dinner. He recalls that at ten o'clock, Packer rose and announced: "You're all wonderful people and you're welcome to stay and visit, but the hour has come at which I tend to turn into a large orange vegetable of the squash family. So I'm going to bed." Mason was given to understand that this was Packer's regular practice on social occasions.

Jazz Music

We would expect a cultured person such as J. I. Packer to be a lover of classical music. What we would not guess is that jazz has been a passion of Packer since his childhood. The taste was first awakened at the age of thirteen. One evening when Packer was listening to the radio while doing his homework, the announcer decided to play jazz music to fill an interval between two programs. The record that was broadcast was *Steamboat Stomp* by Jelly Roll Morton. It was an electrifying and life-changing moment for Packer. Sixty-five years later, he recalled the event in full detail: "I remember getting up and going over to the radio and putting my ear against the speaker and just drinking it in. I was left gasping. My breath was literally taken away."

Packer's interest in jazz grew to the point that when he arrived at Oxford University, he became clarinetist for a jazz band called the Bandits. This was during the same academic term in which Packer was converted. Not only was jazz itself suspect in the eyes of the pietistic members of the Oxford Christian Union, but playing in the band on Saturday nights kept Packer from attending the weekly meetings of the Inter-Varsity group. So he gave in to peer pressure and conscience, sold his clarinet and records, and let his fellow Christians know that he had renounced the "devilish influence" of jazz in his life.

The reference to "devilish influence" in the preceding sentence comes from a 1986 Packer column in *Christianity Today*. In that article, Packer notes that Hans Rookmaaker, a Dutch scholar who was a close associate of Francis Schaeffer, did not renounce his interest in jazz when he was converted, but made it a lifelong area of expertise, and Packer calls him "a wise man" for doing so.

By his thirties, Packer was "ready to shout from the housetops . . . that by Christian standards of judgment, early jazz was among the twentieth century's most valuable cultural products." How can that be? Packer theorizes that early jazz "was essentially fellowship music, group music rather than individualistic display music; that was one Christian value built into it." Another was that "it is happy music." Packer pinpoints the moment that jazz took a degenerative direction. It was the day on which Louis Armstrong carried a trumpet into the recording studio instead of his famous cornet. That marked "the superseding of early jazz's preference for collective polyphony . . . by solo display on more brilliant instruments."

Packer has remained a listener of jazz music. He claims that jazz "energizes you by relaxing you, and its simple climaxes leave you contented and refreshed." Students of former days remember listening to jazz records in Packer's home. Pastor Todd Augustine of College Church in Wheaton first met Packer when Augustine was on the staff of InterVarsity Press. IVP hosted Packer at a Christian Booksellers' Association convention in New Orleans, where Augustine was responsible to get Packer from place to place. Augustine took Packer to a New Orleans jazz concert at Preservation Hall, and he recalls that during the intermission, Packer waxed eloquent about the history of jazz and his own early years of playing jazz music. (On the strength of that fleeting time together in New Orleans, Packer later preached Augustine's ordination sermon at College Church.) Former Tyndale House Publishers editor Wendell Hawley remembers taking Packer to a jazz concert and remarking to him that he seemed to be sitting passively. Packer replied, "But inside I'm enjoying it."

As a final comment on the way in which jazz has spoken powerfully to Packer, I return to the passage in *A Quest for Godliness*, his introduction to the Puritans, in which he catalogs the experiences that awaken a sense of transcendence in him. In addition to five classical composers, he lists "occasional sublimities by Jelly-Roll Morton, Bubber Miley, and Louis Armstrong."

The Nature Lover

Packer does not possess the specialist's knowledge of plants that his wife, Kit, does, but nature has nonetheless been important to him. There are references to hiking in his writing. He visits the botanical garden in Vancouver with Kit and visitors. He has climbed Ben Nevis, the tallest point in the British Isles, in a mist. Jeffrey Greenman recalls that when he was a student and member of Packer's social-pastoral care group at Regent College, he not only listened to jazz records in the Packer home, but also went bird watching with Packer.

Additionally, there is the passage in the introduction to the Puritans in which Packer lists the experiences in life that evoke his longing for and sense of the transcendent. The list includes "the sight of trees, waterfalls, and steam locomotives."

Walking and Stair Climbing

Through the centuries, Britons have been inveterate pedestrians. Packer has been a walker throughout his life, reaching back at least as far as his Oxford University days. Later in life, during his Regent College years, Packer walked to most of the places he went during his daily routine. For Packer, walking is not an amble but a gallop. When the translation committee for the ESV made its daily transition between Tyndale House and the Arundel Hotel, located at opposite ends of the college section of the city, Packer, then in his early seventies, regularly chose to walk rather than ride the van. His walk was nearly a run. Most others would have settled for a slower pace, but that usually proved impossible because Packer was typically in the front of the pack.

Being a bigger-than-life figure, Packer of course has his recorded share of quirks and whimsies. When he taught in Bristol, he was known to go up or down stairs two steps at a time. He never lost the ability to do it until he was in his eighties. David Jones, a former editor for Crossway, remembers that the first time the ESV translation committee met in Cambridge, he twisted his ankle on the cobblestone road and had difficulty walking up the stairs at Tyndale House. Packer saw Jones laden with his computer, notebook, and collection of books, and offered to help. Jones resisted, whereupon Packer replied with mild indignation, "Do you think that because I am seventy-three years old I am too old to help you up the stairs?" He then grabbed Jones's computer and books and bounded up the stairs two steps at a time.

Recreational Reading

"There are plenty of activities that operate as refreshers for the serious work of life," Packer said during an interview that turned to the topic of what he does for recreation. Packer then added, "For me, classic jazz and classic detective stories help do the trick."

J. I. Packer the theologian a reader of murder mysteries? Yes, and his writings contain numerous references to them. The taste for mystery stories was first awakened when his grandmother took Packer on a weeklong holiday at the seacoast town of Torquay to recover from bronchitis. Rain descended on the town, and Packer gravitated to the books on the shelf of the hotel where he was confined. He read a collection of what he calls "spooky short stories" by Agatha Christie entitled *The Hound of Death*. His grandmother had misgivings about Packer's reading of horror stories, but he went on to Christie's *The Mystery of the Blue Train*. He confides that he has been reading mystery authors ever since.

Exactly who makes up the regular fare of mystery writers for the famous theologian? In the interview noted above, Packer provided the following list: Christie, Dorothy Sayers, John Dickson Carr (also known by the name Carter Dickson), Ellery Queen, Erle Stanley Gardner, "and other such authors." Packer then commented that he reads such authors "as recreational resources, just as I listen to music as a recreational resource."

In the same interview, Packer theorized about why and how detective stories work their magic on him. For him, "puzzle stories about crime calm my mind, as crossword puzzles do for others." At bedtime, Packer's mind "is often full of theological and personal problems that would keep me awake." So when he reads "a detective story for five or ten minutes," he knows that it "is of no great importance and it pushes out of my mind all these anxious cares." The result is that "when I switch out the light my mind is blank, and I go right to sleep. This is a good gift of God to me." As the doctor says in the sleepwalking scene of William Shakespeare's *Macbeth*, "Well, well, well."

Packer gives us glimpses of additional detective writers by way of references in his writing. Here is a sampling:

- "One of fiction's great detectives [Sherlock Holmes] laid it down that when you have eliminated all the impossibilities what remains, however improbable, must be true."
- "Detective writer Martha Grimes likes to title each of her books after an unusually named English pub."

But the full disclosure comes in a 1985 *Christianity Today* article entitled "'Tecs [detective stories], Thrillers, and Westerns." In the article, Packer acknowledges, "I devour mysteries." Then he dazzles his readers with his reading list:

> I have read, among others, all the Sherlock Holmeses, Father Browns, and Peter Wimseys. . . . All the full-length stories of Hammett, Chandler, James, and Crispin; and all the work of new arrivals Amanda Cross, Antonia Fraser, Simon Brett, and Robert Bernard, not to mention most of Margery Allingham, Austin Freeman, Freeman Wills Crofts, Erle Stanley Gardner, Rex Stout, Ruth Rendell, and Julian Symons.

"What have I gained?" Packer asks. "Fun, to start with." The enjoyment consists of "the poignant perplexity of the puzzle, the sleuth's superior brainwork, and the doing of justice by clearing the innocent and exposing the guilty."

Just as Packer surprises us by not only enjoying early jazz music but advancing a theory of why it is a Christian form of music, he also articulates a Christian defense of detective fiction. First, even though detective stories are "not great literature," they "are among the most moral fiction of our time" because they clearly distinguish good from evil and assert a principle of justice in the world. But that is not all: "these stories are of a kind that would never have existed without the Christian gospel." They "are Christian fairy tales, with savior heroes and plots that end in what Tolkien called a *eucatastrophe*—whereby things come right after seeming to go irrevocably wrong." The detectives in these stories are "classic Robin Hood figures, champions of the needy, bringers of merited judgment and merciful salvation. The gospel of Christ is the archetype of all such stories." On the surface, that statement seems unlikely from someone who rereads *The Pilgrim's Progress* every year, but once the paradox was put before me, I have found it quite instructive to ponder the connections.

Packer as Endorser of Pleasure

The Packer that I knew before doing the research for this biography was an eminently serious man who wrote on the serious spiritual issues of life. As I spent time with the complete bibliography of published works by Packer, I took note every time I saw a publication on the subject of pleasure. Left to my own designs, I would have given this unit the heading "Packer the Hedonist," but it turns out that Packer does not think that *hedonism* is the right term for his endorsement of pleasure.

I was surprised to find a mini-defense of pleasure in an unexpected place, namely, Packer's book on the Bible entitled *God Has Spoken*. On the opening page of the 1979 edition, Packer introduces the subject of "enjoying your Bible." He then launches into a half-page defense of pleasure, part of which is the following:

> Pleasure, unalloyed and unending, is God's purpose for His people in every aspect and activity of their fellowship with Him. . . . I hold the heady doctrine that no pleasures are so frequent or intense as those of the grateful, devoted, single-minded, whole-hearted, self-denying Christian. I maintain that the delights of work and leisure, of friendship and family, of eating and mating, of arts and crafts, of playing and watching games, of finding out and making things, of helping other people, and all the other noble pleasures that life affords, are doubled for the Christian.

At this point, I start thinking that I am reading one of the original Puritans, and behold, Packer immediately confirms this connection: "As the cheerful old Puritans used to say (no, sir, that is not a misprint, nor a Freudian lapse; I mean Puritans—the real, historical Puritans . . .) the Christian tastes God in all his pleasures, and this increases them."

Pleasure became a small area of specialization as Packer's writing career unfolded. When he agreed to contribute an essay to a *festschrift* for Carl F. H. Henry, he chose to write on "Leisure and Life-Style: Leisure, Pleasure, and Treasure" (in *God and Culture*, 1993). It is a vintage Packer performance—a monograph in twelve pages! Packer provides a Christian defense of leisure and rest, as well as a rationale for pleasure in the Christian life. Having written on the subject myself, I can say with confidence that Packer covers all of the important points in kernel form.

Following a familiar pattern of his writing career, Packer published an article on pleasure in *Christianity Today* in the same year that the essay in the *festschrift* appeared. The article is entitled "Pleasure Principle." To get the ball rolling, Packer asks a question: What does Scripture say to us about our pleasures? He notes that the idea of Christian hedonism has become popular in Christian circles, but he declines to embrace the term because technically it means the elevation of pleasure to the status of the supreme value in life. To do that is to make an idol of pleasure. Packer then proceeds to outline "a positive theology of pleasure." Highlights include the ideas that (1) Paradise was God's pleasure garden and by extension an endorsement of pleasure as God's plan for the human race, (2) we need to let pleasure come unsought instead of pursuing it as a goal in itself, and (3) pleasures are meant to serve as pointers to God.

Despite the visibility of the subject of pleasure in the publications noted above, it turns out that Packer had already sounded the keynotes in his 1988 book *Hot Tub Religion* (Tyndale House Publishers). The hot tub is Packer's metaphor for the feel-good Christianity that dominates contemporary evangelicalism. We might think that Packer is totally opposed to this in every possible way, but he springs a surprise on us by claiming that "hot tub religion is almost right." This is the launching pad for a copious defense of pleasure as God's intention for the human race. "Pleasure is part of the ideal human condition," Packer writes. It "is divinely designed to raise our sense of God's goodness, deepen our gratitude to him, and strengthen our hope of richer pleasures to come in the next world."

The foregoing data seems so massive that it might cast doubt on my inclusion of it under the rubric of "the little-known J. I. Packer." But I have collected the material from lesser-known writings of Packer that the rank-and-file reader of his books is unlikely to have encountered.

Ask J. I. Packer

The little-known Packer has had a side career in the mode of "Dear Abby" and her newspaper advice column. The questions and answers that emerge in situations where he is asked for his opinion sometimes introduce us to a side of Packer that is a foil to the person we think we know. Below is a sampling; the answers are excerpts from longer replies.

Question: "Can the Bible tell me which college to go to?"

> "Look for the college that will give you the best all-round education, the best start. If you're particularly good at a sport, look for a college where you will get the best coaching."

Packer has been a regular speaker at the retreat center Laity Lodge in Texas. A 2008 interview with Packer at Laity Lodge was flowing so beautifully that the host asked a question that was tailor-made to elicit a heartwarming endorsement of Laity Lodge:

Question: "What do you remember of your first Laity Lodge experience?"

> "The family came, that's the first thing to say. We were put into Lodestar, the new house as it was then. The first thing when we walked in was that a scorpion fell to the floor out of the ventilator or the light (I'm not sure which). And there it was wriggling in the contorted way that scorpions do. And that stuck in our minds all the time we were here."

Question: "Do you have any prescriptions for a cure for biblical illiteracy?"

> "The first thing you must do is convince people that it is a wonderful thing to read. . . . Somehow you must make people aware of the benefit of reading, the excitement of reading. . . . Start there."

The element of surprise in the following exchange emerges if we remember that Packer is a professional theologian who was led to choose teaching rather than parish ministry as his vocation and who has made strong statements through the years that he regards his teaching as directed especially toward future ministers:

Question: "When did the guild [of professional theologians] lose its way?"

> "The guild became a reality when seminaries became clergy factories and the professors in the seminaries were no longer expected to be anything other than professors in the seminaries. . . . Able people who have gone through university doctoral programs and have received good doctorates have been snapped up straightaway into teaching. But the pastoral vocation passed them by, or they passed it by. They became pure academics."

Question: "What would you say to a budding writer of Christian nonfiction?"

> "Don't attempt to be a writer unless you have got things to say which you feel must be put on paper and [you are] being called to do it. Writing . . . is as vocational an exercise as becoming a preacher."

Question: "What advice would you give to young men entering the clerical calling?"

> "Dig deep and dwell deep. I think superficiality is a great weakness of the evangelical world today. . . . And then I would say, Expect incomprehension from your evangelical friends. . . . And expect opposition from great sections of the church and from the secular world."

Question: "How should we view secular entertainment such as music, movies, and television?"

> "If there's no place in your life for fun, people will find you wearisome company. . . . God isn't against entertainment. But it had better be decent stuff that entertains you. . . . Don't let entertainment become the biggest thing in your life. . . . You can let music get on top of you, even becoming a slave to music. If you become a slave to anything, that's a sign you ought to pull back from it."

Question: "How can I tell if I'm spending too much time on entertainment?"

> "The principle that applies here is the Sabbath principle of six days' work followed by one day's rest. That gives a proportion of one to six, which means that recreational entertainment may properly take up something like fifteen percent of your time."

Question: "Do you journal as a spiritual exercise?"

> "I have tried but can't do it without posing, and if you can't be real when you journalize it's better not to try. C. S. Lewis' *Surprised by Joy* is bad from this standpoint, and what I wrote was worse."

Question: "What girl should I marry?"

> "Just check that she'd be a good partner, because some girls who are nice to look at would never make a good partner. They're wild, or at least not sensible. Don't marry a goofy girl, because there's no future in it. Ask someone who knows you both whether you would be good for each other."

The following is the lead-in to a letter Packer wrote to a young person who had asked him a list of questions:

> "Short answers to your questions are all I have time for; and while I don't object to sharing I am always a bit frightened if people want to treat me as a role model. . . . I am a sinner who is gifted, or cursed, with ability to talk better than he lives, and I wouldn't want folk to forget that."

Question: "When you were a young lad in England, what did you think you would be when you grew up?"

> "A teacher. . . . I know now that if I'd been properly assessed in terms of potential . . . I'm sure I should have been a lawyer."

Through the years, Packer has been adamant that the words of Scripture are the words of God:

Question: How do the different endings to the Gospel of Mark in various translations "gibe with the inerrancy of God's word?"

> "The inerrancy of Scripture applies to the material as prepared for publication. . . . I want to allow the editor in. In some Old Testament books, it's very evident that an editor has been at work. That's quite all right. It's part of the process. . . . An editorial process that is preparing the material for publication counts as part of the inspiriting process whereby God, in his sovereignty, gave every word."

Question: "How can a person develop a pattern for Bible reading that will help him or her know God better?"

> "Focus particularly on the richer books. . . . There are some books in Scripture which, as words of God to his people, have a richer vitamin content than others. . . . [Additionally,] linger in those books that have a special resonance with you individually."

Question: "Why do so many people find the study of God and the Bible burdensome and boring?"

> "Too often these things have been taught in a rigidly defensive way: 'This is the stuff you are to believe and share; these are the errors

you are to recognize and reject.' Simply projecting orthodoxy that way doesn't give much stimulus to the mind."

Question: "Are you a Calvinist?"

"Well, if what you mean by 'Calvinist' is one who believes there is a God who is in control of all that he has made and lovingly attends to his creation, then, yes, I guess you could say that I'm a Calvinist."

Question: "What is the greatest challenge facing the church today?"

"We are losing younger people. . . . So the church needs to take a deep breath and go for young people. . . . When the church has secured the faith and the loyalty of young people . . . [it] must labor to capture families. Family Christianity is something basic to Bible Christianity. And we've got to try and get it back."

Question: "[Are you] a good role model as a Christian writer?"

"I doubt it."

A Packer Miscellany

There is, finally, a collection of details that do not fit in any of the categories covered thus far. They include the following:

- Why did Packer choose to be called by the imposing initials "J. I."? I had always assumed that it was a pen name, perhaps chosen for its impressive ring. The reason is actually prosaic in the extreme: in the circles in which Packer moved as a youngster, it was simply the custom to go by one's initials instead of one's first name. Packer claims that it never occurred to him *not* to go by his initials.
- Where and when does Packer do his writing? I have seen a photograph of Packer in his office at Regent College that evokes for me a picture (unwarranted by the facts of the matter) of a grand, librarylike office, with a window that looks out at buildings that evoke a cityscape. My imagination runs wild with thoughts of an office that inspires lofty thoughts and great books—perhaps even an upper-floor office of an imposing building! Again the facts of the matter are prosaic: Packer does most of his writing at home, on a typewriter, early in the day.

- Packer's favorite book in the Bible is Ecclesiastes (as it is for me). What the Preacher "says about life's best being an enjoyment of the basics—one's work, meals, marriage" makes Packer "want to laugh and cheer" because this is what he has felt all his adult life. The text "that runs most constantly around [his] heart is Ecclesiastes's exit line—'Fear God and keep his commandments, for this is the whole duty of man,' meaning everybody."
- When Packer was a student, he was convicted by the suggestion from a speaker that a good way to grasp the full meaning of a part of Scripture is to read it ten times. One Sunday, Packer read the book of Hebrews ten times, and it "remains one of the richest books of Scripture" to him.
- In the culinary field, Packer loves spicy food. Former *Christianity Today* editor David Neff has taken Packer to restaurants on numerous occasions, and he attests that a really good meal for Packer is one in which the food is so hot that Packer must take out his handkerchief to wipe the sweat from his face. In Packer's list of experiences that awaken transcendence in him (see references above), one item on the list is curry!
- Another detail related to eating is that Harold Myra of *Christianity Today* remembers Packer as "a big breakfast person." When the editorial staff met with Packer, the person making the arrangements always made sure that breakfast was a full meal instead of coffee and pastries.
- The son of a railroad employee, Packer has an extensive collection of books about trains.
- Packer claims that in his childhood, he "was always an independent kid." One manifestation is that he developed the practice of going on solitary bicycle rides. He once made the hundred-mile round trip between Gloucester and Oxford in a single day. All he had time to do in Oxford was to turn around and head back to Gloucester!
- Packer has been a "contributor of choice" for compilers of anthologies or dictionaries. Some of Packer's contributions have been highly unexpected and (to me, at least) mildly humorous. For instance, here is the list of articles that Packer contributed to the 1975 *New International Dictionary of New Testament Theology* (Zondervan): "Abolish"; "Accurse"; "Arts"; "Carpenter"; "Defile"; "Despise";

"Dirt"; "Firm"; "Present"; and "Ruin." I will refrain from calling it a Calvinist's dream list.

- When Packer was honored on his eightieth birthday (July 22, 2006) in his home church of St. John's Shaughnessy Anglican Church in Vancouver, several speakers, in paying tribute to Packer as their mentor, called him their Gandalf, the wise wizard in J. R. R. Tolkien's *The Lord of the Rings*. When it came time for Packer to respond, he protested that he was no Gandalf, but "much closer to the lowly Sam," referring to the Hobbit gardener in the trilogy.
- In regard to sports, Packer is an enthusiast for the English game of cricket and enjoys talking about it, but he has not actually been a cricket player. A photograph in Alister McGrath's biography of Packer shows him playing table tennis (American Ping Pong) in the common room at Wycliffe Hall, and during his time as a student there Packer served as captain of the college's table tennis team.
- Packer's answers to the question of how he would like to be remembered included the following: "an encourager"; "as a voice that called people back to old paths of truth and wisdom"; and as someone who called into question two deficiencies of contemporary evangelicalism—the personality cult and the short-memory syndrome that privileges the contemporary and forgets the Christian past (as represented by such giants as Augustine, John Calvin, and Charles Spurgeon).
- Packer is a plainspoken man who "tells it like it is." In an autobiographical passage in one of his books, Packer confesses that once, when attending a theological conference in New York City, he "played hooky for two evenings" and went to a jazz club one night and the Metropolitan Opera the next. Why did he play hooky? Because the conference "was boring [him] stiff."
- I have already noted two sayings for which Packer became known during deliberations of the English Standard Version translation committee ("Joe the bus driver" and "good Anglo-Saxon word"). There were additional ones. His standard way of endorsing a change from the Revised Standard Version (the starting point for the ESV) was to say that the change represented "all gain and no loss." His final rallying call to vote for A over B was, "I say, 'Let's do it.'"
- Packer claims that when he mails off a manuscript (usually late), he is the type of person who moves on to his next project so quickly that within twenty-four hours "he forgets what he has written."

- When *Christianity Today* conducted a poll of Christian leaders to name the best religious books of the twentieth century, Packer nominated Tolkien's *The Lord of the Rings* and commented: "A classic for children from 9 to 90. Bears constant re-reading."

Summary

One way to think of J. I. Packer is the paradigm of a major theme and a minor theme. The major theme is the public figure known especially through his writing and public speaking. The minor theme is the man who certainly does not deliberately keep his life secret, but who can be known only through personal acquaintance or research into less familiar sources than Packer's books and public lectures.

16

What Packer's Style and Rhetoric Tell Us about Him

I can imagine that for some, the subject of this chapter is an unlikely entry in a biography of J. I. Packer. But the chapter fits this middle section of the book perfectly, because exploring the way in which Packer expresses himself in his writing and speaking is an avenue toward knowing Packer the man.

Only a minority of people who claim Packer as an influence in their lives have met him in person. They know Packer through his words, chiefly his articles and books. Furthermore, even though I know Packer in person, much of my acquaintance with him is through what he reveals about himself in his writing.

This chapter is not about the ideas that Packer discusses, but about the person who emerges from the pages of what he writes. In my discipline of literary studies, it has been customary in recent decades to speak of an author's "self-fashioning." I have never liked the term, because it implies posturing and manipulation. But there is no doubt that pictures of authors emerge from what they write and that authors make conscious decisions about what they choose to put into their compositions, including what they share about themselves. Additionally, *how* authors package their material tells us a lot about them and is, in fact, one of the ways by which we know them. For any of my readers who remain skeptical at this point, my invitation is to accompany me as I conduct an analysis of Packer's style and rhetoric.

Questions and Answers

In recent years, Packer has emerged as a champion of an ancient practice in the Christian church known as catechesis. In fact, Packer has co-authored a whole book on the subject, entitled *Grounded in the Gospel: Building Believers the Old-Fashioned Way*. Narrowly defined, catechesis consists of a systematic overview of a subject that uses a question-and-answer method of packaging the content (a catechism). It is not surprising that Packer emerged as an advocate of catechesis, because the format of asking and answering questions has long been a favorite rhetorical strategy for him.

A Packer essay (originally a chapel address) entitled "Give Me Understanding" provides an illustration. The point of departure for the essay is the petition that the writer of Psalm 119 prays five times: "Give me understanding." Having provided a brief exposition of Psalm 119, Packer writes, "I turn now to the series of questions which the Psalmist's prayer suggests that we who battle for the Bible need to be asking ourselves." Five questions give shape to the discussion:

- Why does inerrancy matter?
- Under what conditions can the Bible, viewed as inspired and inerrant divine instruction, actually exert authority over us?
- What are the obstacles to our understanding the Bible?
- What is meant by "understanding"?
- How does God give understanding?

I myself learned long ago that one of the best ways to organize a mass of heterogeneous data is to mold it into a series of questions and answers. Packer is a kindred spirit in this matter.

"Is Christianity Credible?" asks Packer in the title of a 1981 essay. He does not structure the entire essay around a series of questions, but intermittently introduces questions at transition points: "What, then, will confirm credibility?" "So I turn to ask what procedures and criteria should decide for us what is an adequate account of authentic Christianity, where various accounts are canvassed and doctors disagree?"

"The question, 'Is Christianity credible?' prompts the retort, 'credible to whom?'"

For a third example, I dipped into *God Has Spoken*. On just two pages, Packer organizes his line of thought around the following questions:

- What is revelation?
- How does God reveal what has to be revealed in order that we may know him?
- Why does God reveal himself to us?
- What is the content of God's revelation?

The question-and-answer method is a specific version of Packer's gift for organization. As a rhetorical form, the use of questions and answers is also an effective way of involving readers in the process of communication, prompting them to ask questions along with an author or speaker. Additionally, the rhetorical format of questions and answers is an embodiment of Packer's devotion to the method of instruction called catechesis.

Numerical Schemes

I once wrote an essay on "reading literature with C. S. Lewis." One of Lewis's skills was organizing masses of data into easily grasped outlines. In turn, he often used a numerical scheme to make the material manageable: Sir Philip Sidney's "defence of poetry will not be rightly understood unless we keep two facts carefully in mind"; "two ways in pastoral lay open before Spenser"; "the prose fiction of this period may be divided into three classes"; "at least five different forms in which evil appears in *The Faerie Queene* may be distinguished"; and the grandeur of Milton's style "is produced mainly by three things." Lewis had specialized in classics at Oxford University, and so did Packer. The imprint on both was thorough.

Packer uses numerical schemes so constantly that it is a rarity to read a book or essay of his that does not employ this method of organization. The following are three specimens, selected arbitrarily:

- From a unit entitled "Romans on Wrath" in *Knowing God*: "We shall end this chapter by analyzing what Romans tells us about

[God's wrath]. 1. The meaning of God's wrath. . . . 2. The revelation of God's wrath. . . . 3. The deliverance from God's wrath."
- From the chapter entitled "Evangelism" in *Evangelism and the Sovereignty of God*: "For a complete picture of what the New Testament means by evangelism, we need not look further than the apostle Paul's account. . . . There are three points to note about it.". . . If we equate evangelism with the holding of evangelistic meetings, "we should be grievously astray, as the following considerations will show" (three numbered considerations are then developed). . . .The evangelistic message is "made up of four [numbered] essential ingredients." . . . The signs of conviction of sin "seem to be three in number." . . . "What is the motive for evangelizing? There are, in fact, two motives that should spur us constantly to evangelize: the first is the love to God and concern for His glory; the second is love to man and concern for his welfare."
- From an essay entitled "Reading the Bible Theologically": "Reading Scripture theologically starts from the truths reviewed above [four points are numbered and listed]. . . . Prayerful theological Bible reading will be pursued in light of three further guiding principles. . . . Three questions [numbered as the discussion unfolds] must govern readers of the inspired Word."

This fondness for brief lists and numerical schemes reinforces two things about Packer. One is the orderliness of his mind. He thinks logically and in a well-organized manner. Disorderliness of organization holds no appeal to him. Additionally, Packer composes with an eye on his audience. Readers and listeners need to be able to follow a train of thought, and numbered points are a great aid to that process. Few authors and speakers have realized that as fully as Packer.

The Personal Touch

As we read Packer's writings, we accompany him to many places and share numerous interesting experiences with him. (This was also one of the points that I elaborated in my essay on reading literature with C. S. Lewis.) As we share these experiences with Packer, we come to know him. This is one of the rewards of reading widely in the Packer canon.

For example, in the preface to Packer's best-selling book *Knowing God*, we relive his experience of being asked by the editor of *Evangelical*

Magazine to write a series of articles on basic Christianity. We share Packer's bimonthly question, "What do I tell them next?" Then we read the chapters of the book to discover how Packer answered that question. When Packer says that the book "is due as much to that editor as to this author," the editor comes alive in our imaginations as a remarkable person to whom the Christian public owes an immense debt of gratitude.

We walk with Packer "in the sunshine with a scholar who had effectively forfeited his prospects of academic advancement by clashing with church dignitaries over the gospel of grace," then hearing the friend say, "But it doesn't matter, for I've known God and they haven't." At the end of the 1973 printing of *Knowing God*, we are present for a fireside chat with the author as he tells us that he finds "nothing I wish to withdraw. In fact, I get help from rereading it."

If we read enough of Packer's books and articles, we relive additional memorable experiences. We are present for Packer's first meal in the Wycliffe Hall dining room, as he sits across the table from "a grinning little Welshman" and announces to his new acquaintance that the Puritans "were magnificent on mortification." Or we find ourselves seated with Packer at the Metropolitan Opera, as he chats about the production with "a youngish woman" sitting next to him. Then we sit with Packer in consternation as the woman's husband, glaring at Packer and clamping his hand firmly on his wife's knee as a sign of ownership, whisks her away to another part of the gallery! We share Packer's theorizing about what lay behind the husband's action. Had he been dragged to the opera against his will and was testy as a result? Did the wife have the annoying habit of being overly friendly with strangers?

We are also present in our imaginations at a Regent College chapel service at which Packer is the speaker. Seated there, we hear Packer's Freudian slip; intending to say, "Remember, this place is a kind of seminary," he instead says, "Remember, this place is a kind of cemetery."

Or we sit with Packer at his desk, looking at "a broadsheet for pastors that begins with the banner heading, 'How Will I Know When I've Succeeded?'" As he ponders the idea of ministerial success in our presence, Packer confides to us: "When I was young, British, and pagan, I thought the sky was the limit and nothing I wanted to do was beyond me. My dreams ranged from being a star cricketer to a distinguished locomotive engineer to a top comedian, with much bizarre stuff in between." As this passage unfolds, Packer further recalls an occasion when he wrote a review of Kent and Barbara Hughes's book *Liberating Ministry from the Success Syndrome*, only to find that "wily editors" entitled the review "Nothing Fails Like Success" and printed it alongside a paid advertisement for "The Robert Schuller Institute for Successful Church Leadership."

Are references such as these an example of "self-fashioning"? That is certainly not Packer's intention. On the other hand, he chooses to give us glimpses into his experiences and thoughts, and in the process we get to know J. I. Packer.

Sometimes a personal anecdote allows us vicariously to live a bit of adventure with Packer. For example, we accompany Packer in our imaginations as he is hiking with Kit and starting to go down a steep, twenty-five-foot embankment to a stream. We see Packer grabbing a small branch of a tree to steady himself and then slipping. We hear Kit yell, "Hang on!" But the branch breaks and Packer continues to slide. Eventually, a tree root stops him and he struggles back up the slope.

Some of Packer's autobiographical anecdotes are a source of humor. We are present in imagination as "two beefy protestors" with pickets invade Regent College and even Packer's office because of something he published in *Christianity Today*. We are present in the Packer residence as Packer peruses a promotional circular that has arrived in the mail announcing the imminent publication of *The Amazing Book of the Packers of Canada*. With Packer, we read that "this is the only book of its kind in the entire world" and that Packer "must order it right away."

Even more hilarious is Packer and Kit's arrival in Manila for the Lausanne II conference. Packer recounts the story in a column cleverly entitled "The Prayboy Club." The conference accommodations are at the hotel that houses the last Playboy Club in the world. In fact, the desk clerk hands the Packers complimentary passes to the club. We look on as Packer's "strong-minded wife grabbed, tore up, and handed back the passes in silence." Packer's laconic final sentence in the piece is, "So back we came to cool-cat, brittle, affluent, self-indulgent, unchurched Vancouver, full of thoughts, and none the worse for our adventure."

The dedications in Packer's books introduce us to a gallery of his friends. They tease us into wanting to know more and are, like the names that Paul mentions in his epistles, a glimpse into the man. "To the Memory of Richard Coates, William Leathem, Alan Stibbs: three mighty men mighty in the Scriptures." We wish we could have known these heroes of the faith from the life of J. I. Packer. "To some friends in Texas [five couples are named], with love and in gratitude." We have no doubt that these are wonderful acquaintances whom we would like to have met ourselves. "To my colleagues at Tyndale Hall and Trinity College, Bristol, 1970–79, with affection and gratitude." "For Fred and Elizabeth in whom so many of Nehemiah's strengths have reappeared." "To Steven Purcell, whose renewed invitation to Laity Lodge sparked my theme; Lane Dennis, who pressed me to publish my material; Scott Barber, who made sense of my messy manuscript." There are untold stories here, and we are glad to have received just a glimpse of them.

The genre of the autobiographical vignette packs a punch out of proportion to the space it is allotted. It is not the main part of an argument. It is simply an experience that an author chooses to share. The personal touch that Packer puts into his writing sticks in the memory and becomes a means by which we know Packer the person.

Logic

Packer has an eminently logical mind. I have long associated this trait with a certain British mindset, and my earliest examples of such a mind playing with an idea and pursuing it to its logical end came from reading the apologetic writings of C. S. Lewis and J. I. Packer.

The first Packer book in which I encountered the play of logic was *"Fundamentalism" and the Word of God*. The chapter entitled "Reason" starts by laying out the charge of liberals that because evangelicals begin with the premise of the truthfulness of the Bible, they do not exercise reason. Having summarized the opponents' argument, Packer writes that "we have now reached the point in our argument at which we can address ourselves directly to this criticism." This confirms that the whole book has been pursuing a line of argument, following a continuous pattern of logical thinking. Packer then defines terms, itself a move toward logic: "'Reason' means reasoning, as 'faith' means believing and trusting. The first is the mark of men, as distinct from beasts; the second, of Christians, as distinct from unbelievers." As we follow Packer's line of thought, we are thinking through the issue, turning the prism in the light. Whereas unbelievers exercise "faithless reason," believers exercise "reasoning faith." Determining the difference between those two is an exercise in reason and logic.

What is "the proper function of reason in relation to faith?" Packer asks in this chapter. It is threefold: (1) it receives and works hard to understand the teaching of God as revealed in Scripture; (2) it exercises itself to apply the teaching of God to life; and (3) it communicates God's truth to others. These three tasks are not unthinking ones; to perform them "requires hard thinking."

What about the alleged conflict between faith and reason, and the charge that Christian thinking is obscurantist? The conflict needs to be resolved, of course. This resolution "always takes essentially the same form. Whereas the logic of faith requires us . . . to challenge and correct secular opinion by the light of revealed truth, the self-styled champions of reason always desire to bring the biblical faith into line with secular ideas." The question at hand "is not whether we should think, but how we should think; whether or not our thinking should be controlled by our faith. The real difference between Evangelicals and those who call them obscurantists lies in the realm of method."

Packer covers much beyond this in his chapter, but I have sketched enough to show that the essential method is to pose a problem (the liberal view that evangelicals abandon reason) and then think the problem through. He pursues a line of logic as he explores the issues related to the problem.

"Fundamentalism" and the Word of God is an apologetic book in which logic is foregrounded. The other main genre of Packer's books is exposition of theology. As a specimen, I have chosen chapter 2 of *Evangelism and the Sovereignty of God*, and instead of reconstructing the argument, I have lifted sentences that show that Packer is proceeding by logical argument (my comments follow the quotations from the book):

- "Our aim in the present study is to think out the nature of the Christian's evangelistic task in the light of this agreed presupposition that God is sovereign in salvation." The need "to think out" is an invitation to exercise logical thinking.
- "It is necessary, therefore, to take the thought of human responsibility, as it affects both the preacher and the hearer of the gospel,

very seriously indeed. But we must not let it drive the thought of divine sovereignty out of our minds." Those two sentences function as a preliminary road sign informing us that we will need to think hard in reconciling two ideas that seem opposite to each other.

- "Let us work this out." This is a command of sorts that we need to be prepared for a rigorous line of inquiry.
- "This shows us the danger of forgetting the practical implications of God's sovereignty. . . . But there is an opposite temptation that threatens us also."
- "Here, then, are two opposite pitfalls: a Scylla and Charybdis of error. . . . What are we to do, then?" Packer poses a problem that requires resolution.
- We must "believe both of these doctrines. . . . We shall proceed now according to this maxim. In what follows, we shall try to take both doctrines perfectly seriously." This is another signpost alerting us to the need to put our logical reasoning on high alert.

Anyone who has read *Evangelism and the Sovereignty of God* knows that it is an extended exercise of reason and logic that requires one's very best thinking. In fact, in his foreword to the book, Packer claims that "it is a piece of biblical and theological reasoning." Not all of Packer's writing requires that much analysis and hard thought, but his approach to every topic is logical, the product of a thinking person pursuing a line of thought and making careful distinctions along the way.

Contrast and Antithesis

From classical times forward, contrast has been one of the most commonly practiced forms of rhetoric. When we set one idea against its opposite, both stand out. Contrast thus serves a clarifying function. Antithesis also lends vigor to a discussion, functioning much as plot conflict does in a story. With Packer, the use of contrast is harnessed in the interests of truth. Truth is the antithesis of error, so Packer regularly uses antithesis in the wars of truth. Much of Packer's writing is polemical in nature as he aggressively debates intellectual positions. It is no wonder that he regularly sets one idea or position against another.

As we would expect, antithesis structures the whole of *Evangelism and the Sovereignty of God*, but not exactly in the form that we might suppose. Ostensibly, the book pits two views of evangelism against each other—the idea that its success depends wholly on human effort and persuasiveness against the view that it relies solely on the sovereign work of God in a listener's mind and heart. In fact, Packer calls these two opposed viewpoints Scylla and Charybdis, meaning two irreconcilable and extreme viewpoints. But that contrast is not the one on which the book is built. Packer considers both of those viewpoints to be errors, so he contrasts them as a pair to the truth, which consists of believing "both these doctrines . . . and [keeping] both constantly before us for the guidance and government of our lives." A subpoint under that format is articulated right at the outset, as Packer announces that he will combat the prevalent view "that a robust faith in the absolute sovereignty of God is bound to undermine any adequate sense of human responsibility. . . . So far from inhibiting evangelism [the false view], faith in the sovereignty of God's government and grace is the only thing that can sustain it [the true view]."

If we fast forward to a book Packer published in 2013 (*Taking God Seriously*), we find that antithesis is still a favorite rhetorical mode. "Much of the church today . . . has two [antithetical] religions in its womb"; they are "the historic faith" and "the alternative Christianity" begotten of modern philosophic and social movements and denial of the historicity of the Bible. "It is often assumed nowadays that Christian ethics . . . spontaneously arise in Christian hearts as the law of universal love is internalized. But no [antithesis]—the rules of Christian conduct are ordinarily determined by facts enshrined in doctrines." Several of the chapters begin with the historic Christian teaching on a subject (e.g., repentance, sexuality, church unity) and end by contrasting that view with contemporary Anglican liberalism. Within the Anglican Church, Packer writes at a certain point, "is a view that can be labeled *liberal*, and the opposite view [antithesis] *conservative*." In all of these instances, Packer could have developed what he regards as the correct view without contrasting it to its opposite, but issues are heightened and truth does battle with error when one view is set against another.

For a third example, I have randomly chosen an early section of Packer's book *God Has Spoken*. As a unit on "new views of revelation and inspiration" unfolds, the following set of contrasts emerges:

- "Up to the nineteenth century, Protestant theology was accustomed to bracket revelation and inspiration together. . . . In the discussion of revelation and inspiration that went on under critical auspices, however [contrast], this neat correlation was given up."
- "Also [another contrast], the centre of interest shifted. Instead of being a mere preamble to the doctrine of inspiration, revelation now became a subject for study in its own right."
- "Hence, unlike their predecessors [contrast], modern Protestant theologians regularly insist that revelation and Scripture are two distinct things."

I need to guard against giving the impression that Packer's use of contrast and antithesis is as abundant as his use of numbered lists or appeals to logic. The point is rather that Packer's mind is attuned to the oppositions in the world, and that a common ploy that he uses in his organizing of material is to set one thing against another. The use of contrast also stems from his career as a polemicist, in which he accepts the task of opposing error with truth.

Analogy and Metaphor

Analogy (including simile) and metaphor constitute a form of logic. They assert a correspondence between two things that needs to be confirmed or denied, as A is compared to B. The test of accuracy is logic and empirical demonstration.

The function of analogy is to shed light on a subject by comparing it to something else. One area of human experience is used to illuminate another area. Analogy is part of Packer's arsenal for clarifying the ideas that he asserts and making them memorable.

To get the ball rolling, I offer the following examples of analogy taken from two early pages in Packer's best-known book, *Knowing God*:

- Trying to live in the world without knowing about God is like flying an Amazonian tribesman to central London and letting him fend for himself.
- Not knowing God is like stumbling through life blindfolded, with no sense of direction.
- Aberrant modern claims about God are like a storm in which we find ourselves and from which we must escape.

- In a cultural climate that denies that we can find accurate knowledge about God, we must become like Bunyan's Christian, putting our fingers in our ears and starting on our journey to find God.
- Getting an accurate picture of God is like climbing a mountain.

A whole subgenre of Packer's analogies and metaphors consists of parallels to subjects taken from the world of literature. These references are more than allusions that enliven the discourse of the moment; they function as parallels or analogies to the subject under discussion. Here are three examples taken from a single book, *Praying*, authored jointly by Packer and Carolyn Nystrom:

- The title of a book by detective writer Martha Grimes, *Help the Poor Struggler*, is offered by the authors as a self-portrait of themselves in the school of prayer—they are like the person named in the book title (who functions as an analogy).
- A statement about a detective in a fictional story that Packer had recently read is adduced as an accurate picture of (analogy to) what often befalls us when our thoughts wander during prayer: the detective was brooding on the crime, but "his thoughts were a blur."
- As a schoolboy, Packer received as a prize the J. B. Priestley book *The Good Companions*; the companions of the title are applied (Packer's term) to the persons of the Trinity, who accompany Christians in their spiritual lives.

Packer's metaphors give us a glimpse into a creative and poetic side of his makeup. Since at least as far back as Aristotle, metaphor has been regarded as the special skill of the poet—"a keen eye for resemblance," Aristotle called it. It is a relatively rare gift, useful not only to poets but to anyone who wishes to express ideas in an original way. Metaphors and similes have arresting strangeness and compel attention. They have the ability to overcome the cliché effect of something that has become overly familiar. Some of Packer's metaphors display these qualities in an off-beat way that quickly seems "quintessential Packer." Here are some random examples:

- John Bunyan's master image in *The Pilgrim's Progress* is the pilgrimage—a journey to a sacred site. It is a great archetype, but it is a cliché to us due to sheer familiarity. Packer gives it an original twist when he tells us that the pilgrimage "could equally be called a hike. There is a constantly changing path, and Christian and his friends have to hike it."

- Some of Packer's metaphors are so daring that they have taken on a life of their own. In his metaphoric imagination, theologians are the plumbers and sewage men of the church, keeping the flow of religious ideas clean (accurate) and getting rid of sewage (mistaken ideas).
- "What would you consider a fit symbol of contemporary Western culture?" Packer asks. His answer: a hot tub—"water at 102 degrees Fahrenheit with an air jet all to oneself." In Packer's metaphoric imagination, "the hot tub perfectly expresses the obsessive passion of the modern West to find" the good life, which is conceived as a comfortable life.
- Spiritual health is analogous to physical health; listening to teaching and preaching is like eating a meal; "spiritual anorexia (not taking in the food we need) and spiritual bulimia (not letting ourselves digest it after we have received it however large the quantities) will keep us from real spiritual health."

My goal in this chapter is to highlight what we know about Packer as a person on the basis of his style and rhetoric. We learn several things about the bent of Packer's mind in his use of analogy as a rhetorical device. Metaphor and analogy are functions of the literary imagination, and they show a literary and imaginative side of Packer. They also demonstrate his concern for the ordinary reader. Packer always writes and speaks with his audience in view, and the typical person is grateful for a comparison to familiar experience as an author discusses ideas. Additionally, Packer's resorting to analogy is yet another manifestation of his quest for clarity. The purpose of a good comparison is to use one sphere of life to cast light on another. And metaphor and analogy are great avenues by which to state the truth in an aphoristic way that is almost impossible to forget.

The Rhetoric of Prophetic Denunciation

Scholars of American literature have identified a literary genre that they call the jeremiad, named after the Old Testament prophet Jeremiah. The heart of the jeremiad is the satiric impulse to denounce human vice or folly. The writer of a jeremiad announces what is wrong in society at large or a subculture (such as the church) within it. Packer does not write full-fledged jeremiads, but his writings are filled with warnings that the contemporary church, modern society, or the human race universally from time immemorial is on the wrong track in many ways. This prophetic voice includes something additional that we find in the Old Testament prophecies—an implied call to people to reform their wrong behavior. Denunciation and reform are the twin thrusts of Packer's prophetic passages.

The following are specimens of what we find regularly in the writings of J. I. Packer:

- "The conviction behind the book [*Knowing God*] is that ignorance of God . . . lies at the root of much of the church's weakness today. Two unhappy trends seem to have produced this state of affairs. Trend one is that *Christian minds have been conformed to the modern spirit*. . . . Trend two is that *Christian minds have been confused by the modern skepticism*."
- "As the years go by, I am increasingly burdened by the sense that the more conservative church people in the West, Protestant and Roman Catholic alike, are, if not starving, at least grievously undernourished."
- "When reason insists on ruling, . . . the results are bleak indeed. In comes relativism. . . . In comes skepticism about all long-standing beliefs; . . . in comes pluralism . . . ; in comes agnosticism. . . . Each of these *isms* is familiar among us today, they creep into churches as well as going on parade outside them, and the church of Christ is sadly enfeebled in consequence. . . . A robust return to the older wisdom about faith's true object is urgently needed."
- "If what we have said is right, our twentieth-century Christian consciousness is already far astray, and the course proposed [by radical theologians] would only lead us deeper into skepticism and spiritual barrenness. It is vain to push on along the wrong road. . . . Our condition will never be eased till we humbly retrace our steps to the point where we first went wrong."
- "Christianity in all its forms has lost its grip on the West, which now leads the world in materialistic, relativistic, and hedonistic secularization. . . . The size of its abortion industry is the measure

> of its paganism. The global culture that has established itself is not a Christian ideology but a technological monster. . . . Our era has turned into an age of atrocity, in which the barbarian obscenities of terrorism, genocide, torture, and religious and political persecution have re-established themselves on a grander scale than ever before."

What is the model for this prophetic strain in Packer's writings? He answers that question himself in his book *Taking God Seriously*: "The books of the prophets constitute about a quarter of the Old Testament and a fifth of the Bible as a whole. . . . When we read them, we find that the prophets are much more moralists than futurologists, and what they speak constantly about is corporate repentance, made necessary by communal sin." That accurately describes a leading trait of Packer's writings as well.

Utopian Rhetoric

To follow the preceding unit on Packer as prophetic denouncer of contemporary failures with a claim that in his writings we can see the rhetoric of utopian idealism would seem to be an impossible case to make. But since I believe that it is the truth, I have gladly shouldered the responsibility of proving it. Despite Packer's pessimistic assessment of the current state of the church and society, he has always shown a tremendous energy of spirit in thinking that Christians can reform their ways. At the heart of the utopian enterprise is the conviction that a better alternative exists than the current way of doing things. The utopian impulse is always to convince us that we have the means to turn our situation around.

The subject of this chapter is what Packer's writings tell us about the man, but before I turn to the utopian rhetoric of his writings, I want to observe that we can see the same utopian impulse in Packer's life. I think, for example, of the decade in which Packer served as warden of Latimer House in Oxford. Latimer House was a clearinghouse for the evangelical initiative within the Church of England. Hopes ran high that the national church could be significantly influenced by the growing number of evangelical ministers and parishes. It was a utopian moment.

Again, as I was composing this biography, I called Packer to interview him and was flabbergasted (British "gobsmacked") to learn that he had spent the preceding two weeks on the West Coast and the East Coast, serving on task forces for the emerging alliance known as the Anglican Church in North America. This, too, is an example of utopian optimism, based on the premise that the Anglican Church in North America can get its act together through a catechism for adults and a liturgy for worship.

Where do we find utopian rhetoric in the books and articles of a man who is often depressed by trends in the modern church? The very books in which he unleashes his jeremiads are mainly devoted to an optimistic program for solving the problems that have been exposed. For example, Packer's book *Truth and Power* sounds the alarm that "the deforming of the church is a constant problem, and a much bigger one than is sometimes recognized." But the main thrust of the book is a call for what Packer calls reformation—a program "for the Bible to form and reform the church." Packer has never given up on the church. He is full of ideas for getting things right. The last essay in the forenamed book is entitled "Life and Health and Peace"—a utopian-sounding note if there ever was one.

In searching for a second example of utopian idealism, I went to my bookshelf and pulled off *Never Beyond Hope: How God Touches and Uses Imperfect People* (2000). The introduction begins with a litany of terrible events and trends in the contemporary world, but the chapters are all about hope—"God's Gift of Hope," "Hope When I Belong to an Unhappy Family," "Hope When I Am Barely Noticed and Not Trusted," "Hope When Everything Has Gone Wrong," and so on. The purpose of the book is to give us a reason for hope.

A third example is the 2010 book *Grounded in the Gospel: Building Believers the Old-Fashioned Way*, co-authored with Gary A. Parrett. Packer has been lamenting the lack of doctrinal knowledge in the church for nearly his entire scholarly life. *Grounded in the Gospel* begins in an awareness that the problem of doctrinal ignorance is widespread in the contemporary church and that the authors' proposed remedy—the practice of catechesis—is out of vogue. But this does not deter the authors in the least. The book outlines an ambitious program of instruction in the church based on catechesis. I do not hesitate to label it a utopian vision of individual and corporate renewal. This is doubly and triply true because utopian thinking is based on the premise of an institutional key that will usher in the good society. *Grounded in the Gospel* offers an institutional key, namely, catechesis. The concluding chapter lists twenty pieces of advice regarding how to implement the vision that the book has cast.

Early in my teaching career I became interested in the literary genre of utopian writing and even taught my senior seminars on the subject. One thing that I quickly learned is that satire and utopia are two sides of the same coin. One literary critic gave me the formula of "dissatisfaction crossed with longing" to describe the utopian genre. The dissatisfaction feeds the longing; the longing provides an antidote to the dissatisfaction. Something of the same rhythm characterizes the life and writings of J. I. Packer. In Packer, we can find much subsurface optimism about what can be achieved, just as we can find in the original Puritans.

A Common Touch

Aristotle theorized that one of the ways in which writers and speakers persuade their audiences is through the image of themselves that they project or share. Aristotle called this *ethos*, and by it he meant that authors generate credibility partly by the authorial person that they create in their audience's awareness. Packer is a famous person and someone of very high intellectual abilities. Knowing that, I have been surprised (and favorably impressed) by the common touch that he possesses. Early in my research for this book, I was captivated by allusions of the following type, which usually occur early in an essay or book:

- "A favorite picture book for three-year-olds, *I Am a Bunny*, looks at life from a rabbit's point of view."
- "'They lived happily ever after.' So say fairy tales of imaginary married couples."
- "The title phrase for this closing reflection comes from a brilliant little poem . . . Rudyard Kipling's *If*."
- "In *The House at Pooh Corner*, the second of A. A. Milne's enchanting collections of Winnie-the-Pooh's adventures, we meet fussy mother Kanga."
- "Let me tell you a story you may not have heard. . . . There was once a man who had a pet gorilla and taught it to play golf . . ."
- "C. S. Lewis wrote a book in the Narnia series called *The Horse and His Boy*. . . . (If you've read the book, you know that the horse Bree is the hero.)"

- "A *Peanuts* cartoon from way back when has Lucy asking a glum-looking Charlie Brown what he is worrying about . . ."

What is going on here? I will answer for myself. I am always a little shocked when I see these references to children's literature. When I pick up a Packer book, I am primed to read a piece of religious or theological writing by a world-famous author, and instead I encounter someone who reads and remembers children's literature! However, in addition to my shock, I find something disarming about this maneuver, and I experience a momentary relaxation from my anticipated exercise in intellectual exertion. For the moment, Packer emerges not as an eminent theologian and thinker but as an ordinary man, in touch with the child within.

Here is a second list of entries in my category of the rhetoric of the typical person:

- "Checkups in the interests of well-being are familiar features of modern life. The servicing patterns of new cars specify periodic checkups."
- "Sheep farms are common in Britain, and that means that walkers in the English countryside become of necessity quite familiar with kinds of trails."
- "'I like [Nehemiah]; he was a construction man,' the old Texan housebuilder told me."
- "I have camped in a tent . . . , and I disliked it very much."
- "'We might have a crash,' said the small girl anxiously, as the family car threaded its way through traffic. 'Trust Daddy; he's a good driver,' said Mommy."

All scholars and theologians have a private life beyond their published books and articles. Some of them show that side of their lives to their reading public, and some do not. Among those who share their private lives, some create a picture of exotic worldwide travel and of moving in a celebrity world—a world remote from the ordinary person. By contrast, Packer's references to his private life show us an ordinary man, reflecting his roots in a blue-collar environment. Packer is someone who takes his car to the garage for periodic checkups, goes on walks in the countryside, rubs shoulders with people in such professions as home construction, goes camping, and drives in heavy traffic with his family in tow.

I will add one more category of references that are cut from the same cloth of appeals to the ordinary person. I refer to Packer's frequent quoting from the traditional hymns of the church. Here, too, the effect is to close ranks with unpretentious readers who, whatever their education and sophistication, do not scorn life at the level of grade school- and high school-educated people. A few tabulations are as follows:

- In *Knowing God*, Packer quotes from familiar hymns twenty-nine times.
- In *Praying*, Packer quotes from the storehouse of Protestant hymns a dozen times.
- In the concluding essay in *Truth and Power*, Packer quotes from eleven different hymns.

Hymns by such writers as Isaac Watts, John Newton, and the Wesleys are the poetry anthology of the ordinary churchgoer. It is entirely to be expected that they are quoted primarily in Packer's "popular" (as distinct from scholarly) books.

Imaginary Questioners and Responders

At many points, Packer's rhetoric reminds me of a genre from ancient Greek and Roman oratory known as the diatribe. This genre is apparent in the epistles of the apostle Paul and the entire epistle of James. The diatribe was originally a form of street preaching and instruction. It was a vigorous form, one in which a common ploy was to imagine someone in the audience raising an objection or asking a question, then to reply to this imaginary person. Here are examples from Packer's writings:

- "'This is all very well,' they will tell us, 'but the fact remains that modern scholarship assures us that the Bible does err.'"
- "You say, 'What do you mean?' . . . And you say, 'What are these things?'"
- "But here someone will interject: 'Exactly; and the thing has now been done. Why do you spend so much time belabouring old-fashioned Liberalism? You are flogging a dead horse.'"
- "'But wait a minute,' says someone; 'your praise of spirituality is all very well, and it's nice to hear, but are you not a theologian?'"

- "'Well,' says someone, 'you are called an evangelical theologian; do you not go along with this passion for system-building?'"
- "It may be that someone is still wondering why I chose to lecture on this somber theme rather than on any other subject."
- "God, they say, is love. This is the real centre of the New Testament revelation, and love must have the last word."
- "At this point, however, appeal will be made to the concept of 'personal encounter.'" (A rebuttal of that position follows.)
- "One sometimes hears it said that by continuing to maintain the plenary divine inspiration, and hence the entire trustworthiness of the Scriptures, Evangelicals are throwing away the gains of a hundred years of scientific inquiry into the Bible."
- "But someone will say: . . . can we not mark off the realm of religion from the secular realm, and let the Bible hold sway in the first, while reason rules in the second?"
- "Our humanist friends will, I think, be equally anxious to assure us that reason claims to rule the whole of life, and that all we believe and do needs to be brought into line with its dictates."
- "'But wait a minute,' says someone, 'tell me this. Is our journey really necessary?'" (From the second page of *Knowing God*, after Packer has proposed the need for Christians to explore theology.)

Replies to imaginary opponents enliven a discourse. They turn the presentation of an author's ideas into a debate. They make the discussion a battle between error and truth. It is no surprise that Packer uses this familiar diatribe strategy in his polemical writings. It is a variation of the question-and-answer format (which appears far more often in Packer's writings and addresses than does the reply to an imaginary questioner or challenger).

The Rhetoric of Practical Advice

Another rhetorical form that I quickly perceived to be characteristic of Packer is the use of the imperative. For Packer, imperatives are not commands, but a form of giving practical advice in a direct way. I liken his lists of imperatives to the sections of application at the ends of Puritan sermons. Having provided reasoned expositions of truth, the Puritan preachers would tell their congregations what they should do in light of those expositions. Or we might think of the imperative mode as an extension of Packer's role as counselor. People who have observed his interactions with students at Regent College describe him as grandfatherly toward them. The rhetorical mode that I am about to illustrate fits this image.

Here are randomly selected examples of lists of what people can profitably do, based on a preceding discussion:

- Packer's co-authored book on the need for catechesis in the church ends with a chapter in which the authors raise twenty questions that need to be asked and answered for a successful implementation of a catechetical program in a church. The last of these questions is elaborated with a list of steps that need to be taken, phrased in the imperative mode: (1) accurately assess the current situation; (2) cast the catechetical vision; (3) cultivate consensus among leaders; (4) start slowly but with resolve; (5) focus on families and children; (6) hone the hymnody of the church; (7) adjust appropriately as needed; and (8) share stories of formation. Anything less direct would lack the punch that these imperatives provide.
- In a discussion of the methods of interpretation that need to undergird preaching, Packer does not simply list the principles, but phrases them in terms of what a preacher needs to do: "hold to the literal meaning"; "hold to the principle of harmony"; and "follow round the interpretive spirals."
- The concluding paragraph of an essay on the Bible as God's Word includes the statements, "Bless God for the light that he has given us for our journey through this dark world. . . . Learn to thank God for the Word and to comment what we believe about it."
- In an essay on preaching, Packer offers three guidelines that can profitably govern the section of a sermon devoted to application, and these guidelines are phrased as a form of imperative: "application should constantly focus on the unchanging realities of each person's relationship to God"; "application should constantly focus on the person, place, and power of Jesus Christ"; and "application should constantly search the hearts and consciences of the hearers."
- In an essay on how we can profitably conceptualize the Bible, Packer turns the discussion into a fireside conversation by using the imperative form of the verb: "think of the Bible as a *library*"; "see the Bible

as a *landscape*"; "look upon the Bible as a *letter*"; "think of the Bible as a *listening post*"; "be clear that Holy Scripture . . . is also a *law* for us"; "always approach Holy Scripture as . . . a *lamp*"; and "our approach to Holy Scripture should be that of a *lifeline.*"

Packer wants to be serviceable to individuals and the church. Giving good advice in a direct mode is one of the things that has endeared him to his readers and listeners.

The Aphoristic Gift

An aphorism is a concise, memorable statement of a great truth. The way in which the truth is expressed is what makes it stick in the mind. Aphorisms have an aesthetic side as well (being examples of beautiful expression). Packer has a gift for aphorism that takes two forms in his writings. One is that his writings are a repository of great quotations from others. Also, Packer himself is capable of stating the apt formula that compels our attention and makes an utterance memorable.

Here are some aphorisms that entered my storehouse when I saw them quoted at second hand by Packer:

- Daniel's three friends refused to worship Nebuchadnezzar's golden image and "smilingly washed their hands of the consequences" (Oswald Chambers).
- Theology is "the science of living blessedly for ever" (Puritan William Perkins).
- When God wanted Paul's letters written, he was not "reduced to the necessity of going down to the earth and painfully scrutinizing the men He found there, seeking anxiously for the one who . . . promised best for His purpose" (B. B. Warfield).
- "Tell me what a man's prayers are, and I will soon tell you the state of his soul" (J. C. Ryle).
- "Most evangelists are not very interested in theology: most theologians are not very interested in evangelism" (Michael Green).
- "We are all beggars" (Martin Luther's last written words, penned two days before his death).
- "Lord, who made me simple, make me simpler yet" (Archbishop William Temple).
- In prayer, we "formulate our souls" (P. T. Forsyth).

Of course, the largest body of aphorisms that Packer quotes comes from the Bible, and a second comes from the hymns that he quotes to drive his points home.

In addition to quoting aphorisms, Packer creates them. Here is a sampling:

- "The question is not whether we should think, but how we should think."
- "All doctrines terminate in mystery; for they deal with the works of God."
- "The Bible excludes the idea of a frustrated Deity."
- "In fellowship, one seeks to gain, as well as to give."
- "What is a Christian? . . . A Christian is one who has God as Father."
- Echoing C. S. Lewis's book title *The Horse and His Boy*: the book of Jonah "is about a man and his God, a merciless man and his merciful God."
- "Santa Claus theology."
- "Hot tub religion."
- "All roads in the Bible lead to Romans."
- "We should read the Bible as if the letters RSVP were written at the head of every page."
- "The Bible appears like a symphony orchestra, with the Holy Ghost as its Toscanini."

Why does J. I. Packer cultivate this aphoristic flair? There are multiple reasons. He is a wordsmith, and the aphorism is one of the natural expressions of a wordsmith. Aphorisms capture a thought at its most penetrating. The aphorism is part of the quest for order and precision. An aphorism makes an insight permanent, which is any writer's goal. And aphoristic thinking values brevity and compression; in the foreword to his book *God's Words*, Packer acknowledges that "I love pregnant brevity, and some of my material is . . . packed tight (Packer by name, packer by nature)."

This is as good a place as any to note Packer's love of alliteration and parallelism as rhetorical devices. Packer acknowledges a proclivity for alliteration in the introduction to *Grounded in the Gospel*, where he uses the formulas "apt alliteration" and "artful alliteration."

Some of Packer's alliteration is subtle and subliminal. For example, in a list of ways in which we should think of the Bible (cited earlier in this chapter), the designations are separated by so much intervening material that it would be easy to miss the fact that they all begin with the same letter—library, landscape, letter, listening post, law, lamp, and lifeline.

More often, the alliteration is foregrounded, as in the following randomly collected examples:

- Headings from a chapter in *Grounded in the Gospel*: Christian Consensus; Evangelical Essentials; Denominational Distinctives; Congregational Commitments
- Truth 1: God is personal. Truth 2: God is plural. Truth 3: God is perfect. Truth 4: God is powerful. Truth 5: God is purposeful. Truth 6: God is promise-keeper. Truth 7: God is paternal. Truth 8: God is praiseworthy.
- "*The first point concerns the* dignity *and* dependence *of the individual.*" "*My second point concerns the* delight *and* development *of the individual.*" "*Third, I want to add to what I have already said about the* design *and* deformity *of the individual.*"

Alliteration fits with several of Packer's primary traits as a speaker and writer: it fixes the attention; it is a mnemonic device; and it is effective as an organizing strategy.

More frequent than alliteration is his use of what in the Bible is known as the verse form of parallelism—using the same grammatical format in successive statements. Here are examples of headings in chapters of various books:

- The inspiration of Scripture as the Word of God; The authority of Scripture as a rule of faith and life; Our dependence upon Scripture as a means of grace
- From a sermon on Samson: Flawed Sexuality; Flawed Humor; Flawed Anger
- Nehemiah's Flaws; Nehemiah's Strengths; Nehemiah's God; Nehemiah's Godliness
- The Call to Christian Unity; Dimensions of Christian Unity; Principles of Christian Unity

As a writer and speaker, Packer is a never-failing ally of the reader and listener. He wants to make the process of communication as easy as possible, and alliteration and parallelism help him do so.

Summary

In this chapter, I set for myself the task of exploring what J. I. Packer's style and rhetorical preferences tell us about the man. It is easy to summarize what we have seen. We have seen the mind of someone who loves order and good organization, especially when a mass of data that has been assembled needs to be made manageable for a reader or audience. We have seen someone who wants to be helpful to those who read or listen to him, and who therefore states ideas plainly, dispenses practical tips for what to do, uses analogies to make unfamiliar or difficult ideas plain, and composes easy-to-follow headings for the modules that make up an address or essay. He writes and speaks with the ordinary person in view, and he endears himself to that person by being a typical man. He is a logician, but there is an imaginative and literary side to him as well. He is paradoxically both a pessimist and optimist: things are bad, but solutions are always at hand.

Did Packer self-consciously cultivate the stylistic and rhetorical strategies that I have explored? I asked him that question, and he said yes. He followed that affirmation with the explanation, "One of the things I am is a communicator."

Part 3

LIFELONG THEMES

Biographies fall into two main paradigms, and I have combined them in this book. One is the chronological model, in which the life events of a person are traced in the order they happened. The focus is on what a person did, with attention to patterns of change and development. If the author is a historian, the impulse is to do so much contextualizing that the biography is partly swallowed up by the documentary history of the subject's era. Part one of this biography ("The Life") is a chronological account of the life events of J. I. Packer.

The other paradigm is the thematic model. This is what I follow in Part 3 of this book. Chronology per se is not a goal, except that in each case I show that the subject of a given chapter has been a central aspect of Packer's life at every point in his adulthood and scholarly career. The topics that comprise this section have been "constants" in Packer's life. In the chapters of this section, I provide a picture of how each sphere permeated Packer's life and of his contributions to each one.

This thematic biography has affinities to the middle section ("The Man"). It takes a heavy analytic hand to find "the man" in the maze of events that comprise Packer's life (Part 1 of this biography), but as I explore the unifying themes in his life, we will feel that we have been brought close to him.

17

The Bible

J. I. Packer had contact with the Bible from his early childhood. The sources of that contact were multiple and included home, school, and church. Of course, mere contact does not instill belief in the Bible as God's Word to people. Packer's childhood encounters with the Bible were a cultural rather than spiritual phenomenon; the Bible was simply part of the English cultural life at home, school, and church. As Packer neared the end of what in the United States is called the high school years, he found himself reading C. S. Lewis's newly released *Mere Christianity*. This, in turn, prompted him to read his grandmother's King James Version of the Bible. (When Packer's grandmother became infirm, she took up residence in the Packer home, and the King James Bible that Packer used was a spare copy.)

How Packer's Relation to the Bible Unfolded

Since it is hard to organize all that might be said about the Bible as a presence in Packer's life, I am grateful to be able to begin with his own survey of the steps through which he passed in regard to the Bible. On July 21, 2010, Packer delivered an autobiographical address at Clare College of Cambridge University. The occasion was an evening banquet during a weeklong meeting of the translation committee for the English Standard Version. The translation committee members and their spouses, selected members of the Crossway family, and invited British locals attended.

Packer entitled his address "One Pilgrim's Theological Progress and the ESV Bible." He was characteristically apologetic about speaking autobiographically, but he resigned himself to it with an awareness that his story is "not so much a story of what I have done with the Bible but of what the Bible has done with me over the years since Christ broke into my life in October 1944." Packer then narrated a four-chapter story with the following headings: "The Authenticity of the Bible"; "The Authority of the Bible"; "The Gospel in the Bible"; and "Teaching Bible Christianity to the Church." The rest of this unit of the chapter is a summary of what Packer presented in this address.

The Authenticity of the Bible

In telling the story of his evolving attitude toward the Bible, Packer began with the high school classmate with whom he played chess. This classmate, the son of the local Unitarian minister, attempted to convert Packer to Unitarianism. But that attempt produced a contrary effect, as Packer became increasingly critical of his friend for not believing more of the New Testament. If one denied the deity of Jesus, Packer wondered, why not deny the whole New Testament? Conversely, if one believed part of the New Testament, why not believe all of it? The broader context within which these early musings about the Bible occurred was one in which "evangelical testimony [in England] was at a very low ebb." There were "few people around who actually did believe that the Word of God is . . . true and trustworthy from first to last."

The breakthrough came six weeks after Packer's conversion during his first year in college. The occasion was a weekly Bible exposition sponsored by the Oxford Christian Union. Packer went to the meeting with the baggage of inherited skepticism about the Bible in his heart. Sixty-five years after the event, Packer could still recall his "feeling of surprise" as he came out of the meeting: "I realized I do believe that Scripture by its very nature is the Word of God and is true and is to be trusted." Upon reflection after many years, Packer believes that he experienced firsthand what John Calvin expounds in the first book of his *Institutes of the Christian Religion*, namely, that the Bible is self-attesting and does not depend on proofs and arguments.

The Authority of the Bible

In the mid-1950s, Billy Graham held evangelistic crusades in England that attracted media attention and liberal hostility. With the debate about evangelicals' alleged "fundamentalism" swirling in British religious circles, an Inter-Varsity group in London asked Packer to speak on the topic "Narrow Mind—or Narrow Way?" As always, Packer took the assignment seriously and spoke for an hour. The brief account of what followed (to be elaborated in a later chapter of this biography on Packer the writer) is that the address became a full-fledged and eventually famous book entitled *"Fundamentalism" and the Word of God.*

In his Clare College address, Packer summarized the effect of this book in his life: "Lo and behold, Packer was now a known author, and the authority of the Bible was the central theme on which people looked to him to expatiate." Later, Packer published additional books on biblical authority. He also became involved for ten years in an American "pressure group" (Packer's label) known as the International Council on Biblical Inerrancy, though Packer professes to prefer the label "truth and trustworthiness of the Bible" over the term *inerrancy*. "All these fifty years," Packer told the assembly in the Clare College dining hall, "I have had [the authority of the Bible] as one of the . . . arrows in my quiver."

The Gospel in the Bible

In his address, Packer gave an additional heading for section three of his story, namely, "Packer Seeking to Expound the Fullness of the Gospel of Jesus Christ." This is a way of saying that the Bible gave Packer the content for his teaching, writing, and speaking. The heart of that content is "the truth about the grace of God saving sinners" through the atoning work of Christ. Packer cited the notion of a Clare College "great" from the past, Charles Moule, that the word *gospel* is "a concertina word" in the New Testament, being regularly woven into the fabric of the argument.

Packer made the evocative statement that "right from the start I found myself unwilling to let any book [that I had authored] go which hasn't got the gospel in it somewhere." In his writings, Packer wrote about the gospel "in a way which surveyed the whole economy of grace and mercy, including those doctrines of grace that give offense to some people—doctrines like the sovereignty of God in calling people to faith."

J. I. Packer speaking on July 21, 2010, at Clare College of Cambridge University on the topic "One Pilgrim's Theological Progress and the ESV Bible." (Photo courtesy of Lane and Ebeth Dennis)

Among the books that Packer highlighted as falling into this genre of "books in which this larger perspective is presented" were *Evangelism and the Sovereignty of God*, *Knowing God* ("a discipling book"), *Keep in Step with the Spirit*, and *In My Place Condemned He Stood*.

Teaching Bible Christianity to the Church

Having written about the gospel in the Bible, Packer came to see himself as "teaching the truths that Christians live by and with that teaching Christians how to live by them." His concern has been that Christians today have "never been taught Christian doctrine in any ordered way." To the Clare College audience, Packer pictured his "last crusade" as attempting to fill the gap that exists in the knowledge base of professing Christians. The method that he now champions is the traditional one of catechesis—a question-and-answer format of packaging Christian doctrine for easy comprehension. The goal is to "get back to teaching doctrine in an ordered way."

Summary

The address to the Clare College audience was a rousing one delivered in a non-air conditioned room on an extremely hot evening. For our purposes, the address is useful for two reasons. First, it shows that Packer sees the Bible as a unifying presence in his life. Second, it imposes a chronological order on how the Bible has entered his life and ministry.

The Bible as the Ultimate Source for Packer's Religious Beliefs

The most continuous way in which the Bible has entered Packer's life is by providing the template on which he bases his beliefs and with which he propounds them in his writings. Of course, this is true for every Bible-believing Christian. On questions of what we should believe and how we should conduct ourselves, we need to know what the Bible says about given topics. I do not claim anything extraordinary for Packer on this point, but it is important that we celebrate how thoroughly he has been a Bible-believing person.

This is seen not only in the books and articles that he has written specifically on the nature and interpretation of the Bible, but also by the way in which the Bible enters Packer's discussions on virtually every subject on which he writes. I am grateful to Packer for recognizing the legitimacy of enlightened proof-texting—adducing verses from throughout the Bible that prove a generalization or doctrine. He continuously offers verses from the Bible as the basis for his assertions about the Christian life or doctrinal beliefs. In this regard, I was struck by Packer's statement in the foreword to his book *God's Words*, where he says that although the technical parts in the opening section dealing with semantic issues can be skipped, "Biblical references in the studies themselves are not . . . skippable; they are part of the argument, and are meant to be looked up."

I have arbitrarily chosen the following three specimens to illustrate the way in which the Bible forms a background chorus to many of the subjects on which Packer has written:

- "In the Old Testament the cry for revival springs from the sense of judgment (*see* Psalms 79:4–9; 80:12–14; 85:4–7; Habakkuk 3:2). . . . *Revival is God stirring the hearts of his people*, visiting them (Psalms 80:14; Jeremiah 29:10–14), coming to dwell with them (Zechariah 2:10–12), returning to them (Zechariah 1:3, 16), pouring out his Spirit on them (Joel 2:28; Acts 2:17–21)." *Keep in Step with the Spirit*, 256

- "The universalist's problem is to circumvent the seemingly solid New Testament witness to the fate of unbelievers, whom Paul declares to be under sin, law, wrath, and death (so says Romans 3:9, 19; 1:18; 5:17), alienated from God and without hope (so says Ephesians 2:12), and facing exclusion from God's presence for non-subjection to what they knew of his truth (Rom. 1:18—2:16)." "The Problem of Eternal Punishment"
- Often Packer quotes the Bible verses right in his text; likewise, in many of his essays and some of his books, the Bible references appear in footnotes or endnotes rather than in parentheses in the text. Thus, a specimen page in *Evangelism and the Sovereignty of God* to which I randomly opened contains four verses quoted from the Bible and four corresponding footnotes at the bottom of the page.

The procedure that I have just illustrated is so common in evangelical circles that its true importance can easily slip past us. The primary importance is that whenever a speaker, preacher, or writer expounds his or her content, *something* is the assumed authority for the ideas that are asserted. If no authority is cited, the implied basis on which the listener or reader is expected to agree is the speaker or writer himself. If written sources other than the Bible are quoted or cited, they become the implied basis for agreement. If the Bible is quoted or cited, the Bible becomes the basis of belief, buttressed by the commentary of the writer or speaker. On religious issues, Packer's listeners and readers encounter the Bible as the continuous and ultimate authority.

This effect is greatly enhanced by the extensiveness of Packer's references to the Bible, and at least two corollaries follow. First, when reading Packer, one quickly gets the impression that the biblical data is very extensive and even overwhelming, and certainly not flimsy. Second, one cannot help but notice how thoroughly Packer knows the Bible. Not being a user of search engines on the Internet, he has obviously relied partly on his own familiarity with the Bible (as did the Puritans).

Publications on the Bible

Before I provide an anatomy of the aspects of the Bible that have most preoccupied Packer, I want to take a global view of how the Bible has been a subject of his scholarly life from the start to the present day. This rehearsal can be taken to encompass his speaking life as well (for which, however, there is no record of addresses). The general pattern is that of a host of essays interspersed with whole books written on the Bible.

Packer's first book was on the subject of the authority and reliability of the Bible, published in 1958. This book made Packer a default authority, not only as a speaker on the subject but also as a writer. Thus, two articles on revelation appeared in 1958, and one on the Bible appeared in each of the next three years.

Packer's second book on the Bible was published in 1965. The British title was *God Has Spoken: Revelation and the Bible*, and the U.S. title was *God Speaks to Man: Revelation and the Bible*. In the wake of that book, there was another wave of essays (some published in magazines and some in edited anthologies): "Hermeneutics and Biblical Authority" (1967); "The Necessity of the Revealed Word" (1968); "The Inspiration and Infallibility of Holy Scripture" (1969); and "Biblical Authority, Hermeneutics, and Inerrancy" (1971).

His next book on the Bible appeared in 1980 and bore the title *Beyond the Battle for the Bible*. This book came near the end of a decade in which Packer served as a leader of the International Council on Biblical Inerrancy. With this book, his focus shifted from the nature and defense of the Bible to its use in the lives of Christians. By this time, it was predictable that Packer would be asked to contribute articles and essays on the Bible after the appearance of a book on the Bible. At least one essay per year appeared from 1982 to 1988.

After that, essays continued to appear from time to time, and these eventually were collected into two books that are among my most treasured titles by Packer. In 1996, Packer polished six previously published major essays to form the book *Truth and Power: The Place of Scripture in the Christian Life*. The final chapter, subtitled "Christians and Their Bibles," is one of Packer's greatest essays (and will be further explored later in this chapter). Three years later, Packer's friends at Paternoster Press did both him and the Christian world a great service by publishing forty years of essays on the Bible under the title *Honouring the Written Word of God* (volume 3 of *The Collected Shorter Writings of J. I. Packer*, reprinted in the United States in 2012 by Hendrickson under the title *Engaging the Written Word of God*).

Another aspect of Packer's career in making the Bible understandable to the Christian public is his work as an editor of Bible materials. In recent years, Packer has been the theological editor for all of Crossway's study Bible versions of the ESV. In that capacity, he has read all of the material (known to scholars as "the critical apparatus") that appears in these Bibles. Additionally, starting in 1993, Packer served as an editor for the Crossway Classic Commentaries series. Not only did he edit the content of the commentaries, but he wrote the introductions to all but two of the volumes. Packer has also been the theological editor for Crossway's more recent Knowing the Bible series of twelve-week studies on biblical books, a position that again involves reading an entire volume and making editorial suggestions. This is part of the behind-the-scenes contribution that Packer has made in many contexts throughout his career, in this case in connection to the Bible.

The foregoing survey shows the degree to which the Bible has been a unifying passion in Packer's scholarly life. In addition to what his publishing history tells us in this regard, we can mention that through the years he has led small-group Bible studies in his home. Many of his conference addresses have been Bible studies. And when he is free to choose his sermon topic, he gravitates toward exposition of a passage from the Bible. It can truly be said of him that he is a Bible man. In this regard, I will also note that hardly any of the courses that Packer has taught through the years have been directly about the Bible. His passion for the Bible in his writing and speaking is part of his concern for the Christian life of believers and not part of his teaching load.

Defending the Bible

"Fundamentalism" and the Word of God covers a much broader swath than its defense of the Bible, but that is what it is best known for and what is relevant to this chapter. The heart of the book is two chapters entitled "Authority" and "Scripture." Packer begins his analysis of authority by noting that there are three possible authorities on which Christians can base their beliefs—the Bible, church tradition, and reason. He then labels these with the adjectives *evangelical*, *traditionalist*, and *subjectivist*. These three, in turn, are identified respectively with confessional Protestants, Roman Catholic/Anglo-Catholic/Orthodox, and modern liberal Protestants. I found this framework very helpful as a college student.

Having provided his threefold grid, Packer proceeds to ask, "Which of these three is the authentic Christian position?" At this point, the argument becomes governed by a strict logic. The New Testament authors regarded the Old and New Testaments as organically one, and regarded the Old Testament as God's authoritative Word. By logic, then, Christians should accept the truthfulness of the Old and New Testaments. How did Christ regard the Old Testament? It was the authority to which he submitted himself and taught others to submit. How did the apostles who wrote the New Testament regard the Old Testament? They accepted its authority. What was the attitude of the early church? It accepted both the Old Testament and the New Testament jointly as a unique authority. The practical conclusion: "the Church must seek, first, to expound Scripture and, second, to reform its belief and practice . . . by the biblical teaching. This is the theological method which Christ commands His Church to follow: to use Scripture as the rule of faith and life."

Taking a further step of logic, Packer proceeds to formulate a position on the authoritative nature of the Bible. His procedure is "to appeal to Scripture for information about itself." The chapter entitled "Scripture" does just that, and Packer takes up three topics in regard to it—the divine origin of the Bible, its nature as the Word of God, and its interpretation. The divine origin of Scripture is synonymous with its inspiration, defined as "a supernatural, providential influence of God's Holy Spirit upon the human authors which caused them to write what He wished to be written for the communication of revealed truth to others." As he elaborates this point, Packer undertakes a continuous refutation of the liberal position as contrasted to the evangelical position. Under the second main subject, the nature of Scripture, Packer discusses the unity of the Bible, its status as the Word of God and a repository of propositional truth, and its infallibility and inerrancy. The argument is copiously buttressed by quotations from the Bible and evangelical scholars, and in my first reading of the book, I found this extremely useful (in fact, it resolved the question of biblical authority for me once and for all). The section of the chapter on Scripture devoted to interpretation is less polemical, but it, too, asserts foundational evangelical principles—literal interpretation, interpreting Scripture by Scripture, the need to avoid allowing science to undermine the authority of the Bible, and the Holy Spirit as a guide to interpreting the Bible.

Further chapters in Packer's landmark book discuss the role of faith and reason in appropriating the Bible. My copiously underlined copy shows how helpful I found these chapters as a college student in thinking about the Christian life, though they move beyond the apologetic defense of the Bible for which the book is best known. Anyone who reads this book with an awareness of Packer's later books on the Bible will see on virtually every page that the later emphases exist in kernel form in this groundbreaking book.

If we look at Packer's total corpus of writing on the Bible, we can see that he has never abandoned his role of defending biblical authority and reliability (though in more recent years the emphasis has been kept alive in books of reprinted essays from earlier in his career). In 1965, Packer published his second book on the Bible, *God Has Spoken* (reprinted in expanded form in 1979). The aim of the book was to "prepare the minds of thinking Christian people to read and study their Bible as Christians should." The centrality of the Bible is not simply taken for granted, however; the apologetic element is interwoven throughout the book.

As with Packer's first book on the Bible, this one establishes the role of modern liberal criticism of the Bible in making evangelicals "unsure, tentative and confused" in regard to the Bible. Liberalism, claims Packer early in the book, "destroys the reverent, receptive, self-distrusting attitude of approach to the Bible." What Packer labels "new views of revelation and inspiration" have resulted, he says, in a diminishment of confidence in the Bible. Within such a context, restoring the authority of the Bible needs to precede anything that we might wish to say about how to read and apply it.

Packer's chosen approach in the early part of this book is to foreground what the historic creeds of the Anglican Church have said about biblical authority: "I shall quote most fully from the Thirty-Nine Articles, Homilies and Book of Common Prayer of the Church of England." We might note in passing that this book was written while Packer was warden of Latimer House, an Anglican clearinghouse. We find sections on the inspiration of Scripture, its authority as a rule of faith and life, and our dependence on it as a means of grace. Later chapters echo the themes of *"Fundamentalism" and the Word of God*—the Bible's claim to be the Word of God, the New Testament writers' acceptance of the authority of the Old Testament, the interpretation of Scripture, and the inerrancy of Scripture.

Inasmuch as Packer invested much of his time over the course of a decade to advance the work of the International Council on Biblical Inerrancy, it is appropriate to note a publication that Packer authored at the end of this time: a thirty-two-page booklet entitled *Freedom and Authority* (1981). Half of the book discusses the issue of authority, showing once again Packer's approach to defending the Bible. My heart soars when I read: "Built into Christianity is a principle of authority. This is because Christianity is revealed religion." Much fell into place for me when, as a college freshman, I read in my Western civilization textbook that Christianity falls into the category of revealed religions (religions that base their beliefs on a text regarded as sacred revelation).

Having discussed the nature of the Bible by placing it into the category of authority, and having defended the idea of authority against modern views of freedom, Packer turns in the last chapter of the booklet to the question of "authority and inerrancy." Brief as the discussion of inerrancy is, it is nuanced. Packer endorses the word *inerrancy*, even though he once disliked it, because it is the only word that makes the claim for the complete truthfulness of everything in the Bible. People who use the words *inspired*, *infallible*, and *authoritative*, writes Packer, eventually show that they believe that the Bible contains errors. Using the word *inerrancy* "is a clarifying thing to do." But Packer sounds two cautions. First, believing in the Bible's inerrancy does not remove the task of exegesis (determining meaning). Second, we are obligated to base our theology on what the Bible says ("however little I may like it") and to "seek actively to live by it (whatever change of present beliefs and behavior-patterns it may require)."

Many of Packer's greatest contributions have grown out of his service on committees that produced important documents. The Chicago Statement on Biblical Inerrancy (1978) is one of those contributions. Packer was a member of the draft committee that formulated the final statement. I remember when it appeared and how impressed I was by its clarity and thoroughness. Despite the fact that the Chicago Statement is a collaborative rather than individual document, it is, from one point of view, the climax of Packer's lifelong career as a spokesman for the authority and inerrancy of the Bible. That Packer "owns" the statement is evident from the way in which the Chicago Statement and surrounding documents appear as an appendix in revised editions of *God Has Spoken*.

It is clear that defending the Bible against modern liberal views was a passion that was sparked early in Packer's scholarly career. This early concentration on the defense of the Bible was then perpetuated partly by books on the Bible and partly by two anthologies that reprinted most of Packer's essays on this subject. If we were to name the top five subjects for which Packer is known, his apologetic for the Bible would be one of those five.

Restoring the Bible to Daily Living

Another leading aspect of Packer's career as a spokesman for the Bible is his unflagging effort to promote the reading and study of the Bible and its application to daily living. "The Bible for the church" would be an accurate heading here, on the understanding that "the church" means the totality of individual Christians. Alternatively, the subtitle of a 1996 Packer book expresses the principle well: *The Place of Scripture in the Christian Life*. Packer has repeatedly articulated the conviction that having the right view of the Bible's authority and reliability is useless if we do not read the Bible and apply it to our lives. He has written on this subject throughout his life.

A good starting point for grasping Packer's passion for restoring the Bible to a position of centrality in Christians' lives is his book *Beyond the Battle for the Bible* (1980). The title itself hints at the argument of the book. It means that winning the battle for inerrancy will achieve little if we do not move beyond the apologetic level.

However, even this book does not abandon the idea that the battle needs to be waged and won. The second chapter is entitled "Inerrancy in Current Debate," and it begins with this statement: "Let no one tell you . . . that the inerrancy debate today is unimportant, a trivial domestic squabble among those quarrelsome evangelicals of the U.S.A. On the contrary, you should see the inerrancy debate as the latest chapter in a great controversy about the Bible which has been going on continuously in the church for the best part of the last 500 years."

Nonetheless, the bulk of the book explores the need to build upon the gains of accepting the inerrancy of the Bible. The opening chapter, entitled "Give Me Understanding," grew out of a chapel address delivered at Wheaton College. To begin with, the need for understanding the Bible reflects Packer's intellectual bent and his Puritan inclination. The Bible cannot be the influence that it needs to be unless Christians understand it with their minds. Four main points emerge: (1) we will not seek to understand the Bible unless we accept its authority; (2) we will understand it only insofar as we interpret it correctly; (3) understanding the Bible means receiving its teaching; and (4) God gives this understanding by his Holy Spirit and by the input of the Christian community and its traditions.

The heart of the matter is then explored in a middle chapter entitled "The Use of Holy Scripture in Public and Private." A historical precedent for what Packer and co-author R. J. Coates envision is provided by the Protestant Reformation, which elevated the Bible to a position of supremacy in the church and individuals' lives. That model, in turn, was preceded by the submission of Jesus and other people in Bible times to Scripture ("Paul's exhortations to Timothy in the Pastoral Epistles suggest to us a picture of the early church as a Bible-loving community"). While this begins at a personal level, the Bible also needs to be read in church services and preached from by ministers. The chapter then proceeds to give detailed attention to the use of the Bible in ministerial work, family life, and devotional life.

Beyond the Battle for the Bible is offered here as a specimen only. Packer's campaign to get Christians on board with his vision of allowing the Bible to pervade all of life has been a lifelong passion. For instance, *Taking God Seriously*, published in 2013, is not a book on the Bible, but the lifelong Packer themes about the Bible are interspersed throughout its pages. Those themes, each accompanied by a summary statement, are as follows:

- The authority of the Bible: "God's authority in and through the revealed truth of the Bible must ever control and shape our belief and behavior."
- The Bible has fallen into great neglect among Christians: "Once, most Westerners knew something of what was in the 'Good Book' to guide us in our lives; nowadays, however, very few know or care what the Bible teaches."

- This is not a minor matter but a major one: "Ignorance of the Bible remains tragic, for it virtually guarantees ignorance of God."
- Restoring the Bible to the center of life is urgent: "To reestablish in people's minds the truth and wisdom of the biblical message . . . is perhaps the church's most urgent task today."

These ideas can be traced backward through Packer's writings over his lifetime.

As already hinted, the context of Packer's prophetic call for Christians to return to the Bible is his observation that most Christians give lip service to the Bible rather than genuinely engaging with it. Virtually every essay that Packer has written on the Bible sounds this note of alarm, which is perhaps stated most explicitly and at greatest length in *God Has Spoken*. The point of departure is Amos's haunting prediction that God "will send a famine on the land—not a famine of bread, nor a thirst for water, but of hearing the words of the LORD" (Amos 8:11). Packer concludes that Amos's "vision of spiritual starvation in Israel pictures ours." The legacy of liberal undermining of confidence in the Bible has led to "the enfeebling of the churches" in five specific areas—lack of biblical preaching, absence of Bible teaching, weakened faith, an absence of lay Bible reading, and hiding Christ from view.

This, then, is a second constant in Packer's lifelong involvement with the Bible—the theme that the eclipse of the Bible from its once-dominant position in the Christian church has been disastrous. The Bible needs to be restored to Christians' daily lives.

How to Interpret the Bible

Packer would not be regarded as a specialist in hermeneutics, but as more of a layman in the field. However, I believe that he is more effective in teaching people how to interpret the Bible *because* he does not write as an expert. I need at once to qualify what I have just said: I can think of numerous points in Packer's writings where, for a moment, he shows that he is thoroughly conversant with current trends in hermeneutics and the technicalities of liberal and evangelical hermeneutics. But his major ministry to the Christian public has been to translate principles of interpretation into helpful tips for reading and analyzing the Bible—something experts on hermeneutics do not always do well.

The starting point for Packer's preoccupation with hermeneutics (not always labeled as such in his writings) is a foundational principle that is often overlooked. Experts in hermeneutics usually turn it into an objective study—the science of interpretation. But in Packer's handling, it is fired by a sense of urgency. Early in his book *Beyond the Battle for the Bible*, he writes: "Scripture can only rule us so far as it is understood, and it is only understood so far as it is properly interpreted. A misinterpreted Bible is a misunderstood Bible, which will lead us out of God's way rather than in it."

Some of Packer's writing on interpreting the Bible takes up broad principles of interpretation. In an essay entitled "Understanding the Bible: Evangelical Hermeneutics," Packer explores four principles that coincide with traditional evangelical categories and that I consider to be more presuppositional than methodological: (1) we must interpret a biblical text in keeping with the author's intention; (2) we must assume the coherence, harmony, and veracity of the Bible; (3) we must interpret individual parts of the Bible by placing them into the context of the entire biblical canon; and (4) we must respond to a biblical text with an increase of our faith (mere knowledge is not the goal of biblical interpretation).

Packer is the ordinary reader's friend, and the entry on "interpretation" in his *Concise Theology* illustrates this. Packer gives a number of rules for interpreting the Bible, each of which expresses a time-honored principle of evangelical hermeneutics, though he avoids the technical name for each principle. The list is as follows (and I have supplied the technical terminology in parenthesis): (1) we must take the human authors of the Bible into account and respect their human intentions (authorial intention); (2) we must not allegorize a text contrary to what the author intended (the literal interpretation of Scripture); (3) the Bible is not a code, but a book that everyone can understand in its main ideas (the perspicuity of Scripture); (4) every passage in the Bible is embedded in a specific historical context (the need to contextualize historically); (5) individual parts of the Bible must be interpreted in light of other parts ("the analogy of Scripture," which Packer the Puritan not unexpectedly names); (6) we must acknowledge that the unchanging truth of the Bible is embedded in historical particulars that we need to reapply to our own situations (the Bible's universal relevance); and (7) no meaning can be read into a biblical text, but must be read out of it (the need for exegesis and an inductive approach to the text).

Even further down the continuum of what I call "concealed hermeneutics" in Packer's writings is an essay that appears in his 1996 book *Truth and Power: The Place of Scripture in the Christian Life*. The concluding essay in the book is entitled "Life and Health and Peace: Christians and Their Bibles." Part of the essay develops a series of ways in which we should view the Bible. Many people would not consider these images of the Bible to be a discussion of hermeneutics at all, but if we pursue the implications of each image to their logical conclusions, we will have an excellent blueprint for reading the Bible correctly. Here is how Packer proposes that we view the Bible:

- The Bible is a library of separate books.
- The Bible is a landscape, that is, "a panorama of human life."
- The Bible is a letter addressed by God to every reader personally.
- The Bible is a listening post where we can hear the voice of God.
- The Bible is a law from God—"his map of the ideal life."
- The Bible is a light for our path.
- The Bible is a lifeline thrown out to drowning people.

Of course, these images need to be unpacked in certain directions before they yield tips for interpreting the Bible, and Packer does so. In the process, he overcomes a common tendency of specialists in hermeneutics to become excessively abstract and technical, and to speak a code language.

Bible Translation: Packer's "Most Significant" Achievement

Packer's lifelong involvement with the Bible has led him to be an apologist for the Bible, a prophet calling Christians to put the Bible at the center of their daily lives, and an interpreter of the Bible. A final chapter in the story of his life with the Bible emerged in the latter stages of his career, and it could not have been foreseen. Packer has not only been a member of the translation committee for the English Standard Version of the Bible, he has been the general editor of the translation and a leading spokesman for it. The external facts of that story were told in my earlier chapter on Packer's career at Regent College. Here I will explore how Packer has shaped and promoted the principles of the ESV behind the scenes.

As a backdrop, I will note that until the ESV project began to unfold, it would have been impossible to predict that Packer would become a champion of the principles that I am about to discuss. In his book *God Has Spoken*, Packer wrote a brief unit on "a variety of versions." He described the entire range of translation philosophies and resulting translations without endorsing any one of them. In fact, he declared that "all the main modern renderings are very good." Packer's final recommendation was a characteristically ambitious one: "I suggest that you try . . . to get the best of all worlds by having four Bibles at hand—the King James, with its majestic language and hallowed associations; a paraphrase; a word-for-word version; and one from the middle—and regularly comparing them."

Then, in 1997, just one year before the English Standard Version project was set into motion, Packer published a column in *Christianity Today* that similarly endorsed all translations and translation philosophies. The title of the piece was "Thank God for Our Bibles," and the summary statement under the title was, "While Scripture comes in many flavors today, we can still trust these translations to give us God's Word." In the article, Packer asked, "Do we need so many translations?" His answer: "Probably, yes, for our world is split into many subcultures." He even endorsed the idea of niche Bibles. As I sometimes say about my own changes of mind and growth in understanding, "That was then and now is now."

In view of Packer's eventual advocacy of an essentially literal translation philosophy (which was used for the ESV), I was initially surprised to find his noncommittal attitude in the sources that I quoted in the preceding paragraphs. But when I looked more closely at the "fine print" of those passages, I could see the seeds of Packer's eventual position on Bible translation. In *God Has Spoken*, for example, Packer notes that paraphrases conceal "the terms, and therefore the existence, of many problems of interpretation, and identify with one current literary culture." In the *Christianity Today* article, Packer writes that "under-translation, in pursuit of an easy English flow, can be more of a problem than is sometimes realized." Again, "Paraphrasing out such semitechnical New Testament terms as *propitiation*, *justification*, *redemption*, *reconciliation*, and *righteousness* keeps readers from realizing that these were among the apostolic teachers' keywords." Additionally, "The rule should surely be: where there is doubt or dispute about the significance of the data, render literally so that readers have access to the wording of the original and so can engage with the problem directly." These latter viewpoints eventually came to tip the scale in the direction of essentially literal translation.

In Packer's Clare College address, cited at the beginning of this chapter, he concluded his narrative of involvement with the Bible by talking about his work on the English Standard Version. He recalled that when he was asked whether he was interested in working with a committee to produce a new translation based on the Revised Standard Version, his "answer was to say yes and yes and yes. I could think of nothing more significant for me to do than share in the work of . . . trying to produce an all-purposes Bible version that would have in our time and perhaps for a century and more, the same all-purposes ministry, the same all-uses fitness that the King James Version had in England for three hundred years." Packer immediately followed that statement with the verdict that other modern translations, even though hailed initially "with great expectations," have all turned out to be niche versions instead of translations for "the whole community."

I have said that some of Packer's published pieces have been collaborative essays produced by committees. These publications are no less Packer's simply because he is not the sole author. I believe that the preface to the ESV, which is a collaborative piece, is a masterpiece. Its primary authors were Packer and Crossway President Lane Dennis, supplemented by minor input from the ESV translation committee. We can distill the contents into a series of principles, as follows:

- continuity with the classic mainstream of English Bible translation (also called "the Tyndale–King James legacy")
- preservation of the full range of meanings that are present in the original text
- faithfulness to the words used by the biblical authors, also known as verbal equivalence (refusal to abandon what the writers wrote and substitute other words in its place)
- concordance—using the same English words in the translation when biblical authors likewise used recurrent words
- preservation of the stylistic variety of the biblical writers instead of flattening their utterances to match the uniform style slanted to a target audience

- transparency to the original text (a particular emphasis of Packer)—removing all obstacles to our seeing what the biblical authors actually wrote
- simplicity, beauty, and dignity of style
- preservation of gender language where required by the principle of faithfulness to the text, and use of gender-neutral language where that was the clear intention of the biblical authors
- use of the best available scholarly lexical resources, and use of the Masoretic (Hebrew) text for the Old Testament

Packer helped to formulate these principles of the ESV, and after its publication, he was an ardent advocate for them.

How does Packer rate the success of the English Standard Version? Very high indeed. In his Clare College address, he said the following:

> It's a Bible that seeks to be both literal and, indeed, transparent, a Bible which seeks to be both lucid and easy to follow. . . . The English Standard Version really is the all-uses version, the all-purposes Bible that our day needs. I believe that it's good for personal reading, it's good for personal study, it's good for public reading . . . , it's good and easy for memorizing.

If that is Packer's assessment of the ESV, how does he view the time and effort that he invested in helping to produce it? He also answered that question in his Clare College address, and it is a very striking statement:

> As I think of the way that God has led me over the sixty-six years of my Christian life, as I thank him for the books I've been able to write and the truth that I've been able to spread during those years, I find myself concluding that the most significant thing that I've been enabled to do . . . has been to serve in the production of the English Standard Version, a reality so much more important for the church than any of the books of Packer.

In an individualistic age, it is refreshing to see an example of the old ideal of communal scholarship.

Summary

This chapter has given the main outline of J. I. Packer's lifelong preoccupation with the Bible in his public life. He has written more than a hundred essays on the Bible, as well as half a dozen books. But that is only the tip of the iceberg. References to the Bible are copious in Packer's writings on multiple subjects. He has taught us how to read and study the Bible, and he has given us a rationale for doing so. He has also been a behind-the-scenes participant in numerous influential movements and publications related to the Bible. Surely there is a logic to Packer's conclusion that to see Christians using the English Standard Version is the culmination of his lifelong encouragement for Christians to make the Bible a reality in their lives.

18

The Puritans

The Puritans of the sixteenth and seventeenth centuries have been a presence throughout the adult life of J. I. Packer. He is a Puritan scholar, and in the academic world, this is one of the things for which he is most famous. We can see this expertise in the frequency with which Packer has been asked to contribute essays for anthologies or journal issues devoted to the Puritans. I will say in passing that I composed this chapter of the biography with special feelings of affinity for my subject because I am also a Puritan specialist of sorts, with my interest in the Puritans growing out of my specialization in John Milton. Packer wrote his doctoral dissertation on a Puritan theologian, Richard Baxter, and the subject of one's dissertation holds a very special place for anyone with a doctorate.

But the Puritans have been much more than an area of professional specialization for Packer. They never would have become an academic specialty for him if they had not first assumed an existential immediacy in his life, serving as his guide and inspiration. The Puritans actually led Packer out of a spiritual wilderness in which he found himself during his second year of college, several months after his conversion. So the Puritans not only gave him a dissertation topic; they also gave him his theological and spiritual bearings when he was wandering. As an epigraph for this chapter, I offer the title of a biographical article that Mark Noll wrote on Packer entitled "The Last Puritan."

The Persistence of the Puritan Presence in Packer's Life

Packer's first foray into the Puritans was an indirect one. During Christmas vacation following his first term at Oxford University, he found himself reading a two-volume biography of George Whitefield that he had checked out of the Gloucester city library. Strictly speaking, Whitefield lived too late (1714–1770) to be a Puritan, but his values, worldview, and lifestyle were such that he was what I call a belated Puritan. An early nineteenth-century reprint of Whitefield's sermons was entitled *The Revived Puritan*. Later in life, Packer called his reading about Whitefield during that vacation a milestone in his spiritual journey. An added note of providence in the story is that Packer came down with a bad case of bronchitis and was confined to bed, where he spent a more-than-ordinary amount of time reading about Whitefield. Perhaps it was the most productive case of bronchitis in history!

Packer's first encounter with an actual Puritan occurred during his second year in college. That Puritan was John Owen, whose influence in Packer's life will be traced in more detail below. The brief story is that Owen's writing on sanctification seized the sovereignty of Packer's mind as an alternative to the Keswick philosophy that was rampant among British evangelicals in general and students in particular.

Once the Puritan seed had been planted, it kept growing. Packer's first three published articles (1952–53) were on Puritan subjects. His doctoral dissertation, completed in 1954, was on Baxter's view of salvation. And then there was the annual Puritan Conference, for which Packer prepared and delivered at least one address per year from 1950 through 1969. These addresses, in turn, were eventually published in one place or another.

When the Puritan Conference was terminated, Packer's publishing on the Puritans became more sporadic, but it did not end. Whenever a speaking or publishing occasion came along that called for a Puritan talk or paper, Packer gladly obliged. Nearly twenty such publishing occasions happened (sometimes in the form of introductions to reprints of Puritan classics). Many of the "fugitive pieces" (as Packer calls them) on the Puritans found their way into his book entitled *A Quest for Godliness: The Puritan Vision of the Christian Life* (Crossway, 1990). Packer's zest for the Puritans has persisted right to the present day, as evidenced by a 2012 book entitled *Puritan Portraits: J. I. Packer on Selected Classic Pastors and Pastoral Classics* (Christian Focus).

It is obvious that the Puritans have been a life obsession for Packer. The origin of that passion is a story of providence that is as exciting as a detective tale (which, in a sense, it is). But Packer's interest in the Puritans has also been a never-failing fountain of delight for him—not only an adventure story, but also a story of friendship.

The Explosion That Started the Lifelong Passion

The starting point was a man with the imposing name of C. Owen Pickard-Cambridge. He had been a student at Oxford University and had become an Anglican clergyman. The same would be true of Packer, but there are more interconnections than that. Pickard-Cambridge had served a stint as vice principal of the Bible Churchmen's Missionary and Training College in Bristol, forerunner of Tyndale Hall, where Packer later taught and served a brief term as principal. Yet another point of similarity is that Pickard-Cambridge, like Packer, was a bookish man with a special interest in religious books from the sixteenth and seventeenth centuries.

When Pickard-Cambridge reached his eighties, a combination of age and diminished eyesight required him to dispose of a library that was no longer of use to him. He boldly decided to donate the library as a collection instead of doling out individual books to interested people. But in an even more striking stroke of providence, he did not give his library to an institution, but to the Oxford student organization known as the Christian Union. This occurred, moreover, in 1944, the year that Packer entered Oxford University, was converted, and became active in the Christian Union.

The foregoing story is only the beginning of wonders. The Christian Union had been given the use of a building on St. Michael's Street in central Oxford as its base of operation. The building, which was of Methodist origin, was called North Gate Hall. The books of the donated library were deposited (Alister McGrath says "piled up"!) in the basement of this building. We might note a certain irony in the fact that North Gate Hall was across the street from the Oxford Union, the famous "Oxford debating society." The Christian Union had a position of senior librarian, and in 1944 that position was filled by a local curate,

John Reynolds of St. Clement's Church. Having observed Packer's interest in old books, Reynolds relieved himself of a burden by designating Packer as junior librarian for the Christian Union during Packer's second year at Oxford. He was a mere nineteen years old.

Packer set about to organize the books (which McGrath describes as "dusty piles . . . in the basement of the North Gate Hall"). If this magical moment had been videotaped for us to watch today, the tension would be nearly unbearable as Packer came upon a twenty-four-volume set of Owen's writings. This collection was a mid-nineteenth century publication edited by W. H. Goold. It is hard to believe but nonetheless true that the pages of the books had never been cut open.

Packer proceeded to explore his treasure trove. The individual treatises printed in each volume were named on the books' spines. As Packer's eyes ran down the spines, two treatises in volume 6 caught his attention—*On Indwelling Sin in Believers* and *On the Mortification of Sin in Believers*. So Packer cut the pages open and began to read.

The personal context in which this drama unfolded was Packer's spiritual struggles with the Keswick view of sanctification. Four decades later, in an introduction to a volume of excerpts of Owen's writings on sin and holiness, Packer described the Keswick philosophy as one that divided Christians into two classes, one "spiritual" and the other "carnal." Keswick taught that through self-denial, consecration, and faith, "spiritual" Christians would find themselves so filled with the Spirit that Christ would banish sin from their lives without any major exertion on their part.

The Puritan idea of "mortifying" sin in one's life by actively resisting it in the strength of Christ was an alternative to the Keswick philosophy. Packer found this alternative true to his own experience, whereas the Keswick motto, "Let go and let God," was, for Packer, "an unreality, a will-o'-the-wisp which no one has ever laid hold of at all." Owen taught Packer to acknowledge rather than conceal that he was a sinner, and also the need to "say no to sin's suggestions and to fortify [oneself] against bad habits by forming good ones contrary to them." The title of an appendix to Packer's book *Keep in Step with the Spirit* is evocative in this regard: "The 'Wretched Man' in Romans 7." When Packer writes about the events that I have just narrated, the concept of Puritan realism is a key concept, as in his statements that "Owen did more than anyone else to make me . . . a moral, spiritual, and theological realist," and that "John Owen helped me to be realistic."

It is impossible to overstate the importance of Packer's reading of volume 6 of the collected works of Owen in his second year at Oxford University. The encounter was a "tipping point" in his life. When he picked up the life-changing book in North Gate Hall, he was a recent convert "trying to make up for lost time" in the Christian life. His emotional life (by his own testimony) "was all over the place," and he was "essentially a mixed-up kid." Without Owen, Packer writes in the introduction to *A Quest for Godliness*, "I might well have gone off my head or got bogged down in mystical fanaticism." Elsewhere, Packer writes that "God used [Owen] to save my sanity." The Puritan doctrine of mortification of sin, another term for sanctification, gripped Packer's mind so thoroughly that the very next year he typed up a twenty-page summary of Owen's arguments and circulated it among his friends! Packer's lifelong passion for the Puritans thus has an existential urgency about it.

Packer's discovery of the Puritans is a story of providence and grace, one that he has retold in many publications throughout his life. No one but God could have orchestrated it. Packer himself has written that "my gracious God sorted me out" with the discovery of Owen. I love McGrath's observation that "Packer could not have made this discovery by browsing in his local bookstore." Among the reasons why this is true is that Puritan books were not in print and were only rarely available secondhand at the time when Packer found Owen's complete works in North Gate Hall in 1945. It was partly Packer's influence that eventually made them readily available (initially through the publishing program of the Banner of Truth Trust, founded in 1957).

Packer's Puritan Publications and Addresses

The twenty-page summary of Owen's views on sanctification that Packer wrote for his college friends was his first Puritan composition. In 1952 and 1953, as Packer was in his final year of seminary and first year of parish ministry, he was thrilled to publish his first three articles, all on Puritan subjects: "The Puritan Treatment of Justification by Faith" (*Evangelical Quarterly*), "Sanctification—Puritan Teaching" (*The Christian Graduate*), and "Great Pastors: Richard Baxter" (*Theology*).

Of course, publication is not the only way to gain a hearing and disseminate ideas. Some scholars manage to become well known and communicate their ideas by means of public lectures. Packer has made his reputation partly through being an indefatigable speaker right from the beginning of his scholarly career. In the first two decades of that career, an important venue for Packer's Puritan scholarship was the Puritan Conference, held at Westminster Chapel in London beginning in 1950.

Packer had been one of two people who conceptualized what became the Puritan Conference. He spoke at three sessions at the first conference, though none of these addresses was published at the time. From 1951 through 1969, Packer helped to organize the annual conference and delivered one address each year. It would be wrong to underestimate the importance of these addresses simply because they were not published until 2000. Just as in the Renaissance the recovery of classical texts held the key to the revival of learning, so in the 1950s and 1960s the recovery of the Puritans provided the vitality for a certain segment of British evangelicalism. This vitality reached to both nonconformist (or free church) and Anglican ministers who attended the annual Puritan Conference. In recent years, we have witnessed a parallel phenomenon in the United States with a movement known as the new Calvinism. In March 2009, the cover story of *Time* magazine was devoted to "10 Ideas Changing the World Right Now," and the new Calvinism was one of the ten.

I know of no scholar who has been more successful than Packer in having his addresses and articles eventually published in book form. All of Packer's addresses at the Puritan Conference from 1956 through 1967 have appeared in a four-volume set that bears the main title *Puritan Papers* (published by P&R Publishing, 2000–2004). The abstracts of addresses from the earlier years are in print today from Reformation Heritage Books.

As noted above, following the demise of the Puritan Conference in 1970, Packer's writings on the Puritans became more sporadic, but the Puritans did not cease to be an important part of his publishing and speaking life. One aspect of Packer as a Puritan writer—and one tribute to his towering stature as a Puritan expert—is the way in which he became the "default author" on the Puritans for compilers of reference books. For example, Packer was tapped to write on "Puritan Ethics" for *Baker's Dictionary of Christian Ethics* (1973), "Theology of the Reformation" for the *Lion Handbook of Church History* (1977), and "The Puritans" for *Eerdman's Handbook of Christian Belief* (1982). Equally indicative of Packer's status as a Puritan scholar is the regularity with which he was asked to write forewords and prefaces to reprints of Puritan classics—to Baxter's *A Christian Directory*, to Thomas Boston's *The Art of Man-Fishing*, and more.

Another sign that a person is an expert in a field is frequent requests to contribute essays on subjects in his expertise for anthologies. Again, Packer shows himself to be a major Puritan scholar: "Richard Baxter on Heaven, Hope and Holiness," in *Alive to God: Studies in Spirituality Presented to James Houston*; "The Glory of God and the Reviving of Religion: The Mind of Jonathan Edwards," in *A God-Entranced Vision of All Things*; "*Pilgrim's Progress* by John Bunyan," in *The Devoted Life*; and "A Puritan Perspective: Trinitarian Godliness according to John Owen," in *God and the Holy Trinity*.

Additionally, Packer has published two books of his own on the Puritans (not counting his dissertation on Baxter, which was published as a book in 2003). The major book is *A Quest for Godliness: The Puritan Vision of the Christian Life* (Crossway, 1990). At the end of the introduction to this book, Packer lists its "sources"—the places where much of the material was previously published. But this obscures an important fact, namely, that Packer massaged the material and wove it into a unity for purposes of the book—a wonderful unity, it should be noted, as an autobiographical introduction explores what the Puritans taught Packer, and a reflective afterword provides a retrospective overview of the emphases that constitute the heart of Puritanism. *A Quest for Godliness* is a major scholarly treatment of the Puritans that covers the territory with admirable scope. There are twenty-three pages of notes that document the sources of Packer's quotations, showing the scholarly rigor that underlies the book.

Packer's second book on the Puritans is entitled *Puritan Portraits* (2012), and it epitomizes much of what I have said about Packer's career as a Puritan scholar. This book brings together previously published introductions that Packer wrote on specific Puritan classics and their authors for a series that Christian Focus Publications printed. In addition to these introductions to Puritan classics, Packer provides an overview of "Puritan Pastors at Work" (actually an introduction to the Puritan movement more generally) and an epilogue that lists the tasks of a minister under the rubric "The Puritan Pastor's Programme." Additionally, William Perkins and Baxter receive biographical chapters.

A final venue for Packer's career as a Puritan scholar is his teaching at Regent College and his assignments as a visiting professor at various seminaries. The best sampling of such lectures is the series on "The English Puritans," available online in audio form. I will note additionally that oral and printed interviews with Packer have included some devoted to the Puritans, such as a printed interview in *Christian History* (vol. 89, 2006; available online).

The sketch that I have provided above is an important aspect of Packer's life and work. It also provides a portrait of Packer the man: he is a belated Puritan.

How the Puritans Helped to Make Packer the Person He Is

I might have entitled this section "The Nature of the Puritans' Influence on Packer," but that would not quite capture the degree to which the Puritans have molded his thinking and being. The Puritans have been an indwelling presence for him, not an outside influence.

Packer's interaction with the Puritans has been a personal and spiritual involvement, as well as an intellectual passion. In his introduction to *A Quest for Godliness*, Packer writes, "Nor is my interest merely academic, though it is not, I hope, less than academic." This is exactly the impression that any reader will carry away from Packer's writings on the Puritans. Indeed, as narrated above, Packer's very first genuine encounter with the Puritans was not primarily an intellectual experience; it was instead a spiritual lifeline thrown out to a floundering soul.

A good starting point for grasping how the Puritans helped to shape Packer is the account that he has given of his "conscious debt" to the Puritans in his introduction to *A Quest for Godliness*. Packer lists seven lessons that the Puritans taught him:

- the need to be realistic about continuing sinfulness and the call to do daily battle with that sinfulness
- "the sovereignty and particularity of Christ's redeeming love"
- the need for regular meditation on Christian truth, application of it to oneself, and turning the truth into praise

- the nature of the minister's calling
- the transitoriness of earthly life and the need to be always ready for death
- a vision of the comprehensiveness and wholeness of the Christian's life in this world
- the need for theology to transform one's spiritual life and not be intellectual only

The first thing to note about this list is that it is personal. Anyone who knows the Puritans can see at a glance that these are indeed leading Puritan ideas. But another person would likely come up with a slightly different list of leading traits of the Puritans or lessons to be learned from them. Related to the personal nature of the list, in Packer's elaboration of each of the "things learned," the experiential note is very strong, showing how close to Packer's heart we come in exploring his Puritan indebtedness. Here, for example, is part of Packer's explanation of how he benefited from the Puritan preachers' preoccupation with putting doctrine to proper use ("the uses," Puritan preachers said in their sermons): "It seems to me in retrospect that by virtue of this Puritan influence on me all my theological utterances from the start, on whatever theme, have really been spirituality (i.e., teaching for Christian living), and that I cannot now speak or write any other way."

An essential feature of Packer's indebtedness to the Puritans is that they came along very early in his Christian life—in his second year at college, as we have seen. Thus, the Puritans were the foundation on which Packer built his growth in Christ and theological understanding. If they had come along later in his life, they still would have been highly important and perhaps even revolutionary, but they would not have been the original light-givers that they were for Packer. Thus, in developing the point about the Puritan conviction that all of life is God's, Packer writes, "I could have learned this ideal of overall evangelical renewal from England's still unappreciated reforming genius Thomas Cranmer or from the nineteenth-century colossus J. C. Ryle (hardly from any more recent Anglican, I think); but, in fact, I got most of it from the Puritans, and principally from the would-be Anglican and reluctant nonconformist Richard Baxter, to whom I owe so much in other areas." Many Puritan ideas are not exclusively Puritan, but since Packer encountered them first in the Puritans, they are for him a Puritan inheritance.

Another example of this indebtedness is too important to omit. Packer's sense of ministerial calling was codified under the tutelage of a Puritan. Packer writes: "My sense of being called to preach the gospel, teach the Bible, and shepherd souls could have been learned from the Anglican ordinal that was used to ordain me, but in fact it crystallised out through my study of Baxter's own ministry and his *Reformed Pastor*. From student days I have known that I was called to be a pastor according to Baxter's specifications."

In summary, then, the first thing to be said about the Puritan influence in Packer's life is that it was formative. The Puritans did not *transform* his life; they *formed* it. Packer without the Puritans does not exist.

A second thing that we can say about the Puritan presence in Packer's life is that it is an extremely broad and comprehensive presence that extends to many different subjects. One of these is theological. Under that heading, we can list the doctrines of salvation and sanctification as particularly important. The Puritan view on the subject of sanctification is one of the most important themes of Packer's life. Few people have written as much on holiness or sanctification as Packer, and when he writes on the subject, the Puritans are likely to be quoted or cited as reliable guides. But a look at Packer's addresses and essays on the Puritans shows that he has valued their views on a myriad of subjects beyond theological ones—family, church life, Sunday observance, preaching, and the Bible to name but a few.

Third, Packer owes his Calvinism primarily to the Puritans, and it is important to stress that Packer is a full-fledged, five-point Calvinist. It is true that Calvinistic theology entered his life from sources beyond the Puritans. For example, the Thirty-Nine Articles that are dear to Packer's heart and mind as an Anglican are Calvinistic in their theological doctrines. But the Calvinism is more submerged in the Thirty-Nine Articles than in the more overt Calvinistic documents of the same era (e.g., the Westminster Confession of Faith). The Calvinism is there for readers who wish to pick up on it, but people are unlikely to become devotees of Calvinism from the Thirty-Nine Articles (and, in fact, since Cranmer's mid-sixteenth century era, few Anglicans have been ardent Calvinists).

In any case, one of Packer's most complete defenses of Calvinism comes in his introduction to Owen's *The Death of Death in the Death of Christ* (chapter 8 in Packer's *A Quest for Godliness*). We cannot remind ourselves too often that the chronology of Packer's intellectual history is important: Owen was the first Puritan whom he read in depth, during his second year in college, and Owen has been foundational to Packer's theological positions throughout his life. In later life, Packer whimsically accepted the claim of a friend that he was "an Owenian," and he claimed that Owen's *Death of Death* turned him "from a four-point into a five-point Calvinist."

As an appendix to what I have said regarding the importance of the Puritans in Packer's life, I will note that they were an ingredient in the situation in which Packer found himself within the British evangelical scene in the late 1970s. The reviving effect of the Puritans among British evangelicals in the 1960s and 1970s was much stronger among nonconformists (especially those in D. Martyn Lloyd-Jones's orb of influence) than among Anglicans. In my experience, very few Anglicans have ever warmed to the Puritans, even when they stand for the same things. After all, most Puritans were hostile to the things that modern-day liturgical Anglicans see as the essence of their church, including a hierarchical church polity and a liturgical worship format. Thus, at the very time when Packer's enduring loyalty to the Anglican Church exiled him from free-church evangelicals, his Reformed and Puritan identity left him stranded among his fellow Anglicans. The very Puritans who had earlier propelled Packer into the mainstream of evangelical circles in which he moved thus left him a relative outsider among those with whom he was officially united.

Packer as Interpreter of the Puritans

Everyone who masters an intellectual area such as the Puritans has a particular "take" on the subject. One expert's view will almost certainly differ slightly from another's. In this section of the chapter, I attempt to provide an anatomy of the angles of vision that Packer brings to the Puritans. By way of lead-in, we should note that Packer's slant on the Puritans is very much influenced by the role that they played in his personal spiritual life. This is true in each of Packer's four major "takes" on the Puritans.

First, Packer sees Puritanism as mainly concerned with holiness. As we have seen, Packer discovered Owen and other Puritans while he was struggling with the specific problem of what constitutes holiness in a Christian's life. The Keswick philosophy of triumphalism had him in turmoil. The Puritans offered a way out of that turmoil. If we fast-forward to a 2006 interview, we find Packer's responding to the question, "What kind of movement was Puritanism?" with this answer: "Puritanism in England was a holiness movement—seeking holiness in church, family, and community, as well as in personal life." That is not an unexpected answer. Many other students of the Puritans would respond similarly. But many devotees of the Puritans would seize most immediately on other principles that unify the movement. Packer sees the essence of Puritanism in keeping with the autobiographical facts of his first encounter with the Puritans.

Second, Packer emphasizes Puritan theology. Again, he stresses this area because of the Puritans' spiritual influence on him. The title of Packer's book on the Puritans is *A Quest for Godliness*, and the chapter titles tend toward (but are not limited to) theological categories. By way of contrast, my own book on the Puritans is entitled *Worldly Saints*, and none of the chapter titles, strictly speaking, is theological. Packer is, by training and profession, a teacher of theology, and that is what most interests him about the Puritans.

Third, Packer regards the Puritans as reliable guides out of contemporary aberrations in the evangelical church and modern culture. In other words, Packer's view of the Puritans is a practical one: the Puritans can actually help us in our own situation. This is exactly what the Puritans did for him. The classic passage in this regard is a statement from one of the volumes of *Puritan Papers* that I frequently have seen quoted as a touchstone of how the Puritans were regarded by those who were transformed by their writings in mid-twentieth century British evangelicalism. Here is the passage—a kind of official "policy statement" of how the ministers attending the Puritan Conference viewed the Puritans:

> The [Puritan and Reformed Studies] Group exists because its organisers believe that historic Reformed theology in general, and the teaching of the great Puritans in particular, does justice to certain neglected biblical truths and emphases which the church today urgently needs to re-learn. This is not, of course, to imply that the Puritan expositions of Scripture are infallible and final, so that the Puritans always succeeded in balancing truth in exactly the right

> proportions; nor is it suggested (forsooth!) that the way to solve the problems which face Christians of the twentieth century is to teach them to walk and talk as if they were living in the seventeenth. What is meant is simply that the Puritans were strongest just where Protestants today are weakest, and their writings can give us more real help than those of any other body of Christian teachers, past or present, since the days of the apostles.

The essay then proceeds to give numerous examples of these generalizations before winding its way back to the statement that "the aim of the Conference is to make a constructive application of what is learned to our own situation."

Fourth, Packer esteems the Puritans for their writings. Packer's way of dealing with the Puritans is influenced by his education in the classics. In my own interactions with the Puritans, I have always regarded myself as performing the ordinary task of literary analysis on Puritan texts, so I was encouraged to find that Packer sees their primary legacy as literary. "Puritanism's most significant contribution to the ongoing life of the church was, and is, without doubt its literary legacy." *Literary* here means "that which comes to us in written form." A history of the Puritans based solely on a narrative of external events would provide an emaciated picture of them. We know the Puritans today chiefly through their writings.

Packer the classical scholar knows that and capitalizes on it. Because he is attuned to the style in which the Puritans write, he asserts, "Form and content though distinct are connected, and here I connect them, saying that by writing *as* they do, no less than *what* they do, these authors fill their books with God for me." Again: "Puritan rhetoric, though always didactic, was as far as possible from being unimaginative, drab and dull. It was brisk and energetic, pictorial and dramatic, within its orderliness often explosive, and always arresting and urgent." Literary students of the Puritans regularly make comments like that, but it is extremely unusual for a theologian to say it.

A final feature of Packer's approach to the Puritans (in addition to the four emphases rooted in his spiritual assimilation of them) is the comprehensiveness of his grasp of the Puritans that emerges from his writings. Perhaps this is best seen in Packer's overview essays on the Puritans. Not only does each of these surveys cover an abundance of material, but the essays tend to be complementary. I have already noted the seven lessons that Packer learned from the Puritans, as developed in the introduction to *A Quest for Godliness*. But in chapter 2 of that book, Packer provides a different list of salient traits of the Puritans: the integration of their daily lives, the quality of their spiritual experience, their passion for effective action, their program for family stability, their sense of human worth, and their ideal of church renewal. Then, in the afterword, Packer gives yet another list of Puritan traits.

As part of his knack for lists that cover the territory in regard to the Puritans, Packer is excellent on the subject of Puritan innovations. From Packer we learn that the Puritans gave us the institution of whole-day Sunday observance. In addition, "They also introduced the Christian family to England, in the sense that they thoroughly worked out the responsibilities of father and mother inside the home, the pattern for family prayers twice a day, how everybody should be taught the Bible and taught to pray on their own." Furthermore, Packer showed that the Puritans developed a system and practice of devotional reading and meditation. And so forth.

I believe that even this tendency to be comprehensive can be linked to Packer's own life. His writing and speaking have been preeminently occasional in nature, meaning that he has prepared essays and addresses as occasions required. This pattern started early with the Puritan Conference, which evolved so as to have a unique theme for each year. This pushed Packer to compose addresses on the Puritans that fit the conference themes. When the editors of an anthology on Puritan devotional writing needed a chapter on *The Pilgrim's Progress*, Packer wrote an essay on a Puritan topic that he might otherwise not have addressed. The typical career path for someone who had written a dissertation on Baxter would have been to become a Baxter specialist, zeroing in on that narrow focus. But Packer is not career oriented; he is ministry oriented. That focus has been a great boon to Puritan studies because it has prompted Packer to diversify his writing and speaking on the Puritans.

Packer's Contribution to Puritan Studies

To appreciate Packer's contribution to what specialists call Puritan studies, one needs to read widely in what Packer has written on the Puritans. Having done so during my research for this chapter, I cannot say enough positive things about Packer as a Puritan scholar. I will develop six points, but they do not exhaust the subject. Again, I do not want my analysis to be divorced from Packer's biography: to grasp Packer's stature as a Puritan scholar is to understand an important part of who he is and what he has done. His contributions to Puritans studies are a major strand in his life story.

One of the most welcome contributions that Packer has made to our understanding of the Puritans is to highlight that Puritanism was the English branch of the Protestant Reformation. It is a particular vexation to me that most people regard the Puritans as a backwater religious movement limited to the island country of England. In fact, the Puritans were part of international Protestantism. Packer's way of underscoring this is unobtrusive but nonetheless effective: he moves with ease back and forth between the Puritans and the Continental Reformers. Packer's 1964 address at the Puritan Conference was on John Calvin, and the next year's was on Martin Luther. Volume 4 of Packer's *Collected Shorter Writings* carries two articles on Luther and two on Calvin. We can hardly miss the point that the Puritans were part of the overall Protestant Reformation.

Second, Packer is a Puritan scholar who writes as an apologist for the Puritans. He does not write primarily as if he is conducting a dispassionate scholarly exploration. Instead, he writes as someone on a campaign to persuade his readers to get on the bandwagon. Packer does not merely describe the Puritans—he defends them. When Packer agreed to write a foreword to my book on the Puritans, I expected a vanilla-flavored endorsement. The title of the essay that Packer wrote was completely beyond that, and it sounded an "apologetic" note: "Why We Need the Puritans." When Packer expanded this essay into a chapter for his own book on the Puritans, he wrote: "The present chapter is, I confess, advocacy, barefaced and unashamed. I am seeking to make good the claim that the Puritans can teach us lessons that we badly need to learn."

We should note in this regard that Packer the Puritan scholar has written for a broad evangelical audience, including laypeople. He is not interested in writing essays that other scholars can quote as they pursue their academic careers. He wants to put genuine Christians on the right path, and he enlists the Puritans as allies in the cause. The Puritans wanted to reform individuals, society, and the church, and Packer's writing and speaking on the Puritans have been part of a similar program of reform. A typical reforming statement, obviously directed to Christians, is that "to recover the old, authentic, biblical gospel, we need to bring our preaching practice back into line with it, . . . and it is at this point that Owen's treatise on redemption can give us help."

Third, and flowing from his apologetic stance toward the Puritans, Packer has produced a vision of Puritanism not primarily or only as a movement from the past, but more profoundly as a movement for the present. This is a very different contribution from the typical historian's enterprise of uncovering the facts about the past. In 2006, Packer wrote an autobiographical piece entitled "John Owen Put Me Straight." As he nears the end of the article, Packer asks, "Does Owen's book minister to others as it ministered to me?" He answers by quoting from a prison inmate who had been converted while reading Owen's *Mortification of Sin*. Packer then concludes the article with the statement, "Owen is one of the dead who still speak," in reference to a comment about Abel made in Hebrews 11:4. In his 2012 book on the Puritans, Packer writes, "The following pages embody the belief that as Isaac re-dug his father Abraham's wells . . . , we today need to re-dig the wells of Puritan wisdom regarding gospel truth, gospel grace, and gospel life." Packer has shown the practical effect the Puritans can have in our present lives. By contrast, Puritan enthusiasts have often given us a picture of the Puritans as specimens from the museum of the past.

Fourth, Packer is a towering figure among Puritan experts in his knowledge of the progression and chronology of the Puritan movement. To me, with my layman's grasp of the movement, Puritanism is one big, timeless mass of great material. Packer knows the exact sequencing of the movement and is therefore able to tell the unfolding story of Puritanism. On a single page (14) of *Puritan Portraits*, Packer tells me the following things that I did not know before: (1) in the second half of the sixteenth century, the church-reform aspect of Puritanism had gradually run out of steam ("they had lost every battle they fought"); (2) but in 1570, Richard Greenham showed the possibility of a grassroots reformation by leaving an academic post at Cambridge University, beginning a successful parish ministry in a farming community, and initiating an apprenticeship system for ministerial students; (3) and then, in the 1580s, William Perkins, "a learned godly man with a flair for speed and clarity as a writer," filled a gap by publishing books on Christian living. None of my copious research on the Puritans laid the situation out with that degree of clarity and sequencing.

Fifth, Packer has shown the importance of individual leaders in the movement. He has done this partly with a biographical flair in his approach to the Puritans. For me, the Puritans are a homogenous movement; for Packer, they are a gallery of unique individuals. He thus sees the nuances and individualizing traits in the Puritans. Related to this is Packer's tendency to choose specific Puritan books or treatises as the focus of many essays. His book *Puritan Portraits* links biographical sketches of seven Puritan authors with classic texts written by each one. One effect of this focus on individual authors and texts is to evoke a sense of excitement about the material. We catch the extraordinary spirit of these people and texts. They are giants, and we might profitably note that the book *A Quest for Godliness* was published in England under the title *Among God's Giants*.

Finally, and complementing what I have just said about his sensitivity to individual authors and works, Packer is able to present Puritanism as a unified movement that cuts across authors and works. In his more recent book on the Puritans, Packer correctly notes that "the Puritans were, to a remarkable extent, a theologically homogeneous school of thought." Although Packer has an admirable ability to delineate the particular contours of thought in Owen, Baxter, or Perkins, he more often discusses topics that cut a broad swath through the Puritans on topics such as the Puritan conscience, the Puritans as interpreters of the Bible, or marriage and the family in Puritan thought.

Summary

It would be wrong to view this chapter on Packer's lifelong involvement with the Puritans as a specialized topic that one can take or leave, depending on one's interest in the Puritans. On the contrary, it is impossible to understand J. I. Packer and his life without exploring the Puritan component. A major part of Packer's professional life has been devoted to the Puritans. But the Puritans have also been an essential feature of Packer's ministry to the Christian world and an important ingredient of his own reforming spirit.

19

Writing

J. I. Packer has taught thousands of students. He has spoken to *many* thousands of listeners. But his writings have been read by millions of people. He has written so much, and on so many topics, that writing this chapter on Packer the author has been a difficult assignment. Still, as with the chapter on Packer and the Puritans, I resonated with the subject of this chapter because my own experience as a writer has embodied many of the tendencies of Packer's writing, though on a much smaller scale.

Packer's Reflections on His Writing Career

It is always good to begin with autobiographical comments from a person about aspects of that person's life. In this introductory section, I have accordingly tapped three sources in which Packer comments about his life as a writer, and I will present them in the order in which I encountered them.

In 2008, Packer wrote an autobiographical column in *Christianity Today* that bore the title "Count Your Surprises: The High Spots of My Life Have Been Anything but Expected." In this article, Packer arranged the high points of his life into a list of five surprises. I was surprised to read, "Soon [after courtship and marriage] came the happy surprise of becoming a published author." One's first book (in Packer's case *"Fundamentalism" and the Word of God*) always comes as a jolt to one's system, but it is nonetheless hard to think of such a widely published author as Packer being surprised by his success as a writer. His comment on his first book is that "its success showed me that writing must henceforth have a central place in the educational work through which I have sought to fulfill my pastoral call."

A fuller explanation of the cursory comments made in the 2008 article can be found in a 1987 article in *Christianity* Today. It bears the intriguing title "An Accidental Author," a takeoff on the title of Iris Murdoch's novel *An Accidental Man*. Regarding his first book, Packer observed: "Behold! I had become an established author." He claimed that to himself he remained "an amateur," a label that he later revised (see below). As an extension of this note of humility, Packer wrote, "I have to remember that God made me a communicator."

This same 1987 article contains an outline of Packer's philosophy of composition, and since it confirms much of what I will say about Packer's career as a writer in the rest of this chapter, I will take time to note what Packer says about writing. First, he regards writing as "both an art and a craft, and you learn it by doing it." Editors and publishers of Packer's works all confirm that Packer is a painstaking wordsmith who labors over the "how" of his writing and not just the "what." (They also confirm that Packer therefore dislikes editorial tampering with what he has written.) Second, he shares "Packer's four rules of writing," and I know that my readers will be interested in them: (1) "Have something to say." (2) "Keep it simple." (3) "Make it flow." (4) "Be willing to redraft as often as is necessary to meet these requirements." (For purposes of comparison, I tell my students that I have managed to publish some fifty books by following two rules: I keep things simple and I use topic sentences.)

Third, in 2008, Packer was interviewed during a speaking trip to Laity Lodge in Texas, where he had become a regular speaker. In the interview, he was asked, "Where did your desire to write originate?" In the ensuing reply, Packer made the following points: (1) He began by observing, "I always enjoyed writing when I was very small" (and we should remember the typewriter that Packer received on his eleventh birthday). (2) During his pre-ministerial days, Packer did a fair amount of writing "to oblige the people who asked me." (3) Despite this early success as a writer, Packer never thought of himself as a professional writer until the success of his first book. (4) In the wake of that success,

Packer came to view himself as "called to be a professional writer" and to look upon writing as "a central activity" of his ministry. (5) Packer also testified that "the satisfaction that [writing] brings me, and I hope the usefulness of it, is on a par with . . . what I do in the classroom" (after which Packer waxed lyrical about how much he loves teaching).

How Much Has Packer Written?

With the foregoing very helpful comments by Packer himself serving as a foundation, we can proceed to an anatomy of his career as an author. The question naturally arises as to how many books, essays, magazine articles, and pamphlets Packer has written. I decided to tackle that question early in this chapter because it is easily answered: Packer has written so much, and in so many different venues or formats, that it is impossible to answer the question of "how many" or even to compile a bibliography of his writings. Packer is so ministry oriented that it is even difficult to determine what counts as a publication, as distinct from a privately circulated piece or a denominational circular.

Nearly two decades ago, historian Mark Noll undertook a preliminary foray into this territory in an essay that explored Packer's role in "the shaping of American evangelicalism." Noll began by acknowledging that "even the simple question of what J. I. Packer has published in America is not as straightforward as it sounds. When someone has been writing as persistently as he has on so many subjects, publishing history becomes a complex matter." Still, Noll does not admit defeat on the matter as readily as I am inclined to do. With the help of "an industrious secretary," Noll concluded that as of early 1995, Packer's published books numbered one hundred sixty-five.

But then a complexity immediately arises: Packer is an absolute genius (aided by aggressive editors and publishers) at publishing books in both England and the United States with different publishers and sometimes under different titles. Additionally, Packer's "fugitive pieces" (a term that Packer taught me) are not infrequently brought together later to form anthologies of essays on common subjects. Or parts of books (such as Packer's introduction to John Owen's *The Death of Death in the Death of Christ*) are sometimes published as freestanding pamphlets. As with numbers of publications, any attempt to quantify the sales figures of books and pamphlets would be obsolete within a month. I propose that we rest content with the knowledge that Packer is an extremely prolific author.

Writing as a Ministry

Taking a look at Packer's earliest publications shows that the trajectory of his writing career was set right from the beginning. It is a pattern that I have followed on a modest scale in my own publishing career, and it consists of entering nearly every publishing door that is opened. I would have been able to see that this is Packer's way of operating by my own observations, but since Packer himself has confirmed the pattern, I will note his comment. Packer states that he got into writing "by being obliging, writing what I was asked to write."

What such a paradigm yields is readily evident from the titles of the first seven articles that Packer published (along with the magazines in which they appeared):

- "The Puritan Treatment of Justification by Faith," *Evangelical Quarterly*
- "Sanctification—Puritan Teaching," *The Christian Graduate*
- "Great Pastors: Richard Baxter," *Theology*
- "Blind Spots," *Discipulus*
- "Baptism: Sacrament of the Covenant of Grace," *Churchman*
- "'Keswick' and the Reformed Doctrine of Sanctification," *Evangelical Quarterly*
- "Some Thoughts on General Revelation," *The Christian Graduate*

We can truly say that the die was cast early. One thing we see is the desire of a beginning young scholar to get into print. We should not minimize this: prolific authors have the urge to publish, and without that urge a person does not become a publishing author. As a fledgling scholar, Packer spun out articles on what he knew best, namely, the Puritans.

Additionally, it is obvious that Packer was not interested in publishing as part of a career path. His writing was an extension of his Christian and evangelical identity. Then, too, while Packer's first articles were on his existing knowledge of the Puritans, we can see what happened after that. He gained a reputation for publishing in evangelical magazines, so editors began to solicit articles on topics about which they wished to publish articles. Then, as the spiral continued, the range of publications began to enlarge. The person who is faithful in little is gradually put over much. The next wave of published articles accordingly appeared in *Banner of Truth*, *Churchman* (a "repeat" venue), *Inter-Varsity*, and *Christianity Today* (a whopping three articles in 1958).

Viewing the writing and publishing of articles as a ministry rather than as a scholarly "contribution to the discipline" (as academicians phrase it) never ceased to be Packer's model. If we fast-forward to 1980, we find him publishing in *Christianity Today*, *Crux*, *Evangelical Quarterly*, and *Churchman*. In 1990, the names have largely changed, but the pattern remains intact: *Mission and Ministry*, *Ashland Theological Journal*, *Crux*, *Evangelical Presbyterian*, *Tabletalk*, and *Christianity Today*. The same thing is true of 1998: *Leadership*, *First Things*, *Crux*, *Christianity Today*, and *Touchstone*. I know from personal experience that when scholars in a secular university look at such a bibliography, they do not know how to make sense of it. It is all ministry oriented and has as its goal the edification of Christians. That does not mean that the articles are of lesser quality than those published in scholarly sources. Anyone who has read Packer's articles knows that he fills them with substantive content. They elicit his best effort. But they are of a general rather than specialized nature.

Who is the audience of ministry-oriented publishing? The worldwide evangelical public has been Packer's readership, and it is very extensive. A career of specialized academic publishing would have garnered a readership of several thousand, mainly fellow academics. Packer's readership has numbered in the millions.

The Range of Venues and Genres

As Packer's reputation grew, the range of publishing venues changed, with magazines becoming proportionately less prominent. I know of no scholar who has published in quite the same range of places and genres as Packer has.

As the number of Packer articles in magazines declined, essays written for inclusion in edited anthologies of essays on common subjects increased. Choosing several representative years yields the following results. In 1966, Packer published essays in anthologies entitled *John Calvin*; *Towards a Modern Prayer Book*; and *Approaches to Reforma-*

tion of the Church. In 1978, he wrote essays for edited books entitled *Foundation of Biblical Authority*; *Evangelical Roots*; and *Law, Morality and the Bible*. In 1995, Packer essays appeared in *Evangelicals and Catholics Together*; *New Geneva Study Bible*; *The Grace of God, the Bondage of the Will*; *The Anglican Evangelical Crisis*; *When God's Voice is Heard*; *The Blackwell Dictionary of Evangelical Biography: 1730–1860*; and *The Bible, The Formation and the Church*. The inclusion of Packer writings in these publications shows how widely known he had become, how much in demand he was, and how diverse was the range of subjects on which he had come to be considered expert.

In addition to articles and essays, we find a genre that became a hallmark of Packer's publishing ministry—introductions, prefaces, or forewords to books authored by other people. They are an expression of Packer's generosity and unselfishness. Again, a selection of representative years will show what happened many times over. In 1985, Packer wrote forewords to books entitled *Biblical Revelation: The Foundation of Christian Theology* and *The Mystery of Marriage*. In 1990, he published five forewords and three introductions. In 2002, he wrote one foreword and three introductions. The subject matter represented by the books for which Packer has written introductory essays is too wide-ranging to yield categorization.

Another grouping within the Packer canon consists of pamphlets and booklets. Most of these belong to Packer's career as a churchman, specifically as a spokesman for the Anglican Church. The following is a list of representative specimens:

- *The Thirty-Nine Articles* (1961): a forty-six-page booklet comprised of revisions of six articles that originally appeared in *The Church of England Newspaper*
- *Keep Yourselves from Idols* (1963): a twenty-page booklet in which Packer responded to Bishop John A. T. Robinson's *Honest to God*
- *The Gospel in the Prayer Book* (1966): an eight-page booklet built out of articles that appeared in a parish magazine inset called *News Extra*
- *Tomorrow's Worship* (1966): a thirty-one-page booklet, part of the Prayer Book Reform Series
- *A Kind of Noah's Ark? The Anglican Commitment to Comprehensiveness* (1981): a thirty-nine-page booklet

- *Explaining Hermeneutics: A Commentary* (1983): an eighteen-page booklet

As I have said, Packer's publishing career is an exercise in ministry, and its goal is the equipping of the church. These pamphlets and booklets served that goal.

A final category is, of course, the books that Packer has published. There is a sense in which his publications in other genres (nearly five hundred such publications) represent the icing on the cake. The "meat and potatoes" of Packer's worldwide influence through the published word is his books. One thing that stands out immediately is how many publishing houses have carried Packer titles. An author of Packer's stature could have become the lead author of a single publisher, but Packer has gone to the opposite extreme of and has extended his largesse to many evangelical publishers. Here is a partial list: InterVarsity Press (American) and Inter-Varsity Press (British); Eerdmans; Zondervan; Baker; Crossway; Harold Shaw; Hodder & Stoughton; Banner of Truth; Tyndale House Publishers; Word; Servant; Vine; Thomas Nelson; P&R; Hillsdale College Press; Regent College Publishing; Lion; and Christian Focus. I laughed inwardly when I heard Packer tell an acquisitions editor that he hoped to give Publisher X one book a year, followed by an added comment that bore a hint of warning: "I hope that [Publisher X] will not become greedy."

The Ad Hoc Nature of Packer's Publishing

I have already given evidence of the occasional nature of Packer's publishing career, but I want to highlight the point. By "ad hoc" I mean an essay or book project that is "occasioned by an event." The occasion might be a professional conference at which an author speaks or a request from an editor for an essay on a particular topic. Alternatively, the author himself might choose to write about a development in the church or world that needs to be addressed.

The annual Puritan Conference, which began in 1950 and lasted for two decades, provided Packer the occasion to publish essays. Packer delivered at least one address at every one of the Puritan Conferences. At least fifteen of these addresses were published. Packer's first book, *"Fundamentalism" and the Word of God*, began as an address to a student group in London. *A Passion for Faithfulness: Wisdom from the Book of Nehemiah* took its origin from a series of conference talks. *Never Beyond Hope: How God Touches and Uses Imperfect People* likewise began as spoken messages delivered in various places.

Often oral presentations become published pieces through the agency of an eager editor or publisher. This chain of events is nicely encapsulated in the dedication of a 2013 Packer publication entitled *Weakness Is the Way: Life with Christ Our Strength* (Crossway): "My special thanks go to Steven Purcell, whose renewed invitation to Laity Lodge sparked my theme; Lane Dennis, who pressed me to publish my material; Scott Barber, who made sense of my messy manuscript."

Another category of occasions that can eventuate in articles or books is requests from editors or publishers. *Knowing God* was occasioned by a request from the editor of *Evangelical Magazine* for Packer to write a series of articles on God. Articles contributed to dictionaries are always the result of invitations from editors, and Packer has contributed entries to such dictionaries as *Baker's Dictionary of Theology*, *New Bible Dictionary*, *New International Dictionary of New Testament Theology*, *Eerdman's Handbook of Christian Belief*, and *The Blackwell Dictionary of Evangelical Biography: 1730–1860*.

An additional category of solicited publications is edited anthologies of essays on announced subjects. Packer has been asked to contribute dozens of essays to edited collections. Five arbitrarily chosen titles that suggest the range of his subject matter are the following: "Infallible Scripture and the Role of Hermeneutics," in *Scripture and Truth* (ed. D. A. Carson and John Woodbridge); "A Christian View of Man," in *The Christian Vision: Man in Society* (ed. Lynne Morris); "A Kind of Puritan," in *Martyn Lloyd-Jones: Chosen by God* (ed. Christopher Catherwood); "The Christian's Purpose in Business," in *Biblical Principles and Business: The Practice* (ed. R. C. Chewning); and "The Preacher as Theologian: Preaching and Systematic Theology," in *When God's Voice is Heard* (ed. John Stott and others).

A subcategory of edited anthologies is *festschrifts*—collections of essays published on the occasion of the retirement or some other milestone of famous scholars or preachers. It is no surprise that editors of *festschrifts* love to be able to include essays by Packer. Here are five representative examples of *festschrifts* and their fortunate editors (including me) who were able to include Packer essays: *God Who Is Rich in Mercy: Essays Presented to Dr. D. B. Knox* (ed. Thomas O'Brien and D. G. Peterson); *Practical Theology and the Ministry of the Church, 1952–1984: Essays in Honor of Edmund P. Clowney* (ed. Harvie M. Conn); *The Gospel in the Modern World: A Tribute to John Stott* (ed. Martyn Eden and David F. Wells); *God and Culture: Essays in Honor of Carl F. H. Henry* (ed. D. A. Carson and John D. Woodbridge); and *Preach the Word: Essays on Expository Preaching in Honor of R. Kent Hughes* (ed. Leland Ryken and Todd A. Wilson).

The occasion for a given publication might also be an event in the world to which an author voluntarily feels called to respond. This has happened many times in Packer's writing career, often because of his investment in the Anglican Church. Sometimes Packer has been moved to stop the inroads of liberalism. On other occasions, he has seen opportunities to steer the Anglican Church in an evangelical direction. Packer's publications during the decade of the 1960s, when he was warden of Latimer House, were dominated by ad hoc writing of this nature. For example, he wrote about "The Revised Catechism" for *Churchman*; about *Tomorrow's Worship*, part of the Prayer Book Reform Series; and about "Anglican-Methodist Unity: Which Way Now?" in *Fellowship in the Gospel: Evangelical Comment on Anglican-Methodist Unity and Intercommunion Today*.

Responding to trends did not stop with Packer's tenure at Latimer House. Packer is a cultural critic who never hesitates to enter the fray in regard to issues that matter to him. Thus, he has published "response" essays or books on such topics as women in the church (e.g., "Let's Stop Making Women Presbyters," in *Christianity Today*), the decline of Christian morality in the West (e.g., "Christian Morality Adrift," in *Society in Peril*), homosexuality (e.g., *The Church and Homosexuality: A Pastoral Approach*, co-edited by Packer), and evangelical abandonment of the doctrine of hell (e.g., "Universalism: Will Everyone be Saved?" in *Hell Under Fire*).

My goal in this section of the chapter has been to paint a broad picture of the occasional nature of Packer's writing career—the extent to which the point of origin for his publications has been events, occasions, or invitations external to Packer himself. As I peruse the list of his publications through the years, my impression is that nearly everything that he has published has been of this ad hoc nature. I speak from personal experience when I say that such a paradigm for publishing has many advantages. It ensures a pleasing variety in one's publishing. It makes publishing an adventure, for it clears space for providence to perform its feats. It frequently makes publishing a collaborative exercise. In at least two ways, it saves a lot of time—it spares a writer from having to decide what to compose next and it ensures placement of essays or books (thereby circumventing that nightmare known as the unpublished piece). Of course, the list of invitations and requests can make life overly busy, and publishers' deadlines have no doubt made life more pressured for Packer than it would otherwise have been. Wendy Zoba observes in her personal portrait of Packer that Kit Packer affirms that he was not always available to the family when he was writing a book.

In my conversations with Packer in June 2014, he confirmed that his writing career has been occasional or ad hoc in nature. He has self-consciously conceived of his writing in terms of filling the gaps—choosing to write on important subjects that no writer has adequately addressed. Packer's summary statement is that "the need at hand fills my time."

Further Dimensions of Packer's Writing Career

For someone who professes to be an introvert, Packer strikes me as the most sociable of people. In the publishing sphere, he has been the opposite of the solitary author reaching unilateral decisions about what to write. As former *Christianity Today* editor David Neff said to me across a luncheon table, Packer "is a great collaborator." Yes, he is, and more needs to be said about his directly collaborative efforts.

For starters, Packer has co-authored numerous articles and books. Specimens include the following: *Christianity: The True Humanism* (with Thomas Howard); *Never beyond Hope: How God Touches and Uses Imperfect People* (with Carolyn Nystrom); "Mind in Motion," in *Christian History* (with Jerry Root); *Praying: Finding Our Way through Duty to Delight* (with Carolyn Nystrom); and "'Go Fetch Baxter': This Feisty Puritan Spent His Life Quieting the Controversies He Started," in *Christianity Today* (with Tim Beougher).

Another feature of Packer's career as a writer is the remarkable degree to which his speaking has fed into his writing. For example, seven of the chapters in *Engaging the Written Word of God* originated as addresses. Five essays in *Celebrating the Saving Work of God* (vol. 1 of *The*

Collected Shorter Writings of J. I. Packer) were likewise addresses before they became published essays. The foreword to Packer's book *Evangelism and the Sovereignty of God* paints a picture that has been reenacted many times in Packer's career as an author: "The nucleus of the following discourse was an address given at the Pre-Mission Conference of the London Inter-Faculty Christian Union on October 24th, 1959. It has been expanded in the hope of giving it a wider usefulness. Its origin, and the practical nature of its subject-matter, accounts for its homiletical style."

Another frequently repeated feature of Packer's writing career is the procedure of publishing the same book in England and America with different publishers and sometimes with different titles. Packer's book on the Puritans was published in the United States by Crossway under the title *A Quest for Godliness: The Puritan Vision of the Christian Life* and in England by Kingsway under the title *Among God's Giants: Aspects of Puritan Christianity*. *Zondervan Dictionary of Bible Themes* (Zondervan) appeared in England under the title *The Hodder Dictionary of Bible Themes* (Hodder & Stoughton). *I Want to Be a Christian* was published in the United Kingdom by Kingsway and in the United States by Tyndale House Publishers with the same title, and then was reissued seventeen years later by Crossway under the title *Growing in Christ*. *For Man's Sake* was printed in England by Paternoster and in the United States by Crossway with the title *Knowing Man*. Marshall, Morgan and Scott (UK) published *Under God's Word*, while in the United States, Cornerstone published the same book as *Beyond the Battle for the Bible*. There are many other examples.

A much larger phenomenon than the ones just noted is Packer's knack for putting material in front of the public multiple times. This happens in several ways. One is the reprinting of material at Packer's own initiative, sometimes in virtually identical form and sometimes with revision. I personally was happy to see the substantial foreword that Packer composed for my book *Worldly Saints: The Puritans as They Really Were* (the preface was entitled "Why We Need the Puritans") reappear as a chapter in his own book on the Puritans (*A Quest for Godliness*), and then as an article in the magazine *Themelios*. Six of the chapters in *Hot Tub Religion* were reworked from previously published material. When Packer contributed an essay entitled "Expository Preaching: Charles Simeon and Ourselves" to the *festschrift* that I co-edited for Kent Hughes's retirement, I said to myself, "I know that Packer is an expert on the Puritans, but how did he find the time to become an expert on Charles Simeon?" Later I learned that Packer had published the material as an article in *Churchman* way back in 1960 (and that the article had originated as an address to ministers).

A less-obvious form of getting double mileage from good material consists of the pattern of a publication on a given subject spawning a second publication on the same subject. Sometimes the germ of an idea in one publication becomes more fully elaborated in a later publication. Packer's metaphor of theologians as plumbers and sewage men was briefly sketched in *Hot Tub Religion* (1987), then developed in a clever column in *Christianity Today* (1992). In 1993, Packer wrote an essay on the subject of leisure for a *festschrift* honoring Carl F. H. Henry, and in the same year he adapted certain ideas from the essay for an article published in *Christianity Today*. In 1987, Packer published an article entitled "The Way of the Weak Is the Only Healthy Way" (*Eternity*); in 2013, he turned a series of conference addresses into a book entitled *Weakness Is the Way* (Crossway).

Packer's own ventures in reprinting or recycling material have been wonderfully perpetuated by what editors and publishers have done on his behalf in recent years. Major books have been released that have given a second life to essays published long ago. Here is a partial list:

- In 1996, Harold Shaw Publishers enticed Packer to rework previously published material for a book of essays entitled *Truth and Power: The Place of Scripture in the Christian Life*.
- In 1998 and 1999, Paternoster Press published four volumes of previously published essays under the series title *The Collected Shorter Writings of J. I. Packer*; the specific titles are *Celebrating the Saving Work of God*, *Serving the People of God*, *Honouring the Written Word of God*, and *Honouring the People of God*.
- In 1999, InterVarsity Press released the one-volume *J. I. Packer Collection*, edited by Alister McGrath.
- In 2012, Hendrickson Publishers re-released *Honouring the Written Word of God* under the title *Engaging the Written Word of God*.
- Starting in 2006, Packer published a series of Anglican booklets that used the formula *Taking ________ Seriously*. Titles included *Taking Faith Seriously*, *Taking Doctrine Seriously*, and so forth. In 2013,

Crossway put all of these into a book entitled *Taking God Seriously: Vital Things We Need to Know*.

All of these books are small libraries of very precious material that would otherwise be nearly inaccessible to the general public. A brief note in the foreword to the four-volume *Collected Shorter Writings of J. I. Packer* gives us a glimpse of how compilations like these have become a reality: "I thank . . . the staff at Paternoster for all their hard work in putting this collection together."

The Immense Range That Packer Covers in His Writing

I was truly surprised to read Packer's self-assessment in his article "An Accidental Author," where he asserts that the range covered in his writings is "absurdly narrow." Packer makes the statement in connection with his claim that he writes "only about ideas and issues of mind and heart before the Lord." But as a reader, I cannot agree that this description does justice to the range of material in his writings. My purpose in this unit of the chapter is to suggest the range of genre and subject matter than characterizes Packer's published work.

I begin with the genres represented, and I will simply list those that I find as a reader and literary scholar, accompanied by either representative titles or other information that gives a brief illustration of the label I have assigned:

- Autobiographical essay, also called informal essay: numerous columns published in *Christian Today* during the era when Packer was a contributing and senior editor
- Published lecture: the Tyndale Fellowship lecture of 1974, entitled "What Did the Cross Achieve? The Logic of Penal Substitution," and the address delivered at the Nottingham Congress of 1977, entitled "Jesus Christ Is Lord"
- Religious pamphlet: a staple for Packer during his decade as warden of Latimer House in Oxford
- Specialized scholarship: Packer's dissertation on Richard Baxter; essays entitled "Encountering Present-Day Views of Scripture" and "The Adequacy of Human Language"
- Sermons and devotional addresses to laypeople (as distinct from conference addresses at professional meetings): the chapters in *A*

Passion for Faithfulness: Wisdom from the Book of Nehemiah and *Never beyond Hope*
- Apologetic books and essays: *"Fundamentalism" and the Word of God*; "Is Christianity Credible?"
- Biography: *Honouring the People of God*; *Puritan Portraits*
- Theological handbook: *Concise Theology: A Guide to Historic Christian Beliefs*; *Taking God Seriously: Vital Things We Need to Know* (a book that also embodies Packer's passion for catechesis)
- Essay of cultural critique: "Hype and Humbug" (a *Christianity Today* article in which Packer criticizes evangelical looseness with truth in such activities as book endorsements); "Christian Morality Adrift"
- History, or historical theology: *A Quest for Godliness: The Puritan Vision of the Christian Life*
- Forewords, prefaces, or introductions
- Book reviews

It is possible to divide the material more minutely than the foregoing, but the categories I have listed provide an adequate picture of the many formats Packer has cultivated in his career as a writer.

The second way to show the diversity and range of Packer's writing is to tabulate the subjects on which he has written, without regard to the genres in which these subjects are packaged. Again steering a middle course between undue specificity and painting the landscape with too broad a brush yields the following:

- theology
- practical Christian living
- the Bible (its nature, reliability, and use)
- the Protestant Reformation, including the Puritans
- the church (including Anglicanism)
- evangelism
- preaching and the ministerial vocation
- the Holy Spirit
- cultural trends
- divine guidance
- leisure and pleasure
- prayer
- sanctification and holiness

I have learned not to make any predictions as to what direction Packer might turn his authorial interests. He has continually surprised me with excursions into writing on pleasure, the fiction of Dostoyevsky, jazz music, or anger.

Packer's Comments on Writing

In the article in which Packer calls himself "an accidental author," he downplays himself as a model for other writers, and he buttresses that verdict by observing that he is "untutored," having "never read a book or [taken] a course on writing." It is not quite that simple, however. There have been several occasions when Packer has been enticed to talk about writing and give advice to writers, and at those times he has shown a sophistication about writing theory that goes beyond the rudimentary.

In July 2012, Tony Reinke interviewed Packer on the topic of what advice he would give to aspiring writers. Among his points were the following: Simply stating the truth is not sufficient. Good writing requires personal communication—"communication that hits the heart." Readers must be made to feel about the writer that "he's talking to me; . . . this person is trying to search me in order to help me, and I must let him do it." "Learn to write for people," Packer said. And again, "There is a certain art and craft in writing in such a way that it gets to the reader's heart." Although Packer did not directly reference William Wordsworth's famous definition of the poet as "a man speaking to other men," he used this formula (by now part of the cultural consciousness) when he said that a writer needs to think of himself or herself as "a person talking to other persons."

Professor Jack Collins of Covenant Theological Seminary asked Packer about how to write during a breakfast conversation as Collins was in the process of writing a book on science and faith. Among the pieces of advice that Collins noted are the following:

- Always write with your intended reader in mind; in fact, it can be helpful to think of a specific person you know as you compose.
- If you state something technical or difficult, follow it up immediately with a short comment that helps to unpack the meaning for the ordinary reader.

- When writing in a polemical vein on currently controversial issues (as Collins was in writing on science and Christianity), it can be helpful to picture one's reader as having just read an opponent's position (for example, in Collins's case, the positions of Richard Dawkins the Darwinian atheist or Stephen Hawking the disparager of Christianity) and now wants to know what to think of the arguments as a Christian.
- Where possible, write with verbs instead of abstract nouns; in fact, help the reader form pictures.
- Remember the humanity of the audience. Packer frequently cites C. S. Lewis as his model in this regard.

When Packer theorizes about writing, he often says something to the effect that "this is what I have tried to do or successfully done," suggesting that he is self-reflective about his writing.

Four Representative Books

I will harness the diffuseness of the material I have covered in the chapter to this point by taking a brief look at four representative books that epitomize Packer's writing career. All four are in the circle of his greatest books.

"Fundamentalism" and the Word of God (1958)

This was Packer's first book. Despite the misleading and overly specific title, the book enjoyed immediate and enduring popular appeal. It sold twenty thousand copies in its first year of existence, and it has never gone out of print. Even more than with most of Packer's books, this one is a story of providence.

Packer tells us about the circumstances surrounding this book. It was written as Packer was midway through his first permanent teaching position as a professor of theology at Tyndale Hall in Bristol. The battle for the Bible was being waged in England, and Packer was a frequent speaker on the subject. In 1957, he spoke to a student group in London on the topic "Narrow Mind—or Narrow Way?" The one-hour address attracted the attention of the publishing director of Inter-Varsity Fellowship, Ronald Inchley, who invited Packer to prepare it for publication as a pamphlet. In typical fashion, Packer kept working on the core ideas of the address, and eighteen months later, he handed over a book-length manuscript to Inchley. Inter-Varsity Press had just cast its lot with mass-market paperbacks for the evangelical public, and Packer's book was an early entry in the field.

The significance of the book extends far beyond its defense of the evangelical view of the authority of the Bible, but we should not therefore minimize that dimension. *"Fundamentalism" and the Word of God* was an influential book for me as a college student in many of the same ways that C. S. Lewis's book *Mere Christianity* was, and as I look at my original underlinings in the book, I can recall the specific ways in which it expanded my understanding.

In regard to the authority of the Bible, two dimensions of the book stand out as particularly important. One is Packer's delineation of the three historic approaches to the question of religious authority. The respective approaches claim that the Bible, church tradition, or human reason is the authority for belief (those are not the terms that Packer uses in the book, but the ones that I supplied as I assimilated the discussion). This is an enormously useful framework for organizing the positions that we encounter in life or in our reading on the question of what constitutes the proper authority for religious belief.

A second reason the book is important on the question of authority is that Packer explores why evangelical acceptance of the Bible as the final authority for religious belief and practice is a valid position. Packer adduces the attitude of biblical writers to the Bible and the practice of the early church, but the really crucial piece of evidence is the attitude of Jesus toward scriptural authority: "Jesus Christ, the Son of God incarnate, who claimed divine authority for all that He did and taught, both confirmed the absolute authority of the Old Testament for others and submitted to it unreservedly Himself." In doing the research for this biography, I found that the attitude of Christ toward the Bible has remained a "constant" in Packer's apologetic for biblical authority.

In what ways does the book go beyond a defense of the evangelical view of biblical authority? One reason why the book gave evangelicals a place to stand is that the author fully identified with the evangelical community. He did not apologize in the least for being an evangelical. The book has a devotional undertow, and the author even capitalizes pronouns referring to God and Christ. Packer (I noticed as a college-age reader) was not at all interested in seeming respectable in the eyes of the secular and non-evangelical world. His interest was in evangelical truth, not academic acceptance. This gave me (and obviously thousands) a model to follow.

While it was not a major purpose of *"Fundamentalism" and the Word of God* to assert the importance of the intellectual life for Christians, I can tell from my original underlinings that this aspect of the book was very important to me. Here are a few specimen statements:

- "The Evangelical is not afraid of facts, for he knows that all facts are God's facts; nor is he afraid of thinking, for he knows that all truth is God's truth, and right reason cannot endanger sound faith."
- "All truth is God's truth; facts, as such, are sacred, and nothing is more un-Christian than to run away from them."
- "The Christian's intellectual vocation is to think about all things in such a way that his life of thought is part of his life of faith and homage to God."

Reason and intellect, however, are not the only or necessarily final authority for religious belief. Faith must also be granted its sphere. As a college student, I found this half of the equation equally illuminating. Here are representative statements:

- "Articles of faith . . . are not in themselves unreasonable, but they are above reason."
- "Reasoning may prepare the mind for faith in these truths, by showing their meaning and biblical basis . . . ; but reasoning alone cannot produce faith, for faith goes further than reason could take it."
- "The logic of faith requires us . . . to challenge and correct secular opinion by the light of revealed truth."

The foreword to *"Fundamentalism" and the Word of God* must be Packer's shortest ever, but it tells us a lot. In it, he describes the book as "a constructive re-statement of evangelical principles in the light of the current 'Fundamentalism controversy.'" The "aim is to fix the right approach to the Bible, to the intellectual tasks of faith, and to the present debate." Packer's hope is that the book will help "evangelical Christians to understand their faith better and witness to it more effectively." He ends by expressing his gratitude to three colleagues who read and critiqued the manuscript, and "most of all" to his wife "for her patience and help."

I want to highlight Packer's endurance in working for eighteen months on a book-length manuscript that carried no assurance of being accepted for publication. The editor had asked for a pamphlet. Would he still be interested a year and a half later? Would he be favorable toward a book rather than the requested pamphlet? Packer was still establishing himself as a professor at his college. Working in solitude and without a contract for a year and a half was a big risk. It was an exercise in trusting providence, as early ventures in publishing often are.

The title of this classic book has baffled most readers through the years. I believe the title obscures the true significance of the book, but it becomes understandable when we place the book into the cultural and religious context out of which it arose. The context that produced the book was growing hostility to evangelicals in England, especially from academics and churchmen. At the hands of liberals, evangelicals were made to appear anti-intellectual. What became known in the public forum as "the fundamentalist controversy" thus formed the context of the book, which is couched as a continuous rebuttal of the liberal position.

Packer did not choose the book's title. He proposed *The Faith Once Delivered*. The Inter-Varsity publishing director, Inchley, believed that the proposed title would be an impediment to the marketing of the book. So he chose to imitate the title of a then-current book attacking evangelicals—A. G. Hebert's *Fundamentalism and the Church of God*. Packer's book has long since been emancipated from its original context, but the title keeps it stuck there. (I will note in passing that I feel myself in numerous ways to be a kindred spirit to Packer, and on this point also: my first book, too, was mistitled by an editor.)

It is impossible to overstate the impact of *"Fundamentalism" and the Word of God* in instilling confidence in evangelicals, especially (but not only) in the sphere of biblical authority. Valentine Cunningham, who became an esteemed Oxford University professor of English literature, recalled that "it felt good to have Packer on one's side." An equally esteemed American professor, Roger Nicole of Reformed Theological Seminary in Orlando, purchased the book for 95 cents, started to read it at ten o'clock at night, and read it for six straight hours! British evangelical Geoffrey Shaw believed that the book was a turning point for his generation, giving evangelicals a new confidence and diminishing the siege mentality that had set in.

God Has Spoken (1965; expanded version in 1979)

The significance of this book escaped me until I did the research for this biography. Its quality and nature make it a representative book, especially in its 1979 reissue. The subject of the book is, of course, vintage Packer, namely, the Bible. With that as the foundation, four additional factors make it an epitome of Packer's writing.

I note first the comprehensiveness of the book. Nearly every subject related to the Bible is covered. The introduction (1979) discusses the Bible in terms of practical Christian living—the enjoyment of reading the Bible, the Bible and salvation, and the variety of English translations available (and regarding which Christians need to make an informed decision). Chapter 2 sounds a prophetic voice as Packer asserts the eclipse of the Bible in the church, the liberal views of revelation and inspiration that have caused this famine of the Word, the negative fallout within the church, and the solution to the problem in the form of historic Reformed teaching about the Bible. This packed chapter is nothing less than a primer on modern attitudes toward the Bible and historical Protestant thinking about it. The rest of the book covers three topics—God's Word spoken, God's Word written, and God's Word heard.

But that simple outline conceals the degree to which each of those subjects is handled in such a way as to cover territory that could yield a book all by itself. This leads to a second characteristic of the book that makes it a typical Packer performance—its compression. Not until I looked at the book closely did I appreciate what I was holding in my hands. Despite the brevity of the book (150 pages) and its comprehensiveness, Packer manages to treat topics with unexpected thoroughness. A chapter unit on the infallibility or inerrancy of the Bible (five pages) manages to (1) introduce the subject and assert its importance, (2) define the words *infallible* and *inerrant*, (3) explain the importance of the concepts, (4) justify their use, (5) explore how the words and concepts can be misunderstood, and (6) refute objections to embracing the concepts of infallibility and inerrancy.

Third, the book is thoroughly scholarly in the specific sense of reaching beyond the Bible itself to broader contexts for the topics that are introduced. Some parts of the book are saturated with references to verses in the Bible. Other parts adduce evidence from the Thirty-Nine Articles of the Anglican Church or Reformed stalwarts such as John Calvin and B. B. Warfield. But the frame of reference is not solely the past: throughout the book, Packer has an eye on the current hermeneutical scene in the world of liberal biblical scholarship, so that the book becomes a primer on non-evangelical contemporary hermeneutics. On the other hand, the footnotes provide very helpful signposts to modern evangelical hermeneutics as well.

Finally, this is a "signature" Packer book by virtue of its rootedness in his institutional ties. The original 1965 version of the book was an expression of Packer's life at Latimer House. In fact, the book was part of a series entitled *Christian Foundations*, designed to promote evangelicalism within the Church of England. In his preface to the re-issue of the book in 1979, Packer reaffirmed his Anglican affiliation. But in quite a different vein, by 1979, Packer was nearing the end of a decade of heavy involvement with the International Council on Biblical Inerrancy. The appendix to the 1979 edition of *God Has Spoken* accordingly reprints the entire Chicago Statement on Biblical Inerrancy and the "Exposition" of it (for a total of sixteen pages).

One hesitates to call any given book by J. I. Packer one of his most important books, since there are many candidates. Nonetheless, I believe that anyone who spends an adequate amount of time with this book will quickly come to see what a true achievement it is.

Knowing God (1973)

This is easily the book for which Packer is best known. It is the book with which he is most frequently linked (for example, in introductions of him or in biographical blurbs on book covers or internet postings). In the preface to the twentieth-anniversary edition of the book (published in 1993), Packer noted that the book had sold more than a million copies. In 2001, according to Wendy Zoba, the book had sold one and a half million copies. In 2006, responders to a *Christianity Today* poll of "the top fifty books that have shaped evangelicals" placed *Knowing God* fifth on the list. The book has been translated into more than twenty languages.

My interest is in how the book epitomizes Packer's writing career, and the first thing to note is that the book was solicited—not as a book, but as a series of magazine articles. This demonstrates what I have called the "ad hoc" nature of Packer's publishing career. The magazine was a little-known publication called *Evangelical Magazine*, which owed its origin in the late 1950s to D. Martyn Lloyd-Jones. The editor was Elizabeth Braund (with Packer as a consulting editor). Braund conceived the idea of a series of articles on the subject of God. In the preface to the 1993 edition, Packer credits the editor with being "the onlie begetter" (a Shakespearean allusion) of the articles and therefore the book. Braund even gave Packer his envisioned audience, namely, people who were "honest, no nonsense readers who were fed up with facile Christian verbiage" and who were "prepared to do some honest and serious thinking." Anyone who has read the book knows that Packer did what his editor requested. The articles appeared in *Evangelical Magazine* over a span of five years. In the preface to the 1993 commemorative edition, Packer notes, "When I sent the manuscript . . . to the publisher just over twenty years ago, I thought of it as a study book that could hardly be of general interest. I was wrong."

Many Packer books are recastings of material that originally appeared in other formats (essays, articles, or oral addresses). *Knowing God* falls into this category. When the magazine series was finished, Packer envisioned the individual pieces as a book. Ronald Inchley, of Inter-Varsity Press, was so intent on Packer's addressing the charismatic movement that was sweeping evangelicalism in England that he refused to consider *Knowing God* until Packer wrote a book on the Holy Spirit. Packer promptly made contact with an editor named Edward England at Hodder & Stoughton, which became the original English publisher for the book. The American editor who acquired the rights to the book was James Sire of InterVarsity Press, who decided to swing through England on a return trip from Switzerland, where he had met with InterVarsity author Os Guinness. He had a fifteen-minute meeting with England during a brief stopover in London. At that meeting, England showed Sire the text of *Knowing God*. Sire latched onto the book and asked for permission to publish it in America. Back home in Downers Grove, Illinois, InterVarsity Press director Jim Nyquist immediately saw the potential of the book to be a major publication.

If we turn from this external publishing data to the book itself, it is easy to see *Knowing God* as a "signature" Packer book. It is a book of theology. This was assured by the subject of the book, namely, the nature of God. Theology is the study of God, and this book is preeminently a study of God. As a theology book, we would immediately call it a traditional book. The categories are traditional—God as spirit (and therefore not to be pictured in physical images), God incarnate in the form of Jesus, the Holy Spirit as the third person of the Triune God, the attributes of God (his unchangeableness, majesty, etc.), and the nature of the redeemed life in Christ (part 3 of the book). The subjects that Packer takes up are familiar to anyone who is conversant with the theological writings of evangelical and Reformed theologians, but I suspect strongly that the reason the book became so widely known is that it was read by people who were encountering many of these theological ideas for the first time. For such readers, the book had the nature of a primer—a codification of "first things" and foundational beliefs regarding God.

Packer has always been temperamentally prone to tackle hard questions and difficult subjects. This trait surfaces strongly in *Knowing God* and accounts for part of its appeal. Subjects that the human race and the Christian world often bypass are prominent in *Knowing God*: God's judgment of sin and sinners, the severity of God, the jealousy of God, God's anger that requires propitiation, and the centrality of repentance in the Christian life. We have an idiom, "hard nosed," meaning "unsentimental and not shirking from facing the tough issues," and it is a dominant strain in Packer's writing.

His writing also shows a practical bent. He is, after all, a latter-day Puritan, and the Puritan outlook is well summarized by John Bunyan's statement that "the soul of religion is the practical part." The Puritan William Ames insisted that it was not enough for a preacher to state the truth; he must also show "the use, goodness, or end" of Christian doctrines. This is what Packer does in *Knowing God*. Each chapter ends with a section that outlines the appropriate spiritual response to the truth that has been delineated in the chapter.

As I have noted, Packer's writing has not been governed by career interests. It has been controlled by ministry concerns. *Knowing God* has ministered to more people than any other of his books. Having praised the book for its serviceableness, I also want to add a note growing out of my own experience as a writer. An author can never predict what writing will prove particularly important or even life-changing in the life of a given reader. It might be an essay published in a little-known magazine or even a pamphlet with such a small profile that it ranks almost as a privately printed document. We should not unduly single out a celebrity book as being what pleases God most.

A Quest for Godliness: The Puritan Vision of the Christian Life (1990)

Even books by Packer that did not have their origin in earlier addresses and publications tend to have the quality of summing up a long-term acquaintance with the subject matter of those books. For example, Packer's interaction with the charismatic and "holiness" segment of British evangelicalism dates all the way back to the early 1960s. Inchley, the Inter-Varsity publishing director, had pressed Packer to write a book on the Holy Spirit in the early 1970s. Packer continued to do research on the subject before publishing a book on it. When his book *Keep in Step with the Spirit* was published in 1984, it was obviously a "summing up" book that had the weight of three decades of thinking and studying behind it.

Likewise, anyone familiar with Packer's lifelong reading and writing on the Puritans knows that *A Quest for Godliness* is this kind of book—Packer's mature thinking about the Puritans. Almost everything in the book had been printed previously (including addresses delivered at the annual Puritan Conference). *A Quest for Godliness* is a convenient library of Packer's publications on the Puritans.

The book showcases Packer's identity as a historian. More specifically, academicians would put the book into the category of historical theology. The impulse to root relevant truth in the past, starting with the Bible, is always present in Packer's writing and thinking. The result is a steady stream of quotations from the Bible, the early church, the Reformation, and the historic creeds of the church (especially, but not only, the Thirty-Nine Articles of the Church of England) in Packer's writings on many subjects. In *A Quest for Godliness*, this impulse is highlighted. The book is an exploration of a movement from the past.

Yet the underlying premise is that this past is for the present and future, with the Puritans serving as reliable guides for today and tomorrow.

An additional way in which *A Quest for Godliness* is a representative Packer book is the authentic tone of personal passion for the subject that breathes through it. All authors have an intellectual passion for the subjects on which they write. But if we compare *A Quest for Godliness* to most books on the Puritans, we find two completely different worlds. We sense throughout *A Quest for Godliness* that Packer's spiritual life was changed and influenced by the Puritans. The Puritans are not simply an intellectual passion for him; they are spiritual mentors to him and sojourners with him on the pilgrimage from this life to the life that is to come.

Summary

I often reflect on the ways in which Richard Baxter's comments about the life of a teacher also fit the life of a writer. Baxter described the calling of a teacher as being "very painful [painstaking], requiring much close attendance." The same is true of a writer. "But yet," Baxter continued, "it is of so great use to the common good, and alloweth the mind so much leisure and advantage to improve itself in honest studies," that it is a better life than one that produces a lot of money. The clinching commendation: "It is sweet to be all day doing so much good."

J. I. Packer can look back on a life of writing that has made him very busy. It has produced a life of labor. An academician needs to swim against the tide to be a prolific author in addition to being a full-time teacher. The most meaningful tangible rewards are the letters that Packer receives from his readers and their comments to him when he speaks publicly. It was also gratifying for Packer to receive a Lifetime Achievement Award from the Evangelical Christian Publishers Association in 1996.

20

Anglicanism

J. I. Packer has been a member of the Anglican Church all his life, and his commitment to that church is as strong today as it has ever been. When I telephoned Packer on October 8, 2013, he had just returned from a week on the West Coast and another on the East Coast, serving on task forces for the Anglican Church in North America (ACNA). The subject of the first meeting was a catechism for adults, and the second dealt with liturgy.

During this telephone exchange, Packer gave me a slant on his lifelong devotion to the Anglican Church that can serve as the umbrella concept for this chapter. It is that he has always had a passion for the revival or renewal of the church. Much of his work for the Anglican Church has been a labor of love and a thankless task, and sometimes a losing battle. But Packer has stayed the course because he wants to reclaim a church that has increasingly lost its theological way.

Packer's Anglicanism finds its way into two other parts of this biography beyond the current chapter. First, the story of Packer's involvement in the Church of England before his move to Canada appears in Part 1, and I will merely summarize that involvement in this chapter. Second, I will explore Packer's involvement in the controversies that have dogged his life in the Anglican Church of Canada in a subsequent chapter devoted to the theme of controversy in his life (chap. 23). My goal in this chapter is to delineate what Anglicanism has meant to Packer during his lifelong participation in it. If we can reach this goal, we will also have answered the question of why he has been such a loyal member of the Anglican community. If we do not understand Packer's conception of Anglicanism, we might misinterpret the nature of his devotion to it. Certainly that devotion has not been to a denomination per se, but rather to an ideal. The right term for the ideal is Anglicanism, which is not synonymous with the Anglican Church as an institution.

Packer's Childhood in the Church of England

The church in which one is raised exercises a formative influence in one's life, and this influence can take two main directions. In the circles in which I move, many adults leave their original denomination for another church or for a life of unbelief. Often the original church influences these people to renounce it for an alternative. But for others, the childhood church continues to draw them, sometimes in mysterious ways. Packer describes himself as "a cradle Anglican who is now one by conversion and conviction." As that statement confirms, the Anglican Church of his childhood has retained its hold over him, even through stormy waters.

The relationship got off to a shaky start. As a child, Packer accompanied his parents to church, but the church represented nominalism in its pure form. He describes going to church on Sunday as being like "regularly cleaning my teeth—a required routine which I was told was good for me." The youthful Packer did not hear the gospel of salvation in Christ in a way that registered with him (and, in large part, the gospel was not directly expressed at all). He was confirmed in the church (somewhat irregularly, as noted earlier), but here, too, nothing was said about repentance from sin and belief in the atonement of Jesus.

Packer's boyhood friend Eric Taylor had been reborn through the ministry of Inter-Varsity at the University of Bristol, but Packer, back home in Gloucester and under the influence of his home church, was mystified by what Taylor wrote in his letters. Packer knew that he was outside the room where the party was going on, but the Anglican Church did not open the door to him. It was opened during Packer's early days in Oxford, again through the ministry of Inter-Varsity. As a new Christian, therefore, Packer was angry at the Church of England for letting him down. In his own words, "I was so cross with the Church of England for never having explained the Gospel to me properly that I spent a couple of years fellowshipping with the Brethren."

But then Packer visits a surprise on us: despite his disillusionment, he refused to repudiate his Anglican roots. Although he mainly attended the local Plymouth Brethren church during his first two years in Oxford, he also attended services at St. Aldate's Anglican Church. He did so even though it cost him favor with the leaders of the Oxford Christian Union, who considered Packer "unsound" when he was nominated for a leadership role in the group. By Packer's third year at Oxford, he had cast his lot with St. Ebbe's Anglican Church for Sunday attendance.

Formal Ties with the Anglican Church

Packer's involvement with the Anglican Church during his undergraduate days quickly intensified beyond mere church attendance. By his third year at Oxford, he reached a conscious decision to seek ordination in the Church of England. Upon graduating, he taught for one year at a theological college (Oak Hill) that had been founded for the education of future Anglican ministers. After that, Packer received his graduate education at Wycliffe Hall, which was likewise devoted to preparing men for ministry in the Anglican Church. Then Packer served as an Anglican minister for two years.

Packer's affiliation with the Church of England did not end when he left the parish ministry. He taught at Tyndale Hall in Bristol and later at Trinity College in Bristol, both of which were Anglican in orientation. In my naïveté, I was shocked by a photograph of the faculty of Tyndale Hall that appears in Alister McGrath's biography of Packer. All of the men are shown wearing the Anglican clerical collar.

Then there is the time that Packer spent as warden of Latimer House in Oxford. Latimer House was the focal point of evangelical efforts to win the Church of England back to its Reformation roots. Latimer House was informally an Anglican institution. To be warden of Latimer House was to be "Mr. Anglicanism," and that was Packer's passion for a decade. During that decade, his life was consumed by the Anglican Church.

Since Packer would have been welcome in the free church world of midcentury British evangelicalism, we need to regard his commitment to the Anglican Church as both consciously chosen and very strong. I was struck by the following passage in Packer's book *Truth and Power*:

"A well-known American reviewer . . . once commended John Stott for not writing in a way that shows him to be an Anglican, as that man J. I. Packer regrettably does. Well, I am indeed an Anglican."

The history that I have sketched requires some explanation. To do so, I propose to explore Packer's writings in which he defines and defends Anglicanism, supplemented by recent interviews and public addresses.

It is safe to say that it was not love of the institutional Anglican Church that Packer found attractive during his years in England (and later as a member of the Anglican Church of Canada). As an evangelical in a liberal-leaning denomination, he was treated as an outsider by the official church boards and the church hierarchy, even during his Latimer House days, when he served on church committees (and was regularly outvoted). What attracts Packer to Anglicanism is the ideals that it represents—the potential that it holds if controlled by evangelicals.

Three Preliminaries

Before I shine the spotlight on Packer's energetic defense of Anglicanism, I want to provide a context that can prevent possible misunderstanding. First, Packer does not disparage alternatives to Anglicanism. For example, on the same page in *Truth and Power* in which he self-identifies as an Anglican (quoted above), he writes, "I admit to thinking that Anglican heritage is the most nourishing in the Christian world, but what I owe to the Puritan tradition from John Owen to Charles Spurgeon and to the Welsh Nonconformist tradition in some of its latter-day representatives is more than I can measure."

The ambiguity is even more pronounced than that, however, as in the following passage from Packer's propaganda piece *A Kind of Noah's Ark?*

> I do not maintain . . . that choosing to be an Anglican is a virtue, or that choosing not to be one or not to stay one is a vice. . . . Anyone may conclude that, rather than be Anglican, . . . he should join one of the smaller groups (Brethren, Pentecostals, . . . etc.) which debar from the ranks of their teachers anyone . . . rejecting major evangelical tenets. . . . These matters are arguable both ways, and neither estimate need be accepted. More important is respect for the other man's deliberate decision, whether or not it coincides with your own.

This is the context within which Packer makes his endorsement of Anglicanism: he himself believes strongly in Anglicanism, but that is a matter of personal conscience that he extends to others equally. The accepted term for this is religious tolerance, and it is here buttressed by the Puritan ideal of obedience to conscience.

A second orienting statement is that Packer is not uncritically accepting of Anglicanism or the Anglican Church. When I conducted research into Packer's involvement with the Church of England before he moved to Canada, I formulated a picture of him as a party-line man and propagandist. That was an inaccurate picture. When Packer served on Anglican committees during his Latimer House days, he was often a solitary evangelical voice trying to defend a castle (Packer's metaphor) from the attacks of liberalism. At such moments, he did not endorse the Church of England as an institution; instead, he deplored it. When Packer was headed for committee meetings, he regularly asked his friends to pray for him, "because I need it."

This attitude is reinforced by recent statements from Packer that I would never have suspected before I began to explore his participation in mainstream Anglicanism (before his move to Canada) as minister, professor, and spokesman. Here are three specimens:

- "In England I got tired of being told that ambiguity was Anglicanism's great virtue, and I hoped when I responded to Canada's call that I was leaving all that tommy-rot behind."
- "No Christian, I imagine, who was around thirty years ago ever dreamed that Anglicanism worldwide would ever be in the state it is in today."
- Two generations ago, "Anglican Christianity . . . became unsure about biblical authority in light of biblical criticism, imprecise regarding the doctrines of the creeds, loose regarding the life of faith in Christ and the discipline of personal repentance, and neglectful of Anglicanism's earlier educational priority of clergy teaching and layfolk learning aspects of Christian truth throughout their life."

When Packer looks at the Anglican establishment as it currently functions in England and North America, it is obvious that his lifelong commitment to Anglicanism as an ideal has been greatly strained.

My third preliminary observation, already implied in the foregoing quotations, is that Anglicanism as an ideal is defined for Packer in terms of Anglicanism as it existed in England in the sixteenth and seventeenth centuries. This is implied by the following statement (arbitrarily chosen from among many) that Packer made in a 2008 interview when he was asked about the feasibility of evangelicals separating from the Anglican Church of Canada: "If the Anglican Church of Canada . . . appealed to the 39 Articles and to the 1662 [Book of Common Prayer] as standards, then I would discourage . . . churches [from leaving] the ACC."

It is customary to think of Packer's rootedness in the Reformation solely or largely in terms of his devotion to the Puritans, but this is misleading. Packer's Reformation loyalty is also Anglican. He loves Thomas Cranmer and the Prayer Book that he authored. The Thirty-Nine Articles, not the Westminster Confession of Faith, is Packer's favorite Protestant creed.

Having stated these three qualifications—that Packer was never an uncritical supporter of the Church of England as a liberal institution, that he has found it increasingly necessary to distance himself from institutional Anglicanism in England and North America, and that his Anglican ideal belongs to the Reformation era—my procedure for the rest of this chapter is to explore what Anglicanism in its Reformation/evangelical form means to Packer. I will look at an apologetic monograph in which Packer defends Anglicanism and his allegiance to it, supplemented by additional defenses and recent interviews and speeches. Despite the qualifications stated above, we need to be clear that Packer's commitment to Anglicanism has been strong enough to persist through all vicissitudes right to the present day. A good summary statement from Packer himself is this: "I cannot say that I ever particularly liked the Church of England as I found it, but I remain an Anglican out of conviction that here is the right place, for here I possess the truest, wisest and potentially richest heritage in all Christendom" (preface to *The Thirty-Nine Articles: Their Place and Use Today*).

A Kind of Noah's Ark?

The foundational text for understanding Packer's pre-Canadian devotion to Anglicanism is a 1981 monograph published by Latimer House under the title *A Kind of Noah's Ark?* (and we should note the question mark). The book was Packer's reply to a letter from a young man who was considering entering the ministry in the Church of England but had reservations. Packer writes in his foreword: "You asked me how an evangelical who takes seriously his stewardship of revealed truth can ever with a good conscience take office in the Church of England when it is such a doctrinal Noah's ark, parading a comprehensiveness under which . . . literally everything goes." Packer accepted the challenge of answering this question with characteristic gusto, boldly asserting that "I'd like the world to have my answer."

In view of the strong endorsement of Anglicanism Packer makes in this monograph, it is surprising to see how much he initially concedes: "Certainly, this has not been a good century for Anglican evangelicals," he writes. He affirms that the traditional Anglican battle cry of comprehensiveness "is obviously right in principle," meaning that the church "should be as wide and tolerant in its embraces as the Christian revelation allows." But what Packer gives with one hand he takes away with the other when he writes that "the present-day reality of Anglican comprehensiveness is not like that," being instead an abandonment of basic Christian doctrines, starting with scriptural authority and belief in the supernatural. Further, "That the liberal theological method has come to stay in the Church of England is . . . not open to doubt."

In view of these melancholy facts, why should a person choose to stay in the Church of England instead of separating from it? Tradition counts for a lot with Packer, as seen in his adducing two role models before he proceeds to offer logical arguments in favor of Anglicanism. His models are Charles Simeon and J. C. Ryle, both of whom remained as clerics in an Anglican Church that opposed them. According to Packer, they were great people who had the right principles and the right program.

The foregoing considerations make up the opening chapter of Packer's monograph. They represent an appeal to experience, and they are designed to gain an initial positive feeling toward the Church of England. Who would not wish to be a latter-day Simeon or Ryle?

Chapter 2 is more analytic. In it, Packer sets himself the task of exploring four distinct conceptions of the principle of comprehensiveness on which Anglicanism has based itself (and we should note that the subtitle of the monograph is *The Anglican Commitment to Comprehensiveness*). One conception of Anglican comprehensiveness is *inclusiveness*, which initially allowed (and ideally still allows) for a broad range of doctrine and practice within the "acceptance of what the Bible, Creeds and Articles contain as normative revelation." The positive twist is that such inclusiveness "expressed doctrinal modesty but not doctrinal indifferentism," but Packer acknowledges that "too many Anglicans have moved beyond this position for it to stand as an account of what Anglican comprehensiveness means today."

A second Anglican definition of comprehensiveness that has been advanced is *integration*, defined as "the synthesizing in action of apparent theological opposites." Packer dismisses this definition as the product of theological liberalism and laxity. A third common understanding of Anglican comprehensiveness is that of union amid a state of *inner tension*—disagreements within the church are tolerated because of the benefits that Anglican comprehensiveness offers. This is seen as the price that Anglicanism "pays for the privilege of fulfilling its unique vocation in reintegrating Christ's divided church." It is an ideal that Packer does not wholly disparage, but in practice it has not yielded what he wants. The fourth modern manifestation of Anglican comprehensiveness is an untenable *relativism*.

Thus ends chapter 2. Packer is three-fourths of the way through his monograph and has mainly disparaged the church that he has set himself to defend to a potential clerical candidate. He gives his third chapter the title "The Hard-Made Decision," borrowing a statement that Ludwig van Beethoven placed above the last movement of his last quartet. The arguments that Packer advances include the following:

- The Anglican Church is no longer the single required religion of the nation, so Anglicans today are Anglican by choice. To choose Anglicanism is an act of Christian liberty.
- "I maintain that a man with his eyes open to the full range of Anglican doctrinal pluralism may yet responsibly choose to be an Anglican, even an Anglican minister, though it may be a hard-made decision bringing misery as well as fulfillment."
- Even in a denomination that has no adequate safeguards against theological liberalism, the *ideal* of Anglicanism remains intact. According to Packer, "evangelicals were right to approve the older type of comprehensiveness, based on common acceptance of the fundamentals of the creed," even though they cannot "condone what that historic comprehensiveness has now turned into."

- Evangelicals who remain within the Anglican Church can serve it by maintaining doctrinal orthodoxy and "tackling off-key views in debate and showing them inadequate."

The concluding statement for the defense is as follows: "The way in which Anglican tolerance obliges you to cope with Anglican doctrinal disorder is, though taxing, the best way both for you and for the Church as a whole." A follow-up statement is that "on the doctrinal front I do not in fact entertain rosy hopes."

The most noteworthy aspect of Packer's defense is that it describes exactly how he conducted his professional and church life in England through the 1970s. *A Kind of Noah's Ark?* is an apology not only for the Anglican Church, but also for Packer's life (an *apologia pro vitae*). Packer worked tirelessly to defend Anglican evangelicalism against liberal forces. He remained hopeful that the denomination was not as liberal as many thought. On the next-to-last page of *A Kind of Noah's Ark?* Packer offers the verdict that "there is no solid reason to suppose that those Anglicans who contend for the historic gospel are fighting a losing battle." Of course, Packer would not make that claim for the mainline Anglican Church in England and Canada today.

The other point to note is that Packer's endorsement of Anglicanism is not an embracing of an institution that has abandoned its orthodox roots. The picture of the Church of England that emerges from his monograph (as well as from recent interviews regarding the Anglican Church of Canada) is overwhelmingly negative. Packer's devotion to Anglicanism is to an ideal and to an institution as it once was—and can be once again, when it returns to its original identity.

A Kind of Noah's Ark? provides a conceptual framework for what Packer means by Anglicanism. Although the book does not mount a defense of Anglican ecclesiology, Packer has always been approving of Anglican church structure and hierarchy. This is made clear in the chapter "Taking the Church Seriously" in his 2013 book *Taking God Seriously*. After taking a paragraph to describe the complex English episcopate, Packer asks, "Is this setup biblical?" In answering that question, Packer's first assertion is that "it is not mandated or exemplified in the Bible." But for Packer, the Anglican ecclesiastical structure does "express New Testament principles and priorities regarding the local church's life" and does "meet the New Testament requirements that everything in the church be geared for edification." This is a principial endorsement only, and in the next paragraph Packer outlines the degree to which the implementation of the ideal has broken down in the Anglican establishment in England and North America.

During a two-day conversation with Packer in June 2014, I asked him if he still endorsed *A Kind of Noah's Ark*? He replied that he did. He added that free-church denominations deal with heresy by disciplining the heterodox in their midst. Then, almost as an aside, he added a statement that explains a great deal of what I cover in this chapter: "Debate is also a form of discipline." The strategy that Packer endorsed in his years in the Anglican Church when he was in England was to engage liberals in debate.

The Thirty-Nine Articles

What does Anglicanism mean to Packer? It means commitment to an institutional church that, in its original and ideal form, he prefers for his church affiliation. It does not mean loyalty to institutional perversions of that ideal. But Anglicanism means more than an institutional church—it includes the embrace of the doctrinal summary of Anglican belief known as the Thirty-Nine Articles.

Every creedal institution or denomination has a founding and normative document that defines and safeguards the beliefs of the group that accepts it as its creed. For Lutherans, it is the Augsburg Confession. For the Dutch Reformed, it is the Heidelberg Catechism. For Presbyterians, it is the Westminster Confession of Faith. For Anglicans, it is the Thirty-Nine Articles, formulated in the middle of the sixteenth century. Packer is Anglican by virtue of his embracing of the Thirty-Nine Articles as his preferred creed of Christian doctrine.

Packer's theology courses have privileged the Thirty-Nine Articles as the source for definitive statements of Christian doctrines. Likewise, in his writings, the most frequent historical references to Protestant doctrine are to the Thirty-Nine Articles. Packer sometimes flags this allegiance in his books, as in the following passage from *God Has Spoken* (1979 introduction):

> The present revised and enlarged reissue is less specifically Anglican in its angle, though its demonstration of the Bible-based, Bible-oriented character of the Church of England formularies (the Thirty-Nine

> Articles of 1563, the 1662 Book of Common Prayer, and the Homilies attested in Article 35) remains intact, as a testimony to my fellow-Anglicans of where their true roots are.

Even when quoting from other traditions, Packer keeps his Anglican allegiance clear, as in the preface to *Concise Theology*: "My frequent quoting of the Westminster Confession may raise some eyebrows, since I am an Anglican and not a Presbyterian. But since the Confession was intended to amplify the Thirty-Nine Articles, and most of its framers were Anglican clergy, . . . I think I am entitled to value it as part of my Reformed Anglican heritage."

But Packer's devotion to the Thirty-Nine Articles is even deeper than I have noted. He has published articles and books on this creed at multiple points in his career. A 1961 monograph entitled *The Thirty-Nine Articles* was a revision of six articles published in the preceding year in *The Church of England Newspaper*. A 1968 book was entitled *The Thirty-Nine Articles Today*, followed the next year by *A Guide to the Thirty-Nine Articles Today*. In 1984, Latimer House published *The Thirty-Nine Articles: Their Place and Use Today* (authored by Packer and with contributions by R. T. Beckwith).

The last-named book is a good summary of why and how the Thirty-Nine Articles have been important to Packer. The book begins by printing the definitive 1563 text of the articles. These are the words that Packer has known for a lifetime and loves. In the introduction that follows, Packer articulates his mission to "help Anglicans both to re-learn and to re-apply some basic biblical truths with which authentic Anglican identity is bound up." The Thirty-Nine Articles "have great theological strength and value" in the pursuit of that goal. Subsequent chapters lament the silence of the Thirty-Nine Articles in the modern Anglican Church, reconstruct the history of the articles, analyze the proper place of the articles in the Anglican Church, and outline a program for using the articles (with the three headings being *assimilate, apply, and augment*).

My interest here is not to reproduce the details of the book, but to accentuate what we learn about Packer from it. The first thing that the book signals is his love for this familiar formulation of the doctrines of the Christian faith. Christians who belong to non-creedal churches or traditions do not experience this, but those who were raised in creedal traditions and have continued in them know the authentic thrill of reading, hearing, and memorizing the words of their preferred creed or catechism. Additionally, Packer is so committed to the Thirty-Nine Articles that he sees their recovery in the Anglican Church as a key to that church's spiritual recovery and health. For Packer, the articles are a point of reference, personally and tactically, for the Anglican Church. The centrality of this document is an important strand in his Anglicanism. Whenever the Thirty-Nine Articles are mentioned, Packer's enthusiasm for them becomes evident.

The Prayer Book and Liturgical Worship

For Packer, Anglicanism means a specific church and its creed. It also means liturgical worship based on Cranmer's Book of Common Prayer. The Prayer Book was part of Packer's earliest experiences of Sunday worship. Even before he attained saving faith, the words of the Prayer Book entered his mind and memory. When he came to saving faith, the words became his heart religion as well.

I will begin with Packer's personal commitment to the Prayer Book and his use of it in daily life apart from the assembled church. In a 2009 interview, Packer outlined the details. He began by noting that his childhood experience in an Anglican church introduced him to the words of the Prayer Book. Then, in the years following his conversion, the Prayer Book "anchored itself deeper and deeper in my conscious life." By now, Packer has "memorized most of the regular services." But that is only the beginning. His current daily routine is to walk for thirty minutes in the early morning. As he walks, he says the Morning Prayer from the Prayer Book. At night, he does "a minimal sign-off after the day's living." When he is asked to give people advice for becoming regular in prayer, he suggests that they pray the Collects of the Prayer Book in private.

This commitment to liturgical "set forms" extends to public worship as well. On Sundays, Packer's present practice is to attend the 7:30 a.m. Communion service at St. John's Shaughnessy Anglican Church in Vancouver, which follows the Book of Common Prayer very closely. He believes that "the whole of the Daily Office—Morning and Evening Prayer both—is admirably angled for corporate use." For Packer, the ceremonial language of the Prayer Book is part of what makes it powerful. The language is ceremonial because "we are addressing royalty when we're praying to our God." The dignity of the language "should be appreciated as making for reverence, rather than treated as some sort of problem." Of course, this requires teaching; "it doesn't come naturally to anyone, just as it doesn't come naturally to understand the Bible the first time you read it."

In a 1966 booklet entitled *The Gospel in the Prayer Book*, Packer explains the meaning of the Anglican Communion service. He stresses the sequence or rhythm of the worship that Cranmer embedded in the liturgy. There are three steps to the sequence in morning and evening prayer: the confession of sin, the announcement of forgiveness through Christ's atonement, and the exercise of faith in praise, testimony, intercession, and receiving instruction. It is not hard to imagine that this sequence appeals strongly to the orderly mind of J. I. Packer. The 1662 Communion service follows the same three-part paradigm, only it gives it to us three times:

> Like most masterpieces, the Prayer Book Communion service has a basic structure that is extremely simple; just three repeats of the sin-grace-faith cycle, like three turns of a screw, each going further than the last in fixing the Gospel in our hearts and drawing out our response to it. The second adds to the first a sharpened application; the third adds to the second a sacramental confirmation.

Obviously, Packer has analyzed the Anglican liturgy very carefully. It has been a passion of his life to see it implemented in Anglican churches much more thoroughly than it has been in recent times.

Packer's Troubles with the Anglican Church of Canada

I want to return to the story of Packer's involvement with the institutional Anglican Church. When Packer moved to Canada, he lived out his Anglicanism in the Anglican Church of Canada, even though his official clerical investiture remained with the Church of England. I will explore Packer's conflict with the Anglican Church of Canada in the final chapter. What I need to establish here is that Packer's participation in the Anglican Church of Canada was far more antagonistic than his churchmanship in England had been.

In England, Packer was tolerated as a minority voice on church committees. He was regularly outvoted, but there was never the threat of being defrocked. All of that changed when the Canadian church decided to make the sanctioning of homosexuality a requirement for remaining an ordained cleric in the Anglican Church of Canada. One can trace the gathering storm step by step over the period of a decade. All that I need to say in this context is that Packer and other evangelical clerics were ejected from the Anglican Church of Canada.

We might expect, with the Canadian suspension of Packer's license, that his participation in the institutional Anglican Church would have declined and perhaps become extinct. That is what I assumed before I did the research for this biography. After all, Packer's side lost, and he was deprived of his license to minister. The situation is actually the reverse of this. The case can be made that Packer's influence in the institutional Anglican Church world is now at an all-time high.

When we look at the story of Packer's Anglicanism after his move to Canada, we can discern three successive phases, and these will constitute the outline for the rest of this chapter. The phases are: (1) continuing in the long-held position of remaining active and hopeful in the mainstream of the Church of England; (2) forced separation from the liberal wing of Anglicanism; and (3) the flowering of Packer's Anglicanism in an alternative Anglican Church.

Attempted Continuation of a Longstanding Modus Operandi

When Packer arrived in Vancouver, he became a participating member and honorary assistant on the ministerial staff at St. John's Shaughnessy Anglican Church. For some twenty years, he continued to practice and advocate what he had as an evangelical within the liberal Church of England; that is, he remained within the fellowship and served a voice for orthodoxy in whatever ways he could. The position that he articulated in 1981 (*A Kind of Noah's Ark?*) was a rejection of "ecumenical idealists on the one hand and evangelical separatists on the other." Citing the biblical example of the unruly church at Corinth, Packer argued that conflict over doctrine has always been part of the church, yielding "the far-reaching principle that God will regularly allow divisions of one sort or another to enter the churches." Not to worry, as the British say. The risks of "unending pluralism, constant muddle, public vacillation and embarrassment" should be embraced by evangelical Anglicans as "part of the package deal which they accepted when they chose Anglicanism." Their positive mission is to remain Anglican, take as positive a view of the mainline church as possible ("though disorderly," it "is far from dead"), and "persist" at the parish and individual levels.

Packer followed this game plan for two decades when he moved to Canada. One can see this continuity in a 1995 address delivered at a church conference in England. Despite the storm clouds that were gathering in the Anglican Church of Canada, Packer reaffirmed his belief "that Anglicanism embodies the richest, truest, wisest heritage in all Christendom." Having asserted that, Packer immediately conceded that Anglicanism "is sinking" everywhere in the West (Canada, Britain, the United States, Australasia), but this truth needed to be balanced by the fact that "the church grows and the gospel advances by leaps and bounds" under Anglican auspices in Africa.

Faced with the onslaught of the homosexual lobby in the West, what should evangelical Anglicans do? Packer outlined three options. The first two were pietistic acquiescence and separation. Regarding the latter, Packer's advice was, "Weigh the loss before you go." People leaving Anglicanism would lose "a heritage." In Packer's view, "the loss would far outweigh the gain."

Packer's preferred course was what he called "the inner mission." Its program was as follows: "Evangelicals get together within the church, establish their own links of fellowship and joint action. They are together for the renewal and invigorating of the church." None of this envisioned the development of the alternative Anglican Church that eventually materialized.

Separation

The original Puritans provide a model for what Packer advocated—and for what happened to him. Most Puritans remained within the Anglican fold, even though many of them (such as John Milton) totally opposed the official Anglican Church and its worship rituals (such as vestments and the use of the Prayer Book). They were nonconformists ("not conforming to Anglican church practices"), but most of them attended worship services at local Anglican churches on Sundays. If the local parish church was under the control of Puritans, they were content to retain the title of Anglican. But as the seventeenth century wore on, many Puritans found themselves in the position of being separatists, because they were not allowed to practice their Puritan preferences. The most notable example was the Great Ejection of 1662. In that year, the Act of Uniformity resulted in the eviction from the pulpit of two thousand ministers who refused to conform to dictates from the Church of England.

This is what gradually happened to Packer in the Anglican Church of Canada, confirming again that his life has often followed Puritan contours. One can trace a gradual separation that was under way in a series of statements that Packer made about the Anglican Church as the homosexual lobby became more and more coercive. Below, I have collected specimen statements that Packer made in interviews and public addresses. Anyone making statements such as these was in a process of separating from the church that he criticized.

- "If the gospel is at stake there must be division. . . . In the case of a division like New Westminster [the Vancouver diocese that condoned same-sex unions as official Anglican policy] this is a necessary split."
- "We [evangelical clerics who refuse to accept same-sex unions] were put in a situation comparable to the Puritan clergy in 1662."
- "If [the Anglican Church of Canada] continues to shrink at the present rate—this, of course, is comparable to the situation of the Church of England, too—it will be extinct by the middle of [the twenty-first century]."
- "The Church of England appears to be much weaker . . . than it was in 1960. That year, in my reckoning, was the top year, the most fruitful year, in the venture which God brought into being, and in which I found myself caught up, for restoring evangelical truth to leadership in Anglican affairs. Things, I believe, are different today."
- In the church in the West, "you have a remnant who are standing fast while the rest of the church, the much larger community, . . . are basically selling themselves down the river. But the remnant stands fast. It's a remnant situation."
- "Why did I walk out [of a meeting of the synod of the Anglican Diocese of New Westminster when it officially sanctioned same-sex unions]? Because this decision . . . falsifies the gospel of Christ, abandons the authority of Scripture, jeopardizes the salvation of fellow human beings, and betrays the church in its God-appointed role as the bastion and bulwark of divine truth."

All of these statements stand as a foil to the optimistic and accepting statements that Packer had made until the homosexual lobby gained dominance in his diocese in the official Canadian Anglican Church.

It is obvious that Packer ended up doing what he refused to do under pressure from D. Martyn Lloyd-Jones in 1966: he separated from the mainline Anglican Church of Canada and its official church hierarchy. Packer himself has referenced the link with Lloyd-Jones and his current situation: "In England, when Dr. Martyn Lloyd-Jones called on evangelicals ministering in doctrinally-mixed denominations to leave them, I resisted the idea. I did not expect that in Canada withdrawal from the diocese and province that had welcomed me would become an issue of conscience, but so it is. Like other Christians, I find peace in doing what I believe I have to do, but I cannot always find pleasure in it."

Of course, the situation in England was not exactly parallel to the one in Canada. Lloyd-Jones had proposed voluntary separation from the Church of England. In 2002, Packer was suspended by his diocesan bishop and thus, in effect, evicted, like many Puritan clergy in the seventeenth century were. Also, in England in 1966, the only alternative if one separated from the Church of England was to become a member of the free (nonconformist) church in one form or another (Congregational independency or Protestant denominationalism, such as Baptist or Methodist). In Canada, Packer remained Anglican by affiliating with an alternative Anglican federation. Still, we should not downplay what a momentous shift happened in Packer's Anglicanism.

Would Packer have separated if the axe had not fallen in the form of suspension in the wake of official sanction of same-sex unions? It is inconceivable that he would have. Although Packer never condoned doctrinal heterodoxy within the denomination of which he was a member, he consistently endorsed leniency regarding the presence of liberal forces within Anglicanism as opposed to separating from the church. Here is a sampling of such statements:

- Evangelicals in the Church of England "give every viewpoint which claims, however freakishly, to be in line with Scripture and reason, opportunity to make its claim good."
- "They are prepared to show conscientious goodwill to a good deal of experimental theology which would, perhaps, be looked at askance in doctrinally unmixed churches."

- "They see that in the providence of God much insight, stimulus and help in understanding spins off from work done by good scholars whose claim to be interpreting Christianity is marred by some seemingly heterodox opinions."
- "They conclude that the church gains more from continuing to accept these men on the basis of their good intentions, while looking to its orthodox scholars to correct any oddities, than it could do by officially outlawing them and declining to pay serious attention to their work."
- "While welcoming what insights they find in the work of the heterodox, they approach the excrescences of current Anglican over-comprehensiveness from the standpoint of the original comprehensiveness to which they adhere as their ideal."
- "So it is best . . . not to treat those who seem heretical on one key point in a way that keeps the church from benefiting by their insight on other points."

As part of this relaxed attitude toward the presence of liberalism within the Church of England, we should also note that Packer has always rejected the concept of guilt by association, which he labels "a nonsense notion, which has been given an unhappy airing during the past two decades."

Packer makes it clear that he changed his mind on retaining membership in a liberal denomination because the situation changed. In a 2008 interview, Packer was asked: "You were criticized [in previous days] for staying in a pluralist denomination. What is different now?" He replied: "The difference is that in those days the discussion by heretics was purely notional. You could disclaim the errors of the errorists and seek to persuade people to turn their back on them. . . . Guilt by association didn't apply. But this is different from" what has happened in regard to the gay issue more recently, with the official sanctioning of erroneous practice. "This was not happening in England [when I was there]."

A New Lease on Life for Packer's Anglicanism

Despite his eviction from the denomination to which he gave some of his best efforts and a great deal of time, Packer today remains more of an Anglican than ever. His separation from Anglicanism in Canada has not meant separation from Anglicanism. All of this is possible because of the emergence of an alternative Anglicanism (my term). It exists in several institutional forms, but the one to which Packer has committed is the Anglican Network in Canada (ANIC), which is now a branch of the Anglican Church in North America (ACNA). There were various intermediate and temporary steps leading to the establishment of ANIC, including a conference held in Montreal called Essentials '94, and Packer was very involved with them.

Packer has made clear in interviews that he has not ceased to be an Anglican, but has instead affiliated with what he identifies by such terms as "realignment" and "parallel jurisdiction." This refers to new associations of Anglican Churches such as GAFCON (Global Anglican Future), ANIC, and ACNA. For Packer, these Anglican federations "are not disrupting the Anglican Communion, we are keeping it together by ensuring that people in it are kept in fellowship with a biblically based version of . . . Christianity. You thus make it possible for the faithful to stay together. . . . Parallel jurisdiction and realignment is the only way to keep the Anglican Communion together."

In a 2007 address delivered at the Anglican Network in Canada Launch Conference, Packer contrasted "Anglicans Adrift" (the liberal Anglican establishment) to "Anglicans Anchored." The latter, an alternative Anglican association, is in the true lineage of the Anglican Church that was put in place in England in the middle of the sixteenth century. It (and not the liberal Anglican Church) is the body that upholds "historic Anglican standards" as defined "in our foundation documents and expressed in our Prayer Book." Packer's lifelong enthusiasm for the Anglican Church is still present: "We rejoice to know that the more than 90% of worshipping Anglicans worldwide outside the Old West [Britain, North America, Australasia] are solidly loyal to the Christian heritage as Anglicanism has received it, and we see our realignment as among other things an enhancing of our solidarity with them." In fact, Packer claimed in the address that "what we are doing is precisely not leaving Anglicanism behind."

When I first encountered statements by Packer to the effect that he is today more an Anglican than ever, I was very surprised in view of his expulsion from the Anglican Church of Canada. But in the context of his high stature in the alternative Anglican church, the sentiment strikes me as easily provable. For once, Packer is on the majority side of the Anglican church group to which he belongs. Heretofore, he has always been a minority evangelical voice in a denomination that as a whole disregarded him. I am reminded of the Anglican cleric who examined Packer for ordination and expressed a "profound distaste" for Packer's theology. That is the kind of milieu within which Packer was an apologist and activist for half a century.

All that has changed with the Anglican realignment. The Anglican world in which Packer now moves looks to him for leadership and hangs on his words. He has been a regular and influential speaker at ecclesiastical meetings devoted to forging new Anglican structures. Interviewers latch onto him for comments at every possible opportunity. Packer is the "poster boy" for Anglican bloggers and speakers as they make their pitch for their preferred denomination. Todd D. Hunter, the author of *The Accidental Anglican*, an apologetic book, predictably asked Packer to write the foreword. Packer serves on working committees for the Anglican Church in North America, and while this work might seem like a throwback to his Latimer House days, this time his opinions actually carry weight and make an impact (as in a recently formulated catechism for the church).

Summary

The story of J. I. Packer's Anglicanism has been such a long and complex one that writing this chapter has required endurance. The dominant thread has been his extreme passion for Anglicanism and willingness to devote time and energy to the institutional Anglican Church. Few academicians and authors have ever given as much time to working on church committees as Packer has. For a quarter of a century, the work of people such as Packer gave evangelicals within the Church of England a stay of execution, during which many Anglican parishes carried on their work untrammeled by hostile decisions being made at the bureaucratic level. Then, when Packer was suspended by the Anglican Church of Canada, it appeared that he had finally lost out to the liberal establishment. But he emerged from that low point in his Anglican history to enter what might be his finest moment as an Anglican. He is finally in an Anglican federation that honors him and heeds his wisdom.

I want to finish this chapter with a caution that we should not overemphasize Packer's Anglicanism. Until I did the research for this chapter, I had no conception of the depth of his commitment to Anglicanism. To me, he was primarily an evangelical in the "mere Christianity" mode (a formula popularized by C. S. Lewis, but coined by Packer's hero, Richard Baxter). I am not alone in seeing Packer this way. Hunter (author of *The Accidental Anglican*) confides that "as Packer was having this big effect in my life, I never thought of him as an Anglican. . . . All I knew was that Packer was English and one of the most influential evangelicals in the Western world. . . . I thought that Packer must be one of us." While Hunter finds this embarrassing, he should not, for Packer largely agrees. In the preface to his 2013 book *Taking God Seriously* (a book written for Anglicans), Packer writes, "Before I am an Anglican I am an evangelical, and I have tried to write in such a way that all evangelicals . . . will benefit."

21

Theology

"By trade," wrote J. I. Packer in 2001, "I am a theologian." Likewise, "James Innell Packer is a British-born Canadian Christian theologian," a biographical site informs us; "he currently serves as the Board of Governors' Professor of Theology at Regent College in Vancouver, British Columbia." In a 2014 conversation, Packer encapsulated his life calling in the formula "theological education and formation." There are other labels that can be accurately applied to J. I. Packer, but the dominant one is that of theologian.

As I stand on the threshold of this chapter on the role that theology has played in Packer's life, I need to remind my readers that I am writing a biography, not conducting a dissertation-style analysis of Packer's theology or theological method. My goal is to tell the story of how theology has given shape and substance to Packer's life and career (both academic and ecclesiastical).

The early sections of this chapter are built around the framework of three areas in which theology has been important in Packer's life. First, theology has been a foundation of his own spiritual life. Second, theology has been Packer's profession—the area of his academic and teaching specialization. Third, theology has been more than a profession for Packer; it has also been part of his platform for reforming the church.

Theology in Packer's Personal Spiritual Life

Packer's lifelong involvement with the Puritans is rooted in his early experience after his conversion in college, and the same is true of his calling as a theologian. After his conversion, Packer's personal spiritual life became his passion, and secondarily, service in the Oxford Christian Union. That was his general religious orientation, but it took a specifically theological turn almost at once. When confronted with the triumphalist holiness position of the Keswick school, Packer providentially stumbled upon the account of mortification of sin, or sanctification, propounded by the Puritan John Owen. Anyone who has read Owen knows how thoroughly theological his writing and thinking are. For Owen to have solved Packer's first spiritual crisis after his conversion means that from the beginning Packer's interest in theology has had an existential urgency about it. Packer became a theologian partly because theology rescued him spiritually.

The theological compass was thus set early in Packer's life as a Christian. When I asked him whether he became impatient with his study of classical languages and literature during his undergraduate days, he replied that he did not because he knew that he would pursue theological studies after he graduated from the Oxford classics program. In fact, he felt at the time (and continues to believe) that studying something beyond theology would make him a better theologian than he would be without it.

As planned, Packer did pursue graduate study at a theological college. Then he studied for a doctorate, and his choice of subject for his dissertation was thoroughly theological—not just Richard Baxter, but Baxter's doctrine of redemption. The official title of the dissertation spells this out: "The Redemption and Restoration of Man in the Thought of Richard Baxter: A Study in Puritan Theology."

Called to Be a Professional Theologian

In 1992, Packer published an article in *Christianity Today* in which he developed the metaphor of the theologian as a plumber and sewage man. The article confirms the thoroughness with which Packer self-identifies with theology as a profession. He begins the article by saying, "Since I am paid to teach theology, I get typed as a professional theologian." By itself, that sentence might be interpreted as having a note of protest, but at the end of the article, Packer fully embraces the label "theologian." He writes, "Most of all, I want to be a plumber and sewage man." Packer had already put this metaphor before the public in his 1988 book *Hot Tub Religion*, and there, too, he had identified himself as belonging to the group he had just described: "This book might be called *I Am a Theologian*, for this is precisely what I am attempting to do."

The *Christianity Today* article also develops a profile of the professional theologian. It is not so much an outline of a method or task as a description of the temperament that characterizes a theologian. Anyone reading the article naturally assimilates it as Packer's self-portrait, and that is how I propose to treat it here. He begins with the thesis that "professional theologians are curious creatures." In fact, "curiosity drives them." From that starting point, he makes the following points:

- Theologians "have a consuming interest in conceptualizing God and working out what is or might be true about him." Of course, all people "are theologians . . . who venture to think and say things about God," but "the professional's job is to help us do it right."
- We should applaud theologians for having an innate "curiosity in wanting to know all you can about the works and ways of your heavenly Father."
- Theologians are a professional group; they "form societies, talk professional jargon, publish books and journals addressed to each other," and interact with each others' ideas.
- Modern non-evangelical theologians have done the church a great disservice by pursuing the wrong kind of curiosity and thereby losing the respect of ordinary Christians. These theologians "marginalize themselves by endless concedings and relativizings of revealed truth." They become less and less relevant "for real Christian life," until finally "the saints lose patience and write off their theologians as curiosities in the sense of freaks."
- Ordinary Christians need to value what their theologians do: "they instruct today's and tomorrow's clergy; they pontificate to synods and conferences; they lobby leaders; they take up causes and challenge systems."

The entire article displays a strong apologetic stance, showing the degree to which Packer identifies with the group that he is describing. He does more than describe a professional group; he also paints a portrait of himself, showing us the temperamental makeup of J. I. Packer, the professional theologian.

Because Packer possesses the inclinations of a theologian, the approach that he takes to various subjects is often theological, even when other approaches are possible. Packer's writing and speaking on the Puritans, for example, are often theological, as seen in the titles of specimen addresses that he delivered during the two decades that the Puritan Conference was held: "Richard Baxter as a Theologian"; "The Puritan Theology of the Christian Life"; "The Puritan Idea of Communion with God"; and "Jonathan Edwards and the Theology of Revival."

Again, the *ESV Study Bible* contains a series of articles under the rubric "reading the Bible as . . ." (subsequently republished by Crossway as a free-standing book entitled *Understanding Scripture*); Packer could have written on several of the topics, but he wrote on the subject with which the editors most naturally associated him—"Reading the Bible Theologically." An anthology of essays on preaching entitled *When God's Voice Is Heard* (Inter-Varsity, 1995) covers a broad span of topics related to preaching, but we could guess which chapter Packer wrote from the title: "The Preacher as Theologian: Preaching and Systematic Theology."

We might say that Packer's mental predisposition—his default mode—is theology. This was impressed on me when I consulted Packer's book *God's Words*. Because my own intuitions are literary, I expected to find something similar to a book that I co-edited entitled *Dictionary of Biblical Imagery*. Instead, I found the type of word study that theologians compile. Even though the same words appear as entries in *Dictionary of Biblical Imagery* (e.g., *death*, *holiness*, *justification*), Packer's approach is ideational, as he unpacks the theological and conceptual content of the words.

This "default" theological mode constantly reveals itself in Packer's writings. In his co-authored book *Praying*, it would have been entirely plausible to begin by adducing biblical data on the subject of prayer. Instead, Packer begins with a thoroughly theological chapter ("This Is Your God") that develops eight ideas about the God to whom we pray—God is personal, plural, perfect, powerful, purposeful, a promise-keeper, paternal, and praiseworthy. An essay entitled "Encountering Present-Day Views of Scripture" does not begin where we would expect. It opens with a unit entitled "Theology and Religion," on the rationale that when encountering a present-day view of Scripture, "you encounter more than a view of Scripture. What you meet is a total view of God and the world, that is, a total theology."

An obvious way to illustrate Packer's professional theological orientation is to note the degree to which theological topics have formed the substance of his publishing career. This is not to say that theology dominates his total corpus. Although theology is the largest single topic, Packer's repertoire encompasses so many subjects that theological subjects do not outweigh the other topics when they are placed together into a composite group.

Packer's first two published articles were on theological topics—"The Puritan Treatment of Justification by Faith" and "Sanctification—Puritan Teaching." In the 1950s, Packer published articles with the titles "'Keswick' and the Reformed Doctrine of Sanctification" and "God's Justification of Sinners." A sampling of titles from the 1960s and 1970s includes "The Bible in Modern Theology"; "Fellowship: The Theological Basis"; "Thomas Cranmer's Catholic Theology"; "Reservation: Theological Issues"; "Taking Stock in Theology"; and "Theology of the Reformation." If we fast-forward to the first decade of the present century, we find that theology remains a preoccupation for Packer: "Maintaining Evangelical Theology"; "Theology and Wisdom"; "The Glory of the Person of Christ"; and "Incarnate Forever: What Is the Scriptural and Theological Support for the Teaching that Jesus, the God-Man, Remains Eternally Incarnate?"

If we turn to the books that Packer has published over the course of his writing career, theology is again a foundation (along with the Bible) that undergirds the entire edifice. *Knowing God* is a book of theology that explores the character of God; we can call this theology—the study of God—in its pure form. *Evangelism and the Sovereignty of God* combines a practical topic—the nature of evangelism—with a theological one—how the sovereignty of God (a divine attribute) relates to summoning people to salvation. *Keep in Step with the Spirit* is an inquiry into the person and work of one person of the Trinity. The title *Concise Theology* speaks for itself.

We do not ordinarily limit the label *theology* just to the study of God, but extend it more broadly to encompass Christian doctrine generally. In the bibliographic overview that I have sketched above, I have kept the focus narrowly on articles and books devoted to the nature and work of God. But we can extend the label *theological* to many of Packer's articles and books beyond the cluster that I have delineated. His publishing career has represented the output of a theologian first and foremost.

Doing Theology for the People of God

I have taken the title for this section from a book of essays published in honor of Packer in 1996. The title *Doing Theology for the People of God* strikes exactly the right note. Theology has been more than a personal passion and profession for Packer (as sketched above). The flavor of his theological writing is different from most such writing that I have read. The distinctive feature is that for Packer, theology has been an important part of an envisioned program for church reform and renewal. The audience of theology *professors* is the students seated before them; the audience of most theological *authors* is individual readers; but the audience of Packer's theological writings is the institutional church and its congregants, with special attention to church leaders who are in a position to steer their churches locally and nationally in the direction of theological knowledge and orthodoxy.

This is a large subject, and my way of organizing it is as follows. First, I will note that Packer continuously places his theological writing into the context of the current neglect of sound theology and of theological thinking. In other words, the paucity of doctrinal knowledge in the church is the starting point for his theological writing. Then I will theorize that the churchwide focus of Packer's theological writing was influenced by his early professional years, when he was active in the Anglican Church at a denominational level. Third, I will note how the two foregoing considerations lend a tone of existential urgency to his theological writing. For these explorations, I have chosen Packer's theological *writing* because it is the body of data that is accessible; his speaking on theological topics can be assumed to have the same qualities that his theological writing possesses.

A Context of Theological Neglect

The impetus behind Packer's theologizing is more than a professional interest in the subject. It is fueled by alarm over the theological state of the institutional church and its members. Two main factors have contributed to this crisis. One is ignorance, or the lack of theological knowledge. The other is the inroads of liberal theology into the church. I will quote four passages that illustrate the platform from which Packer puts theology before the public:

- "The eclipse of doctrine among liberal Protestants and those they have influenced has reflected a somewhat confused notion that following Christ is in fact one form (other religions offer other forms) of everybody's natural and even instinctive religion. . . . The orthodox have often failed to see where liberal notions—no Trinity, no virgin birth, no objective atonement, no bodily resurrection and ascension, for starters—would take them." We are faced with "the doctrinally uninstructed condition of very many middle-aged and young attendees at Anglican worship services."—*Taking God Seriously*
- "Superficial smatterings of truth, blurry notions about God and godliness, and thoughtlessness about the issues of living . . . are all too often marks of evangelical congregations today, particularly, if we may dare to say it, some newly planted ones. . . . A far-reaching change of mindset about this is called for."—*Grounded in the Gospel: Teaching Believers the Old-Fashioned Way*
- "Clearly, we can only start [our quest to know God] from where we are. That, however, means setting out in a storm, for the doctrine of God is a storm center today. . . . Knowledge about God is strictly a nonentity. Types of teaching which profess such knowledge are written off as outmoded. . . . If we postpone our journey till the storm dies down, we may never get started at all."—*Knowing God*
- "Few children today, however, are brought up on the Westminster Shorter Catechism, and few modern worshipers will ever have heard a series of sermons covering the doctrine of the divine character. . . . Few, too, will ever have read anything simple and straightforward on the subject of the nature of God, for scarcely any such writing exists at the present time."—*Knowing God*

All evangelical theologians desire to see their audiences embrace truth about God and the Christian faith. But that is different from where Packer begins his theological mission. For reasons I will note shortly, Packer has the entire landscape of evangelicalism in view when he writes about theology. He writes under the great burden of the shipwreck most Christian churches and parishioners today have brought on by indifference to theology on corporate and individual levels.

This sense of angst is heightened because as a person with a strong historical sense, Packer is aware that the situation was once the reverse of what it is today. I am reminded of the anecdote of a Frenchman who visited England during the Puritan Reformation and returned home with the amazed announcement that "in England, everyone is a theologian." As a Puritan scholar, Packer knows that theological ideas that are little known today "were not always so to the people of God. There was a time when the subject of God's attributes (as it was called) was thought so important as to be included in the catechism which all children in the churches were taught." As an advocate of the instructional method known as catechesis, Packer is thoroughly aware that the systematic teaching of Christian doctrine in the church "was a staple item in the church life of the first Christian centuries and also of the Reformation and Counter-Reformation era."

The Church Context of Packer's Theologizing

If we ask how Packer arrived at this "global" (as opposed to individual) platform for plying his vocation as a theologian, I believe that the answer lies in the early decades of his life as a Christian. Packer identified with the Church of England almost from the start. He became an Anglican minister. Then he taught at an Anglican theological college. Most decisive of all was the decade during which he served as warden at Latimer House, a semiofficial arm of the Church of England. The whole scope of his work at Latimer House was directed to the institutional church.

This is readily apparent when we look at Packer's theological publications during his tenure at Latimer House. His 1963 booklet *Keep Yourselves from Idols* was a refutation of the theological errors disseminated in Bishop John A. T. Robinson's book *Honest to God*. Given Packer's position at Latimer House, this was more than a private response; it was perceived as a position paper representing evangelical

Anglicanism. Packer published books with the Church Book Room entitled *The Thirty-Nine Articles Today* and *A Guide to the Thirty-Nine Articles Today*. When Packer addressed the 1967 Keele Congress on the subject "The Good Confession: Our Crisis and God's Christ," he did not speak simply as a theologian addressing a conference of professional theologians; he spoke as an influential Anglican who hoped to influence the theological direction of his denomination.

Not all of Packer's theological writing and speaking was this overtly denominational, but Packer has plied his theological trade in an environment that prompts him to think in terms of the church and its structures. Systematic theologies by Louis Berkhof and Wayne Grudem (for example) inform us about correct doctrine; Packer's theological writings are part of an organized plan for church reform, and at this point I am reminded of a similar orientation in the English Puritans. In a chapter on "Taking Repentance Seriously" (in *Taking God Seriously*), when Packer turns to application, he does not have the individual Christian in view, but the church: "I turn now to the implications for our corporate life of the things I have been saying." And the subheading that immediately follows is "The State of the Church," referring specifically to the Anglican Church in Canada.

The Urgency of Theology

Because Packer believes that the future of the church is at stake in the theological enterprise, he "does theology" with a great sense of urgency. For example, starting in 2006, Packer published a series of booklets as part of the Anglican Agenda Series in Canada. The individual pamphlets were brought together in book form in *Taking God Seriously* (Crossway, 2013). In the preface to the book, Packer writes, "As an Anglican, I write with a sense of urgency in response to recent trends in my own church context." He then adds, "But readers who are not Anglicans will recognize many of the same trends in their own denominational circles, and may find that this book speaks pointedly to their situations, challenges, and concerns." The unifying motif of taking an individual doctrine "seriously" (as in the titles of the pamphlets and chapters of the eventual book) is not something that is foregrounded in a typical book of theology. Most theological writing aims only at conceptual accuracy; Packer's theology aims at the renewal of the church.

Packer's book on the theology of the Holy Spirit (*Keep in Step with the Spirit*) provides a good illustration of how this note of urgency works itself out. The book is one of Packer's "occasional" writings. The occasion was the sudden prominence of charismatics in the evangelical wing of the Church of England during the 1970s. (That something needed to be said to clarify thinking about the Holy Spirit is suggested by the fact that John Stott had published *The Baptism and Fullness of the Holy Spirit* already in 1964.) Packer's book is thoroughly documented; in fact, he resisted outside pressure to write the book until his thinking had had time to reach closure on the subject. Packer says in the preface that his book will cover "encounters with Wesley's perfectionism, classic Keswick teaching, and contemporary charismatic spirituality." These topics were important in Packer's personal life, but also on the Anglican evangelical scene at the time. A lot was "up for grabs" in regard to thinking about the Holy Spirit as he composed the book on his typewriter. Packer's book spoke with urgency to the controversy of the moment.

For a second illustration, I will cite the Leon Morris Lecture that Packer delivered in 1990 in Melbourne, Australia. The address (available in printed form in *The J. I. Packer Collection* edited by Alister McGrath) was occasioned by the assault of several prominent evangelicals on the doctrine of hell. Packer entitled his address "The Problem of Eternal Punishment." The address has the urgency of a rebuttal in a formal debate. Why did Packer choose this subject for this address when other topics were available? He answers that question himself:

> It may be that someone is still wondering why I chose to lecture on this somber theme rather than on any other subject. This is the moment for me to explain why. In today's Christianity, what I am now calling the divinely executed retributive process that operates in the world to come is becoming more and more a problem area for belief. Uncertainty is growing, and growing in a way that has a very weakening effect on Christian witness.

Packer then outlines the theological crisis that he is attempting to correct. His conclusion is that universalism "cannot but impoverish a Christian . . . and limit his usefulness to the Lord." This address does not come across as a chapter in a systematic theology book; it comes across as an attempt to salvage a segment of the evangelical church that is heading in the wrong direction.

How Packer Views Theology

I have devoted the first half of this chapter to *the theologian*—the person who composes and disseminates theology. I am ready to turn from the person to theology—how Packer regards the nature of the theological task and the methodology involved in performing that task.

When I first encountered Packer's metaphor of the theologian as a plumber and sewage man, I was mainly struck by the offbeat cleverness of it. The more I have pondered the metaphor and the passages in which Packer unfolds what he means, the more helpful it has seemed to me. So I will begin by scrutinizing how Packer explains this metaphor in his book *Hot Tub Religion*.

Packer starts by comparing theologians to water engineers and sewage specialists. He then elaborates the analogy as follows:

> Their role is to detect and eliminate intellectual pollution, and to ensure . . . that God's life-giving truth flows pure and unpoisoned into Christian hearts. Their calling obliges them to act as the church's water engineers, seeking by their preaching, teaching, and biblical exposition to make the flow of truth strong and steady; but it is particularly as disposers of spiritual sewage that I want to portray them.

This is very revealing in regard to Packer's theological writing (as we will see). In the passage from which I have quoted, he goes on to define the task of theologians-as-sewage-experts as being "to test the water and filter out anything they find that confuses minds, corrupts judgments, and distorts the way that Christians view their own lives."

Packer has dropped hints as to how he envisions the theologian's task in other places as well. Part of the task is to restore theological truth to a contemporary world and church that have abandoned their past. Thus, Packer criticizes theologians who do not take up the yoke of "reaffirming and vindicating the Christian heritage against all forms of unbelief and alternative belief." As we will see, Packer's theological writing and speaking have consistently turned to past traditions (starting with the Bible) as a reliable repository of theological truth. It is possible to read right past the subtitle of Packer's *Concise Theology*, but it points in the direction I have just noted: *A Guide to Historic Christian Beliefs*.

Packer's metaphor of the theologian as mapmaker is also instructive. According to Packer, when they are facing theological problems, theologians "should make a map of each problematical life-situation, with all the human factors involved, and then superimpose all the relevant biblical teachings and Bible-based considerations." The purpose of the resulting map is to provide guidance on life's journey—"to enable the walker to find his way." Because the issues of life are many, "the scale of the map will need to be fairly large." On the other hand, "technicalities (sometimes unavoidable . . .) will be pursued only for the sake of simplicity. Simplicity of principle, once it is achieved, makes for straightforwardness of practice." I cannot think of a more accurate description of Packer's theological writing. In the preface to his *Concise Theology*, he reinforces his method of simplicity: "I have aimed to keep things as simple as possible."

If the task of theology is getting rid of error, supplying pure doctrine, and providing guidance, the ultimate goal is something different. The final outcome is to be doxological—"giving God glory for his glorious achievements." In the preface to *Concise Theology*, Packer writes, "Theology is for doxology and devotion—that is, the praise of God and the practice of godliness."

I will conclude my analysis of Packer's theorizing about the theologian's task by looking again at his metaphor of the theologian as a plumber and sewage man. This two-fold paradigm provides an excellent overview of his theological writing. It is easily demonstrated that from the beginning of his career as a theologian, much of Packer's writing and speaking has been directed toward opposing theological error. Since much of this refutation has taken its cue from current happenings on the religious scene, we can detect a loose chronology to Packer's career of "eliminating theological effluent" from the church (quotation from the *Christianity Today* article). Here is a brief chronology of what Packer the theologian has combatted:

- the Keswick view of sanctification (triumph over sin by "letting go and letting God")

- the liberal view of the Bible and general disparagement of evangelicalism
- ecumenical appeals for church unity that ignore theological disagreements
- incorrect thinking about the sovereignty of God, including how it affects evangelism
- theological confusion about the person and work of the Holy Spirit
- unscriptural claims about divine guidance
- universalism (denial of the doctrine of hell)
- the sanctioning of homosexuality
- the success ethic and its infiltration into the church

Of course, there have been additional skirmishes along the way. The lengthiness of the list shows the degree to which Packer has taken seriously his self-defined theological task of ridding the church of theological sewage.

But getting rid of sewage is only half of the theological task as Packer envisions it. The other half of the equation is ensuring a supply of clean water. In this regard, we should note that in the very articles and books in which Packer joins battle with the errors noted above, he also supplies the antidote. Additionally, I believe that we can look at Packer's publications and see the theological ideas that have particularly seized the sovereignty of his mind. The list is as follows:

- sanctification and holiness
- salvation or redemption
- the atonement
- the sovereignty of God (and the related doctrines of grace in Calvinistic theology)
- the nature of revelation and the Bible
- the sacraments
- the nature of the church and church unity
- the attributes of God
- the person and work of the Holy Spirit
- the nature of man (the theological category of anthropology), with due attention to human sinfulness

Here, too, there have been many excursions into additional theological topics.

Practical Theology

One of the most consistent themes in Packer's comments about theology is the need to make it practical, and once we have assimilated his passion in this matter, we can see that in his theological writing, he has practiced what he has preached. There is a phrase in the "Plumber and Sewage Man" article that one easily could read right past, but that actually packs a tremendous punch. In criticizing modern theologians for trivializing their profession and "muddying the waters" for churchgoers, Packer observes that these theologians make theology matter less and less "for real Christian life." In other words, theology is no more than an intellectual game and pastime unless it equips ordinary people to live out their faith.

This view of theology as needing to be practical is everywhere evident in Packer's theological writing. "Theology's proper goal," he writes, "is to equip the disciples of Jesus Christ for obedience." The maps that theologians draw are "not simply to be possessed as so much intellectual wealth, but rather to be used for the believer's route-finding in his personal pilgrimage of following his Lord." Likewise, "Good theology," writes Packer, "constantly calls for deliberate, responsible decisions about how we are going to live." Most theology books are not fired by this vision; they are mainly oriented toward imparting correct thinking about God, people, and the world. I do not disparage them for this; I consult theology books to find answers to my questions. But when I read the theology of J. I. Packer, I become aware that a different approach to theology exists.

When we turn to Packer's theological writings, we can see his theory in practice. *Keep in Step with the Spirit* is a good illustration. In the preface, Packer pays his disrespects to readers "who are just curious to know what the author thinks these days about the Holy Spirit." The book "has been put together to help Christians who mean business with God."

Keep in Step is intellectually demanding, as Packer carefully weighs various views of the Spirit's work (especially in sanctification) and examines the biblical data on the Holy Spirit. The book would be complete with those ingredients. But in the preface, Packer foreshadows an additional element—"some thoughts about the work of the Paraclete in reviving the body of Christ," a section that Packer predicts readers might find "bittersweet." The chapter, when it comes, has something to unsettle everyone. It challenges non-charismatics for lack of fervor and for undervaluing the role of the Holy Spirit in their lives. It criticizes charismatics for going beyond anything that the Bible reveals about the Holy Spirit. For both groups—those who expect too little of the Holy Spirit and those who expect the wrong things—the chapter stands as a call to Christians to bring their lives (not just their thinking) into line with what the Bible says we should expect in regard to the Holy Spirit.

Conflation of Theological Traditions

The template within which Packer has conducted his theology is the Anglican tradition (as noted in the preceding chapter). His early classroom teaching was in Anglican theological colleges, with an interlude at Latimer House as a semi-official spokesman for the evangelical wing of the Church of England. Packer's default theological creed in those contexts was the Thirty-Nine Articles of the Anglican Church. Additionally, in his theological writing, Packer has foregrounded his allegiance to the Thirty-Nine Articles, the Prayer Book, and Anglican theologians such as Thomas Cranmer.

Packer is not an ordinary Anglican theologian, however, and I will note two complexities in this regard. The first stems from Packer's lifelong devotion to Puritan theology. That does not make Packer any less Anglican, inasmuch as Packer has always viewed the Puritans as Anglicans who wished to bring the Church of England into line with a more Protestant and less Roman Catholic position. The right label for Packer's theological tradition at this point is "the Reformation tradition." We should note in this regard that Packer's cooperation with Roman Catholics at various times has never been a complete theological assent, as he has consistently made clear.

A second important deviation from mainline Anglican theology is Packer's solid adherence to Calvinism. Although Anglican theology was originally Calvinistic, the thoroughness of Packer's devotion to that tradition makes him seem less Anglican and more Reformed. Packer himself has written theology in the Calvinistic vein in so many places that naming them is superfluous.

A good testimony to Packer's Calvinistic theology is the degree to which Calvinistic and Reformed people claim him as a spokesman and apologist for their own views. Through most of his career, Packer's greatest influence has been in the Reformed and Calvinistic wing of evangelicalism. In 2009, *Time* magazine claimed that one of "10 Ideas Changing the World Right Now" was new Calvinism. Mark Dever subsequently wrote a blog post in which he asked, "Where Did All of These Calvinists Come From?" He attributed much of the resurgence to the writings of J. I. Packer, whom he called the "current grandfather of this Reformed movement." Dever also attributed the rise of book titles using a gerund-plus-noun construction to the model of Packer's *Knowing God*—titles such as *Desiring God*, *Trusting God*, and *Loving God*.

We can see the dual track of Packer's theology (Anglican and Calvinistic) reflected in his speaking career. Packer has moved with equal ease and frequency in both Anglican and Reformed circles. In a conversation with me, Packer said that he "never made comparisons" between those two worlds and instead "desired to see both worlds together and influence both." Packer observed that a certain division of duties emerged between the two venues—Bible exposition at rallies in the free-church tradition, and fellowship and evangelistic rallies for the Anglicans. We can add a third paradigm as well: addresses on Reformed theology at conferences such as the Philadelphia Conference on Reformed Theology and those sponsored by R. C. Sproul's Ligonier Ministries.

Knowing God as Packer's Signature Book of Theology

As I have composed this chapter on Packer as theologian, it has become increasingly clear to me that Packer's most famous book—*Knowing God*—sums up his theological theory and practice. I have accordingly decided to allow a brief excursion into this book to bring together the various strands that I have covered up to this point in the chapter.

With my analysis earlier in this chapter on our radar screen, we can see a submerged theory of the theologian's task in the preface. "The conviction behind this book," writes Packer, "is that ignorance of God—ignorance both of his ways and of the practice of communion with him—lies at the root of much of the church's weakness today." In that sentence, we can see (1) Packer's eye on the condition of the church (and not simply individual Christians) and (2) his sense of urgency about what is at stake in the theological enterprise, namely, the health of the church. Faced with contemporary ignorance of theological truth, Packer proposes that we need to "ask for the ancient paths, where the good way is; and walk in it" (Jer. 6:16). "Such is the invitation which this book issues," writes Packer. The book itself is "a straightforward recall to old" paths.

Why should the reader embark on the theological journey toward a knowledge of God that the book promises? Packer encourages his reader to ask, "What do I intend to *do* with my knowledge about God, once I have it?" He warns, "To be preoccupied with getting theological knowledge as an end in itself . . . is the direct route to a state of self-satisfied self-deception." Later in the book, Packer makes his famous distinction between knowing about God and knowing God. The purpose that Packer envisions for his book is the same that Psalm 119 offers for the study of Scripture—"biblical teaching and theology, not as ends in themselves, but as means to the further ends of life and godliness."

What kind of theology book is *Knowing God*? It is not a systematic theology; it is a piecemeal or topical theology. Many of the familiar categories of systematic theology are present, though they are informally arranged instead of following the usual outline of a systematic theology book. These familiar categories are the attributes of God—his majesty, love, grace, justice, and such like. But many of the familiar topics of systematic theology are missing. I believe that systematic theology would have been an impediment to what Packer does best. The chapters in most theology books do not end with sections of application and prompts to suggested responses, but the chapters of *Knowing God* do. Chapters on the goodness and severity of God and the adequacy of God (an exposition of Romans 8) appear in *Knowing God*, but are rarely if ever found in a book of systematic theology. A piecemeal approach enabled Packer to be flexible in his choice of subjects and the order in which he presented them.

In the preface to the 1993 re-issue of *Knowing God*, Packer describes how he composed the original articles, which appeared in *Evangelical Magazine* at two-month intervals. He "was prompted each time [note well] by the question, *What do I tell them next*?" If he had written a systematic theology, the agenda of topics would have been predetermined, and Packer would have lacked the freedom that he experienced when writing the articles and then the book. *Knowing God* comes across as a series of fireside chats with the author, and I have regularly seen it put into the category of a devotional book rather than a theology book.

Most theology books are written for and read by theologians and people of sophisticated theological orientation. *Knowing God* is a theology book for the ordinary Christian. It illustrates the implied claim of a book title designed to capture the essence of Packer's career as a theologian—*Doing Theology for the People of God*. As I conducted my research into Packer's writing about the theological task, I encountered some exceedingly technical articles aimed at professional colleagues, showing that Packer can write at the level of specialized scholarship. Here is a specimen sentence: "Stanley Grenz urges that we shall be better placed to [speak theologically to our own age] if as trinitarian, communitarian (meaning, churchly), and eschaton-oriented believers we reposition ourselves clearheadedly in a Pannenbergian type of coherentism." The point I am making is that Packer's choice to write theology for the ordinary person is a conscious one. In fact, in the very essay from which I quoted the technical sentence, Packer writes, "It is vital to realize that truth is for people, and therefore, the pastoral function of theology is ultimately primary."

The Biblical Foundation of Packer's Theology

The starting point for Packer's theological methodology is the premise that the Bible alone is the reliable authority for all religious belief. In an essay on theological method published in *New Dictionary of Theology*, Packer claims that there are three methods of doing theology. These three methods are none other than the three views of authority that Packer first popularized in *"Fundamentalism" and the Word of God* (showing how foundational that paradigm has been for him). Furthermore, all three views are formulated in relation to the Bible. The three views of authority and therefore of theological method are: (1) the Bible alone as the ultimate source of belief; (2) the Bible plus church tradition; and (3) human reason and knowledge, with the Bible viewed as a human and culturally conditioned document. Packer endorses the first as following the pattern set in Bible times, the early Christian centuries, and the Protestant Reformation. It is the evangelical position. I was struck by an "aside" in an essay that Packer contributed to an anthology entitled *The Use of the Bible in Theology*; he mused that "I would have felt freer and happier altogether if the title of our symposium could have been, 'How *the Bible uses me* when I do theology.'"

It is easy to see what this scriptural orientation looks like in Packer's theological writing. It produces an absolute abundance of biblical quotations and parenthetical or footnote references to verses in the Bible (the positioning of the biblical data in Packer's writing depends on the nature of what he is discussing at a given moment). I consider this to be enlightened proof-texting, and I will note in passing that I myself have never shared the pejorative attitude that some scholars display toward proof-texting. The chapter entitled "The Holy Spirit in the Bible" in *Keep in Step with the Spirit* refers to three hundred Bible passages. In public lectures, Packer naturally feels less free to quote extensively from the Bible, but we find nearly fifty biblical references in Packer's Leon Morris address on "The Problem of Eternal Punishment."

Of course, theologians can base their beliefs on the Bible without quoting directly from it in their theological discourse. But when theologians quote extensively from the Bible, they keep the record clear that the authority for their theological ideas is Scripture and not themselves. Additionally, whenever we read theological writing, we absorb (however unconsciously) a methodology for conducting theological inquiry ourselves. Anyone reading the theological writings of J. I. Packer gets the point that our ideas about God and religion need to find their ultimate origin in the Bible. In his own words, "If Scripture is indeed God himself preaching and teaching, . . . the first mark of good theology is that it seeks to echo the divine Word as faithfully as it can" (preface to *Concise Theology*).

Looking to the Theological Past

A main element of the theological legacy Packer has bequeathed to evangelicals is the model of looking to past theological traditions as a reliable guide in the present. This is Packer's theory as well as his practice. In a very learned essay in which Packer articulates how he envisions the task of theology (entitled, we should note well, "Maintaining Evangelical Theology"), Packer asserts that one of the "marks of Christian theology" is "direct engagement with its own heritage." He criticizes modern theologians for not "reaffirming and vindicating the Christian heritage against all forms of unbelief and alternative belief." In a unit labeled "My Practice of Theology" in an essay entitled "In Quest of Canonical Interpretation," Packer writes: "Like Calvin, I theologize in constant dialogue with the whole Christian heritage of study, proclamation, and belief. . . . Theology is a cooperative enterprise, and the fellowship of its practitioners has a historical as well as a contemporary dimension."

Anyone familiar with the professional career of literary scholar C. S. Lewis knows the inaugural address that Lewis delivered when he left his teaching position at Oxford University and accepted a chair at Cambridge University. In this speech, Lewis stepped forward aggressively as a spokesman for what he called the Old Western Culture. It is highly significant that when Packer gave his inaugural lecture upon assuming the position of Sangwoo Youtong Chee Professor of Theology at Regent College, he referenced Lewis's lecture at the beginning and end of his talk. Packer was explicit in saying, "My theology, I know, is old-fashioned . . ."

The outworking of this in Packer's theological writing and teaching is a heavy incidence of quotations from past theologians. In fact, his writing on theological topics often becomes a primer on what famous theologians have said on the same subjects. I actually enjoyed tabulating the fifty authors that Packer quotes or cites in *Knowing God*. They were a virtual roll call of famous pillars of the evangelical tradition—Charles Spurgeon, C. S. Lewis, John Bunyan, Oswald Chambers, John Newton, William Gouge, Richard Baxter, Leon Morris, Louis Berkhof, John Murray, and more. In the chapter devoted to the subject of faith in *God's Words*, we find references to the Anglican Thirty-Nine Articles, Martin Luther, J. C. Ryle, John Berridge, A. W. Pink, and a familiar hymn. The effect of adducing a cloud of witnesses like this is to instill confidence that Packer has read widely and can therefore speak authoritatively, and also to awaken a certain excitement in us that we can join a high-level discussion on ultimate issues.

From what traditions does Packer draw most often? That question implies a correlative question: with what traditions is Packer eager to acquaint his readers? The answer is threefold: Packer draws on Anglican sources (especially the Thirty-Nine Articles) and on Calvinistic or Reformed sources, and beyond that (my third answer) he is refreshingly eclectic, showing that he agrees with G. K. Chesterton's view that "tradition asks us not to neglect a good man's opinion," regardless of who the person is. In his preface to *Concise Theology*, Packer affirms the first two traditions: "My frequent quoting of the Westminster Confession may raise some eyebrows, since I am an Anglican and not a Presbyterian. But since the Confession was intended to amplify the Thirty-Nine Articles, and most of its framers were Anglican clergy, . . . I think I am entitled to value it as part of my Reformed Anglican heritage, and to use it as a major resource." As for Packer's eclecticism beyond Anglican and Reformed sources, a few minutes of browsing uncovered references to Augustine (Roman Catholic), Charles Wesley (Methodist), Elisabeth Elliot (nondenominational evangelical), Hannah Whitall Smith (Quaker/Plymouth Brethren/Methodist), Oswald Chambers (Baptist), and F. F. Bruce (Brethren).

The Interdisciplinary Nature of Theology

In Packer's theorizing about theological method, he repeatedly asserts that theology must intersect with other disciplines. The most obvious intersection is with Christian living (as noted in multiple places in the foregoing discussion). But academic disciplines are included as well. Packer's vision for what a theologian needs to master is idealistic and utopian in the extreme. In the preface to *Concise Theology*, he outlines an ever-expanding list of ten activities that theologians need to incorporate into their job descriptions:

> elucidating texts (exegesis), synthesizing what they say on the things they deal with (biblical theology), seeing how the faith was stated in the past (historical theology), formulating it for today (systematic theology), finding its implications for conduct (ethics), commending and defending it as truth and wisdom (apologetics), defining the Christian task in the world (missiology), stockpiling resources for life in Christ (spirituality) and corporate worship (liturgy), and exploring ministry (practical theology).

Packer himself, in his life and work, shows that all of this can be done, but how many J. I. Packers are there in the world?

An example of how theology can enter our daily routine is outlined in Packer's essay "Reading the Bible Theologically." He begins by defining the enterprise he is about to describe: "To read the Bible 'theologically' means to read the Bible with a focus on God: his being, his character, his words and works, his purpose, presence, power, promises, and precepts." Later, Packer describes this as "a quest for God," then he adds the idea of theological reading of the Bible as "the quest for godliness." Additionally, "The goal of theological Bible reading," writes Packer, "is not just to know truth about God . . . but to know God personally in a relationship that honors him." Within those parameters, the right theological information to seek as we read a passage from the Bible is (1) what the passage shows about the triune God, (2) what it tells us about the world, and (3) how it can serve as a guide for daily living.

Another sphere that theology can infiltrate is preaching. Packer has accordingly written an essay entitled "The Preacher as Theologian: Preaching and Systematic Theology." The first two sections of the essay outline the ten activities required of a theologian (as summarized above) and the nature of preaching, and a third section brings those two together. Packer's thesis here is that "a preacher needs to be a theologian of some competence in order to do his job." Some specific gifts that theology confers on the preacher are: adequacy of coverage in the topics on which one preaches, accuracy of exposition, and adequacy of application. Packer's parting shot is that theology is to the preacher what a coach is to a tennis player; just as a tennis player will perform his sport better for having been coached, a preacher will preach better "when helped by theology."

Teaching Theology in the Church and Family: Catechesis

This chapter on theology is the best home for a discussion of Packer's lifelong passion for teaching Christian doctrine in the form known throughout the Christian centuries as catechesis. Because of the high value that Packer places on theology, it is no wonder that he has given his thought and effort to how theology can be disseminated in the church and family, not just individually. In recent years, he has risen to visibility in evangelical circles on the subject of catechesis, but he has actually championed this method for a very long time.

In the preface to his 1977 book *I Want to Be a Christian*, for example, Packer wrote: "Christianity is not instinctive to anyone, nor is it picked up casually without effort. It is a faith that has to be learned, and therefore taught, and so some sort of systematic instruction (*catechumenate*) is an essential part of a church's life." Packer then lists some famous examples of catechisms and instructional documents from church history. All of this leads to the conclusion that "one great need today is a renewal of systematic Christian instruction—catechetical teaching—for adults."

There has been a steady stream of such statements in Packer's writings, culminating in a co-authored 2012 book entitled *Grounded in the Gospel: Building Believers the Old-Fashioned Way*. It is a full-scale presentation of Packer's beliefs that (1) theological ignorance and illiteracy lead to great weakness of faith individually and corporately, (2) the church today suffers from exactly that form of weakness, and (3) we can devise a program of instruction in families and churches that will teach the content of Christian theology in a systematic manner that will cover all of the essential facets of the faith.

Earlier in this chapter, I claimed that Packer's approach to theology in his writing is topical instead of adhering to the roadmap laid out by traditional systematic theology. But I need to guard against leaving the impression that he does not want the teaching of Christian doctrine to cover the whole content of theology presented in an organized way. Packer is open to a range of formats for achieving such an organized coverage of Christian doctrine. He is quite sympathetic to the Westminster Shorter Catechism and the Westminster Confession of Faith. The Anglican Thirty-Nine Articles are a constant point of reference for Packer, who has written pamphlets and books based on it. In *I Want to Be a Christian* (reissued by Crossway in 2007 under the title *Growing in Christ*), Packer uses the Apostles' Creed, the Lord's Prayer, and the Ten Commandments as an organizing framework for his exposition of Christian doctrine.

Packer's Unwritten Systematic Theology

Something needs to be said about Packer's projected but unwritten systematic theology, so I will say something about it. Packer signed a contract with Tyndale House Publishers approximately three decades ago to write a book of systematic theology. The idea did not originate with Packer, but with acquisitions editor Wendell Hawley. Hawley heard such glowing endorsements of Packer's courses in theology at

Regent College that he became determined to get a book from Packer based on his lectures. After the contract was signed, Hawley pursued the project aggressively. He met with Packer when Packer made his quarterly visits to Wheaton as part of his work with *Christianity Today*. He visited Packer in Vancouver once or twice a year, partly to get the book of systematic theology under way. Packer's daughter Naomi was identified as someone who had the expertise to do the spadework for the book. According to bloggers, Packer gave indications through the years that he was at work on a book of systematic theology. Some Packer devotees continue to stand on tiptoe for the appearance of this work.

In the corridors of Tyndale House Publishers, the unfulfilled contract is today regarded with wry humor and a sense of resignation, but in a certain segment of the scholarly world (chiefly British), the unwritten book is a very sore point. The myth of the great book that Packer did not write perhaps began with D. Martyn Lloyd-Jones. In his 1970 letter informing Packer that the Puritan Conference would be discontinued, Lloyd-Jones took a swipe at Packer for allowing himself to be diverted into the "ecclesiastical affairs" of the Anglican Church. As part of that criticism, Lloyd-Jones wrote, "I had expected that long before this you would have produced a major work in the Warfield tradition." Not doing so, said Lloyd-Jones, is "nothing less than a great tragedy and a real loss to the Church."

Gerald Bray voiced the same view in a 1997 review of Alister McGrath's biography of Packer. Bray pictured himself as speaking for many British evangelicals. Whereas McGrath celebrates Packer's move to North America as a doorway to enlarged opportunities, Bray claims that "this perception is the exact opposite of the one generally held by Dr Packer's admirers in England." Writes Bray: "It was widely assumed (or at least hoped) that Dr Packer was in the process of writing a great theological synthesis which would be the definitive work of evangelical theology for the next generation. What we were looking for was a new Charles Hodge . . . , but what we got was *Knowing God*." Bray further claims that "when I meet like-minded friends in England, we sometimes talk about this and wonder whether Dr Packer will ever find time to write this missing volume. . . . It has to be recorded that this has been the expectation of his English friends and admirers, and that so far we have felt let down." Like Lloyd-Jones, Bray chastises Packer for investing himself with Anglican issues when he should be writing the great book: "We fervently wish that [Packer] would spend less time on ephemeral projects like *Essentials 94* . . . and devote himself to activities of long-term value and impact."

Carl R. Trueman is in the same lineage of British evangelicals who are critical of Packer for not writing a systematic theology. In an essay lamenting that Packer did not become a leader in the nonconformist British church, Trueman adds: "Further, it is surely disappointing that he has never produced a full systematic theology. . . . Packer has a brilliant mind, full of theological footnotes; indeed, only a brilliant mind could write deep theology in such a profoundly simple way; yet he should have given us much more."

I will note first that the rank-and-file Packer devotee is quite unaware of this great gap in his publications. The preoccupation with the missing book of systematic theology belongs to professional systematic theologians. This does not automatically make it inappropriate, but we need to acknowledge that in terms of numbers, the people who are metaphorically missing an arm or leg over the unwritten book are statistically insignificant. In both Bray's review and Trueman's essay, the complaints about the unwritten book come in the context of Packer's refusal to provide leadership to British evangelicalism (Trueman) and Packer's move from England to North America (Bray); I note a certain irony in the fact that both Bray and Trueman followed Packer's pattern of leaving England to teach in the United States. (Of course, not all British evangelicals lament the move from England to Canada: Dick Lucas, retired rector of St. Helen's Bishopsgate Church in London, writes, "I can only be thankful for the move, surely providential, that gave Jim the scope he needed, in a freer environment, to realize his so great potential.")

I believe that the criticisms of Bray and Trueman unintentionally help us understand the phenomenon of the unwritten systematic theology. Trueman's longing for "all those footnotes that [Packer] holds in his head" is code language for specialized scholarship. From time to time, Packer indulges his ability for specialized scholarship, but he has deliberately subordinated it to mid-level scholarship that makes a difference "for real Christian life" (Packer's stated ideal for theology). If we ask whether the kingdom benefits more from esoteric footnotes or the kind of writing Packer has predominantly done, I think the answer is obvious.

Bray heaps scorn on *Knowing God*. He writes, "The chapters of this book attracted little attention" when they were published in England. "It was really only when [the book] hit the American market that it took off," and this says more about the superficiality of "much American Evangelicalism than it does about the value of the book itself." I suggest that this is a self-revealing statement that tells us little about Packer's book. Furthermore, Bray's disparagement of Packer's Anglican activities helps us to see Packer's commitment to the Anglican Church in high relief. We do not need to agree with that commitment, but Packer is bound by his conscience and not answerable to us. Packer's commitment to the rank-and-file Christian is so far from the conventional career trajectory of an academician that most professional theologians find it hard to understand and fully value it.

How does Packer regard his unwritten systematic theology? A partial answer can be found in a 2004 interview that appeared in *Resurgence*. On the one hand, Packer observed that "there are already quite a number of evangelical systematic theologies written by professors, presumably on the basis of their class notes for teaching students." All of them are intended for a specialized audience—"clergy [and] people studying to get their M.Div. degree in seminary." Packer then confided, "I see no need to add to their number because, as a mainstream Reformed thinker, I haven't anything fresh to say." This is exactly the conclusion to which I had come. Packer's books are noteworthy for their fresh angle on the subjects that he addresses, whereas the course packets for his theology courses follow familiar contours.

However, that was only half of Packer's answer. He further theorized that if God gives him more years, "I would like to survey the whole of Christian doctrine at what I call the 'higher catechism level'—the level [at] which one addresses thoughtful laypeople who are not technically educated in theology, but who want to know their faith accurately and to have a solid grounding in Christian basics." Packer is, in fact, making progress on this book, which has "reconceived itself in [his] mind" from when he first signed a contract for it. His recent interest in catechism has "given the project new life."

Theologians Assess Packer as a Theologian

Since I am not myself a professional theologian (though I have been encouraged by scattered comments from Packer to the effect that all Christians are incipient theologians), I have decided to end this chapter with a sampling of what professional theologians have said about Packer's theological contributions. These assessments provide an apt summary of what I have covered in this chapter from people more knowledgeable than I am.

- Donald J. Payne, "J. I. Packer's Theological Method" (for fuller documentation, see the bibliographic notes at the end of this book). After a scholarly survey of Packer's theological premises and practices, Payne highlights the following "conclusions" at the end of his essay: (1) "Packer's theological method reflects an unwavering commitment to the controlling principle of biblical inerrancy and authority"; (2) Packer's further commitments are to "a covenantal, canonical, and christological orientation" rooted in a theocentric method governed by the idea of God's self-revelation as the basis of theological truth; (3) Packer's emphasis on the role of reason in the theological process is greater than he acknowledges; (4) evangelicalism is greatly indebted to Packer's theological writing and teaching for its blend of erudition, accessibility, scholarly rigor, and warm-hearted piety; and (5) Packer's theological methodology needs to be continuously analyzed and critiqued (not necessarily negatively) because no matter how correct his theological ideas are, he also influences how people perform theological analysis themselves ("Packer's method matters because his influence is more multifaceted than merely the theology that he teaches").
- Carl R. Trueman, "J. I. Packer: An English Nonconformist Perspective" (in which one of the sections bears the heading "Packer's Theological Contribution"). Trueman's purpose is to place Packer the theologian into a twentieth-century British evangelical context. Packer's first great contribution to his generation was the recovery of Puritan and Reformed theology, which held the key to revival in a certain segment of British evangelicalism (especially, but not only, the non-Anglican segment). But despite Packer's prominence in British evangelicalism, he was a theological anomaly—not quite fitting into the Anglican scene because of his strong Reformed iden-

tity and not wholly acceptable to the free church world because of his Anglicanism. When Packer rejected Lloyd-Jones's 1966 call for evangelicals to leave the Church of England, he lost most of his influence among British nonconformists. For Trueman, Packer "is the lost leader of English nonconformity," the man who could have provided theological and ecclesiastical leadership to a whole era of evangelicalism in England. Packer "was the one man who had the theology and . . . ecclesiology to have potentially offered [a] positive church vision" for nonconformists.

- Mark Noll, "J. I. Packer and the Shaping of American Evangelicalism." Noll's essay parallels Trueman's by assessing Packer's influence on evangelicals in the United States. Noll is completely positive about Packer's theological influence in America. His contributions have been those of an "educated, Reformed, Anglican evangelical." Part of Packer's greatness is his erudition and wide knowledge base. He "has embodied the virtues of a weighty theological tradition." Also, he has been "a sturdy Calvinist," but at the same time an Anglican and an evangelical. It is the combination of these and the balance among them that is Packer's triumph. "Packer's theological horizon is wide," writes Noll. Among Packer's contributions is the blend of head and heart that he has championed, sending a call to evangelicals "to sharpen their wits, even as they guarded their hearts."
- Alister McGrath, "James I. Packer: An Assessment." McGrath begins his essay with a somewhat startling statement: "Some would say that Packer is a great theologian; it would probably be more accurate to say that he is a great 'theologizer.'" McGrath does not spell out what this means, but we can infer that it points to what I have asserted in this chapter—that Packer does not go about his theological task as a systematic theologian does, and is instead "ad hoc" and piecemeal in his published theology. The first theological contribution that McGrath highlights is Packer's historical sense: "Packer embodies the distilled wisdom of the theological ages," thereby exposing evangelicalism "to the riches of the past." In a section entitled "The Primacy of Theology," McGrath notes that whatever topic Packer takes up—evangelism, church renewal, spirituality, prayer, preaching—he "reaffirms his fundamental belief that all are grounded in theology, and must be justified by theology." In

a unit entitled "The Coherence of Theology," McGrath claims that "Packer's theology is strongly integrative, in that he sees theology as offering both a foundation and coherence to Christian thinking and living." The tendency among professional theologians is to turn theology into a primarily intellectual exercise; for Packer, theology is "a transforming and renewing encounter with the living God."

- Packer's comment on the effect of McGrath's labeling him a theologizer: McGrath "didn't want to call me a theologian and he ended up calling me a 'theologizer.' It was after that that I realized I'm a catechist." Packer adds, "I am an adult catechist; it was quite a discovery."

22

Preaching and the Minister's Calling

Many people know that J. I. Packer has made a practice of filling pulpits around the world, often linking a preaching occasion with a visit to an area for another reason. Some people know that he was a parish preacher before he became a lifelong teacher. Neither of those two facts, however, would have prompted me to regard preaching as a "life passion" for Packer. After all, he has taught at institutions that call themselves colleges rather than seminaries. As I worked on this biography, various bits and pieces gradually led me to see that preaching and the ministerial calling have been a continuous thread in his life. Here are some of those bits and pieces:

- When Packer felt that he had reached the end of his usefulness at Latimer House, he pondered various options for a next step. His eventual decision to teach at Tyndale Hall in Bristol was accompanied by this revealing statement: "I really am called, if I know anything at all, to make ministers and establish consciences . . ."
- In a chapel address to Regent College students, Packer said that Regent "is a kind of seminary."
- In reflecting on his life, Packer wrote: "Soon after my conversion I was made vividly aware that I would only ever get job satisfaction from a life of pastoral ministry, shepherding my Savior's sheep along their path of life, and that is still a fixed point. . . . [During

my year of teaching at Oak Hill Theological College] I found that adult teaching was in my blood, and I became sure that my future pastoral ministry would involve much of it, both in congregational settings and in teaching and pastoring the teachers and pastors of tomorrow within a seminary or seminary-type community."

- In addition to how Packer himself views his involvement in preaching, it is obvious from Internet sources that preachers worldwide look to Packer as an authority on preaching. In fact, when a homiletics professor asked thirteen famous preachers to write an essay expressing their views of preaching and then provide a sample sermon of their own, Packer was one of them.
- When Packer asks and then answers the question, "How do I prepare my own sermons?" I am made aware that he is a practitioner of preaching, as well as a commentator on the subjects of preaching and sermons.
- In paying tribute to Richard Baxter as an influence on him, Packer wrote that "my sense of being called to preach the gospel" was learned from Baxter, and that "from student days I have known that I was called to be a pastor according to Baxter's specifications."

Even though Packer did not become a lifelong parish minister, he has maintained a continuous commitment to preaching and the preacher's calling. The purpose of this chapter is to flesh out what that commitment has looked like over the course of his lifetime.

The Person in the Pew

Preachers are only half of the equation in preaching. The other half is the people who listen to preaching. Just as it is easy to think of education in terms of what administrators and teachers do, it is a permanent tendency to think of preaching in professional terms as what preachers do. But just as the heart of education is what happens to students, so, too, the "bottom line" in regard to preaching is what happens in the minds and hearts of the people in the pew.

Packer's involvement with preaching began as a listener to sermons rather than as a preacher. During his college years in Oxford, Packer's choice of a local church to attend was determined mainly by the preachers and the preaching. During the first two years, Packer gravitated to the local Plymouth Brethren church because its preaching was better than what he found at the two Anglican churches in the city center. But during his third year, when St. Ebbe's landed a superior preacher named Maurice Wood, Packer attended that church. During his year of teaching at Oak Hill Theological College in London, Packer made it a regular practice to attend the Sunday evening service at Westminster Chapel, where D. Martyn Lloyd-Jones preached his famous sermons.

From the beginning of his Christian life, Packer was a devotee of great preaching and could not conceive of life without it. Although he has preached hundreds of sermons, he has listened to more than he has preached. This is part of his lifelong (if undocumented) interest in preaching and sermons.

One spillover effect of Packer's experience of listening to sermons is that when he is asked to theorize about preaching and sermons, he never loses sight of the person in the pew. When preachers write about preaching or speak about it at conferences attended by preachers and seminarians, the content of the discussion tends in the direction of professional "shop talk." That is not necessarily bad, but the discussion can become disconnected from ordinary laypeople. I believe that Packer's writing and speaking about preaching never lose sight of those who hear.

The essay that covers more of Packer's views of preaching than any other is entitled "Mouthpiece for God." Two sections in this essay take up the subject of listening to sermons. One of the two takes up the subject of application. In a manner reminiscent of the Puritans, Packer provides an anatomy of likely categories of listeners in a typical congregation. Then he provides an anatomy of types of application. To explore application in this way requires an understanding of the person hearing the sermon. A well-known professor of homiletics has cast application in a negative light by saying that it is in application that preachers introduce error and heresy. Packer does not agree that application is suspect. He believes that "half the message should be in essence instruction in biblical truth about God and man and half should be in essence specific application of that truth."

The second unit devoted to listening to sermons in the essay "Mouthpiece for God" is entitled "How to Hear Sermons." The question that Packer addresses in this unit is, "How are we to hear sermons as the

Sword of God and benefit from them in our ongoing relationship with God?" In answering the question, Packer goes right to his Puritan hero, Baxter, who wrote about "Directions for . . . Understanding the Word which you Hear" in his massive work *A Christian Directory*. After surveying what Baxter said, Packer adds three pages of his own suggestions for listening to sermons and making them a means of grace in our lives. He raises the bar high for the person in the pew, and we get the sense that he does so because listening to sermons has been a central part of his own life.

Packer's Brief Career as a Parish Minister

Although Packer did not become a lifelong minister, he would not have become the authority on preaching and the ministerial calling that he has been if he had never been a parish minister. He quickly landed on teaching as his calling, but it was not a foregone conclusion that this would be the direction of his life. Soon after his conversion, Packer began moving toward ordination as an Anglican minister. During his third year in college, he devoted a Sunday afternoon to listing reasons for entering the ministry and reasons for not doing so. He decided to seek ordination, and shortly thereafter found himself at a three-day selection conference for young men intending to become ministers in the Church of England. Even after his successful year of teaching at Oak Hill Theological College, which steered Packer in the direction of a career in teaching, he continued to think in terms of becoming a parish minister. Part of the context was that it was an unwritten rule of the time that a stint as a minister was a desirable preparation for teaching in a theological college.

Packer spent approximately two years as a minister at St. John's Anglican Church in Harborne, a suburb of Birmingham. Although he was busy writing his dissertation during much of those years, he shared in a full round of ministerial duties. He preached at church services. He taught in the middle of the week, including a doctrine class that became popular with young people. He became an unofficial youth minister to boys in the congregation and spoke at a Boys' Brigade summer camp. He taught at women's meetings in the church. This was all valuable experience for someone who would become a spokesman for the minister's calling throughout his life.

Packer's Lifelong Investment in Preaching

After Packer left the parish ministry for a career in teaching, his lifelong investment in preaching and the ministerial calling took three forms. One was his own preaching, which has never been absent from his life. I have heard Packer preach only twice, but he has left a convenient sampling of his sermons in various publications. It is tempting to look at them immediately, but I will resist the impulse and end the chapter by looking at specimen Packer sermons.

A second way in which Packer has pursued his commitment to the minister's calling is his teaching. It would be possible to teach at the colleges where Packer has served without viewing the enterprise primarily as the preparation of future ministers. This is especially true of Regent College, which I have always viewed primarily as a "marketplace" institution designed to educate laypeople for their callings in the workaday world. But Packer has viewed his colleges as seedbeds (to use a Puritan word) for future ministers. As already noted, Packer regards Regent College as "a kind of seminary." What do theologians do? Packer's answer is that "they instruct today's and tomorrow's clergy." For Packer, teaching and preaching are nearly synonymous. His advice to young clergy is that they "have three priorities: teach, teach, and teach."

To stay one more moment with this motif of how Packer has viewed subjects from a ministerial perspective when other approaches are possible, we can note his scholarship on the Puritans. One can be a Puritan scholar without making preachers and preaching part of one's interest. But the subject of ministry is a permanent part of Packer's writing and speaking on the Puritans. In his primary book on the Puritans, *A Quest for Godliness*, one of four sections is a three-chapter unit on "The Puritans in Ministry." More recently, Packer's book *Puritan Portraits* (2012) bears the subtitle *J. I. Packer on Selected Classic Pastors and Pastoral Classics*. This book has a unit on "Puritan Pastors at Work" and an epilogue on "The Puritan Pastor's Programme"

A third way in which Packer has continued to fulfill his ministerial calling (in addition to his preaching and teaching) is his public speaking and writing. Preaching has not been the primary subject on which Packer has been asked to lecture, but it has been a consistent topic. That fact shows that preachers regard him as an influential member of the guild. To show that preaching and the ministerial calling have been a unifying thread in Packer's life, I offer the following list of publications (some of which began as public addresses):

- "Great Pastors: Richard Baxter" (1953)
- "Expository Preaching: Charles Simeon and Ourselves" (1960)
- "The Puritan Approach to Worship" (1964)
- "Ministry of the Word Today" (1965)
- "Training for the Ministry" (1970)
- "Preaching as Biblical Interpretation" (1980)
- "Why Preach?" (1986)
- "Packer on Preaching" (1987)
- "From the Scriptures to the Sermon" (1990)
- "Authority in Preaching" (1991)
- "The Preacher as Theologian: Preaching and Systematic Theology" (1995)
- "Some Perspectives on Preaching" (1999)
- "God's Triple Team: Preaching the Trinity" (2006)

The list speaks for itself: preaching has been a continuous passion for Packer and a subject on which the world regards him as an authority.

The Preacher's Vocation

For the remainder of this chapter, I will divide the overall subject into its obvious subpoints. I will begin with a wide-angle view of the minister's calling in general. To be a minister, especially today, entails much beyond preparing and delivering sermons; it requires filling numerous roles. To fill them, the minister needs to be broadly educated and resourceful as a person.

Packer is well aware of the demands. When he started out as a preacher, the whole institution of preaching stood much higher in public opinion than it does today. In 2009, Packer spoke at Oak Hill Theological College in London and agreed to be interviewed by the principal of the college on the education and calling of a minister. One of the subjects covered was the cultural standing of the minister. Packer observed that "in the world in which I was brought up, there was still a Christian culture [and] sympathy for the church," as well as an "understanding of the position of the clergyman, . . . who had a role in society, [and there was a] willingness to listen to him." However, "that willingness has been replaced by incomprehensibility" that anyone would do the things a minister does. The minister, said Packer, is today viewed "as a visitor from outer space." "You can't change that," he added; "you have to live with it."

What can a minister do about the situation? Packer's advice: "If you're going to live with cultural skepticism of this kind, you've got to be very sure of who you are, very sure of what you stand for, and you've got to be very clear in your mind and with your mouth as to how you say it." All in all, "Yes, it's a very difficult time in which to minister."

As the interview unfolded, Packer began to sketch how he thinks a minister should proceed with his task. He believes that ministers should do what they always have done and not change the job description to match current trends. When a Christian minister moves into a congregation, he "has first of all to make sure that there is a willingness on the part of the congregation to learn the Bible." Given the prevailing negligence in our culture and the contemporary church in this matter, a minister "may have to work at generating that willingness. But he cannot achieve much until the church becomes a Bible-learning community." The second major task is "to mobilize the congregation to go and make disciples in their own area."

If that is the task, what prepares a minister for it? Packer has always cast his lot (and did so in the interview) with the need for two or three years of residential training in a seminary-type setting. A clergyman needs "to know his stuff very thoroughly indeed." For Packer, there are three primary areas of knowledge that comprise the education of a minister—"solid Bible teaching, solid theological teaching, and good, thorough teaching of church history." In regard to the Bible, what a person needs for the ministerial task is not esoteric biblical scholarship and critical theorizing about the composition of the Bible, but knowledge of the content of the Bible itself. One of the benefits of knowing church history is that it provides models for how to effect change. Without a vision for how to challenge the status quo as the pioneers in church history did, ministers become mere maintenance men, and "a clergyman can't be a maintenance man." In the second tier of prerequisites, would-be ministers need to pick up "basic skills for handling pastoral situations," and additionally, "you have to know a certain amount of church administration."

Packer provides a convenient summary of his views on the clerical vocation in the concluding paragraph of his book *Puritan Portraits*:

> The pastor should see himself as a man set apart to preach Bible truth, to teach Christ and to counsel the spiritually perplexed in light of the written Word; to convert, nurture, watch over and care for sinners; to pray for them, bring wisdom to them, model godliness before them, and lead them into and in doxology, fidelity, purity, humility, maturity, and joy in Christ; and to fight in whatever way particular situations might require for the fullness and forthrightness of the faith.

Packer's Views on Preaching

When Packer expresses his views on the ministerial calling, there is never any doubt that he believes that preaching is the minister's primary task. In a 2009 interview for *Christianity Today*, Packer was asked to respond to a prevalent contemporary view that making preaching central—to the point of placing the pulpit front and center in the church sanctuary and making the sermon the centerpiece of the church service—is part of the problem with the church today. Packer rejected the suggestion, defending the traditional view of the primacy of preaching and taking a swipe at "all this moaning and groaning about preaching being an old-style form of behavior that is unfashionable in these days." We need to credit Packer with having a nuanced view of the matter. He nowhere implies that preaching is a minister's only task. Additionally, he has a view of preaching that is not completely traditional. For example, in the Oak Hill interview, Packer buttressed his strong endorsement of seminary education with the comment that the preacher "has got to teach and teach and teach" (not "preach and preach and preach").

How does Packer envision preaching? For starters, he assumes that the content of preaching will come from the Bible. In his defense of theological education, Packer claims that a preacher needs to know the Bible and instill in his congregation a desire to learn it, because the preacher "is there to teach from the Bible." If the Bible needs to form the chief content of preaching, it is no wonder that Packer is critical of preaching that elevates anything besides the Bible to the central position. In topical preaching, as opposed to expository preaching from the Bible, ministers "take a topic, they appeal to one or two Scriptures to illustrate the topic, they tell stories from their experience and other people's experience to illustrate the topic," and all the while the focus of the sermon shifts from the Bible to the preacher. The authority by which a listener is expected to believe what the preacher says "is the human authority of a knowledgeable person," and nothing more. Needless to say, Packer is opposed to this procedure of using "the texts . . . as a convenience for illuminating the topic" instead of the Bible "being expounded as the Word of God." In topical preaching, according to Packer, preachers do not regard themselves as being "mouthpieces for messages from biblical texts." When the Bible is not at the center of preaching, "biblical content is made to appear as part of the speaker's own wisdom," instead of emerging as the authority for what is said.

What is at stake here is the question of what constitutes the authority for what a preacher says, and that in turn relates to why the person in the pew should regard what the preacher says as being true. When a preacher speaks in his own voice only, the listener has only one option in regard to authority, namely, that the preacher is the authority for what is said. By contrast, when a preacher allows the Bible to provide the primary frame of reference for a sermon, the Bible emerges as the authority and reason for belief. But, of course, the Bible speaks through the mediation of the preacher. Particularly helpful here is Packer's metaphor that "the activity of preaching the Bible . . . unlocks the Bible to both mind and heart."

Building on a lifelong preoccupation with the authority of the Bible, Packer is a strong exponent of the view that the preacher needs to speak the truth of God, not of himself. This is a bold claim to make today, but it was not so in bygone eras of the Christian church. One of Packer's well-known essays on preaching is entitled "Speaking for God." A published interview of Packer on preaching bore the title "Preaching as God's Derivative Word." In the interview, Packer was asked, "Can we rightly say that when the preacher speaks, God speaks?" Packer's answer was that we can indeed say that *if* the preacher roots his message in the Bible. Here is how Packer expands that thought:

> Calvin understood the preaching office as a matter of relaying what God is saying through the text. That is, you expound the text as you discern its flow and its meaning. You state it, you break it down into

> little bits and then put it together again. . . . [The preacher can say] God speaks to you, each one, through the word that I speak to you because the word that I speak to you is my attempt to echo what's there in the text.

Such a conviction makes sense only if one shares Packer's view of the authority of the Bible. He himself highlights this: "In the books that I've written about biblical authority, I have tried to make clear that Scripture should always be preached and listened to, read, reflected on as the word of the God who here and now is saying what Scripture says."

An important concomitant of this view of the preacher as God's mouthpiece is that the minister, too, places himself under the Word that he preaches. Packer's objection to preaching removed from biblical content is that the preacher becomes the authority—the one who says, "Listen to me, learn from me, I've got it, I give it to you." The only way for a preacher to avoid making himself the authority is for him to see "himself as no less under the authority of the Word than the congregation." A preacher needs to tell his congregation: "With God's help, I am going to try and open up this passage so that we may all hear what God is saying. I want myself to be the first to hear it, and then I want you all to hear it." Such a procedure creates a "link between text, preacher, and congregation."

Packer's first axiom is thus that preaching must be biblical in content, deriving its authority from the Bible as God's Word to the congregation.

His second axiom is that preaching should follow the pattern of the Puritans. There is nothing magical about the Puritans; they simply got it right in regard to preaching. In his chapter of *A Quest for Godliness* on "Puritan Preaching," Packer shares his "conviction that the well-being of the church today depends in large measure on a revival of preaching in the Puritan vein."

In elaborating this thesis, Packer writes, "Four axioms underlay all Puritan thought about preaching." They are as follows:

- The primacy of the intellect. "It follows that every man's first duty in relation to the word of God is to understand it; and every preacher's first duty is to explain it. The only way to the heart that he is authorized to take runs via the head." Additionally, "the minister who does not make it his prime business, in season and out of season, to teach the word of God, does not do his job."

- The supreme importance of preaching. For the Puritans, "the sermon was the liturgical climax of public worship." It was "the prime means of grace to the church" and "a very solemn and momentous enterprise." To follow the Puritan example requires that "both minister and congregation should recognize that their Sunday sermons are the most important and significant events of the week."
- Belief in the life-giving power of Holy Scripture. "The Puritans insisted that the preachers' task is to *feed* their congregations with the contents of the Bible." In elaborating this point, Packer writes that "the Puritans defined *pastoral* work in terms of *preaching* first and foremost." In contrast to the modern tendency to regard ministerial work in terms of visitation and personal relations as opposed to preaching, for the Puritans, "faithful preaching was the most basic ingredient in faithful pastoring."
- Belief in the sovereignty of the Holy Spirit. The preacher's task is "to be faithful in teaching the word; it is God's work to convince of its truth and write it in the heart." The Puritans "would have criticized the modern evangelistic appeal, with its wheedling for 'decisions,'" and at this point we catch echoes of Packer's book *Evangelism and the Sovereignty of God*.

Preaching never stood higher in people's estimation than it did during the Puritan era, and as a Puritan scholar, Packer knows that. It is no wonder that he wants to recapture as much of the Puritan success in local churches as possible.

In his lead-in to the discussion of Puritan principles that I have just noted, Packer paints a picture of Puritan sermons in their overall qualities. The idealized picture does not totally fit my own impression of Puritan sermons, but it is a great passage that I think captures what Packer himself wants to see in preaching: "Practical biblical exposition was the actual substance, and liveliness was a regular mark of the style. Puritan preaching prolonged the down-to-earth raciness of presentation, with verbal pictures, narrative illustrations, and allusions to Bible stories scattered throughout in abundance." Puritan ministers "preached the Bible systematically and thoroughly, with sustained application to personal life, preaching it as those who believed it, and who sought by their manner to make their matter credible and convincing."

In an earlier chapter, I ascribed a prophetic voice to Packer in the sense that he sounds a warning about the contemporary church. This is evident in his writing and speaking on the subject of preaching. Because Packer has a clearly defined ideal for preaching, he is critical of much (probably most) preaching that occurs in evangelical churches today. He addresses this in numerous places, and the following points from a section in an essay entitled "Why Preach?" can serve as a summary. Packer's analysis is built around the following assertions:

- "First, there has been much non-preaching in our pulpits." The most prevalent forms of this malady are preaching that does "not open Scripture," preaching in which a preacher expounds his own opinions, or preaching in which a preacher offers the requisite teaching of Scripture but not the application of it to the lives of the listeners.
- "Second, topical preaching has become a general rule."
- "Third, low expectations are self-fulfilling." The fault lies with both preachers and listeners.
- "Fourth, the current cult of spontaneity militates against preaching."
- "Fifth, the current concentration on liturgy militates against preaching." This criticism might seem surprising from an Anglican such as Packer, but the argument is mainly directed toward people who have come to Episcopalianism from other Protestant denominations and are so captivated by liturgy that it "seems to have elbowed all concern about preaching out of their minds."
- "Sixth, the power of speech to communicate significance has become suspect." The chief culprit is the influence of the media and a general mindset that does not value "the use of words to create a sense of the greatness and weight of spiritual issues."

At no point does Packer imply that preaching, in the traditional sense that he advocates, will be popular in today's cultural and church climate. Still, Packer is a utopian idealist at heart, and he never loses his enthusiasm for the ideal that he portrays for preaching.

How Packer Views a Sermon

Packer has written so much on the content and shape of sermons that the material makes up a small library within his writing and speaking corpus. In this section of the chapter I have distilled and codified what I believe to be most important, in an awareness that much more exists in Packer's writing and speaking about sermons.

I have already noted that Packer believes that the content of a sermon should be derived from the Bible, but that only sets an overall parameter for preaching. Many additional matters need to enter our analysis of how the Bible can form the basis of a sermon. The process starts with correct interpretation of a biblical text. Haddon Robinson believes that it is the application part of a sermon that is most likely to introduce error into it, but I disagree. The problem is as likely to begin at the very basic level of determining what a Bible passage is about. Throughout my life, when listening to sermons, I have repeatedly scratched my head and asked myself: "How did you get *that* from this text? Where did you get the idea that this text is about *that* subject?"

Packer recognizes that a biblically based sermon needs to interpret the biblical text correctly. One of his striking statements articulates a principle that is easy to overlook: "A misinterpreted Bible is a misunderstood Bible." That is why seminary education and a degree of sophistication in matters of hermeneutics are necessary parts of genuine biblical preaching. Packer makes a preliminary foray into this territory in an essay entitled "Preaching as Biblical Interpretation." The principles of interpretation that he advocates are a beginning list and somewhat global, but they are foundational:

- Hold to the literal meaning. To do so means to avoid the allegorical approach to a biblical text. A synonym for *literal* is *natural*—the straightforward, obvious meaning of a word, event, or character.
- Hold to the principle of harmony. This, in turn, is based on the presupposition (accepted by faith and the inner conviction brought to the believing heart by the Holy Spirit) that the Bible is inerrant. If we believe that the Bible is without error or contradiction, we have a motivation to look for inner coherence of its subject matter and explanations of apparent contradictions.
- Follow the interpretive spirals. This is a somewhat elusive concept, but it becomes concrete when Packer lists subordinate points under

> it: explore the Bible from within; allow the Bible to enlarge our culturally bound ideas and, as a result, to bring our ideas into line with itself; and allow our self-knowledge to grow through knowledge of God.

These can be supplemented by the general principles of interpretation that Packer advocates elsewhere (see the chapter on "The Bible").

One of the more daring claims that Packer makes is that "the preacher, rather than the critical commentator or the academic theologian, is the true interpreter of Scripture." How can this possibly be true? It is true because the commentator and biblical scholar tend to teach only, and interpretation is more than teaching. It "means among other things, bringing literary and artistic legacies to life and showing their significance" in the lives of people today. "Commentaries and theologies are resources for this task, but only preachers can fully perform it; and they perform it fully only as they apply their text in a rational and realistic way."

My heart soars when I see the emphasis that Packer places on application as a major part of every sermon. He even defines a sermon in terms of application: "a sermon . . . is teaching plus . . . application of truth to life." In my view, Packer is absolutely correct when he says that application is "a largely forgotten part of the evangelical heritage with regard to preaching." His "rule of thumb for pastoral sermons" is that half of the sermon should be exegesis of the Bible and instruction in its message, and half should be application. If a preacher observes these proportions, claims Packer, he "cannot go far wrong."

If half of a sermon is going to be application, we need to subject the topic to analysis and codification. I would not hesitate to speak of the *science* of application, and although the Puritans did not use that phrase, they were *the* great systematizers in regard to application. Packer knows this well, and sometimes he takes over their grids directly. In his book on the Puritans, for example, Packer cites the categories of listeners that William Perkins delineated in his *Arte of Prophesying*, with the assumption being that a preacher must apply the truth of a text to all of these categories. On the same page (287), he quotes the taxonomy of types of application that was formulated in the Westminster Directory for Publick Worship. Not surprisingly, Packer believes that the Puritans' emphasis on application is not only "the most striking feature of Puritan preaching," but "the most valuable legacy that Puritan preachers have left to those who would preach the Bible and its gospel effectively today."

Elsewhere, Packer follows the Puritan model in compiling his own taxonomy in regard to application. In his essay entitled "Mouthpiece for God," Packer offers these guidelines:

- "Application should constantly focus on the unchanging realities of each person's relationship to God."
- "Application should constantly focus on the person, place, and power of Jesus Christ."
- "Application should constantly search the hearts and consciences of the hearers."

In elaborating the third of these, Packer delineates six categories of listeners in a typical congregation: unconverted and self-satisfied; concerned and inquiring; convicted and seeking; young Christians; mature Christians; and people in trouble.

Then—true to his temperament to organize material into numbered categories—Packer provides a taxonomy of types of application, each of which can be applied as occasion requires to the six categories of listeners. The types are: (1) application to our mind; (2) application to our will; (3) application to our motivating drives; and (4) application to our condition. Obviously Packer has thought through the subject, and the overall lessons we can carry away is that he believes that preachers need to be self-conscious about application in their preparation of sermons and that the space allotted to application in sermons should be major, not minor. Where application is lacking, "something less than preaching occurs."

Packer has also codified his thoughts on sermon preparation. He finds two chief starting points for a sermon—the known needs of a congregation and the personal insights that a preacher has and desires to pass on to a congregation. External occasions (including the annual church calendar) can determine the substance or angle of vision for a sermon. Packer proposes that sermon outlines are a crucial part of the process of preparation. He himself turns to commentaries and homiletic materials only after he has settled on an outline for a sermon. He shows his traditionalist bent when he confides that he finds older commentaries and printed sermons more helpful than modern ones, and he garners his illustrations from the Bible and everyday events.

Finally, how much of a minister's personality and experience should form the substance of a sermon? More than we might think from the preceding discussion. Packer accepts Phillips Brooks's definition of the sermon as "truth through personality," going so far as to say that "the preacher is, indeed, half of his sermon." But this is not true in the form encouraged by the contemporary celebrity syndrome, with its self-focused preachers. Packer is looking for authenticity in preaching. The preacher is not the authority that the congregation is asked to accept as the basis for belief; the Bible is the authority. But the congregation needs to see that the preacher "manifests both the mentality of a messenger [from God] and the disposition of a disciple."

Influences on Packer's Views

It is natural to wonder how Packer came to the conclusions about preaching and the ministerial calling that have been outlined above. One answer is that many famous preachers from the past have been a cloud of witnesses to him. A glimpse into this eclectic circle can be found in the catalog of giants adduced by Packer in his essay "Mouthpiece for God." He lists examples of preachers whose "preaching career and sermonic legacy" are reliable models for us today: John Chrysostom, Augustine, Martin Luther, Hugh Latimer, John Knox, Richard Baxter, John Bunyan, George Whitefield, John Wesley, Jonathan Edwards, Charles Simeon, Robert Murray McCheyne, Charles Spurgeon, John Charles Ryle, D. Martyn Lloyd-Jones, and Billy Graham. These men have been guiding lights, but more specifically, two influences have had the most impact on Packer the preacher, and both reach back to the beginning of his Christian life.

The Puritans, first of all, helped Packer to codify his thoughts on the nature of the ministerial calling and the preaching of sermons. The Puritans became an intellectual specialization for Packer during his college years, and we all know that preaching was a hallmark of the Puritan movement. In fact, a modern Puritan scholar has called the minister "the hero" of the Puritans. Since Packer was himself heading for a life of ministry, he naturally picked up on this aspect of Puritanism. Packer writes regarding Baxter that he "focused my vision of the ordained minister's pastoral office," especially in his treatise entitled *The Reformed Pastor*. Similarly, when Packer lists the traits of Puritan sermons, it is obvious that he is also describing his own ideal for a sermon: Puritan sermons were expository in method, doctrinal in content, orderly in arrangement, and popular in style.

The second great influence on Packer was Lloyd-Jones. Packer has affirmed this in numerous places in his writings. Here is one: "For several months during 1948 and 1949 I sat under the Sunday evening ministry of the late Dr. Martyn Lloyd-Jones. It seems to me in retrospect that all I have ever known about preaching was given me in those days. . . . What I received then still shows me what to look and hope and pray for in listening, and what to aim at and pray for in my own preaching." He later adds that "it was Dr. Lloyd-Jones's ministry that under God gave me my standards in this matter."

When I look at Packer's own sermons (see below), I feel a very large disconnect between them and Packer's professed models. The Puritans and Lloyd-Jones did not preach what I define as expository sermons. They preached topical and doctrinal sermons. I can think of no tradition more guilty of what Packer calls "doctrinal overload" than the Puritans. It is true that the content of the sermons preached by the Puritans and Lloyd-Jones derived ultimately from the Bible, but such sermons do not, in my view, automatically rank as expository, and are in any case not the types of sermon that Packer preaches. I infer, therefore, that the veneration that Packer feels toward Lloyd-Jones is a comment on the latter's oracular presence in the pulpit and the tremendous sense of biblical authority that came through. I have been told of an American who visited a service at Westminster Chapel and sat in a trance when Lloyd-Jones finished his sermon, overwhelmed by a sense of the spiritual transcendence he had just experienced.

Sermons by Packer

J. I. Packer's sermons give us actual examples of what he advocates in his theorizing about preaching and sermons. I believe that the most noteworthy thing to emerge from Packer's sermons is the literary inclination that he shows in them. When Packer *writes* about the Bible, his orientation is overwhelmingly theological (whereas mine is literary).

But when he preaches sermons, his approach to the Bible is governed by literary intuitions.

Packer's literary inclination is seen first in the parts of the Bible to which Packer gravitates for his sermons. Most seminary-trained preachers seize upon the most heavily conceptual and theological parts of the Bible and are, in fact, content to preach almost solely from the Epistles. Packer gravitates to the narrative parts of the Bible. Within that parameter, he feels most natural in preaching about the characters in the biblical narratives. The resulting sermons are what I call character studies—a thoroughly literary approach. I will look at three sermons to see what they tell us about J. I. Packer as preacher.

A Sermon on Mary and Martha

I first heard Packer preach a version of this sermon at Bethel Presbyterian Church in Wheaton, Illinois. In the weeks leading up to Packer's appearance, the sermon was pitched to the congregation as a Puritan sermon, perhaps because Packer was in town to speak at a Puritan conference. The published version appears in a book entitled *Never Beyond Hope*, where it bears the title "Hope When False Priorities Have Betrayed Me: Martha." The part of the sermon that I remember most vividly after all these years is Packer's entering into the mind of Martha and empathizing with her frustration when Mary ignored any sense of domestic duty and was content to spend her time listening to Jesus.

That the published sermon is a character study is confirmed by the fact that Packer brings together three separate stories in which the shared element is the presence of Mary and Martha (a unity of character, not of plot). They are the stories of Jesus's visit to the home of Mary and Martha (Luke 10:38–42), of the death and resurrection of Lazarus (John 11:1–44), and of Jesus's visit to Bethany a few days before his crucifixion (John 12:1–8). Packer adopts a literary approach by reliving these texts as they unfold, not by asserting a series of theological generalizations and dipping into the text for illustrations of them. The first item on Packer's agenda is telling the story as it unfolds sequentially, making it come alive in our imaginations and allowing us to be vicariously present at the event.

Packer begins with the episode that is known to us as "the story of Mary and Martha." The subject of literature is universal human experience, and Packer implicitly acknowledges that subject in his handling of the text. The characters of Mary and Martha come alive as types that we all have known. Martha is the archetypal hostess, intent on managing the occasion as a hostess naturally would. We have experienced or observed her personality type hundreds of times. But Martha finds that serving as hostess, not only to Jesus but also to the twelve disciples, is more work than a solitary person can manage. Packer helps us experience the event:

> There behind the semicircle, glaring over the disciples' heads, is Martha with her hands on her hips. She's got a red face. She breaks into the conversation and says in a loud, strident, edgy voice, "Lord, don't you care that my sister has left me to do the work by myself? Tell her to help me." She's blowing her top. She's making a scene. She's lost control.

Having relived the moment, Packer subjects it to analysis. According to Packer: "If you look at Martha's words, she's really saying three things. One is that she wants to be noticed." She also "wants to domineer her sibling." Third, she "is actually trying to manipulate Jesus."

Packer knows that a literary text like this is a picture of life universally, and he retells the story in such a way as to make that transparent. In regard to the sibling rivalry, for example, Packer muses that in real life "the elder brother or sister will try to set the agenda for the younger siblings and push them around and control their lives. For the younger siblings it can be a rough experience." Further: "In this instance I am sure that it was a rough experience for Mary. Can you imagine her looking at the floor and going very red in the face as she hears Martha say these things? I can."

Martha's complaint constitutes Act 1 of the story. Act 2 is Jesus's response to her. In Packer's explication of the text, Jesus replies to each of the three implied complaints. When he says, "Martha, Martha, you are anxious and troubled about many things," he lets Martha know that she has been noticed and that he is grateful for her efforts on behalf of her guests. Second, Jesus implicitly rebukes Martha's attempt to take Mary into the kitchen when he affirms Mary's choice with the statement, "Mary has chosen the good portion, which will not be taken away from her." In that same statement, Packer sees Jesus's refutation of Martha's attempt to use him as her tool against her sibling.

In view of Packer's championing of the need for application in a sermon, I will note that he mingles application with his analysis of the text. Regarding Jesus's assurance to Martha that she is noticed, Packer states: "You and I should bear in mind that our Lord Jesus always knows. . . . He never in fact forgets us." In regard to Jesus's commendation of Mary, "You and I ought to be glad to give someone else the opportunity to learn the things of God from the Scriptures."

The simple reading of this story is that Mary is commended and Martha rebuked. But the aspect of the sermon that intrigued me when I first heard it was Packer's follow-up claim that Martha and her mindset are not condemned per se. In Packer's view, "Jesus is not rebuking Martha for not being in the learning group." Again: "Jesus approves of the fact that Martha is out in the kitchen making them a meal, just as he approves of the fact that Mary is there sitting at his feet and learning from him. Situational responsibilities are not to be ignored for the sake of devotional exercises, any more than vice versa." The application: "The lesson that we all have to learn is to be Martha and Mary by turn. . . . We ought to have space in our lives for doing what Mary did: spending time with the Word of God, learning from Jesus. . . . But let us also learn that from time to time we are to be doing the practical helpful things that are needed around the house and for that matter around the church."

That would be an adequate sermon for many preachers, but Packer is in the Puritan mold, so he keeps going. He next relives the story of the death of Lazarus, as narrated in John 11. Martha rises in Packer's and our estimation when Jesus says to her: "I am the resurrection and the life. Whoever believes in me, though he die, yet shall he live, and everyone who lives and believes in me shall never die. Do you believe this?" Martha responds with her great confession: "Yes, Lord; I believe that you are the Christ, the Son of God, who is coming into the world." But then Martha becomes an obstructionist again by trying to counter Jesus's command to open the tomb, thereby showing that she does not understand that Jesus will raise Lazarus now, not just at the last day.

The third narrative of the triptych is the John 12 account of Jesus's visit to the home of Mary and Martha for a dinner at which Mary anoints his feet. The text says that "they gave a dinner for [Jesus] there. Martha served . . ." In this "last glimpse we have of Martha, the devoted disciple, what we see is Martha truly honoring Jesus. She honors Jesus, and he accepts the honor." When Mary makes her extravagant gesture of adoration to Jesus, "Martha doesn't say a word. Martha accepts that Mary has a right to express her worship of Jesus in her own way." In Packer's handling, this event is a foil to the earlier story of Mary and Martha in Luke, showing how Martha has matured while never losing her identity as one who serves by being a hostess. The difference is that "she doesn't lose her temper this time."

The sermon ends with application (of which there has already been an abundance). One lesson is that "Jesus values all of our backstage ministry that few if any notice, and nobody thanks us for." To clamor for attention is a form of self-centeredness and pride that "disfigures our discipleship and makes us . . . a burden to our families and friends." But Jesus "led Martha beyond it, and that gives us hope that he . . . will do the same for us."

I remember thinking when I heard this sermon that it was not the message I was expecting when I saw the biblical text listed in the church bulletin. I expected to see the heroic figure of Mary offered as an ideal. Instead, I was introduced to the Martha no one knows—a very human figure (one of us), but also a figure of hope and even inspiration. Mary seems too heroic for me, but Martha, who serves in the kitchen, is someone toward whom I can aspire. As I worked with the published version of the sermon, I found myself very moved by the figure of Martha. In its glorification of the ordinary, the sermon displays a strong Puritan orientation.

A Sermon on Samson

Packer's sermon on Samson is another one that I can attach to a real-life event. Retired Anglican Bishop Wallace Benn remembers hearing a version of this sermon when he was a student at Trinity College, Bristol, in the early 1970s. Packer preached on Samson in a chapel service. It was such a rollicking address, replete with a reference to Samson's hot women and fast chariots, that Benn remembers Trinity Principal Alec Motyer laughing so hard that he had to take out his handkerchief and wipe the sweat from his face. In its published version, the sermon bears the title "Hope When My Strength Brings Weakness with It: Samson." In that version, Packer shares that "in my travels I have spoken many times on the character of Samson" (adding that the story is always up to date in our own society and churches).

The sermon is another character study. Its dual thrust is to make the character of Samson come alive and to extract the lessons for living that the author of Judges embodied in the story. Packer's means of achieving these two ends are the same as I, with my literary intuitions, would use—conduct a close reading of the text, extract principles from the story and its protagonist, and apply those principles to everyday living.

Samson emerges as a person with whom we all can identify. He is a deeply flawed man, one whose misdeeds are larger than but not essentially different from ours (at one point, Packer speaks of Samson's flaws as "Samson's and ours"). Samson's faults are flawed sexuality, flawed humor, and flawed anger. However, the news is not all bad regarding the delinquent Samson, who is God's person despite his failings, who oddly has things about him that remind us of Jesus, and who can teach us about being weak when we are strong and strong when we are weak.

All of the foregoing traits are found in the sermon on Martha as well, so I will concentrate on additional characteristics of Packer the preacher that we find in the sermon on Samson. One of these is that Packer, classically trained and liberally educated as he is, shows an awareness of literature and literary scholarship. The sermon begins this way: "No one, surely, can read the Samson story without thinking, *This is tragedy*. Tragedy is a waste of good, a squandering of potential." Well, people without a literary education *do* read the story without thinking that, but Packer is nonetheless correct about the nature of the story. In the course of my teaching, I regularly take up the story of Samson as a literary tragedy, and part of the definition of literary tragedy that I share with my students is the sense of waste that the tragic hero's choice introduces into the lives of himself and others. I was alerted to this dimension of tragedy when reading the famous Shakespearean scholar A. C. Bradley, in his book *Shakespearean Tragedy*. The idea that literary tragedy incorporates a sense of waste is one that we are likely to encounter in literary discussions of tragedy, not by looking up a dictionary definition.

Packer is also well aware that he is dealing with a hero story. In such a story, what the storyteller wishes to say about life is embodied in the central character (the hero) and his exploits. This is the unstated premise of Packer's sermon, and it dictates his methodology. The principle underlying literary narrative is that every story is, at some level, an example story. Literary theorists from time immemorial have operated within a framework of "example theory," based on the premise that stories present us with positive examples to follow and negative examples to avoid. A tragedy always holds up a negative example that we should avoid, and Packer treats Samson as a many-sided example of what we should avoid. Packer calls the story "a cautionary tale" and a biography that stands as a warning.

In addition to showing a literary flair, Packer shows an ability to "bridge the gap" between the ancient world of the text and the modern world of our own experience. This bridging of the gap is an omnipresent trait of great preachers who rise above the common field. Knowing this (and having written on it), I took immediate note when Packer claims in his essay "Mouthpiece for God" that the preacher must "bridge the apparent gap between the Bible and the modern world by demonstrating the relevance of what Scripture says to the lives of those whom he addresses."

To bridge the gap requires a keen eye for similarities between the ancient text and the modern world. This is an exercise in the imagination, which is adept at seeing connections. *How* we phrase our analysis of a text is a crucial factor in this regard. Here is an example from the sermon on Samson: the story is "very much like the sort of thing you read in paperback thrillers: women and fights all the way." When stated that way, we immediately see the contemporaneity of the Samson story. Again: "The book of Judges tells us of a people who lived in a permissive society. . . . 'Permissive society' is a description that applies very directly to modern North America." Such touches abound in the sermon. Delilah is Samson's "good-time girl." Samson is a "buffoon." As the foxes with their tales on fire run through the fields, Samson stands "laughing his head off." Samson is like "powerful and successful males" we know, who think of "sexual pleasure as a recreation to which their achievements somehow give them a right."

The Samson sermon is one in which Packer makes good on his proposed proportions of fifty percent interaction with the text and fifty percent application. In arriving at that figure, I count the extraction of principles as application (since I immediately see how they apply), but I am sure that some readers would not see the matter in quite that way. In any case, there is so much wonderful application in the sermon that I cannot hope to reproduce it here. Most of the application flows from the nature of the story as a tragedy and a cautionary tale. So the story primarily yields a harvest of application in which we see what we should avoid in our lives and ministries. I dislike an overload of abstraction and generalizing in a sermon, but I love application. I dislike moralizing, but I want to be edified. I like convicting sermons rather than feel-good, inspirational sermons. Packer hits the target on all these counts because he chose a literary text and treats it in a literary way. There is no free-floating generalizing; Packer ties everything to the character of Samson.

A Sermon on the Tower of Babel

This sermon was Packer's contribution to an anthology entitled *Inside the Sermon: Thirteen Preachers Discuss Their Methods of Preparing Messages*. The book was compiled by a homiletics professor, and the fact that Packer was asked to be one of thirteen esteemed preachers contributing chapters confirms that the world at large regards him as a preacher. Contributors were asked to write essays that expounded their views of preaching and sermons, then follow them up with sample sermons. The preliminary essay that Packer wrote, entitled "Speaking for God," is a concise summary of what I have covered in the present chapter in this biography. The biblical text for his sermon is the story of Babel as recorded in Genesis 11:1–9. Packer records that he originally prepared a sermon on this text because someone assigned him the passage, and also that the printed sermon is shorter than the originally preached version.

We should note that in this sermon, Packer is in his typical stance of preaching on a narrative text. This is what he does most naturally. He begins by looking at the story as recorded. He does so in abbreviated form in the published version, but this is not as important as it might seem because he continues to interact with the text as he proceeds with the sermon.

The primary thrust of the sermon is that "the Babel story is a mirror of the modern world." The very project of building a tall building to make a name for a nation is something that "we still do," and Packer notes modern instances. The premise that we can see universal human experience in the particulars of a text is at the heart of the literary enterprise, and Packer accepts it as his working premise in this sermon.

In this sermon, Packer simultaneously explicates the text and shows its universal themes, demonstrating that what happened at Babel is what always happens. Alternatively, we can envision Packer's procedure as teasing out the symbolic meanings of a central image (the tower). The chief principles embodied in the building project are human pride, the passion for power, self-absorption, unrest ending in paranoia, and foolhardy unrealism. All of that is embodied in the part of the story dealing with human ambition and technology. But God is the supreme character in the story, and his judgment against erring humanity resolves the plot. Packer believes that this strand in the story yields the truth that the purpose of divine providence in the world "is preservation of the present order of things until God's eternal plan for bringing sinners to faith in the Savior and so gathering and building his universal church has been completed."

The foregoing is the exegetical half of the sermon, which is managed in such a way that application is intertwined with the analysis of the text. The application becomes explicit halfway through the sermon. Packer builds that application around "three heart-searching questions." Those questions are: Do we embody the attitude of Babel? Do we experience the anathema or curse of Babel? Do we embrace the alternative to Babel? The alternative started at Pentecost, which began a spiritual reversal of the confusion that came at Babel: "Life in fellowship with Christians completes the reversal of Babel that life in fellowship with Christ begins."

Summary

J. I. Packer has spent more of his time on, and is better known for, pursuits other than preaching—writing, teaching, delivering addresses at conferences, and acting as a spokesman for groups and causes. Yet this chapter on preaching is one of the longer chapters in this biography. This fact signals something important.

Packer's theorizing about preaching is one of his major contributions. Preachers have looked to him for leadership and inspiration. In this regard, Packer views himself as a coach. He says about his preaching and theorizing on preaching and sermons that "you can sometimes do a useful job as a coach even when you are not one of the best players."

But we should not underestimate the importance and impact of Packer's sermons. He has preached in hundreds (possibly thousands, by his own testimony) of pulpits to *many* thousands of churchgoers. And we have a handful of choice published sermons to give us a taste of Packer the preacher.

23

Controversy

Part three of this biography is devoted to unifying themes in the life of J. I. Packer. Coverage of that subject would be incomplete if it did not paint a picture of the way in which controversy and conflict have been part of his life, from his college years to the present day. Packer has not sought controversy, and his life would have been a great deal easier without it. On the other hand, he has not avoided controversy when he has felt called to defend a cause or enter a conflict involving truth and error.

Packer himself has made a revealing statement that can serve as an epigraph for this chapter. He once confided that "like a good pietist I've always wanted peace, and like Richard Baxter I've been involved with trouble, trouble, trouble, all the way." The purpose of this chapter is to trace the contours of the "trouble" that Packer references.

Two facts will provide a helpful context for the controversies that have beset Packer. First, while he has never courted controversy for its own sake, there is something about his temperament that does not back off from conflict. People of a more passive temperament could have avoided some (not all) of the controversies that Packer has sparked simply by keeping certain opinions to themselves and not rocking the boat. Second, Packer is a high-profile person. Some of the attacks that he has elicited would not have occurred if a less-famous person had been involved.

College Years

We can see the seeds of Packer's life of controversy in his religious affiliations during his college years at Oxford. On the one hand, he buckled under peer pressure in regard to his interest in jazz music. The pietistic strain in the Oxford Christian Union regarded jazz as worldly. Within a short time of his conversion, Packer renounced jazz and let his fellow students know that he had done so. He sold his jazz records. This was not entirely due to peer pressure, inasmuch as Packer was also under conviction because playing clarinet in the Bandits jazz band on Saturday evenings kept him from attending weekly meetings of the Christian Union.

But Packer showed an individualistic streak in his church attendance. Even though he followed the approved path for Christian Union members in frequently attending services at the local Plymouth Brethren assembly during his first two years at Oxford, he also accompanied the Christian Union representative at his own college to services at St. Aldate's Anglican Church. That awakened disapproval from leaders in the Christian Union—so much so that when Packer's name was put forward as a potential candidate for leadership on the executive committee, the suggestion was squelched by senior members because of the suspicion that attached to attending St. Aldate's.

Packer's Attack on the Keswick View of Christian Living

The first really large controversy of Packer's public life was his attack on the Keswick theology. The controversy happened during his first year of teaching at Tyndale Hall, Bristol. Packer stirred up a hornet's nest with a review of Steven Barabas's book *So Great Salvation: The History and Message of the Keswick Convention*, which explained and promoted the Keswick view of the Christian life. That view had sent Packer into a tailspin soon after his conversion at the start of his college years. Discovering the Puritans had provided him with an escape from the defeatism that had been engendered in him by the triumphalist position of the Keswick view of the sanctified life (and we can note the paradox of a triumphalist view of the Christian life engendering defeatism in Packer's Christian life).

A book review seems an unlikely spark for a firestorm, but we should let it register that the review was no fewer that thirteen pages in length (published in *Evangelical Quarterly*). Obviously this was much more than a book review. By a slight stretch, it might labeled a "review article," but it would be highly irregular for a review article to be devoted to a single book (a review article is more likely to be occasioned by multiple books on a common subject). It is accurate to say that Packer's attack on the Keswick philosophy was a polemical article occasioned by Barabas's book. Packer agreed with the suggestion of a recent interviewer that this review was one of the few times he has drawn his sword.

Packer's article caused an explosion in the circles in which he moved (for details, see chapter 7 of this biography). It was Packer's initiation into his life as a controversialist. His half of the controversy was fueled by characteristic energy. In later years, Packer called his article a "fiery onslaught" against the Keswick viewpoint. When I asked Packer whether he was aware that his article would provoke such intense controversy, he replied that he was not. He accompanied that verdict with the statement that he felt like a crusader for a cause. That metaphor can stand as an umbrella for this chapter devoted to Packer's career as a controversialist: when he has found himself engaged in controversy, he has viewed himself as being on a crusade. He takes naturally to the role. I will note in passing that Packer has continued his attack on the Keswick viewpoint in polemical asides in his writings and interviews throughout his life.

Controversy with Lloyd-Jones, Part 1

Probably the most famous controversy of Packer's life was his conflict with D. Martyn Lloyd-Jones in the mid-1960s in connection with an event that was a watershed in the history of evangelicalism in England. Before I look at the conference where this crisis occurred, I want to take time to observe that the roots of conflict between Lloyd-Jones and Packer on the issue of Anglicanism vs. separation existed under the surface for several years before the precipitating conference of 1966. This disagreement occurred, moreover, in an arena where Packer and Lloyd-Jones ostensibly agreed, namely, the English Puritans as role models for today. In summarizing the underlying tension that existed between Lloyd-Jones and Packer in regard to the Puritans, I am indebted to an essay by John Coffey that uncovers the relevant data (see sources listed at the end of this book).

That Lloyd-Jones and Packer mutually revered the Puritans is well attested. The most visible monument to this joint veneration was the Puritan Conference, which Packer helped to instigate and which was held for twenty years at Lloyd-Jones's church, Westminster Chapel in London. But if we look closely at what each of these men highlighted in the Puritan movement, a definite fissure emerges. The starting point for Packer's appropriation of the Puritans was his Anglicanism, and we should note again that Packer's Reformation roots are as much Anglican as Puritan. In fact, Packer viewed the Puritans as Anglicans. Whereas in much of Anglicanism today (according to Packer in the early pages of *A Quest for Godliness*) people specialize in the individual strands of Anglicanism (doctrinal orthodoxy, liturgical worship, aspects of personal sanctity, social witness, congregational structures, or revival of piety), the Puritans provide a model for combining all of these. In other words, the Puritans were ideal Anglicans.

If we look at what Packer stressed in his twenty years of annual lectures at the Puritan Conference, we find that he showed little interest in ecclesiastical issues and focused instead on what the Puritans called practical divinity ("practical writings" was a common Puritan category, and Packer has written an excellent essay entitled "The Practical Writings of the English Puritans"). More specifically, Packer explored Puritanism as a devotional movement, a theological renewal movement, and a movement that aimed to reform the Anglican Church. In the introduction to his book on the Puritans, Packer acknowledges that his interest in the Puritans for more than forty years centered on "Puritan theology and spirituality," including the "devotional quickening" that the movement sparked. By contrast, Packer implies that the well-traversed "ecclesiology and politics of the Puritans," as well as "their nonconformist and republican stances," do not interest him. In the same source, he claims that the Puritan movement "was essentially a movement for church reform. . . . The Puritan goal was to complete what England's Reformation began: to finish reshaping Anglican worship, to introduce effective church discipline into Anglican parishes"—in other words, to promote personal and communal godliness.

All of this seems vanilla-flavored until we set it alongside Lloyd-Jones's conception of the Puritans. For Lloyd-Jones, the Puritans were essentially separatists and nonconformists, not people who remained, either contentedly or discontentedly, within the Church of England. Whereas Packer was interested in the spirituality of the Puritans and their desire to reform the national church, Lloyd-Jones saw them as fiery separatists who were glad to have left the Established Church behind. Coffey writes that for Lloyd-Jones, "Puritanism was the drive for a pure church," achieved through leaving what Lloyd-Jones called a doctrinally mixed denomination (harboring both orthodox and aberrant groups). Coffey further notes regarding Packer and Lloyd-Jones that "at the Puritan Conference, the two men promoted their rival visions," Packer by simply speaking about his perception of the Puritans, and Lloyd-Jones in the combative way of "polemically charged lectures that directly challenged the Anglican vision." Lloyd-Jones's polemics reached their climax in his closing addresses at the Puritan Conference in 1963, 1964, and 1965, when he lectured on (1) John Owen's defense of independency or separation from Anglicanism, (2) the failure of the idea of "*ecclesiola in ecclesia*" ("a small church within the church"), and (3) the Puritan Henry Jacob, founder of Congregationalism.

Packer confirms Coffey's analysis of the situation. In his well-known biographical essay on Lloyd-Jones entitled "A Kind of Puritan," Packer quotes from an essay by Lloyd-Jones in which the latter rejects "the Anglican view" (i.e., Packer's view) of Puritanism as "essentially pastoral theology." For Lloyd-Jones, Packer writes, "the Puritan study of piety and pastoral care was, as a matter of history, 'subsidiary to the desire for true reform of the church,'" that is, a church that had separated from the Church of England. Packer's alternative viewpoint is muted but nonetheless stated: "It was tempting to Dr Lloyd-Jones and his admirers to think of their own preferred options within the Puritan spectrum as 'really' Puritan in a way that other options were not. But such temptations have to be resisted, at least by those for whom history is more than a resource for propaganda."

Controversy with Lloyd-Jones, Part 2

The sparring over rival interpretations of the Puritans was relatively subtle, and probably most attendees at the Puritan Conference were unaware of what we can now see as a conflict. Once we are aware of it, however, we can trace an arc of increasing tension as the 1960s unfolded.

The inciting moment for open conflict between Lloyd-Jones and evangelical Anglicans (including but not limited to Packer) came at the Second National Assembly of Evangelicals, held at the famous Central Hall in Westminster, London, on the evening of October 18, 1966. This assembly was a melting pot of evangelical affiliations in England, with the two large groups being the free church or nonconformist wing and the Anglican wing. Ironically, in view of the outcome, the conference had as its goal the pursuit of the "unity of the Spirit" (Eph. 4:3). Alister McGrath's analysis of the crisis that the conference engendered is that "the cause of the split was a public confrontation between Lloyd-Jones and [John R. W.] Stott." My focus will be on the conflict between Lloyd-Jones and Packer. We should note that the conflict occurred midway through Packer's tenure as warden of Latimer House, where he was perhaps the leading spokesman for the evangelical wing of the Church of England.

Lloyd-Jones gave the opening address of the conference. He chose to talk about the doctrine of the church. As a context, the ecumenical winds of church mergers were blowing across the world of liberal Christianity. Packer was embroiled in the controversy over a proposed merger between the Methodists and Anglicans in England. Packer represented an evangelical resistance to the proposed merger, and that viewpoint eventually won. An even broader context was the worldwide split that was occurring between liberal and conservative views of the Bible and the gospel. In the United States, this split had tended to lead conservatives to separate from liberal mainline denominations. A litmus test was whether a given church or denomination retained affiliation with the liberal World Council of Churches.

The atmosphere in the audience was electric as Lloyd-Jones made an appeal for evangelicals to separate from the Church of England. This call was couched in terms of an appeal for unity among evangelicals—a visible unity that would match their spiritual unity. "You and I are evangelicals," Lloyd-Jones told the audience. "We are agreed about these essentials of the faith, and yet we are divided from one another" by different church affiliations. Many are "united with people who deny and are opposed to these essential matters of salvation. We spend our time with them. We have our visible unity with them. Now, I say, that is sinful." According to Lloyd-Jones, the day might come when evangelicals would actually "thank God" for the ecumenical movement, "because it has made us face our problems on the church level . . . and really brought us together as a fellowship, or an association, of evangelical churches."

Stott was on the platform as the presiding official for the session. When he got up to announce the closing hymn, he was so alarmed over the prospect of ministers in the audience heeding Lloyd-Jones's call to separate that he said: "I hope no one will make a precipitate decision after this moving address. We are here to debate this subject and I believe that history is against Dr Jones in that others have tried to do this very thing. I believe the Scripture is against him in that the remnant was within the Church and not outside it."

What role did Packer play in this drama? The first thing to say is that Packer was solidly of the same opinion as Stott. In a 1995 address, Packer recalled the evening in the Central Hall as though it had happened the night before. Among the points he made were the following:

- Lloyd-Jones was guilty of "two bad arguments. Bad argument number one was that if we stay in the Church of England we're guilty by association of all the theological errors that any Anglican may be propagating anywhere at all."
- "It was a sad thing that a great mind like that of the late Dr Martyn Lloyd-Jones should ever have toyed with an argument as bad as this one."
- Second, Lloyd-Jones said, "Don't you see that the times call us to leave all the doctrinally mixed congregations and form a pure new one."
- "I and others looked around and couldn't see that the times called us to do any such thing."
- "We asked what do the times call us to do? It seemed clear that the times called us to stay put and work for Reformation, renewal and fresh life in the church that has this rich heritage."

These recollections tell us the thoroughness of Packer's rejection of Lloyd-Jones's appeal.

There is a strong emotional undertow in the statements I have quoted. So far as I have been able to ascertain, the two ascriptions to Lloyd-Jones are self-revealing of Packer in the sense that they go beyond what Lloyd-Jones said. It is true that Lloyd-Jones spoke of guilt by association, but not in this address. Further, I have seen nothing to the effect that Lloyd-Jones believed that someone who remained a member of the Anglican Church was guilty by association of all the doctrinal aberrations held by all heterodox Anglicans. Similarly, the consensus of scholarship is that Lloyd-Jones was extremely vague on what he wanted evangelical Anglicans to separate *to*. Lloyd-Jones's terminology in the address was "a fellowship, or an association, of evangelical churches," not a single pure church. What we can conclude is that Packer was extremely opposed to Lloyd-Jones's position. His recollections of what Lloyd-Jones said express emotional truth (Packer's passionate opposition), even if they are not quite literally accurate.

Disagreement with someone does not by itself produce a break in personal relations, nor does it add up to controversy. We need to look at the fallout from Packer's disagreement with Lloyd-Jones to get that picture. There was no immediate break in relations between the two men. Packer did not attack Lloyd-Jones publicly; he simply remained in his post as warden of the Anglican Latimer House. The Puritan Conference went on as usual for four more years. Packer spoke on John Owen and communication from God, the Puritans and spiritual gifts, Arminianism, and the doctrine of justification among the Puritans. Lloyd-Jones, who always gave the closing address, spoke on independent clergyman Robert Sandeman, Welsh Calvinistic Methodism, and learning from history. In the last of these, Lloyd-Jones proposed that "we really must say farewell once and for ever to the idea of a national church" and its vision of a "comprehensive model" of church unity, embracing instead "the evangelical view" of unity among people who believe the fundamentals of the faith.

Although the conference continued during these years, tensions ran high, and in July 1970, Lloyd-Jones wrote to Packer to announce that the Puritan Conference had been terminated. For all practical purposes, this was the end of direct personal contact between Lloyd-Jones and Packer.

It was not only Packer's refusal to separate from the Church of England, however, that brought the Puritan Conference to an end. It was also Packer's continuing work in the Church of England, and in particular an event that sparked controversy well beyond Lloyd-Jones. Before I turn to that controversy, I need to sum up the long-term effect of the break with Lloyd-Jones in Packer's life.

The first thing to note is that relatively few Anglican evangelicals heeded Lloyd-Jones's call to separate from the Church of England. Conversely, then, most evangelical Anglicans remained in the Established Church. The hostility that Lloyd-Jones and his nonconformist followers showed toward Packer did not extend to these other Anglican loyalists. In particular, many have pointed out that Lloyd-Jones did not shun Stott as he shunned Packer. Why did Stott remain in relatively good standing with Lloyd-Jones?

The explanation is probably that Packer's refusal to leave the Anglican Church was seen as a betrayal, whereas Stott's refusal was not. Stott was never regarded as a candidate to heed the call to separate, but that was not the case with Packer, whose Puritanism and evangelical ecumenism had made him a champion in nonconformist circles. Packer had moved with ease in non-Anglican evangelical circles, beginning in his Oxford days. He spoke to evangelical groups regardless of their denominational affiliation. The parachurch organization Inter-Varsity had been a home to him, and he was a father figure to its students.

In view of these close ties with non-Anglican evangelicals, it was probably inevitable that Packer's refusal to leave the Anglican Church was regarded as a drawing back from what had appeared to be a sympathetic identification with non-Anglican evangelicals. Those who experienced it that way saw an element of betrayal in it. McGrath notes that "some have argued that Packer was a bold reformer who somehow lost his nerve over the period 1966–71 (a view especially associated with the circle around Lloyd-Jones)." McGrath also correctly notes that Packer was actually "following his own consistent reforming agenda" for the Church of England.

Forty years after Packer's refusal to be dissuaded from his reforming agenda for the Church of England, Carl Trueman of Westminster Seminary subjected the decision to analysis and popularized the view in an essay and in Internet postings that Packer became the lost leader of the nonconformist movement in the second half of the twentieth century in England. In other words, Packer's choice remains a subject of controversy and criticism. According to Trueman, if Packer had heeded the call to secede, he would have become the eventual leader of non-Anglican evangelicals in England. He might have provided a ballast to Lloyd-Jones's dominance among the free-church constituency. He could have helped that same segment to see the value of historic Christian creeds and the unity that ecclesiastical tradition and structures can supply to what otherwise becomes (and did become) a tendency toward independency and fragmentation. Trueman's conclusion: "But Packer remained an Anglican. That was, I believe, a mistake and greatly impoverished the British evangelical scene. He failed to be the leader that he should have been because he simply refused Lloyd-Jones's call rather than building on it. He was the one man who had the theology . . . and ecclesiology to have potentially offered some positive church vision to which others might come out."

Growing into Union: Controversy among Evangelicals

The simplistic view of the falling out with Lloyd-Jones and the nonconformist community in England is that it stemmed from the great evangelical split of 1966. This is a misrepresentation. After all, the Puritan Conference went on for another four years. Something beyond the secession controversy was unfolding at the same time, and the controversy that it spawned was not limited to the Lloyd-Jones circle but embraced Anglicans as well.

In his role as warden of Latimer House, Packer served on numerous Anglican committees. In what was to be his last report to the Latimer House Council (October 1969), Packer mentioned several projects that were on the verge of completion. One was a book-length committee report, authored by four people, that Packer whimsically called "a mixed Willesden-Mascall-Buchanan-Packer grill." Little did he realize what a controversy it would create. The subject of the book, entitled *Growing into Union* (1970), was church unity in England. The occasion was a major ecumenical push of the 1960s to merge the Anglican and Methodist churches in England. This was perceived as highly undesirable by Anglican evangelicals on both doctrinal and procedural grounds. Over a span of several years, Packer sank a lot of time into working to thwart the union, a venture in which he was successful.

During the course of these efforts, it became clear that two wings of the Anglican Church shared "common cause" in seeking to resist the merger. They were certain members (not all) of the Roman Catholic-leaning wing (Anglo-Catholics) and the evangelicals. In a move that was prophetic of a later venture in cooperation with Roman Catholics known as Evangelicals and Catholics Together (see below), Packer and his evangelical cohort Colin O. Buchanan were glad to join hands in writing the document with the Anglo-Catholics Graham Leonard (bishop of Willesden) and E. L. Mascall. The shared ground of opposition to the Anglican-Methodist merger was doctrinal, and in particular a desire to hold the line for orthodoxy and resist the triumph of liberalism in the proposed united church.

We can infer that Packer proceeded with no awareness that the resulting joint publication was beset with a huge potential for misunderstanding and controversy. For starters, it was unusual (McGrath says "highly unusual") for evangelicals to join with Anglo-Catholics in producing a joint document. Second, Packer was probably naive in believing that *Growing into Union* would be received as a provisional statement, not a final position paper. He himself viewed the document as a "tract" rather than a "treatise." (It should be noted, however, that the book is two hundred pages in length.) When Packer cast a retrospective look at the book a decade later, he explained that it was no more than an exercise of what Francis Schaeffer called "co-belligerence" (co-operation against a common opponent). In Packer's words, "we made common cause on particular issues without committing ourselves to agree beyond that point."

The discovery of like-mindedness between the two pairs of authors came as a surprise to them. Just a few years previously, both sides had published books that were hostile to the other's affiliation (Packer's edited book was entitled *Fellowship in the Gospel*, 1968). As the four discussed matters, they were surprised by the spirit of cooperation that descended on them. *Growing into Union* was fired by enthusiasm for this newly found agreement. The authors noted that "we are not what we were [before we found ourselves agreeing with each other]. There has been a joy and a mutual benefit in tackling this task together."

There were two dimensions to *Growing into Union*. One was a doctrinal section in which all four authors expressed as much agreement as their different personal beliefs allowed, and more than most of their fellow Anglicans had thought existed. The other dimension of the book was an alternative vision for a Methodist-Anglican merger than had been proposed by the mainstream bodies. The doctrinal section evoked the ire of evangelicals, and the proposal for an alternative method of proceeding in regard to the merger (along with unflinching attacks on the official scheme) provoked attacks from ecumenically minded Methodists and Anglicans (see the next section).

The book placed Packer squarely in a public controversy among evangelicals. *Evangelical Magazine* subjected the book to scrutiny in three successive articles, showing the magnitude of the opposition to Packer and the others. The author was David N. Samuel of the Protestant Reformation Society, who made a snide comment about how "the differences that have divided Christendom for four hundred years" had been "resolved by four Anglican clergymen, and that all within the space of six months." Paul Helm, writing in *The Banner of Truth*, claimed that *Growing into Union* was "muffled and muted" on the important doctrine of justification. According to an article in *Peace and Truth*, the book was an insult to Protestantism, while the *Evangelical Magazine of Wales* claimed that Packer and Buchanan had departed from "historical, biblical Evangelicalism," leaving evangelicals "betrayed and abandoned." A threesome of Alan Stibbs (former vice principal of Oak Hill Theological College), Oliver Barclay (general secretary of Inter-Varsity), and Nigel Sylvester (general secretary of Scripture Union) issued a joint memorandum charging that "most evangelical Anglican clergy are now so committed to the Church of England that they are unwilling to fix certain points beyond which they cannot go. . . . Denominational loyalties, which are without clear biblical warrant, seem to take precedence over questions of truth." Packer dismissed the accusation as reflecting "a siege mentality."

The criticism came from previously friendly Anglicans as well. Packer's longtime associate Roger Beckwith called the book "deplorably weak." Even Stott joined the chorus of criticism. He saw the book as intensifying the "alienation" between Anglicans and nonconformists after the 1967 Keele Congress, and expressed a worry about "signs and symptoms of an underlying doctrinal compromise." He acknowledged that the furor represented a new departure in which "Free Church (and some Anglican) evangelicals" were not simply questioning the post-Keele policy, approach, and preoccupation with secondary issues, "but our theology itself." Stott wrote, "We must not blind ourselves to the fact that our theological orthodoxy and integrity as evangelicals are being called into question."

Of course, Lloyd-Jones was appalled by the seeming Anglo-Catholicism of *Growing into Union*. Its publication did what Packer's refusal to secede from the Church of England had failed to accomplish—it brought an end to the twenty-year Puritan Conference. In the letter announcing that fact to Packer, Lloyd-Jones said nothing about Packer's failure to leave the Anglican Church. Instead, the catalyst he cited was *Growing into Union*. The three planners of the conference who terminated it agreed that "the doctrinal position outlined in that book cannot be regarded as being evangelical, still less puritan." To continue the Puritan Conference with Packer's involvement would at the least "cause great confusion in the minds of all Free Church evangelical people and indeed also a number of Anglican people." As a parting shot, Lloyd-Jones wrote, "You must have known that the views expounded in the book concerning Tradition, Baptism, the Eucharist and the Bishops, not to mention the lack of clarity concerning justification by faith only, could not possibly be acceptable to the vast majority of people attending the Puritan Conference."

In light of the furor that *Growing into Union* caused in many circles, it ranks as a major chapter in the story of J. I. Packer as a controversialist. Compared to it, his non-secession from the Anglican Church by itself is a relatively minor matter. It is probably accurate to say that *Growing into Union* provides a gloss on Packer's continuing loyalty to the Church of England, based on a concept of comprehensiveness within his denomination.

Growing into Union: Controversy among Liberal Ecumenists

The current chapter mainly reviews Packer's run-ins with fellow evangelicals. But there is another side from which Packer has been attacked as well, namely, liberals. For the most part, these skirmishes have occurred within the world of liberal Anglicanism. In that world, Packer has all along been an evangelical outsider whose views have irritated the liberal establishment. Having looked at how *Growing into Union* ignited evangelical protest by its sympathetic stance toward the Anglo-Catholic viewpoint, I want to explore how the same book brought down the scorn of liberal Anglicans on Packer and Buchanan.

There were two arenas for that scorn. One was the Anglican convocation at which a final vote was scheduled on the proposed Methodist-Anglican merger. Negotiations had been under way for sixteen years.

The convocation, which occurred in the summer of 1969, bore the official title of the Convocations of Canterbury and York. Even though this was a year before the appearance of *Growing into Union*, the four authors were already viewed as a united voice at the convocation. In fact, the four had publicly petitioned the convocation to reject the official proposal, "not in order to bury all hopes for unity," but because a "better way" could be found to achieve unity. The position of the four was highly controversial. Packer himself later recalled that the plea of the four was treated like "the ecclesiastical equivalent of rotten eggs and raspberries. . . . Incredulity was voiced in many memorable ways."

It needs to be said that the tone of the statements submitted before the convocation and stated in the book is combative and polemical. The team of authors wrote as people engaged in a life-or-death struggle, and they made no attempt to provide the proverbial "soft voice" that turns away wrath. For example, in commenting on the lax view of scriptural authority in the official plan of merger, the authors observed that "the way was deliberately left clear for anyone to treat Scripture as he pleases. Here the cloven hoof of doctrinal minimalism seems to appear, if not indeed of doctrinal indifferentism, which is worse." Or: "We are told that its [the Anglican-Methodist Unity Scheme] rejection would lead to widespread cynicism and despair. We are ourselves convinced that attempts to implement it as it stands would produce great disruption and harm." When I read the book as a conservative evangelical, I find the experience invigorating (do I dare say "and entertaining"?), but all the while I am busy imagining how angry the book would have made the ecumenists who read it.

To catch the flavor of the scorn that was heaped on the viewpoints espoused by Packer's group at the conference, here is a list of specimen statements:

- "I do not believe that there are any workable alternatives to the present proposals. Let the minorities [i.e., the quartet], who disagree among themselves, tell us what their scheme is. But they won't, they won't, they won't."—Archbishop Michael Ramsey, after the official proposal failed to receive the 75 percent vote required for passage.
- "The idea that the Bishop of Willesden (High) and Dr Packer (Low) can find an agreed solution is the product of the Mad Hatter's tea-party in the Old Mitre tavern."—Bishop Mervyn Stockwood

- "The way of doing theology which was common to the new alliance . . . was authoritarian in temper, it was highly mathematical in structure, and it was based on a restricted use of language. . . . Their castles in the air might, in fact, be built on theological sand."—Unidentified speaker at the convocation
- "Now look what you have done. The unholy alliance of Low and High extremes has rebuffed the consensus of reasonable, hopeful, theological, faithful, expectant church opinion. How dare you!"—Unidentified clergyman from Devon

In this way, Packer and his cohorts found themselves at the center of controversy at the Anglican assembly.

But even more vehemence surfaced when *Growing into Union* was published a year later. The book was published by SPCK (Society for Promoting Christian Knowledge) and launched at a press conference in London. Packer defended the book in an article published in *The Church of England Newspaper*, writing that "we found in each other a common concern in opposing the 1968 plan, a common thrust in basic theology, and a common radicalism regarding present church structures." It did not take long for reaction to erupt. Here is a sampling of the opposition that the book elicited from liberal critics:

- Six Methodist officials published a twenty-two-point indictment that dismissed the book as "an Anglican book for Anglicans (perhaps an old-fashioned Anglican book for old-fashioned Anglicans), showing a profound ignorance of Methodist structures, ideas, procedures and ways of thinking and acting."
- "The plan proposes no solution at all to the inveterate problem of the ministry which has dogged all our negotiations with the Church of England. . . . It shows no sign at all of appreciating the ideas or wishes or hopes of Methodists."—Rupert Davies, principal of Wesley College, Bristol
- "A fiasco."—Anglican Bishop Kenneth Riches of Lincoln
- "Irrelevant."—Lord Fisher
- "You seem to have . . . the illusion that you, the remnant, are the only ones left with a concern for divine Truth! The rest are liberals, expedient opportunists or confused thinkers. You hadn't really listened to what we were saying."—Simon Barrington-Ward, Anglican cleric

Enough has been said to show that *Growing into Union* elicited as much controversy among liberal ecumenists as it did among evangelicals. Andrew Atherstone, author of a marvelously researched essay on the subject, calls *Growing into Union* "one of the most controversial ecumenical tracts in recent decades"—a book that "provoked vociferous reactions, polarizing opinion amongst English ecumenists caught up in the heady reunion debates of a generation ago."

The Move to Canada

Packer's decision to leave England for Canada in 1979 is a major subject among people interested in his life. The primary attitude that the public takes to the decision is one of mystification: why did such a prominent and quintessentially British person as Packer make the move? I propose that "wondering why" has an element of controversy in it. People are not necessarily critical of the move (though some are), but they are baffled by it. To be the object of so much public inquisitiveness is akin to being at the center of controversy.

The circumstances surrounding Packer's acceptance of a position at Regent College give us a clue that he knew the move would be controversial. James Houston's original letter of invitation to Packer to teach at Regent came in 1976. We might say that for the next three years, Packer conducted a delicate balancing act that included an element of secrecy. As he weighed the likely fallout of a move to Canada, he did not want to leave immediately after the Nottingham Congress of 1977, toward which he had negative feelings. Packer feared that moving hastily after the conference might be interpreted as leaving in a "huff."

As far as the recruitment process was concerned, Packer's first visit to Regent College was a secret twenty-four hour visit in 1977 during a routine speaking trip in North America. Then Packer taught at the Regent summer school in 1978, which aroused no suspicion, since he taught regularly on a short-term basis in North America. At the end of the summer session, Packer accepted the offer to teach permanently at Regent. When Packer returned to Bristol, he informed Trinity College Principal Alec Motyer of his decision. No formal announcement was made, but the news spread informally and quickly to students and staff. The surprise and controversy that ensued are not, by and large, a matter of public record. McGrath provides the following picture, which we can well imagine without a written chronicle of responses:

> The news that Packer was to leave England for Canada surprised and distressed many back home. It came like a bolt from the blue. Many were saddened that the English church was to lose Packer's gifts and talents. Some, perhaps with inflated views of the importance of England, felt that his move was to the general loss of Christianity.

Part of the reason the move remains controversial is the rival explanations that people offer for the decision. For some, the move was the result of a sinister exclusion of Packer within British circles, and especially the evangelical wing of the Anglican Church, that was now firmly under the influence of Stott. Others point to the shunning and loss of influence that Packer experienced in the free-church circles dominated by Lloyd-Jones. In either case, Packer was "frozen out of certain evangelical circles in which he had once been a welcome participant" (McGrath's summary).

A further dimension of the controversy surrounding Packer's move to Canada is disagreement about whether it was a good or bad thing. It is safe to say that no one in North America thought the move was anything less than a godsend. But it was otherwise in England. Long before Packer's move became a fact, even the prospect of it had struck his colleague John Wenham as "perhaps the greatest disaster that has ever overtaken the Evangelical cause in the Church of England." Stott marked Packer's departure from England with an article in a religious periodical in which he praised Packer's "enormous contribution to the cause of Christ" and lamented the loss of its continuance in Anglican evangelicalism. But—and this is part of the controversy surrounding the move—others celebrated the expansion of opportunity represented by the move. Dick Lucas, longtime rector of St. Helen's Bishopsgate in London, someone who (like Packer) was critical of the liberal fallout after the Nottingham Congress of 1977, offered the verdict that he could "only be thankful for the move, surely providential, that gave Jim the scope he needed, in a freer environment, to realise his so great potential."

Assorted Controversies

Before I take up the controversies that engulfed Packer's life after he moved to Canada, I want to give brief coverage to other controversies that happened during the middle of Packer's career. One of these was the Anglican congress held at Nottingham University in 1977, an envisioned repeat of the acclaimed congress held at Keele a decade earlier. Stott was keen on staging a follow-up conference. Packer was not. At the first planning meeting for the conference, Packer offered the view that the proposed conference would be a distraction from grassroots evangelical efforts at the parish level. Packer's view was rejected. At the second planning session, Packer pushed for a study-style conference that would address doctrinal subjects on which the church was then deficient. Stott wanted another general conference that would serve the function of what in the United States would be called a rally. Packer's proposal lost. Packer further warned that if such a conference produced a published report, the document would be intellectually thin and would thereby perpetuate an unwanted view of evangelicals as being simplistic in their approach. Packer's caution went unheeded.

It is obvious that right down the line, Packer's minority viewpoint was regarded by the majority as an unwanted obstruction to their enthusiasm for the envisioned conference. Whatever word we might use for this—*controversy*, *dissonance*, *disagreement*—it fits into the pattern of Packer's views being a subject of controversy.

Another controversy that Packer endured was the turmoil surrounding the demise of Tyndale Hall and the formation of Trinity College. In addition to certain elements of controversy, there was simply the emotional wear and tear and the dashing of hopes that entered Packer's life when Tyndale Hall was terminated after he had successfully introduced organizational and curricular changes into the college.

The controversy arose when a merger of the three theological colleges in Bristol—Tyndale Hall, Clifton Theological College, and Dalton House—was mandated by the Anglican House of Bishops. This decision immediately introduced questions of turf, especially regarding who from the three colleges would provide leadership at the new college. Packer was active in exploratory meetings of an Interim Council. He had already been approved as dean of studies at the new college, and from that premise, Packer's goal was to see how the administration of the new college might look. However, the Clifton candidate nominated to serve as a member of the "three-dean" arrangement for governing the new college interpreted Packer's contributions as an attempt to dictate how Trinity College would be run. The Clifton representative wrote a letter of complaint to the bishop of Bristol. Packer protested what the letter said. Urgent missives ensued, including a hand-delivered letter from the bishop to Packer. The bishop's final conclusion was "that Packer had not misled anyone; the problem was that Packer simply seemed to have difficulties in dealing with people" (McGrath's summary)!

I offer the foregoing simply as a specimen of the turmoil, controversy, and rumors that swirled during the process of merging the three colleges. As negotiations unfolded, it became clear that the Clifton contingent did not want Packer to have a significant administrative position at the new college. A Clifton representative even suggested that Packer not receive a position, but this was soundly rejected by Tyndale representatives. I have said enough to establish that one of the bypaths in Packer's unsought career as a controversialist was the merger of the three colleges in Bristol.

Packer has also entered the fray in controversies that existed before his involvement in them. One of these is the charismatic movement, which achieved prominence in the 1960s and 1970s. The situation in England was different from that in the United States. In the United States, the charismatic movement largely unfolded in Pentecostal churches and denominations, off by themselves, where the practice of the charismatic gifts was simply allowed to flourish. But in England, the charismatic movement became prominent within the Church of England, where it needed to be addressed.

McGrath chronicles a portion of the flurry of dialogue and organized meetings that unfolded as Anglicans attempted to understand what was happening within their ranks. What matters for this biography is that Packer was a very active participant in the controversy surrounding the spiritual gifts in the Church of England. According to McGrath, Packer was not only "a significant voice" in the Anglican response to the charismatic movement, but "at times . . . a lonely voice." From the vantage point of distance, we can discern two roles that Packer played in the controversy.

One was that of facilitator and coordinator among those who disagreed about whether the charismatic gifts have a legitimate role in the normal Christian life today and about the relation between the Holy Spirit and the written Word of God as religious authorities. At a 1974 meeting of an evangelical Anglican group known as the Senior Eclectic Conference, Packer delivered an address in which he expressed the view that there was enough "essential evangelicalism" in the charismatic movement that non-charismatics needed to cooperate with charismatics. From this suggestion came a "Gospel and Spirit" group that met over an eighteen-month period and issued a joint statement.

The second role that Packer played in this movement was that of mediator between rival positions. This is best seen in his book *Keep in Step with the Spirit* (1984). It is one of Packer's major books—fully researched, comprehensive in coverage, and packed with references to the Bible and theological traditions. Although Inter-Varsity Press Publishing Director Ronald Inchley pressed Packer to write a book on the Holy Spirit when the working committee that came to be known as the "Gospel and Spirit" group produced its report in the mid-1970s, Packer refused to write such a book until he had thoroughly researched the subject a decade later. *Keep in Step with the Spirit* won a Gold Medallion award from the Evangelical Christian Publishers' Association, and McGrath is correct when he calls the book "unquestionably one of Packer's more significant works, repaying close reading."

What immediately strikes a reader of this book is that Packer is pursuing a reasonable middle way between extremes. On the one hand, he holds the line against simply accepting all charismatic experience and theology as true and normative. Sticking with the Bible as his source, Packer says much that a non-charismatic wishes to be said. There is plenty of material that would make him an ally of the skeptics of the charismatic experience. But Packer's criticism of various charismatic positions (including his longtime nemesis, Keswick triumphalism) is handled in such a conciliatory manner that people of charismatic conviction would see Packer, at some level, as their ally, too. Packer finds much to affirm in various Holy Spirit movements.

I have uncovered no evidence that Packer became the object of widespread criticism as a result of his participation in the charismatic debate of the 1960s and 1970s. It is more a matter of his not hesitating to enter a sphere that he knew to be controversial. In doing so, he played the role of mediator between opposed and sometimes hostile camps. Most evangelicals in the Church of England did not know how to respond to the teaching on the baptism of the Holy Spirit that was a leading ingredient in the charismatic movement. According to McGrath, many Anglicans viewed the charismatic movement "with hostility." Packer did not.

Years later, when Packer was active in the Christianity Today Institute, he was still serving a mediating role. David Neff, former editor of *Christianity Today*, shares the following remembrance: "As we sat together for several hours talking about the Holy Spirit, I saw Jim and [Pentecostal leader] John Wimber grow remarkably chummy, and I heard John Wimber giving vigorous assent to Jim Packer's Owenesque statements about the Holy Spirit." Neff then adds, "That wasn't supposed to happen, but Jim presents his theology in such a way that even those who are supposed to disagree with him can't seem to help themselves."

Packer's mediating role in the charismatic controversy contrasts with the strong stand that he has taken on the question of women in the church. The publication that proved most controversial was a 1991 article in *Christianity Today* entitled "Let's Stop Making Women Presbyters." Before I look at that article, though, I want to note that it did not suddenly spring from Packer's typewriter; he had been publishing his viewpoint on the different roles that he believes the Bible prescribes for men and women for two decades. Here is a sampling:

- "Representative Priesthood and the Ordination of Women," in *Why Not? Priesthood and the Ministry of Women: A Theological Study* (1972; second edition 1976)
- "Thoughts on the Role and Function of Women in the Church," in *Evangelicals and the Ordination of Women* (1973)
- "Understanding the Differences," in *Women, Authority and the Bible* (1986)

But the "big one" was the *Christianity Today* article of 1991.

Packer begins the article by affirming that he is "as emphatically for women's ministry as I am against turning women into substitute men by making presbyters of them. To confine women to domestic and menial roles when God has gifted them for ministry and leadership would be

Spirit-quenching." From that starting point, Packer turns his attention to the contemporary feminist movement, which demands equal roles for women and men. Packer's conclusion is that "the present-day pressure to make women presbyters owes more to secular, pragmatic, and social factors than to any regard for biblical authority." Since the Bible is Packer's authority, the bulk of the article addresses biblical data. Among the controversial assertions that he makes are these:

- "That Jesus' maleness is basic to his role as our incarnate Saviour is a matter of biblical revelation. Jesus was not, and is not, merely a symbol of something else. . . . To minimize the maleness shows a degree of failure to grasp the space-time reality and redemptive significance of the incarnation."
- "God made humanity in two genders. Both males and females bear his image and in personal dignity are equal in every way, but God has set them in a non-reversible relation to each other."
- The "distinctive quality of womanly ministry" is that "it is maternal rather than paternal in flavor and style," and "this quality should permeate all the activities that make it up."
- Gender roles "are complementary, and the true enrichment comes when they are being fulfilled side by side."
- "The creation pattern, as biblically set forth, is: man to lead, woman to support; man to initiate, woman to enable; man to take responsibility for the well-being of woman, woman to take responsibility for helping man."

It is obvious that these views have made Packer a champion among evangelicals who hold to a complementarian view of men and women. Equally, they have cost him favor with feminists. Some individuals and institutions have risen above their disagreement on the gender question and continue to view Packer as a worthy authority, but others have stopped association with him.

A final controversy that I will note under my rubric of "Assorted Controversies" is one that has simmered in evangelicalism for a long time, but that became especially prominent in the 1980s—the rejection of the doctrine of hell. Several labels can be used for the view that Packer opposes, including annihilationism (belief that unbelievers experience annihilation instead of punishment in hell after death), universalism (belief that all people will be saved or at least that no one will be consigned to hell), denial of eternal punishment, and conditional immortality (only the saved are immortal). I will note in passing that this subject was an area of importance for Packer as early as a 1959 article in *Christianity Today*.

These views became a major controversy in evangelicalism in both England and America in the 1980s, and remain such to this day. They gained prominence when certain high-profile evangelicals published works denying the traditional Christian doctrine of hell. These included Stott, Philip Edgcumbe Hughes (one-time librarian at Latimer House in Oxford), Packer's longtime colleague John Wenham, and Packer's predecessor at Regent College, Clark Pinnock. Packer has expressed rebuttals to the viewpoints of these men in many places, including the Leon Morris Lecture that Packer delivered in Melbourne, Australia, in 1990. (I would also particularly recommend Packer's essay "Evangelicals and the Way of Salvation," published in an edited anthology entitled *Evangelical Affirmations* in 1990.)

It is not my purpose to reconstruct the details of Packer's argument. It is a recapitulation of the biblical data on eternal punishment and of the traditional statements of the doctrine through the centuries. My purpose is to convey the flavor of the controversy that Packer inevitably accepted as part of his endorsement of the traditional doctrine of hell and his public disagreement with scholars who argued against it. Here is a sampling of Packer's statements in which he refused to avoid the controversy:

- "Universalist speculations, hazardous and unconvincing as they are, continue to gain ground. . . . I confess that it troubles me greatly."
- "Does it matter whether an evangelical is a conditionalist or not? I think it does: for a conditionalist's idea of God will miss out on the glory of divine justice, . . . and in his preaching of the gospel he will miss out on telling the unconverted that their prospects without Christ are as bad as they possibly could be."
- "If you think of this lecture as a dissuasive from universalism and conditionalism, . . . you will be correct."
- "It is distasteful to argue in print against honored fellow-evangelicals, some of whom are good friends."
- "When John Stott urges that 'the ultimate annihilation of the wicked should at least be accepted as a legitimate, biblically founded

alternative to their eternal conscious torment,' he asks too much, for the biblical foundations of this view prove on inspection . . . to be inadequate."

- "The feelings that make people want conditionalism to be true seem to me to reflect, not superior spiritual sensitivity, but secular sentimentalism."

In these statements, we see, once again, J. I. Packer the crusader. In that role, he has regularly carried out the dual tasks of defending a position and arguing against its opposite.

Evangelicals and Catholics Together

J. I. Packer entered the sphere of cooperation with Anglo-Catholics in his role as an activist on Anglican issues during the 1960s (see above). The alliance that Packer forged with them was driven by the need to join forces in an effort to thwart attempts at an Anglican-Methodist merger in England. A later venture in cooperation, however, was one that Packer voluntarily undertook. This time the alliance was not with Anglo-Catholics, but Roman Catholics.

The venture was called Evangelicals and Catholics Together (ECT). The movement was a child of the 1990s. At least two triggers can be identified. One was a growing tolerance of Roman Catholicism among certain segments of evangelical Protestantism. The second was anxiety among traditional Roman Catholics and conservative evangelicals about the growing secularism, materialism, and moral collapse of Western society. The concept of "common cause" or "co-belligerence" (cooperation to combat a common foe) was fully operative. To certain influential evangelicals, the prospect of cooperating with Roman Catholics on a limited range of issues despite deep theological and ecclesiastical differences held great appeal. All that was needed to produce a movement was a catalyst.

The catalyst came in the form of two men—Roman Catholic cleric and author Richard John Neuhaus and evangelical author and speaker Charles Colson, a former White House staffer under President Richard Nixon who was converted after the Watergate scandal. Neuhaus had authored a best seller entitled *The Naked Public Square* (1984) in which he documented the degree to which religion had been systematically excised from public life in the United States. Colson had published a book that covered similar territory—*Kingdoms in Conflict* (1987). It became clear that the two authors shared a common agenda in regard to the need for Christians to put up a joint front against the erosion of Christian values.

Neuhaus and Colson accordingly began to assemble a network of evangelicals and Roman Catholics. Packer, who was both famous and someone with a track record of ecumenical cooperation with Anglo-Catholics, was eventually (but not initially) included. A working group assembled in September 1992. An ambitious joint document, with which Packer publicly identified, was made public in May 1994. Summarizing the content of the document is beyond my purpose, but the paper is readily accessible. As criticism was expressed, further meetings occurred and more documents were produced. By that time, Packer was in the middle of all that happened (as chronicled in McGrath's biography).

Why did Packer pour himself into this movement, and how did he defend that involvement? Packer answered those questions in an article entitled "Why I Signed It" (*Christianity Today*, December 12, 1994). The most salient points that he made are the following:

- "I was surprised at the violence of initial negative Protestant reaction." Packer attributed the criticism to fear.
- Why did Packer sign the final document? "Because it affirms positions and expresses attitudes that have been mine for half a lifetime, and that I think myself called to commend to others every way I can."
- Packer himself "could not become a Roman Catholic because of certain basic tenets to which the Roman system . . . is committed."
- Why did the collaborative effort appeal to Packer? For three reasons: because of the kinship that he had felt with many Anglo-Catholics and Roman Catholics; because collaboration would strengthen Christian social witness in a hostile secular world; and because collaboration would acknowledge a togetherness that had already begun.
- ECT is not (as alleged) a "sellout of evangelical Protestantism." Packer's answer to the question, "Does it not always put you in a false position to work with people with whom you do not totally agree?" is, "Not if you agree on the specific truths and goals

the proposed collaboration involves, and if the points of nonagreement and therefore the limits of togetherness in action are well understood."

Many evangelicals applauded the work of ECT and praised Packer's involvement. The controversy surrounding his participation lies with those who were critical of him. McGrath correctly observes that some of the criticism verged on personal abuse, and I agree with McGrath that Packer elicited such vehemence because "of his high profile and status within evangelicalism." Packer's involvement with ECT was a virtual repeat of his efforts in the Church of England during the 1960s (eventuating in *Growing into Union*, as noted above), and the fallout among conservative evangelicals was nearly identical to what happened then. Packer's cooperation with non-evangelical Anglicans cost him his relationship with D. Martyn Lloyd-Jones, and when Packer identified with ECT, he lost his working relationship with R. C. Sproul, at whose conferences Packer had become a regular speaker and with whom he had collaborated in writing projects.

To catch the flavor of the opposition that Packer elicited by his involvement in ECT, I offer the following statements gleaned from online postings:

- When the publication of the joint statement "Evangelicals and Catholics Together" provoked a firestorm of protest among evangelicals, Colson tried to douse the fire by meeting with prominent evangelical leaders in Florida. In the wake of that meeting, radio and television host John Ankerberg interviewed three people who had attended the "summit"—Sproul, James Kennedy, and John MacArthur. The three-part roundtable was devoted entirely to criticizing the "Evangelicals and Catholics Together" document. The following statement by Sproul captures the spirit of the broadcasts: "My fondest hope was that these men [Packer, Colson, and Bill Bright] would remove their names from it, and if they couldn't do that, if they couldn't recant of it, that they would at least revise the document itself."
- "The framers of ECT have done a disservice, first and foremost to the gospel of Christ, and secondarily to their communities. We call upon such men as [five men are mentioned] and especially J. I. Packer to rethink their position, and withdraw their support

from a document that can do nothing more than cause confusion and 'give aid and comfort to the enemies of the cause of Christ.'" —James White

- "It appears to me as if Packer is the one who ought to brush up on the doctrine of regeneration." This appears in a posting by Ken Silva, in which he pursues a list of specific criticisms of Packer under the umbrella question, "But is this the same J. I. Packer?" The general drift is to cite positive endorsements of Packer or contributions by him in the past and then ask, "Would this then be the same J. I. Packer who signed the *Evangelicals and Catholics Together* document?" The effect of this rhetoric is to portray Packer as guilty of evangelical treason.
- "We are very pleased to quote Dr. Packer's earlier writings, for in them he clearly describes the danger of 'taking up' with much of the thinking in the modern Christian world. Somewhere along the way his priorities seem to have changed, for now he puts the need for 'Christian unity' above the need for doctrinal purity. We sincerely hope that he may one day re-evaluate his position; we would like nothing better than to see him regain his reputation as one of those terribly divisive fellows who is constantly concerned about doctrinal exactness."—Arie den Hartog

There can be little doubt that Packer's involvement in ECT took a large toll on his standing among American evangelicals. By contrast, the movement was barely noticed in Britain.

Evangelicals and Catholics Together belongs to Packer's career as an ecumenist rather than social activist. The thrust of ECT was toward determining theological boundaries and bridges between evangelicals and Roman Catholics. Once Packer had participated in these discussions and seen how controversial his participation was, he poured himself into defending the venture and his part in it. Although ECT was formulated to combat the moral decline of the West, I have not been able to uncover any evidence that this goal was achieved in a major way (or that it was even pursued). The goal became ecumenical unity between evangelicals and Roman Catholics. I believe that Packer in effect acknowledges this in the following sentence from his article entitled "Why I Signed It": "I have long thought that informal grassroots collaboration with Roman Catholics in ministry is the most fruitful sort of ecumenism that one can practice nowadays." Packer has always been ecumenical in his leanings, and he cannot rest content for long without engaging in some form of ecumenism.

Homosexuality and the Anglican Church of Canada

A final large area of controversy in J. I. Packer's life has centered on the Anglican Church of Canada. The issue of controversy has been homosexuality, which Packer has resolutely opposed. This time, the controversy arose between Packer and the liberal wing of Anglicanism. Evangelicals who resist granting sanction to homosexuality have viewed Packer as their absolute champion, and I think it fair to say that by his actions in this controversy, Packer has regained some of the stature that he lost through his involvement with Evangelicals and Catholics Together.

The climax of his run-in with the Anglican Church of Canada came on the day in 2002 when Packer was one of a dozen evangelical clergymen who walked out of a diocesan synod that voted in favor of blessing gay unions. The dissidents declared themselves "out of communion" with the bishop and the synod. But the battle had been raging for at least two decades before that. The chief antagonist for evangelical Anglicans in Vancouver was Michael Ingham, who became bishop of New Westminster in 1994. For a decade before that, he had been a parish clergyman in the diocese and had urged full acceptance of homosexual couples. Over the years of his service as bishop, Ingham promoted and engineered the policy of blessing same-sex unions through official Anglican channels. Even though the bishops of the worldwide Anglican Communion had rejected such sanction by a majority of seventy-five percent at the Lambeth Conference of 1998, Ingham ignored that mandate and nurtured his plan at the level of the synod. When the synod approved the plan, Packer and others walked out.

The disintegration of relations between Packer and the New Westminster diocese dragged on for a number of years. As it became clear that evangelicals would lose their struggle with the mainline denomination, Packer felt liberated to say what he believed and felt. While speaking at Holy Trinity Church in Eastbourne, England, Packer was asked what he would say if he could spend five minutes with then-Archbishop of Canterbury Rowan Williams. Packer replied that he would tell the archbishop that since he had affirmed in print that gay relationships are potentially holy, "he is not qualified to lead the Anglican Communion" (in other words, he should resign). The battle with the liberal denomination officially ended in 2008 when Packer was "suspended" (i.e., had his license revoked) by Ingham, whom an online source correctly calls a revisionist Anglican bishop. Packer, however, was relicensed by the archbishop of the Southern Cone and received into the Anglican Church in North America.

Packer's fullest explanation of why he flouted the Anglican Church of Canada as an apostate body is an article that he published in *Christianity Today* (January 2003). The following is a summary of the main points that Packer made:

- Packer walked out "because this decision . . . falsifies the gospel of Christ, abandons the authority of Scripture, jeopardizes the salvation of fellow human beings, and betrays the church."
- What does Paul say in 1 Corinthians 6:9–11? "Those who claim to be Christ's should avoid the practice of same-sex physical connection for orgasm."
- Paul "is not speaking of inclinations, only of behavior."
- As always, Packer rejects the practice of homosexual advocates who "let experience judge the Bible."
- "Homosexual inclinations are a spiritual disorder, one more sign and fruit of original sin in some people's moral system."

It is obvious that Packer did not simply walk out of a meeting; he has repeatedly denounced homosexual practice and explained the reasons for that condemnation.

Controversy as a Constant in Packer's Life

From his college years onward, Packer has been engaged in public controversy. What conclusions might we draw from the history that I have narrated in this chapter?

First, Packer would never have been involved in the controversies I have noted if he were not a person of strong convictions. A person who held his viewpoints with less passion would have sidestepped some of the controversies that Packer has embraced. He told me that when he takes a stand on controversial issues, he regards himself as a crusader.

When he believes strongly in something, Packer is willing to campaign for it and is not deterred by the wear and tear of being at the center of a battle. Packer has been a very public figure, and controversy has gone with the territory.

Does Packer enjoy controversy? Is he, in fact, a natural-born controversialist who courts it? There is no evidence that would allow us to answer those questions affirmatively. Packer told Wendy Zoba that he has been dogged by "trouble, trouble, trouble, all the way." People do not enjoy trouble. By Packer's own testimony, he early found himself "being criticized all the time and getting used to it." He professes to have found it "wearying." His summary of his life as a controversialist is that he "is not a controversialist by nature but by necessity."

Yet we should not concede too much along these lines. I believe that Packer finds that controversy (experienced as crusading) focuses his energy. A friend of Packer offered an opinion, held by others also, that Packer is at his best intellectually when he is exercised or agitated by an issue. There is a level at which Packer thrives on controversy.

One index to this willingness to engage in controversy is the strong polemical strain that has characterized Packer's writings. Many of his books are entries in public debates. Packer's career as a polemicist began with his very first book, *"Fundamentalism" and the Word of God*. From start to finish, this book is a reply to liberal disparagement of evangelicals and to the liberal view of authority and the Bible. Packer's second major book, *Evangelism and the Sovereignty of God*, is scarcely less polemical as it defends Calvinistic theology and criticizes non-Reformed methods of evangelism. *A Kind of Noah's Ark?* is a propaganda piece for Anglican comprehensiveness—a book tailor-made to put non-Anglicans in a bad mood. *Keep in Step with the Spirit* charts a middle course between extremes, but in the process, Packer continuously expresses disagreement with those extremes. And all of this is to say nothing of the numerous polemical articles and pamphlets that Packer published during his years as upholder of evangelicalism in the Church of England.

Has being at the center of controversy taken a toll on Packer? Of course it has. The opening pages of Packer's book *The Evangelical Anglican Identity Problem* are revealing in this regard. The very first sentence of the monograph reads, "Let me begin with some brooding." The "brooding" is a gratuitous piece of autobiography (not required by the book that follows) in which Packer rehearses the issues on which his evangelicalism had been called into question as of that date (1978). The controversies that he names are the jointly authored book *Growing into Union* (regarding which three separate controversies are identified), a Church of England report entitled *Christian Believing*, Packer's leniency on evolution, and his refusal to separate from the liberal Church of England. The background chorus of this opening chapter is that Packer's evangelicalism had been called into question on all of these issues. I assimilate the chapter as Packer's baring the wounds he has received at the hands of conservative evangelicals.

An added dimension is that Packer has been singled out for a more-than-ordinary degree of criticism. In one of the quoted online sources cited above, James White named several evangelicals who should recant their participation in Evangelicals and Catholics Together, "and especially J. I. Packer." Trueman, in his essay offering "an English nonconformist perspective" on Packer, speaks of "the suspicion and the bile that was directed toward Packer in post-1966 nonconformist circles in so many informal ways, over cups of tea after church, in conversations, in sermonic asides, and so on," a body of data "not documentable but nonetheless real." This accords with Gerald Bray's picture of evangelicals in England routinely sharing criticisms of Packer—for not writing a systematic theology, for involving himself in Anglican issues, or for not devoting himself "to activities of long-term value and impact." When neither Stott nor Packer assented to Lloyd-Jones's appeal for evangelicals to leave the church of England, Packer was shunned by Lloyd-Jones, while "Dr. Stott remained a warm, loving personal friend of Dr. Lloyd-Jones to his death in 1981, and visited him regularly" (Gaius Davies). Packer's Anglican defense entitled *A Kind of Noah's Ark?* includes a statement of complete tolerance for evangelicals who choose not to separate from the Church of England ("these matters are arguable both ways, and neither estimate need be accepted"). It is hard to ask for more than that, but Helm devoted an entire Internet posting to taking Packer to task for not being decisive on the issue. Why are certain groups and individuals so angry at Packer? I speak of a great mystery.

Of course, in every controversy, there are two sides. If one camp is angry at Packer for landing on a given side of a controversial issue, the people who have agreed with his position have viewed him as an ally and often as their champion. In terms of numbers of supporters, though, Packer's crusades have often been a thankless task, and some of them have been losing causes in terms of long-term effect. For example, throughout most of his life, Packer has defended the Church of England in principle, yet few British Anglicans have paid attention to that defense, and it has been a cause for rejection among nonconformists. Roman Catholic-leaning people have been happy to see Packer praise them, but Packer cannot be said to be influential among Roman Catholics or Anglo-Catholics.

I do not feel qualified to conduct an exercise in virtual history of the type that Trueman conducts very ably. I will simply leave my readers to ponder my unanswered question: What would the career and ministry of J. I. Packer have been like if he had not thrown himself into so many controversial ventures? Packer himself provides an angle on this question in a 1991 column in which he discusses how he wishes to be remembered. He writes: "Discussions of biblical inerrancy, secular humanism, abortion, signs and wonders, women's ordination, prophecy, and Christian healing [a list that covers much of Packer's career of controversy] have to be maintained, but they tend to be barren fields for the soul. I should like to be remembered as one who pointed to the pasturelands."

Afterword

J. I. Packer Reflects on His Life

Well do I recall the jolting moment when young Alister McGrath, sitting across the aisle from me in an Oxford-to-Cambridge bus, gazed intently at me and said, more or less out of the blue, "I must write your life." He did so, and to my mind most skillfully, covering with perceptive precision all the main intellectual concerns of my first seventy years.

This time around, it was a little different. Once more I was surprised to find that someone wanted my life written while I was still living it, but publishers are persuasive people, and the chosen biographer was a fellow evangelical believer—a blood brother, bonded to me by the cross of Christ, as I might say; also, a fellow academic; also, a fellow Puritan-lover; and one who is more than a match for my rather disorderly sense of humor. And once more I am left thinking that a very skillful job has been done.

Christian biography is an art form that began to emerge in the days of the first Christian martyrs; that blossomed in the seventeenth century; and that has flourished mightily in more recent times. As biography, it explores what made its subject tick; as Christian biography, its framing question always is: How did this person seek to honor God? Doxological concern dominates it; human interest comes second, though good products of the genre blend both. To have had two very competent biographers dissect me under their respective microscopes is something of a privilege, and I very much appreciate their efforts.

All of us think we know exactly why we say and do what we do,

J. I. Packer (second from left) and his wife, Kit (right), with Lane and Ebeth Dennis of Crossway during an ESV translation committee meeting in Cambridge, England. (Photo courtesy of Lane and Ebeth Dennis)

but above and beyond our conscious motivations, we are all subject to influences of which we are unaware, or a least not fully aware, and one of the tasks of a biography is to trace in full the subject's reasons for action and show how these might appear to a discerning outside observer. When your portrait is painted, you pose to order, but it is the painter who decides how you finally look, and when your biography is written, it is the biographer who makes that decision, projecting you the way he or she sees you. You supply information, answer questions, and express opinions, but your biographer calls the shots. Whether in fact McGrath's and Ryken's friendly accounts of me help in, add to, or detract from an appropriate perception of me is more than I know, or can know, so I remit that question to their readers and move on. What I want to do here is simply express my gratitude to them both for the meticulous care and goodwill that went into their work, and my pleasure that both biographies now exist.

If asked to profile myself at this stage of my life, I should begin by highlighting my ongoing sense of being called by God, as a sinner saved by and owing everything to his grace, to serve his people as a minister-teacher who is as a communicator of life-giving Bible truth concerning the providence, goodness, and knowledge of the Father, the Son and the Holy Spirit, and hereby a furtherer of spiritual formation and a helper of troubled souls. That sense of vocation has been with me since I was nineteen. I would explain that though professionally a professor, my main trajectory of concern has always been ministerial and ecclesial rather than narrowly academic, and my aim as preacher, teacher, and writer has always been to promote present and forward-looking fellowship with God—in other words, faith, love, and hope according to the Scriptures. Then I would share my sense that over many years, my theology, which has stood steady in other respects, has deepened on two points: first, the pervasive corruption of sin in all human lives; second, the equally pervasive centrality of the Lord Jesus Christ in all the plans and actions of God. And I would spell out the fact that from very early on I have seen myself as an historico-theological generalist, trying to catch up with John Calvin as an overall delineator of Christianity, and with a special interest in the evangelical heritage of Reformational, Puritan, revival, and renewal piety.

As I read Leland Ryken holding up his mirror to some of these facets of my life, I am drawn to thank God again for what he has led me to discern and attempt thus far, and to ask him to raise up other saved sinners who will travel further and faster along these trails to serve the church of tomorrow. So may God be glorified; amen.

J. I. Packer

Sources

Chapter 1

Material in this chapter comes from nine sources. The major source is pages 1–12 of Alister McGrath's *J. I. Packer: A Biography* (Grand Rapids: Baker, 1997). This is supplemented by the personal profile of Packer in Wendy Murray Zoba, *J. I. Packer Answers Questions for Today* (Wheaton, IL: Tyndale, 2001), 93–95. The remaining material comes from Packer himself, in the following sources: telephone interview, September 9, 2013; "What Lewis Was and Wasn't," *Christianity Today*, 15 January 1988: 11; "Still Surprised by Lewis," *Christianity Today*, 7 September 1998: 54–60; "Books of the Century" poll, *Christianity Today*, 24 April 2000 (http://www.christianitytoday.com/ct/2000/april24/5.92.html); "Count Your Surprises: The High Spots of My Life Have Been Anything but Expected," *Christianity Today*, March 2008: 66–67; *Praying: Finding Our Way through Duty to Delight* (Downers Grove, IL: InterVarsity, 2006), 63; online interview of Packer by Carl Trueman (http://thegospelcoalition.org/blogs/justintaylor/2012/05/18/carl-trueman-interviews-j-i-packer/).

Chapter 2

Information on the key events in Packer's life at college was taken primarily from Alister McGrath's *J. I. Packer: A Biography* (Grand Rapids: Baker, 1997), 13–28. Second in importance is Wendy Murray Zoba, *J. I. Packer Answers Questions for Today* (Wheaton, IL: Tyndale, 2001), 95–99. Also used: private interview of Lady Elizabeth Catherwood (née Elizabeth Lloyd-Jones) by her children Christopher and Paulette Catherwood. Personal statements by Packer, in addition to those quoted or cited in McGrath and Zoba, are from scattered sources, including the following: telephone interview, October 9, 2013; "Count Your Surprises: The High Spots of My Life Have Been Anything but Expected," *Christianity Today* March 2008: 66–67; online interview of Packer by Carl Trueman (http://thegospelcoalition.org/blogs/justintaylor/2012/05/18/carl-trueman-interviews-j-i-packer/).

Additionally, statements by Packer about his conflict with the Keswick view of the Christian life comprise a small corpus of their own, as follows: "'Keswick' and the Reformed Doctrine of Sanctification," *Evangelical Quarterly* 27 (July–Sept. 1955): 153–67; preface to centenary edition of J. C. Ryle's classic *Holiness* (Welwyn: Evangelical Press, 1979), vii–viii; *Keep in Step with the Spirit* (Old Tappan, NJ: Revell, 1984), 145–63; introduction to John Owen's *Sin and Temptation: The Challenge of Personal Godliness*, ed. James M. Houston (Minneapolis: Bethany

House, 1996), xvii–xxx; Packer interview with John Armstrong, *Reformation and Revival Journal* (Fall 2004), 163–96 (http://www.biblicalstudies.org.uk/pdf/ref-rev/13-4/13-4_interview.pdf).

Information about Eric Nash and his "Bash campers" comes from McGrath (noted above) and Alister Chapman, *Godly Ambition: John Stott and the Evangelical Movement* (Oxford: Oxford University Press, 2012), 17–18.

Chapter 3

The only substantial source of information about Packer's life during the 1948–49 academic year is Alister McGrath, *J. I. Packer: A Biography* (Grand Rapids: Baker, 1997), 34–39 and 49–54. I hereby record my gratitude to McGrath for his painstaking "primary" research and uncovering of data through interviews and personal contacts. A few additional details about the origin and importance of the Puritan Conference are provided by W. Robert Godfrey in his foreword to *Puritan Papers, Volume 1 1956–1959*, ed. D. Martyn Lloyd-Jones (Phillipsburg, NJ: Puritan and Reformed, 2000), ix–xii. The history of Tyndale House and Fellowship that I reference is by T. A. Noble, *Research for the Academy and the Church: Tyndale House and Fellowship, the First Sixty Years* (Leicester: Inter-Varsity, 2006), 64. An additional source is a telephone interview of Packer conducted on October 29, 2013.

Chapter 4

Alister McGrath is again the chief source: *J. I. Packer: A Biography* (Grand Rapids: Baker, 1997), 40–49. Biographical data on Geoffrey Nuttall appears in David L. Wyke's entry in *Oxford Dictionary of National Biography* (http://www.oxforddnb.com; subscription required). Packer's account of his first meeting with John Gwyn-Thomas appears in *God's Words: Studies in Key Bible Themes* (Downers Grove, IL: InterVarsity, 1981), 180. Packer's dissertation was published in book form as *The Redemption and Restoration of Man in the Thought of Richard Baxter* (Carlisle, Cumbria: Paternoster, 2003); in a "note from the author," Packer states that "the present text of this work is almost exactly as submitted to Oxford University for a doctoral degree in 1954." Additional source: telephone interview with Packer, October 29, 2013.

Chapter 5

Most of the factual data for this phase of Packer's life has been assembled by Alister McGrath, *J. I. Packer: A Biography* (Grand Rapids: Baker, 1997), 59–65. I again record my admiration of McGrath's research. The following sources provided just a little more data: Wendy Murray Zoba, *J. I. Packer Answers Questions for Today* (Wheaton, IL: Tyndale, 2001), 102–3; the website of The Westminster Conference provides a list of speakers and addresses from the Puritan Conferences (http://www.westminsterconference.org.uk/pastpapers/); and *Never Beyond Hope* (Downers Grove, IL: InterVarsity, 2000), 30–31, contains Packer's account of William Leathem's telling him to use humor in his sermons.

Chapter 6

The sources of information for this chapter are as follows: Alister McGrath's *J. I. Packer: A Biography* (Grand Rapids: Baker, 1997), 65–69; Wendy Murray

Zoba, *J. I. Packer Answers Questions for Today* (Wheaton, IL: Tyndale, 2001), 105–6; Packer interview with John Armstrong, *Reformation and Revival Journal* (Fall 2004), 163–96 (http://www.biblicalstudies.org.uk/pdf/ref-rev/13-4/13-4_interview.pdf); J. I. Packer, "Count Your Surprises: The High Spots of My Life Have Been Anything but Expected," *Christianity Today* March 2008: 66–67; J. I. Packer with Carolyn Nystrom, *Guard Us, Guide Us: Divine Leading in Life's Decisions* (Grand Rapids: Baker, 2008), 51.

Chapter 7

Material for this chapter comes from the following sources: Alister McGrath's *J. I. Packer: A Biography* (Grand Rapids: Baker, 1997), 70–98; Wendy Murray Zoba, *J. I. Packer Answers Questions for Today* (Wheaton, IL: Tyndale, 2001), 107–8; "Bibliography of the Works of J. I. Packer," in *J. I. Packer and the Evangelical Future: The Impact of His Life and Thought*, ed. Timothy George (Grand Rapids: Baker, 2009), 187ff.; Jonathan Perry, "Introduction," *Reformation and Revival in Eighteenth-Century Bristol* (Stroud: Alan Sutton, 1994), viii; T. A. Noble, *Research for the Academy and the Church: Tyndale House and Fellowship, the First Sixty Years* (Leicester: Inter-Varsity, 2006), 111–15; a list of speakers and addresses from the Puritan Conferences appears on the website of The Westminster Conference (http://www.westminsterconference.org.uk/pastpapers/).

Additional material comes directly from Packer in the following sources: *Keep in Step with the Spirit* (Old Tappan, NJ: Fleming H. Revell, 1984), 145–64; "An Accidental Writer," *Christianity Today*, 15 May 1987: 11; "Count Your Surprises: The High Spots of My Life Have Been Anything but Expected," *Christianity Today* March 2008: 66–67.

Chapter 8

Alister McGrath, *J. I. Packer: A Biography* (Grand Rapids: Baker, 1997), 99–137; Timothy Dudley-Smith, *John Stott: A Global Ministry* (Downers Grove, IL: Inter-Varsity, 2001), 65–103; Iain H. Murray, *Evangelicalism Divided: A Record of Crucial Change in the Years 1950–2000* (Carlisle, PA: Banner of Truth, 2000), 79–148; Carl R. Trueman, "J. I. Packer: An English Nonconformist Perspective," in *J. I. Packer and the Evangelical Future: The Impact of His Life and Thought*, ed. Timothy George (Grand Rapids: Baker, 2009), 115–29; Iain H. Murray, *Lloyd-Jones: Messenger of Grace* (Carlisle, PA: Banner of Truth, 2008), chapters 8–9; "Bibliography of the Works of J. I. Packer," in *J. I. Packer and the Evangelical Future*, 187ff.; J. I. Packer, "A Kind of Puritan," in *Martyn Lloyd-Jones: Chosen by God*, ed. Christopher Catherwood (Westchester, IL: Crossway, 1986), 33–57; Wendy Murray Zoba, *J. I. Packer Answers Questions for Today* (Wheaton, IL: Tyndale, 2001), 111–12, 116–17; Alister Chapman, *Godly Ambition: John Stott and the Evangelical* Movement (Oxford: Oxford University Press, 2011), 18, 81–82; John C. King, *The Evangelicals* (London: Hodder & Stoughton, 1969), 56; John Wenham, *Facing Hell: An Autobiography 1913–1980* (Carlisle: Paternoster, 1998), 172. Information about specific books by J. I. Packer was taken directly from those books. Packer's address delivered at the Keele Congress is printed in the conference book edited by Packer: *Guidelines: Anglican Evangelicals Face the Future* (London: Falcon Books, 1967), 11–38.

Statistics regarding the percentage of evangelicals in the Church of England are taken from the following sources: Dudley-Smith, *John Stott: A Global Ministry*, 82, 97; Randle Manwaring, *From Controversy to Co-Existence: Evangelicals in the Church of England 1914–1980* (Cambridge: Cambridge University Press, 1985), 193 and 204.

Chapter 9

Nearly all of my material for this chapter comes from Alister McGrath, *J. I. Packer: A Biography* (Grand Rapids: Baker, 1997), 134–79; although McGrath chronicles the events in much greater detail than fits my needs, I hereby record my admiration for how much data he uncovered from primary sources. Also consulted: Wendy Murray Zoba, *J. I. Packer Answers Questions for Today* (Wheaton, IL: Tyndale, 2001), 113–14; "Bibliography of the Works of J. I. Packer," in *J. I. Packer and the Evangelical Future: The Impact of His Life and Thought*, ed. Timothy George (Grand Rapids: Baker, 2009), 187ff.; various online reference sources; telephone conversation with Wallace Benn, August 22, 2013.

Chapter 10

Alister McGrath, *J. I. Packer: A Biography* (Grand Rapids: Baker, 1997), 180–217; "Bibliography of the Works of J. I. Packer," in *J. I. Packer and the Evangelical Future: The Impact of His Life and Thought*, ed. Timothy George (Grand Rapids: Baker, 2009), 187ff.; J. I. Packer, "What Did the Cross Achieve? The Logic of Penal Substitution," in *The J. I. Packer Collection*, ed. Alister McGrath (Downers Grove, IL: InterVarsity, 1999), 94–136; T. A. Noble, *Research for the Academy and the Church: Tyndale House and Fellowship, the First Sixty Years* (Leicester: Inter-Varsity, 2006); J. I. Packer, *The Evangelical Anglican Identity Problem: An Analysis* (Oxford: Latimer House, 1978), 4–5; J. I. Packer, "A Long War: Fifty Years Battling for the Bible," in *Truth and Power: The Place of Scripture in the Christian Life* (Wheaton, IL: Shaw, 1996), 97–125; telephone conversation with Wallace Benn, August 22, 2013. A complete survey and bibliography of Packer's defense of biblical inerrancy can be found in Roger Nicole, "James I. Packer's Contribution to the Doctrine of the Inerrancy of Scripture" in *Doing Theology for the People of God*, ed. Donald Lewis and Alister McGrath (Downers Grove, IL: InterVarsity, 1996), 159–89. Additional references about or from books by J. I. Packer are taken directly from those books.

Chapter 11

Alister McGrath, *J. I. Packer: A Biography* (Grand Rapids: Baker, 1997), 217–37; Wendy Murray Zoba, *J. I. Packer Answers Questions for Today* (Wheaton, IL: Tyndale, 2001), 116–17; "Bibliography of the Works of J. I. Packer," in *J. I. Packer and the Evangelical Future: The Impact of His Life and Thought*, ed. Timothy George (Grand Rapids: Baker, 2009), 187ff.

The quotation from David Wells regarding the decline of Puritan influence is from "On Being Evangelical: Some Theological Differences and Similarities," in *Evangelicalism: Comparative Studies of Popular Protestantism in North America, The British Isles, and Beyond, 1700–1990*, ed. Mark A. Noll *et al.* (New York: Oxford University Press, 1994), 398. Carl Trueman's assessment of the move to Canada appears in "J. I. Packer: An English Nonconformist Perspective," in *J. I. Packer and the Evangelical Future*, 125.

The autobiographical statements about the move to Canada come from J. I. Packer, "Count Your Surprises: The High Spots of My Life Have Been Anything but Expected," *Christianity Today* March 2008: 66–67; and chapter 6 in *Truth and Power: The Place of Scripture in the Christian Life* (Wheaton, IL: Harold Shaw, 1996), 230–31.

Material by or about John Stott comes from two biographies: Timothy Dudley-Smith, *John Stott: A Global Ministry* (Downers Grove, IL: InterVarsity, 2001), 103; and Alister Chapman, *Godly Ambition: John Stott and the Evangelical Movement* (Oxford: Oxford University Press, 2012), 97–111.

Chapter 12

Alister McGrath, *J. I. Packer: A Biography* (Grand Rapids: Baker, 1997), 237–79; "Bibliography of the Works of J. I. Packer," in *J. I. Packer and the Evangelical Future: The Impact of His Life and Thought*, ed. Timothy George (Grand Rapids: Baker, 2009), 187ff.; emails from Jeffrey Greenman, Loren Wilkinson, and Christopher Hall; Mark Noll, "J. I. Packer and the Shaping of American Evangelicalism," in *Doing Theology for the People of God: Studies in Honor of J. I. Packer*, ed. Donald Lewis and Alister McGrath (Downers Grove, IL: InterVarsity, 1996), 191–205; online reference sources (including websites of Regent College and Crossway Books).

Chapter 13

Interviews with Harold Myra and David Neff (longtime leaders at *Christianity Today*); emails from Myra and Neff; a notebook of memoranda lent by Myra; Neff, "Pumping Truth: J. I. Packer's Journalism, Theology, and the Thirst for Truth," in *J. I. Packer and the Evangelical Future: The Impact of His Life and Thought*, ed. Timothy George (Grand Rapids: Baker, 2009), 43–54; "Bibliography of the Works of J. I. Packer," in *J. I. Packer and the Evangelical Future*, 187ff.; research in the bound volumes of *Christianity Today* in the Wheaton College library.

Chapter 14

This chapter encompasses so many individual sources that tabulating them does not serve a useful purpose. Wherever I thought that my source was one that a reader might wish to explore further, I have given enough information about it in the chapter to enable a person to pursue it.

Chapter 15

This chapter encompasses so many individual sources that tabulating them does not serve a useful purpose. Wherever I thought that my source was one that a reader might wish to explore further, I have given enough information about it in the chapter to enable a person to pursue it.

Chapter 16

All material has been taken from published sources authored by J. I. Packer. Any attempt to document every source would have collapsed under its own weight, so I have not made the attempt.

Chapter 17

The books authored by J. I. Packer that are referenced in this chapter were consulted directly, and I have chosen not to list them here after naming them in the chapter. Additional sources include the following: an unpublished written copy of the address delivered by Packer at Clare College, Cambridge, July 21, 2010; "Bibliography of the Works of J. I. Packer," in *J. I. Packer and the Evangelical Future: The Impact of His Life and Thought*, ed. Timothy George (Grand Rapids: Baker, 2009), 187ff.; "Thank God for Our Bibles," *Christianity Today* 27 October 1997: 30–31.

Chapter 18

Works by J. I. Packer: *A Quest for Godliness: The Puritan Vision of the Christian Life* (Wheaton, IL: Crossway, 1990); *Puritan Portraits: J. I. Packer on Selected Classic Pastors and Pastoral Classics* (Ross-shire, UK: Christian Focus, 2012); "Introduction" to *Sin and Temptation: The Challenge of Personal Godliness*, ed. James M. Houston (Minneapolis: Bethany House, 1983, 1986), xxv–xxix; "John Owen Put Me Straight," *Christian History* 89 (2006), http://www.christianitytoday.com/ch/2006/issue89/johnowenputmestraight.html; "Physicians of the Soul," *Christian History* 89 (2006), http://www.christianitytoday.com/ch/2006/issue89/1.12.html; "Introduction" to the 1958 Puritan Conference, as published in *Puritan Papers*, Volume 1, 1956–1959, ed. J. I. Packer (Phillipsburg, NJ: Presbyterian and Reformed, 2000), 169–76; *Honouring the People of God* [vol. 4 of *The Collected Shorter Writings of J. I. Packer*] (Carlisle, UK: Paternoster, 1999).

Works from other sources: Alister McGrath, *J. I. Packer: A Biography* (Grand Rapids, Baker: 1997), 24–26; "Bibliography of the Works of J. I. Packer," in *J. I. Packer and the Evangelical Future: The Impact of His Life and Thought*, ed. Timothy George (Grand Rapids: Baker, 2009), 187ff.; the list of addresses delivered at the Puritan Conference, as posted online by The Westminster Conference (http://www.westminsterconference.org.uk/pastpapers/).

Chapter 19

The myriad of references in this chapter to individual writings by J. I. Packer are based on direct reading of those sources; providing bibliographic information on every quotation and citation is of course impractical. However, I would not have been able to compose this current chapter in the form in which it appears without access to "Bibliography of the Works of J. I. Packer," in *J. I. Packer and the Evangelical Future: The Impact of His Life and Thought*, ed. Timothy George (Grand Rapids: Baker, 2009), 187ff. Packer's comments on his own writing were taken from the following three sources: "An Accidental Writer," *Christianity Today*, 15 May 1987: 11; "Count Your Surprises: The High Spots of My Life Have Been Anything but Expected," *Christianity Today*, March 2008: 66–67; interview of Packer conducted at Laity Lodge, accessed at http://spurgeon.wordpress.com/category/ji-packer/. Mark Noll's tabulations about the numbers of Packer's writings appear in "J. I. Packer and the Shaping of American Evangelicalism," in *Doing Theology for the People of God: Studies in Honor of J. I. Packer*, ed. Donald Lewis and Alister McGrath (Downers Grove, IL: InterVarsity, 1996), 193–95. Also consulted: Tony Reinke interview of Packer, accessed online at http://www.desiringgod.org/blog/posts/j-i-packers-advice-to-aspiring-writers; Wendy Murray Zoba, *J. I. Packer*

Answers Questions for Today (Wheaton, IL: Tyndale, 2001); Alister McGrath, *J. I. Packer: A Biography* (Grand Rapids: Baker, 1997).

Chapter 20

Books by J. I. Packer: *A Kind of Noah's Ark? The Anglican Commitment to Comprehensiveness* (Oxford: Latimer House, 1981); *Taking God Seriously* (Wheaton, IL: Crossway, 2013); *The Thirty-Nine Articles: Their Place and Use Today* (Oxford: Latimer House, 1984); *The Gospel in the Prayer Book* (pamphlet published in 1966; accessed online at http://www.stpaulsanglicanchurch.org/prayer_book_links.php); additional references as indicated in the text of this chapter. Also, the foreword to Todd D. Hunter, *The Accidental Anglican* (Downers Grove, IL: InterVarsity, 2010).

Interviews with J. I. Packer: by Julie Lane-Gay of *The Anglican Planet*, on the subject of the Prayer Book, 2009, http://anglicanplanet.net/interviews/2012/11/24/advent-2012-ji-packer.html; by John Richardson and Chris Sugden for *Anglican Mainstream*, July 1, 2008, http://anglicanmainstream.org/interview-with-j-i-packer/; and by Matthew Block for the *Canadian Lutheran*, November 18, 2011, http://www.canadianlutheran.ca/interview-j-i-packer-on-biblical-authority-world-anglicanism-and-ecumenicism/.

Addresses by J. I. Packer: "Global Realignment: Who We Are and Where We Stand," delivered in 2007 at the Anglican Network in Canada Launch Conference, http://www.globalsouthanglican.org/index.php/comments/global_realignment_who_we_are_and_where_we_stand_ji_packer; address on the problems of the Church of England from a Canadian perspective, delivered June 30, 1995, at the Bishopsgate Conference of Reform, http://trushare.com/04SEP95/SE95PACK.htm.

Chapter 21

Packer's comments about the nature and task of theology are nicely codified in the following sources: "In Quest of Canonical Interpretation," reprinted in *Honouring the Written Word of God* [vol. 3 of *The Collected Shorter Writings of J. I. Packer*] (1985; rprt., Carlisle, UK: Paternoster, 1999), 213–29; *Hot Tub Religion* (Wheaton, IL: Tyndale, 1988), 11–17; "Method, Theological," in *New Dictionary of Theology*, ed. Sinclair B. Ferguson *et al.* (Leicester: Inter-Varsity, 1988), 424–26; "God's Plumber and Sewage Man," *Christianity Today* 6 April 1992: 15; preface to *Concise Theology: A Guide to Historic Christian Beliefs* (Carol Stream, IL: Tyndale, 1993); "Maintaining Evangelical Theology," in *Evangelical Futures: A Conversation on Theological Method*, ed. John G. Stackhouse Jr. (Grand Rapids: Baker, 2000), 181–89. The opening quotation in this chapter is from Wendy Murray Zoba, *J. I. Packer Answers Questions for Today* (Wheaton, IL: Tyndale, 2001), viii.

References to Packer's books can be directly consulted and are too numerous to list here. Essays for which my readers might wish identification are as follows: "Reading the Bible Theologically," in *Understanding Scripture*, ed. Wayne Grudem *et al.* (Wheaton, IL: Crossway, 2012), 29–36; "Encountering Present-Day Views of Scripture," in *Honouring the Written Word of God*, 3–22; "The Problem of Eternal Punishment," in *The J. I. Packer Collection*, ed. Alister McGrath (Downers Grove, IL: InterVarsity, 1999), 213–25; "An Introduction to Systematic Spirituality" (Packer's inaugural lecture upon assuming the position of Sangwoo Youtong Chee Professor of Theology at Regent College), in *The J. I. Packer Collection*, 197–207; "The Preacher as Theologian: Preaching and Systematic Theology," in *Honouring the Written Word of God*, 301–16. As always, I benefited from "Bibliography of the Works of J. I. Packer," in *J. I. Packer and the Evangelical Future: The Impact of His Life and Thought*, ed. Timothy George (Grand Rapids: Baker, 2009), 187ff.

The sources on which I drew for the unit on the unwritten systematic theology were as follows: interview of Wendall Hawley, former Tyndale House Publishers acquisitions editor, August 14, 2013; Iain H. Murray, *Lloyd-Jones: Messenger of Grace* (Carlisle, PA: Banner of Truth, 2008), for the D. Martyn Lloyd-Jones letter; portions are excerpted at http://banneroftruth.org/uk/resources/articles/2010/the-end-of-the-puritan-conference/; Gerald Bray's review of Alister McGrath's biography, *Churchman*, 1997, http://churchsociety.org/docs/churchman/111/Cman_111_4_Bray.pdf; Carl R. Trueman, "J. I. Packer: An English Nonconformist Perspective," in *J. I. Packer and the Evangelical Future*, 115–29. Packer's self-assessment of his unwritten book appears in *Resurgence*, 2004, http://theresurgence.com/files/pdf/reformation_and_revival_2004-10_james_i_packer_interview.pdf.

The four excerpts from theologians on Packer's contribution to theology are as follows: Donald J. Payne, "J. I. Packer's Theological Method," in *J. I. Packer and the Evangelical Future*, 55–68; Trueman, "J. I. Packer: An English Nonconformist Perspective," in *J. I. Packer and the Evangelical Future*, 115–29; Mark A. Noll, "J. I. Packer and the Shaping of American Evangelicalism," in *Doing Theology for the People of God: Studies in Honor of J. I. Packer*, ed. Donald Lewis and Alister McGrath (Downers Grove, IL: InterVarsity, 1996), 191–205; Alister McGrath, "James I. Packer: An Assessment," in *J. I. Packer: A Biography* (Grand Rapids: Baker, 1997), 280–90. Packer's comment on the quotation from McGrath appears in Joel Belz's interview with Packer entitled "J. I. Packer: The Lost Interview," *World Magazine*, posted online on December 7, 2013, http://www.worldmag.com/2013/12/j_i_packer_the_lost_interview.

I took the Mark Dever material from two online sources: http://thegospelcoalition.org/article/where-did-all-these-calvinists-come-from/ and http://9marks.org/article/whered-all-these-calvinists-come-from/.

Chapter 22

Most of what Packer has written about preachers and preaching can be found in the following sources: seven essays that form the third section (entitled "Preaching the Word") of *Honouring the Written Word of God* [vol. 3 of *The Collected Shorter Writings of J. I. Packer*] (Carlisle, UK: Paternoster, 1999), a book that was printed in the same year by Hendrickson under the title *Engaging the Written Word of God*; "Mouthpiece for God," in *Truth and Power: The Place of Scripture in the Christian Life* (Wheaton, IL: Harold Shaw, 1996), 157–85; "Puritan Preaching," chapter 17 in *A Quest for Godliness: The Puritan Vision of the Christian Life* (Wheaton, IL: Crossway, 1990), 277–89; chapter 12 of the anthology *Inside the Sermon: Thirteen Preachers Discuss Their Methods of Preparing Messages*, ed. Richard Allen Bodey (Grand Rapids: Baker, 1990), 185–200. I also drew upon two interviews: one conducted by the principal of Oak Hill Theological College, accessed at http://thegospelcoalition.org/blogs/justintaylor/2010/01/09/an-interview-with-j-i-packer-on-theological-training/; and one conducted by *Christianity Today*, accessed at http://www.preachingtoday.com/skills/themes/preachingwithauthority/jipackeronpreachingasgodsderivativeword.html. The list of Packer publications on preaching was extracted from "Bibliography of the Works of J. I. Packer," in

J. I. Packer and the Evangelical Future: The Impact of His Life and Thought, ed. Timothy George (Grand Rapids: Baker, 2009), 187ff.

The three sermons explored at the end of the chapter can be found in *Inside the Sermon* (see above) and in J. I. Packer and Carolyn Nystrom, *Never Beyond Hope: How God Touches and Uses Imperfect People* (Downers Grove, IL: InterVarsity, 2000).

Chapter 23

The following summary encompasses most (but not all) of the sources from which I have drawn data for the controversies in Packer's life. At various points, I have drawn upon Alister McGrath, *J. I. Packer: A Biography* (Grand Rapids: Baker, 1997). Packer's statement about having endured "trouble, trouble, trouble" is quoted from Wendy Murray Zoba, *J. I. Packer Answers Questions for Today* (Wheaton, IL: Tyndale, 2001), 111.

On controversy with D. Martyn Lloyd-Jones: Lloyd-Jones, "Evangelical Unity: An Appeal," in *Knowing the Times: Addresses Delivered on Various Occasions, 1942–1977* (Carlisle, PA: Banner of Truth, 1989), 246–57; Lloyd-Jones, *The Puritans: Their Origins and Successors* [addresses delivered at the Puritan and Westminster Conferences, 1959–1978] (Carlisle, PA: Banner of Truth, 1987); John Coffey, "Lloyd-Jones and the Protestant Past," in *Engaging with Martyn Lloyd-Jones*, ed. Andrew Atherstone and David Ceri Jones (Nottingham: Inter-Varsity, 2011), 293–325; Andrew Atherstone, "Lloyd-Jones and the Anglican Secession Crisis," in *Engaging with Martyn Lloyd-Jones*," 261–92; J. I. Packer, address delivered at Reform Conference of 1995, quoted at secondhand from Roger Steer, *Guarding the Holy Fire* (Grand Rapids: Baker, 1999), 225; J. I. Packer, "A Kind of Puritan," in *Martyn Lloyd-Jones: Chosen by God*, ed. Christopher Catherwood (Westchester, IL: Crossway, 1986), 33–57; Carl R. Trueman, "J. I. Packer: An English Nonconformist Perspective," in *J. I. Packer and the Evangelical Future: The Impact of His Life and Thought*, ed. Timothy George (Grand Rapids: Baker, 2009), 115–29; Gaius Davies, *Genius, Grief and Grace* (Ross-shire, UK: Christian Focus, 2001), 325–69.

On the controversy surrounding *Growing into Union*: Andrew Atherstone, "A Mad Hatter's Tea Party in the Old Mitre Tavern? Ecumenical Reactions to *Growing into Union*," *Ecclesiology* 6 (2010): 39–70; also, the Atherstone essay cited above.

On assorted controversies: in addition to McGrath, the sources cited in the chapter itself. Similarly for the controversy surrounding Evangelicals and Catholics Together.

On homosexuality and the Anglican Church of Canada: assorted news items accessed from archives on the Internet; numerous interviews posted on the Internet; J. I. Packer, "Why I Walked: Sometimes Loving a Denomination Requires You to Fight," *Christianity Today*: January 2003, 46–50.

Sources used for the concluding section (in addition to ones cited above): J. I. Packer, *The Evangelical Anglican Identity Problem: An Analysis* (Oxford: Latimer House, 1980); Gerald Bray, review of McGrath's biography, *Churchman* (1997), http://churchsociety.org/docs/churchman/111/Cman_111_4_Bray.pdf; Paul Helm, online posting in Helm's Deep, December 14 2009, http://paulhelmsdeep.blogspot.com/2009/12/ji-2.html; J. I. Packer, "How Will I Be Remembered?" *Christianity Today*, 24 June 1991: 11.

Index

This entire book is about J. I. Packer, so this index does not include an entry for his name, with several pages of topics under that heading. Users of this index should go directly to an alphabetized entry such as "Bible" or "conversion of Packer." Page numbers that appear in bold signify a concentrated or major block of material on a topic (sometimes even an entire chapter). Only the most frequently referenced books by Packer have been included. An index is designed to supplement but not replace a table of contents and headings within chapters. The sources for the various chapters appear in concentrated form on pages 416–424 and have not been incorporated into the index.